Following The Grand Tour

TO ITALY, FRANCE & SPAIN

ANYA NIELSEN

Publishing Details
The Grand Tour by Anya Nielsen

Published by Anya Nielsen

1st Edition 2024, paperback.

ISBN: 978-1-923038-36-3 paperback
ISBN: 978-1-923038-37-0 eBook

Publishing services by: PublishMyBook.Online
A catalogue record for this book is available from the National Library of Australia.

The gulf between holidaying and travelling gets wider every day.

Anon

Contents

Chapter 1: Bari 7
Chapter 2: Matera 17
Chapter 3: Roma. 28
Chapter 4 : Still Rome. 43
Chapter 5: Southern Sunshine 59
Chapter 6: Pompeii 76
Chapter 7: Calabria 88
Chapter 8: Sicily 98
Chapter 9: Ancient Mosaics 111
Chapter 10: Palermo 122
Chapter 11: The Eternal City 134
Chapter 12: Three Coins in the Fountain 142
Chapter 13: IL Bella Nord 153
Chapter 14: Michelangelo 165
Chapter 15: Harry's Bar. 176
Chapter 16: Torino. 191
Chapter 17: La Scala. 210
Chapter 18: Florence Again 225
Chapter 19: A Feast Day 233

Chapter 20: All Good Things Must End 245
Chapter 21: Madrid España 254
Chapter 22: Barcelona. 268
Chapter 23: Flamenco. 279
Chapter 24: Carcassonne 289
Chapter 25: Avignon 293
Chapter 26: Paris 300
Chapter 27: Old Friends 309
Chapter 28: Champagne 315
Chapter 29: Loire Valley Chateaux 322
Chapter 30: Impressionists 332
Chapter 31: A High Day 344
Chapter 32: Cabaret 354
Chapter 33: Versailles and Water Lilies 364
Chapter 34: Ballet de l'Opéra 373
Chapter 35: Food, Glorious Food 377
Chapter 36: Nice. 386
Chapter 37: The Finale 399
About the Author 414

Chapter 1
Bari

The romantic idea of taking the Grande Tour[1] was a notion I conceived during school days but delayed until 2012. I'd dreamt of paying homage to the haunts of my favourite writers and artists—seeing where they lived and worked—and to experience for myself the locations and cultures that had inspired their creativity.

I'd been to the Holy Lands, Egypt and Greece. This time I planned to spend a month in Italy and a month in France, where I would meet my dear friend, Marina.

When I told my daughter of my plans, she insisted I extend my trip to include Barcelona, specifically to traipse through *Parc Güell*—a world heritage site. She said the collaboration between Antonio Gaudi, the architect, and Count Güell, an entrepreneur who'd backed Gaudi's ventures, was a remarkable achievement.

---

1 A Grande Tour of Europe was a rite of passage for young British nobility of the 18th and 19th centuries, a sort of finishing school to gain culture and sophistication. Typically, the itinerary included classes in riding, dancing, the French language and fencing. Youngsters toured with a tutor to facilitate their knowledge of art, architecture, archaeology and music. Vestiges are still evident today in these destinations and include Italy, France, Switzerland and sometimes Basel, where one can take the waters.

Once the bones of the trip were decided, I began to examine the details. What I most wanted to do in Italy was to visit the relics of St Nicholas located in Bari, a port city on the Adriatic east coast. St Nicholas the Wonderworker[2], as he is called, is one of the most revered saints of the Christian world. I based my whole trip around this pilgrimage. I discovered that his relics were kept at a Catholic church, the *Basilica di San Nicola*.

Quite soon after sending my enquiry to the email link on the church website, I received a most encouraging response from a Fr Gerardo. In his reply, he explained that the relics of St Nicholas are kept in the crypt below the church. Although he would be away until early September, he wrote that a visit to the relics could be made at any time. He also said that the most frequent visitors were pilgrims from Russia. They had permission to serve a Divine Liturgy every Thursday in the crypt. Fr Gerardo was a bit unsure regarding the protocols surrounding this event. However, he said I should contact Fr Andrei from the *Chiesa Russa San Nicola* for details.

This was easier said than done. Many phone calls and unanswered emails tested my resolve. How badly did I want to get there? St Nicholas was part of my culture, part of my childhood, and I knew that this would be my only opportunity to make such a pilgrimage. I decided to put my trust in St Nicholas and let him decide if it should happen.

2 Beloved throughout the Christian East, St Nicholas is called wonderworker for his help during his life and the miracles that continue to occur when those in need pray for his intercession. He is patron saint of children, travellers and seafarers. Many of his miracles were recorded. My father used to tell of the icon of St Nicholas at the wharf on the Sungari River in Harbin. One day, a Chinese fisherman got caught in a terrible storm on the river. He remembered the icon and how the people venerated it, and he called out, 'Old man of the river, help me.' The storm abated and the man returned to shore to tell of his miraculous rescue.

So I confirmed my other tours and bookings for Italy and France, all based on the assumed Bari dates. If my plans for Bari fell through, then like dominos, the rest of my trip would be in jeopardy. As time progressed, I began to worry. I shared my trepidation with a friend.

'Have you tried anyone in our own diocese?' she asked. 'Ring Fr Gabriel in Brisbane. He's been to Bari. He'll advise you.'

I immediately sent him an email, then prayed to St Nicholas. Moments later, Fr Gabriel responded. He happened to be in transit somewhere overseas when he received my email. As it happened, he even had Fr Andrei's mobile number on him. I was elated. I knew this was the first miracle.

Not to lose momentum, I immediately rang Fr Andrei and was surprised when he answered straight away. I told him I wanted to attend a liturgy at the relics and asked if he could also recommend accommodation nearby.

'You've just caught me,' he said. 'I'm about to board a plane for Russia. We offer basic rooms for pilgrims in the hostel that is on our church grounds. If you wish, you may stay there.'

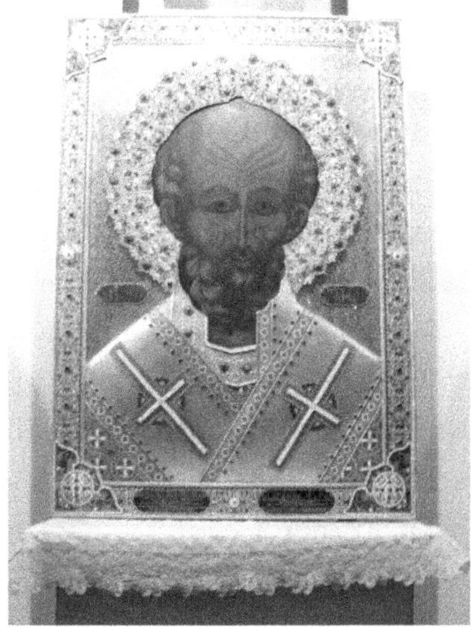

'That would be ideal,' I replied. Fr Andrei's welcoming words had the power to lift the stress I'd been carrying from my shoulders. 'How do I organise it?'

'By the time you arrive, I will be back,' he said. 'Come straight to the church. I will arrange everything.' Then hurriedly added, 'We have vespers each Wednesday night if you wish to make a confession. The following morning, we'll all go together to the crypt. It's not far.'

This was the second miracle. I was so fired up, I could hardly breathe. A new energy coursed through my veins and I began to dance around the room, chanting, 'I've cracked the code, I've cracked the code.'

The economy hotel I'd selected in Dubai was located on the outskirts of the skyscraper-filled city. Most people use this stopover as a transit point. I know that the threat of deep vein thrombosis occurs due to long flights, so to minimise this happening, I take an overnight stopover. The first time I was in Dubai I stayed two nights and even had a short, but terrifying excursion four-wheel driving through the sand dunes. This time I only had one night but knew it would make an enormous difference to my well-being.

I sat in the back seat of the taxi and gazed through the windows. Along the route, I noticed that several changes had occurred since my last stay. An IKEA had popped up in the burbs. Further on, we passed a billboard advertising the opening of an underwater aquarium and SECA World in the newly extended Dubai Mall. What hadn't changed was the intense, dry heat. People remained indoors during the day and came out at night to shop and socialise.

That evening, I meandered across the road from my hotel to the Mall of the Emirates for a bit of window shopping and to find something tasty for dinner. I was surprised to see an additional attraction inside. An indoor ski field had recently been installed, complete with chair lifts and a ski run. All were enclosed within a glass arena. Outside, it had cooled to a bearable 43°C but inside people wore parkas while skiing the *faux* snow at the mall. *Now that's quintessential Dubai.*

The next morning at the airport, I was surprised to find that my prebooked seat to Rome had been upgraded to business class. The woman at check-in said, 'It's a long flight. You'll enjoy the upgrade. Go straight up the stairs when you board.'

I smiled to myself. *A six-hour flight is hardly enough time to scrutinise the list of inflight movies on offer. Not like the gruelling 14-hour leg from Sydney to Dubai.*

First up, one of the cabin crew brought around champagne.

'French or Italian?' the hostie asked, as she showed me the labels.

'French, please.' *An easy decision,* I thought as she poured Bollinger into a fine glass flute. I'm not sure if it was the feel of the fine glassware on my lips or the unrelenting bubbles that tickled my nose that impressed me the most.

We received a printed wine list and menu for dinner. There were Arabic and continental options. The meal was served with real cutlery on a linen-covered tray with a starched napkin to match. For the entrée, I chose plump and juicy king prawns on a bed of crisp salad greens with a tiny jug of tangy coconut dressing. The hostess offered wine that she poured from a bottle with an impressive but unfamiliar French label.

The main course followed—pale pink salmon, pan-seared to perfection, the crisp skin resembling a flat bit of corrugated iron roofing, balanced at a daring angle over the top of the fish. A platter of assorted vegetables was offered for individual selection. There were wedges of potato, tiny golden marrows, purééd eggplant, roasted red capsicum and pale green courgettes. A Bearnaise sauce, which complemented the assortment of vegetables, was available in sachets. For sweets, honeyed baklava and other similar sweetmeats accompanied coffee brewed to order. I decided on Turkish coffee and was not disappointed.

Afterwards, I stretched out on the soft mattress that lined my sleeping capsule and rested my head on a down-filled pillow encased in a silken smooth pillowcase. As I closed my eyes, I decided I could easily become accustomed to travelling in this manner.

I recall my first time at Rome's Fiumicino Airport. It was in 1986 and the place was crawling with military personnel their rifles and submachine guns at the ready. This was in response to the bloody terrorist attacks on Rome and Vienna airports some four months earlier. To prevent another incident, the military was stationed all over the airport to ensure peace and security. At the time, I thought their demeanour menacing.

It was a disquieting first impression, which left me intimidated. I was in transit and swore I would never return to Rome. Now, some 26 years later, in the comfort of business class, I was back to enjoy a whole month in Italy. I hoped this time to find a calmer, more welcoming country.

Rome airport seemed twice the size I'd remembered. My greatest fear was getting lost as I scurried around the herds of sauntering people. *Am I the only one in a hurry?* I searched for the domestic terminal and the departure gate for my one-hour flight to Bari, which was due to depart shortly. Beads of sweat covered my brow as I scrutinised the unfamiliar signage. Finally, I arrived at the gate, only to find my flight had a two-hour delay.

All the seats in the lounge were occupied but I spied one hidden by luggage in the far corner of the room. I must have appeared determined as I made a bee-line to claim it because the man sitting nearby quickly removed his things so I could sit. I felt agitated and found it hard to relax. My mind raced and I fidgeted with my phone. *I should confirm my accommodation.* However, my Australian SIM card wouldn't work. I noticed a vending machine nearby. *Promising idea. I'll buy a local phone card.* While I was doing that, I lost my seat. When I tried the new phone card, it didn't work. I was not a happy camper and being on my own, there was no one to listen to me sounding off my frustration.

When I arrived in Bari[3], it was already dark. I put my trust in the taxi driver even though he didn't speak a word of English. *Just as well I did an Italian for Travellers course in preparation for this trip. Here goes, I hope he understands me.* I visualised St Nicholas by my side as I said a little prayer to ask for his help before I attempted to speak to the driver.

'Per favor, portami in Chiesa Russa Santa Nicola,' I said.

'Si. Corso Benedetto, Croce? No problemo,' he replied.

'Quanta Costa?' I enquired.

'Trente euro, Senora.'

---

3 Bari is an important port city and the capital of Puglia region. Here, ferries connect Italy with Albania, Montenegro, Croatia, Greece and the Ionian Islands, including Corfu.

And so, the deal was done. We drove along unfamiliar roads into Old Town, where the street lighting was dim. I'd been warned by friends that Bari was known for crime—mugging of tourists was the preferred sport; an unsettling thought.

When we arrived at the church[4], the gate was locked and there was not a soul to be seen. I was crestfallen. *I've come this far and I'm stopped at the gate. I can't stay here in the street by myself. I'll have to get the taxi driver to take me to the nearest hotel and hope they have a room.*

'*Senora*,' the driver pointed to the building, '*una luce nella finestra*.'

He pointed at a sliver of light in one of the downstairs windows of the building next door to the church. As he rattled the gate wildly, I called out, 'Hello? Hello?'

A youngish couple emerged from the building. 'Hello, is Fr Andrei there?' I asked in Russian. 'He's expecting me. He said I could stay at the hostel. Can you open the gate, please?'

'Fr Andrei is not back from overseas,' replied the thin young lady.

I was much relieved when a man stepped out from behind her and said, 'We are expecting you. Please enter. Your room is ready.'

That was the third miracle. The taxi driver stood waiting for the result of our exchange. I paid him the agreed amount and gave him a good tip for all his help.

The young lady extended her hand in greeting. 'I am Katerina and this is my husband, Sergei,' she said, turning to

4 In the 19th and 20th centuries, many Russian churches were built all over the world for the benefit of Russian pilgrims. The majority were designed in the Moscow-Yaroslavl style. This church is of the rare Pskov- Novgorod style.

the gentleman, who had already picked up my luggage. 'He will take you to your room. When you are ready, come down to the kitchen and have some supper with us.'

My room was basic but clean, and the shared bathroom was at the end of the hall. It was certainly not the Ritz but it was modest accommodation, sufficient for pilgrims.

When I returned downstairs, I discovered that autumn was their off-season. May and December were the main months for pilgrims. St Nicholas Day is celebrated on 6 December by the Catholic or Western rite, who follow the Gregorian calendar while the Orthodox or Eastern rite follows the old Julian Calendar, so it falls on 19 December. Translation of the relics[5] from Myra to Bari is likewise celebrated on 9 or 22 May. Katerina explained that during quiet periods like these, Fr Andrei often took the opportunity for a short sabbatical. She said he'd be back in the morning.

In the kitchen, I met Zena, a Vietnamese lady who was both cook and housekeeper. Around the table sat Matushka, Katerina, Sergei and Yuri—a handyman and driver. Zena served us a nourishing vegetable soup with freshly baked bread, followed by a stew. We were encouraged to help ourselves to tea and fruit.

'What are your plans for tomorrow?' Zena asked.

5 In 1071, Myra was invaded by the Seljuk Turks and a period of subjugation followed before the Ottomans overthrew the Byzantine Empire. Then on 9 May 1087, under the guise of protection, the relics of St Nicholas were stolen by Italian and Venetian raiders and taken to the port city of Bari, where they remain to this day. This day is commemorated annually as the date of the translation of the relics to the new site.

'I have no plans,' I replied. 'I might have a wander around the city centre.'

'You must take the train to the UNESCO Heritage site of Matera. Don't worry, you'll get back in time for Vespers,' she assured me.

Yuri joined in our conversation. 'Matera?' he asked. 'Yes, you must go. I take you to train station after breakfast.'

I could rest easy now that the program for my one free day in Bari had been decided.

Chapter 2
Matera

After breakfast, Fr George, a priest who'd come straight from the airport with two chanters, joined our group. A minibus was at our disposal, and we made our way to the Basilica for a short memorial service in the crypt.

The Romanesque style, limestone *Basilica di San Nicola,* is located within the ancient, fortified citadel near the ferry wharf. Originally built in 1087, it has been refurbished and altered several times through the ages. However, the towers, like *Cathédrale Notre-Dame de Paris,* have not been crowned with the intended spires.

As I walked in, I was struck by the immense size of the nave. An avenue of tall columns flank the main aisle. Each architectural feature remains plain. White. Austere. The only colour to be seen is in the features of the ornate paintings that cover the ceiling. My gaze continued to the canopy-covered altar. To the right of it, a large icon of the Crucifixion[6] adorns the wall and further on I could see a humble secondary altar where an image of Our Lady of the Passion is depicted standing between St Nicholas and St John the Evangelist.

6 Painted in 1304.

Two wide stairways in the lateral aisles lead down to the crypt where the relics of St Nicholas are kept. As we made our way there, half a dozen other people joined us. The crypt is supported by 28 columns decorated with carved capitals.[7] The relics, which lie in a raised marble sarcophagus, are positioned directly under the altar of the main church. A 14th-century Byzantine icon hangs on the wall behind the reliquary. This small compound is fenced off by a metal screen.

The presence of an Orthodox chapel in the crypt is noteworthy as a rare[8] example of the coexistence of two religions. Indeed, the crypt houses two altars: one dedicated to the Catholic rite and the other to the Orthodox rite. This ecumenical vocation is unique and is due to the continued pilgrimages over the centuries of the faithful from all over the world, but particularly from devout Orthodox Russia.[9]

Our small group gathered in front of the reliquary for the short service of petition to St Nicholas. We asked for his intercession on behalf of those present and those who had requested prayers. The sincerity and concentration of our group made it a very moving experience. As the lists of names were many, I worried whether I'd have enough time to visit Matera.

At the conclusion of the service, we were only able to reach through the metal screen to touch the cold marble dais on which

7 The purpose of columns is to support the weight of the ceiling. At the top of the column is an entablature, which can be plain or decorative, called the capital. The capital mediates between the column and the load of the ceiling being thrust upon it, thus broadening the area of the column's supporting surface. The ancient order of capitals are Doric, Ionic or Corinthian.

8 I know of no other such instance anywhere.

9 The first recording of Russian pilgrims was in 1459. That group was led by Fr Varlaam, a monk from Rostov.

the sarcophagus stood. I was hoping to be able to venerate the sarcophagus but had to console myself with just being there.

Yuri drove me to the railway and left me on my own. The train[10] I was supposed to catch must have recently departed. I couldn't help but notice that very few trains and even fewer people used this station. There was a cool breeze, which added to my feeling of uneasiness.

Matera is 70 km south of Bari and the journey takes approximately two hours. I confess I had second thoughts about going, but wondered if this might be one of those unplanned gems that serendipitously present themselves. So I decided to take the chance.

Finally, after an hour of waiting, an old and shabby train arrived. I thought it could do with a thorough hose out. The people using the train looked tired. Some dozed but others sat with their eyes downcast.

Through the window, I watched the countryside roll by. We seemed to travel straight through plantations of old and gnarled olive trees, and orchards of fruit trees, followed by farm sheds and further on dried-up disused land. *The trains are so infrequent most likely because it is a single track,* I mused. *I wonder if the train must first reach its destination before it can return.* I didn't have enough Italian to ask anyone.

Stations seemed few and far between. As the train gathered speed, the buildings appeared smaller, unadorned and without signage, akin to quaint outhouses. Commuters wandered across

10 Privately-run trains to Matera leave from the FAL station situated next to the main railway station.

the tracks to get onto the platform. No one seemed in a hurry—*domani*—tomorrow, as in Dean Martin's song 'Forget Domani'.

Presently, we stopped at a station where an elderly couple boarded. Both used walking sticks and supported each other. The conductor offered to give them a hand. They spoke briefly, then the three of them trundled over to the ticket machine. The lady scratched around in her handbag as we sat inside the train, watching and waiting.

I was enthralled to see the conductor help them, but equally perplexed at how the train would maintain its schedule. The passengers sat patiently, unconcerned by the delay. *No wonder I had to wait so long for the train. I can't imagine something remotely like this scene happening anywhere else in the world.*

The conductor tried several times, even gave the machine a bit of a kick, but it refused to budge. I almost laughed aloud. Having given up, the trio made their way back into the carriage. The conductor blew his whistle, and the train resumed its journey.

When we arrived at Matera, I followed a small group of people to the exit. *There's no one here to collect our tickets. How ironic.* As I glanced back, I noticed the elderly couple tootling along behind me. *They'll have had a free trip. Good luck to them.*

Out in the street, a colourful sign indicated the way to the 16th-century Castello Tramontana. The path led to a turreted medieval castle perched high on a hill. But alas, the castle was closed for renovations.

In the distance, spires punctuated the horizon. I headed in their direction. The road brought me to an ancient piazza, where a fountain graced the cobblestoned square. The *bibliotheca communale* or municipal library, together with the town hall and a church, bound the perimeters of the square. Laneways radiated from the piazza. I followed one, the *Strada Panoramica dei Sassi,* not knowing what lay beyond. To my surprise, the path led to an amazing sight—a whole village of makeshift dwellings gouged out of the mountainside.[11]

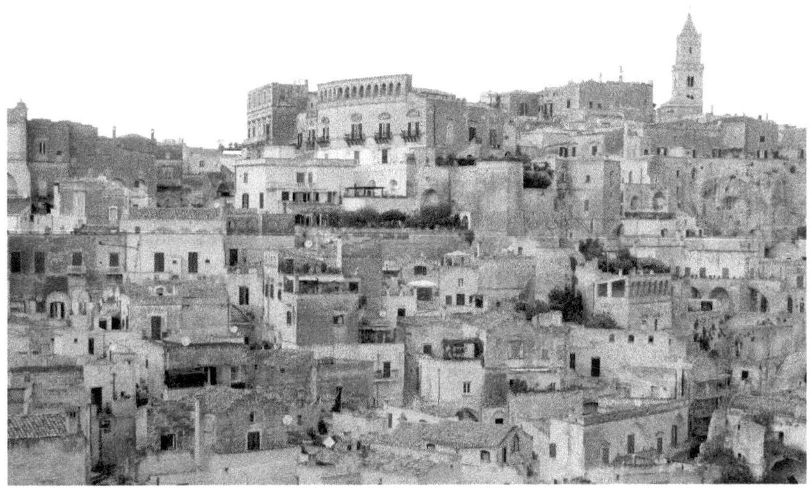

The main town is perched on the top of a ravine while the lower slope, pockmarked with caves, is called the Sassi district. These two districts, at odds with each other, make Matera the most fascinating city in Southern Italy. *So this is what Zena wanted me to see.* She'd told me that from the 8th to the 13th century, Greek monks had originally occupied the caves. Later, these were taken over by refugees. Gradually, the area became gentrified and by the 18th century, was quite grand.

During the 1950s and '60s, they'd been taken over by squatters and soon returned to their original squalid state. The

11 Inhabited since 10 BC.

municipality forcibly rehoused the occupants and cleaned out the area to make it habitable again. Today, Sassi is a tourist area with many boutique hotels and chapels.

The narrow alleys, lined with stone buildings, lacked trees or any sort of greenery. It reminded me of the old city of Jerusalem. Nearby, a signboard indicated the town dated back to the 12th century.[12] Indeed, movies like Mel Gibson's 2004 *The Passion of the Christ* and Bruce Beresford's *King David* in 1985, were filmed there because of the similarity to ancient Jerusalem.

Though already autumn, I hadn't expected the sunlight that reflected off the stonework to make me feel so warm and thirsty. Up ahead, a sign over a nondescript door read *Café*. I remembered that my meagre breakfast of tea and toast was some time ago and it was time for a break—gelato, coffee and a clean loo. In my experience, public loos are disgusting and I prefer to use one attached to a restaurant.

Time ticked by and I began to worry about returning in time for Vespers. I stepped outside but had lost my direction. Fortunately, some kind locals noticed me looking lost and pointed the way. Soon after, I was on a train heading back to Bari. By the time I arrived at *Chiesa Russa San Nicola,* it was ten to six. I'm used to Vespers commencing at six but in Bari, they start at five. The service, in the lower chapel, was already far advanced.

Katerina noticed me arrive flustered and red-faced. She came over and whispered in my ear, 'It started at five o'clock, but don't worry, there'll be time enough tomorrow for confession,' she said. 'You can help me lock up when this is finished.'

---

12 In 1993, the Sassi was deemed a UNESCO World Heritage site. It's now a tourist location with boutique hotels, museums and chapels where once the early monks, hermits and cave-dwellers lived.

The small yet cosy chapel was erected in honour of St Nicholas's home in Myra. It is dedicated to St Spyridon, a Greek saint.[13] I helped Katerina douse the candles. As we walked around, she showed me some of the more ancient icons, which had adorned the original church and had been transferred when this one was built.

'Many precious church items were donated by the more well-heeled early pilgrims,' she said. 'The iconostasis in the main church is the work of Alexandre Benoir. You'll have time to see it tomorrow. We'd better go straight to the kitchen now; the others will already be there.'

After supper, as we sat in the cosy warm kitchen, Zena told me the church complex was going through a huge refurbishment, funded by the local municipality.

'It is due for completion next year when we celebrate our centenary. The land was bought in 1911 and the foundation stone laid in 1913. Maybe you will return for the celebration?'

'That would be nice,' I replied, 'but unlikely. Australia is a long way, and the fare is extremely expensive.'

The following morning saw an early start. No breakfast. Confessions were scheduled to take place from 8:00 am and the liturgy to begin at 10:00 am.

As we waited for our group to converge, I started to worry about missing my flight to Rome. My thoughts were interrupted

13 When the Turks overthrew the Byzantine Empire, the Greek town of Myra became part of Turkey. They turned churches into mosques, including the most important church in Christendom, Santa Sophia's cathedral, located in the capital of Constantinople, now known as Istanbul. President Erdogan, in defiance of world heritage, has recently changed the use of the cathedral from a museum to again becoming a working mosque.

when a shiny black sedan pulled up in the church courtyard and a well-groomed young man with a trimmed beard and hair stepped from the vehicle. He looked as if he'd come straight out of a *Vogue* magazine in his designer jeans, sparkling white open-necked shirt and RM Williams boots. He was toting a small leather overnight bag. *That pilgrim is cutting it fine. Good looking,* I thought. *I should extend my time in Bari.*

Katerina, who was standing behind me, said in a soft undertone, 'That's Fr Andrei.'

'Oh. He's very handsome.' I gulped as the warmth of a blush coloured my cheeks. I had expected him to look like the other cassocked priests who had alighted, their beards[14] wafting in the morning breeze.

Fr Andrei was sharp. He saw an unfamiliar face and strode towards me. 'You must be the one from Australia,' he said, smiling. 'Welcome. My flight was late. We'll be off in a minute.'

'Good morning, Fr Andrei,' I replied. 'I am a little worried about getting to the airport after liturgy in good time for my flight to Rome.'

'Don't worry, it will all work out. You'll see.' And with that, he went inside to leave his bags.

Meanwhile, a young, long-bearded priest with dancing eyes approached me. He introduced himself as Fr Mikhail. He had a cheeky smile and seemed full of life. 'Are you staying long?' he asked. 'I'm taking a group of pilgrims to the holy sites in Italy. Will you be joining us?'

'Thank you. Unfortunately, I wasn't aware of it and have an itinerary already booked.'

'That's too bad,' he said. 'You must have a copy of my DVD from a recent trip. I'll autograph it. What is your name?'

14 It's traditional for priests to emulate Christ.

'I'm named after St Anna of Kashin.'[15]

'Ah, she was a princess, and her consort was Duke Mikhail.' He laughed. 'I'm one of the drivers today. Hop in,' he said. 'I'd be glad to drive Anna Kashinskaya around.'

We were the first to arrive at the basilica and made our way directly to the crypt. I left my bags behind an alcove near the Russian iconostasis to the far left of the crypt.[16] Fr Mikhail ushered us up to the main church, where they were setting up for confession. A dozen Catholic tourists had arrived for their scheduled short memorial service in the crypt.

Our group congregated in the basilica, where more people began to arrive. I wondered which hotels they'd stayed at or if there'd been several tourist buses. Orderly queues formed for confession. I ended up in the line for Fr Mikhail. As he dismissed me after absolution, he said, 'Yes, yes, Australian sins, not serious. Go in peace to Holy Communion.'

With a light step, I proceeded to the crypt, where several people had already positioned themselves facing the reliquary. The wire gate was open now and we were able to approach the relics for veneration. Meanwhile, the number of people was

15 Anna of Kashin was a princess from the Rurik dynasty. She married Prince Mikhail of Tver. Both were devout Christians. When her son and husband were murdered by the Mongol horde, she retreated to the monastery, where she is remembered for her kindness and piety. She died in 1368. People continued to come to her grave to ask for help. Since 1611, miracles of her intercession have been recorded.

16 In 1966, a vault in the crypt was dedicated as an Orthodox chapel with an iconostasis built to commemorate the lifting of some anathemas that had existed since the Great Schism of 1054, when Christianity split into two camps—Catholic and Orthodox. The discord was about papal supremacy, Nicene Creed alteration and a few local differences. In 2017, Pope Francis allowed a portion of the relics of St Nicholas to travel to Christ the Saviour Cathedral in Moscow, then on to St Petersburg. More than a million people lined up for a moment of veneration.

building. Yesterday, where eight of us had stood, this day, an extraordinary sea of humanity had gathered. Soon we were shoulder to shoulder in silent contemplation, waiting for the liturgy which, due to the vast number of penitents, began at 10:30 am.

Eight priests, several deacons and readers, resplendent in gold-coloured vestments, conducted the service. They used the reliquary sarcophagus as the altar. The choir of four consisted of soprano, alto, tenor and bass. Their voices resonated in the confined space of the crypt, taking me somewhere into the stratosphere, somewhere not time-bound—a place where peace and calm reigned. The atmosphere, filled with such fervent prayer, was palpable.

There were so many people I struggled to cross myself. When the congregation joined in the singing of the Creed, followed by Our Father, the atmosphere was electric. Some people were clearly moved, some wept, several with their eyes closed appeared trance-like, as if in another place altogether. I will never forget the feeling. Even though I'd stood without breakfast in one spot for two hours, I felt no tiredness, hunger or thirst.

There were eight chalices for Holy Communion, as most everyone was partaking. As in the parable of the loaves and fishes, all were attended to. By the time I said my farewells, it was half past twelve. I left with a feeling of invincibility and elation; I was already flying, although I still had to get to the airport. Katerina phoned for a taxi and sent me on my way with a small parcel.

The taxi was prompt and I was at the airport half an hour later. Fr Andrei had been correct when he'd said everything would work out all right.

There was not too much formality at this provincial airport. Customs were busy chatting to each other, the cleaners and baggage handlers. They were very laidback, the equivalent of any big family at a picnic.

I opened Katerina's parcel. She'd given me a small bottle of fragrant holy oil to take back to my church. Also in the parcel was some holy bread—my breakfast. Up until then, I'd forgotten my hunger, but was glad for the tiny piece of bread to break my fast.

That was when I realised it was time I had some lunch. A takeaway stand nearby displayed a stack of warmed rolls—panini, with salami, cheese and salad. I ordered a *Caffè americano*. They don't have flat white coffee in Italy. Still, I loved the little jug of milk to the side of the black coffee. It tasted delicious and after a few sips, I knew I'd returned to this planet.

Bari was unforgettable. Some people say it's old and grotty, but it has a charm that can only come from an ancient place—a place with history, a place with a past. I never felt unsafe, even while on my own.

The locals say Bari is fine. It's Naples where one must be aware of crime.

Chapter 3
Roma

The plane landed smoothly and thankfully, there was no gun-bearing military to greet me. I found a taxi and made my way from Rome airport to my accommodation, which was located close to the Vatican.[17]

Fr Gerardo had given me a contact for *Santa Maria alle Fornaci*, a *pension* run by one of the Catholic orders, which can be found next to the church of the same name. It was built in the 14th century as a Jesuit monastery and is now a guest house for visitors. Owned and run by the Order of the Holy Trinity, they provide basic but well-appointed single accommodation with an excellent buffet breakfast included. All this for under $100 per night, which I believe is phenomenal value. However, the most important attribute is the location—a comfortable five-minute stroll to the Vatican and the Metro.

Elation enveloped me as I strode briskly to St Peter's Square. To get my bearings, I did a 360° turn in the empty forecourt. The massive elliptical area is paved in travertine, its focal point the broad façade of the Vatican Palace[18] and the red granite Egyptian

18 A design attributed to Bernini, it took 400 years to build, so the architectural style varies from late Renaissance to Roman Baroque.

obelisk at the centre. I paused at the trapezoidal[19] entrance, where the colossal Doric-columned cloisters encircled me in an architectural embrace by the mother church.

The upper and lower stories of the building are linked by pilasters. At the centre of the façade, a grand triangular pediment is set over the central balconied window. This is where the pope gives his blessing to those gathered in the square. A distinctive balustrade replete with statues of Christ and the apostles crowns the building.

My first organised tour was to the Vatican museums, St Peter's Basilica and the Sistine Chapel. I walked around to the entry, where a group of 10 had already gathered. Sabrina was our guide. We began at the Gallery of Tapestries, where we paused several times while she pointed out some of the unique features.

'These tapestries were designed by Raphael in 1530,' she said, 'but were manufactured in Brussels. They were hung in the Sistine Chapel until 1830 and then moved to this gallery.' Sabrina gently but firmly demanded our attention. She pointed up to the ceiling. '*Allora*, look at the beautifully sculpted architectural reliefs and cameos above you.'

We gawked at the highly decorative coffered ceiling, replete with caissons of ornamental gilded mouldings, which reflected the luxury and splendour of the Vatican Palace.

'However, it is an optical illusion—a special work of art, discovered by the genius of these 18th-century artists, to trick the eye into seeing a flat surface appear like 3D. We know this as *trompe l'oeil*, and this is a most stunning example.'

19 A convex quadrilateral trapezium, only two sides are parallel.

We were amazed and impressed. I'd seen this technique on the exterior of buildings during my visit to the ancient ring towns outside of Moscow, but it still tricked the eye and captured my imagination. However, I've been known to smell a bunch of flowers that turned out to be artificial. Though I've not taken a bite of any plastic fruit as yet.

'Is it possible to go back after the Sistine Chapel?' asked one of the ladies who'd been busy taking photos of the ceiling.

'No. It's strictly one-way traffic through a prescribed route that will lead us into the Sistine Chapel. If you get lost, we can't go back to look for you,' she said. 'Please stay together. This hall is 250 metres long and we have much more to see today.'

A man, who I surmised was the lady's husband, grabbed her elbow and gently directed her back to the group.

'You're lucky,' said Sabrina. 'It's early and there are few people crowding your view. Pay attention to the 12 tapestries along the left of this hall. They depict the life of Christ. When you get to the Resurrection tapestry, please notice how Christ's eyes follow you down the hall.'

She then ushered us through large doors that led into the Hall of Maps.

'*Allora*! Here you see the largest collection of geographical paintings and surprisingly accurate maps—the three-year work of Ignazio Dante in the 15th century. Take a little time to look closely at the decorations—tall ships, barques, galleons, all interspersed with enchanting mythical sea monsters.'

Some of the group were distracted by the ornate frescoes on the ceiling and were busy photographing them.

'This is the second, most photographed ceiling in the Vatican complex. Some people even mistake it for the Sistine Chapel. You must remember photography is forbidden inside the Sistine.'

The most avid photographers in the group came to a halt. They'd hoped to gain a swag of memories through their lenses. Sabrina waved us forward and we went through to the next area of special interest.

'*Allora*! These next rooms are a suite of four reception rooms.[20] The frescoes are the work of Raphael. They are interrelated through thematic tradition in honour of the four faculties of knowledge—philosophy, theology, law and poetry.'

'I know this one,' said a tall gentleman. We all peered at him.

'Yes,' Sabrina said. 'It is famous. Called the School of Athens. Here, the most celebrated philosophers—Plato, Aristotle and Socrates,' she pointed out each one. 'They're deep in discussion, debating important views of the age.'

She motioned us to another fresco. 'Now look at this fellow,' she said, pointing out another figure. 'Who does he remind you of?' We all concentrated. 'Some people say it's the movie actor Al Pacino.' We laughed at the uncanny likeness, although this had been painted centuries before Pacino's time.

Sabrina led us down a staircase. 'We have arrived at the doors to the Sistine Chapel, named after Pope Sixtus, who commissioned the building of the chapel. Can anyone tell me who built it?'

A young fellow raised his hand to get her attention. 'Was it built by Michelangelo?' he asked.

'No. Bramante built it. But he recommended Michelangelo to repaint the original star-studded blue ceiling. Thinking he'd not agree to do it, Bramante planned to give the job to his friend and relative, Raphael. Michelangelo was well-known as a cantankerous and poverty-stricken sculptor and not a painter

20 Commissioned by Pope Julius II in 1509.

at all. However, Michelangelo agreed to take on the project and it became his crowning glory.'

'He did the work lying on his back,' the young fellow added.

'That is another misconception,' Sabrina corrected. 'Michelangelo designed his own scaffold, which allowed him to stand while painting, though he still suffered neck and back pain. He painted for four years, not letting anyone enter until he had finished.'[21]

By now my excitement was at a fever pitch, and I wondered how much more information I could manage.

'There is a time limit inside the chapel and there are strict rules,' she said. 'We must be quiet inside. So stay close to hear me whisper. Remember, no photos, or you will be escorted straight outside.'

We moved into the Sistine Chapel. I was overwhelmed by the rich palette of colours that covered every surface. I knew I'd have to return to see it a second time. Every wall is covered in frescoes. On the one side the story of the life of Christ, and on the other, the life of Moses. My neck felt strained from looking up at Michelangelo's ceiling and I became dizzy both with the perspective and the excitement of being in this hallowed chapel. *How could the master hold his head in position for so long?*

Sabrina motioned us to gather close, then whispered, 'The wall frescoes are by Botticelli, Signorelli and Perugino. Of course, the ceiling is the story of the creation, with Adam at the centre.' We all looked up; she held a finger up to her lips to remind us not to speak.

21 The Sistine ceiling was finished in 1512, and the unveiling overshadowed the 68-ft wall frescoes of Jesus and Moses. The ceiling's main scenes were the Creation of Adam, the Expulsion of Adam and Eve from Eden, and the story of Noah.

'Look at the *Last Judgment,* behind the altar. Michelangelo specially designed it to ensure the judgement would be at eye level for the priests to reflect upon.'

We smiled at her observation. *I agree. With position comes power and exposure to many temptations—greed, avarice and lust.*

'I will show you two faces and then leave you for 20 minutes to look around,' said Sabrina. 'I'll be waiting for you on the other side of the exit.'

We followed her. She pointed out Michelangelo's self-portrait on a cloth held by St Bartholomew. Then she headed for the far wall, to the *Last Judgm*ent.[22]

'This fresco is based on chapter 20 of St John's Gospel, although many liken it to Dante's *Divine Comedy*. In any case, it's considered to be the most powerful work of art in existence here.'

We strained to take in Sabrina's whispered description. Security guards stood nearby to maintain order and decorum in what is a working chapel.

'There was much controversy,' Sabrina said, crouching in conspiratorial fashion. 'Some people were affronted by all the nude figures. Cesena, the pope's Master of Ceremonies, was the most vocal. Michelangelo repaid him by painting Cesena's portrait as the face of Minos—the judge of Hell. When Cesena protested to the pope, the pope said, "I don't have influence over Hell." Eventually, another painter was commissioned to paint modesty drapery over the offending parts.'

We had a snigger at this snippet of tit-for-tat. Sabrina then left us to enjoy the paintings in peace.

---

22 Michelangelo was well into his sixties when he painted this example of High Renaissance art. It took him seven years to complete and was finished in 1541.

After three hours of such intense colour and wonderment, I needed a good break. I found a quiet little café nearby, somewhere I could sit outdoors at a small table with a panini and coffee to watch the world go by.

Presently, a beautiful young lady, as if on a catwalk, strode towards me. She was slim, long-legged and wore tight white jeans. Her skinny, yellow crop top accentuated her ample bosom and tiny waist. *It must be difficult,* I thought, *for her to walk along the uneven cobblestones in her precariously high, stiletto heels.* Young men gawked at her as they drove past in their sports cars. She walked along, smiling smugly at all the adulation she was receiving. Meanwhile, her long dark hair fanned out behind her in the breeze.

When she was almost a metre away from me, she stopped, produced a bike helmet from nowhere, threw her leg over a shiny, new Ducati motorbike as easily as if she were a young farmhand, then disappeared into the traffic. She left with a mere hint of French perfume in her wake.

After lunch, I went to the Vatican post office to buy postcards to send to myself and to my other avid stamp collector friends. This is the only place where you can obtain a *Vaticano* stamp.

Having completed that bucket list detail, I stopped alongside a group of people positioned in front of the Swiss Guards, resplendent in their brightly coloured uniforms of red, yellow and dark blue.[23] They looked as if they were on their way to a fancy-dress party in their voluminous pantaloons and feather-

23 These were the colours of the Medici family, a prominent family of bankers who ruled Florence.

topped metal helmets. The notice nearby indicated that the guards and their uniforms dated from 1506. They are the oldest and smallest military unit, protecting the smallest country and its head of state—the pope. Suddenly there was movement and the crowd gathered to observe the ritual of the changing of the guard.

In the afternoon, I strolled around to the far corner of St Peter's Square, where bus tours commenced. Several people were already boarding the bus with the sign 'Basilicas of Rome' above the windscreen, so I climbed aboard too. Our tour guides were Rebecca and Lindy.

When the bus moved off, Rebecca took the microphone. First, she set out a laundry list of protocols and rules, such as the covering of shoulders and knees inside the basilicas.

Respect. All common sense you'd think. Though I suppose common sense is not very common.

She spoke in a clear and commanding voice that captured everyone's attention. 'There are four major basilicas in Rome: The Basilica of St Peter in the Vatican, St Paul Outside the Walls, St John Lateran and lastly, St Mary *Maggiore* or Major,' she said.

'Will we visit all four?' asked someone across the aisle from me.

'You can see St Peter's by yourselves,' Rebecca replied. 'Today we will visit the other three, starting with St Paul's Outside the Walls. This name was used to distinguish it from other churches dedicated to the Apostle Paul. It's two kilometres outside of the city boundary or walls of the Vatican compound, hence its name.'

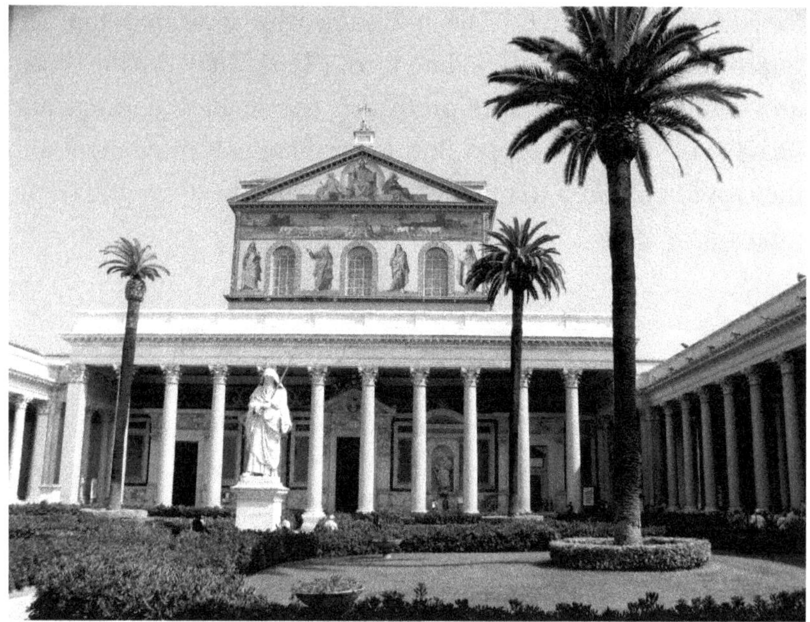

One of the ladies seated near Rebecca asked, 'When can you touch the holy doors to receive absolution?'

'During holy years,' the guide replied. Then she turned to the rest of us to explain the discussion. 'This rare event occurs every 25 years. The holy doors of the four basilicas always remain closed except during the holy years, when they are opened. It is said that by visiting and prayerfully touching all four doors, the faithful may receive absolution.'[24]

There was a buzz of discussion amongst the group as the bus drew to a halt outside a building bound by many Corinthian columns. *More like a Greek temple, I reckon.*

Lindy took over the commentary as she led us to the entrance. 'St Paul's Outside the Walls was built in the 5th century over the burial place of St Paul the Apostle. It features Roman columns. The mosaic pediment dates to the Middle Ages and features Christ with St Peter and St Paul.'

The same lady asked, 'Wasn't the original church burnt down?'

'That's right. After the fires of 1823, the church was faithfully restored,' replied Lindy. 'The fires all but razed this church. Most of the mosaic tiles from the pediment were collected, cleaned and put back together, like doing a jigsaw. Little remains of the original church except for the cloisters. Those columns are an example of the finest workmanship from the Middle Ages. Here you see there are a variety of designs, some with smooth shafts, others fluted and twisted like climbing boughs.'

I loved the feeling of space at this basilica. It felt that way because of the lovely gardens that surround the compound.

Lindy motioned us inside.[25] The interior was even more spacious and the shimmering mosaics more spectacular. Each surface vied for our attention: the ceiling white and gold, the marble floors inlaid in a tan and cream geometric pattern. The spectacular apse and a triumphal arch are also encrusted in mosaic. The arch that framed the gilded canopy over the altar was especially memorable.

Back on the bus, Rebecca took over the microphone. 'Our next destination is the Basilica of St John Lateran. The attached monastery, known as the Lateran Palace, was originally a *palazzo* belonging to the Lateran family, hence the name. The palace served as the papal residence until the 14th century. It is the most important basilica because it is the seat of the ruling bishop, who now happens to be the pope.'

The old fellow with a moustache, who was sitting up the back, interrupted. 'Are the Holy Stairs[26] in there too?'

25 There is a gallery of portraits that chronicles every pope up to the present.

26 You can attain forgiveness of a sin by climbing the entire staircase on your knees

'Their correct name is *Scala Sancta*. They're located across the road,' Lindy replied.

Rebecca, who was seated closer to the enquirer, added, 'After this visit, there will be time for you to have a look but unfortunately, not time to climb the stairs. If you wish to climb, you can return another time.'

'*Allora*,' Lindy announced. 'The Basilica of St John is some four kilometres from the Vatican. It is a Byzantine church built originally by Emperor Constantine and is the oldest and highest-ranking of the four major papal basilicas. The main entrance, the same as St Peter's, is crowned by statues of Christ and the apostles.'

'Is that the church with the obelisk in front?' The question came again from the man at the back of the bus. His view was partially obscured by those in front of him who were preparing to alight.

'Yes, the square is graced by an Egyptian obelisk[27] from the temple of Ammon in Thebes. The monolith was brought to Rome by Constantine's son.'

The bus drew up to the piazza and we assembled by the obelisk. 'Until 1870, the Basilica of St John Lateran was the church where all popes were enthroned.[28] Now the pope celebrates only the Thursday Mass here,' Lindy explained. 'As we walk to the entrance, look up to see a balustrade and statues. The statues represent Christ, St John the Baptist and

---

while meditating on the Passion of Christ and reciting the Creed, Our Father, Hail Mary, Glory Be and making a sacramental confession, receiving the Eucharist, praying for the intentions of the Pope and being free of all attachment to sin.

27 This obelisk is the tallest of all the obelisks that stand on various piazzas in Rome.

28 Upon ratification of the Lateran Treaty, the papacy recognised the state of Italy, with Rome as its capital. Italy in return recognised papal sovereignty over Vatican City, a minute territory of 44 hectares (109 acres) and secured full independence for the pope.

the Doctors of the Church. Inside the portico, you'll notice bronze doors. Those at the far right are the Holy Doors. Now, let's go in.'

Inside the church, we inhaled the aromas of incense and beeswax. The nave is a long gallery bound by marble and granite arches, columns and pilasters. This bank also houses niches with larger-than-life statues of the 12 apostles.[29] High above is a heavily gilded caisson-covered ceiling. I was mesmerised, in a world of my own, until Lindy's soft voice called us to attention and I joined the group as they moved closer to hear her.

'The pope's cathedra, his throne, is located under the beautiful mosaic-decorated apse,' she said.

We all peered in admiration at the magnificent mosaic.

'The scene you see portrays Christ surrounded by angels and a cross symbolising the crucifixion. From the left are St Paul, St Peter, St Francis of Assisi and then a much smaller figure.' Lindy pointed to the remaining figure. 'This is Pope Nicholas IV, who was responsible for ordering the work to be done.'

Human nature, the artist, the designer, is not opposed to self-promotion. In a way, this is his signature, his billboard, an example of his work.

I could hear our guide continue. 'See how gently, even motherly, the Virgin places her right hand over the pope's coronet. On the right is St John the Baptist, a smaller figure of St Anthony of Padua, then St John the Evangelist and St Andrew.'

Lindy added, 'The artists were Franciscan monks, hence the inclusion of St Francis and St Anthony, who were of the same

29 Judas Iscariot is replaced by St Paul, who was converted after the Resurrection of Christ.

order, together with Pope Nicholas, their patron, who was the first Franciscan pope.'

When outside, several of us spontaneously crossed the road to see the Holy Stairs. Rebecca hadn't planned to accompany the group. I'm sure she wasn't happy with this turn of events but it was her duty to ensure we crossed the busy road safely.

'*Sancta Scala* is a sacred place,' she said. 'Not only for Catholics and Orthodox Christians but even people of other faiths like Hindus and Buddhists. They say they are drawn to the sanctuary's spiritual atmosphere,' said Rebecca. 'The stairs are white marble, said to be the same ones which led to the praetorium of Pontius Pilate in Jerusalem and were sanctified by Jesus Christ during His Passion.'[30]

We noticed several people climbing the stairs on their knees while reciting prayers.

'The stairs are encased in wood to protect them from being worn down by this traditional practice,' said Rebecca. 'They lead to a small chapel, which is the only building retained from the old Lateran Palace. We don't have the time to see it today; the bus is waiting.'

On the bus, Lindy took the microphone. 'Our last stop will be the *Basilica di Santa Maria Maggiore*. In AD 356, the Virgin Mary appeared in a dream to Pope Liberius, instructing him to build a church at the place where, on the following day, it would snow.'

'It's too warm to snow in August,' sniggered a young fellow. His mother shushed him. When his cheeks coloured, I knew he was embarrassed.

30 They were taken from Jerusalem to the Lateran Palace in the 4th century by Empress St Helena, who was Constantine's mother.

'That's right,' said Lindy, 'but snow it did—a miracle. And the church was built[31] on that very spot. A mosaic of the miracle can be found in the *loggia* of the portico. This basilica is the fourth largest in Rome and the largest of 26 churches dedicated to the Virgin Mary.'

The bus pulled up and we alighted onto a piazza near a very tall column. Rebecca ushered us in quickly. By now, I was getting a bit weary with all I'd seen and heard. Thankfully, this was the last item on my agenda for that day.

'As you enter, you'll see that this church[32] is also resplendent with mosaics. They adorn the ceiling, walls, apses and particularly, the triumphal arch. Beneath the arch is the beautiful baldachin or canopy, which is supported by four porphyry columns. The altar is a sarcophagus holding the relics of Apostle Matthew.'

As Lindy paused to point out exceptional areas, I gazed vacantly from one feature to the other. I was interested but in need of a break.

'In front of the high altar is another reliquary. It holds pieces from the crib in which baby Jesus lay. I'll leave you to wander around before we get back onto the bus for our return journey.'

'Lindy, I hope you don't mind, but I'd rather stay and make my own way home.'

'That's fine,' she said. 'I hope you've enjoyed the excursion today and wish you well for the remainder of your stay.'

I wanted to have a better look at the side chapels, the beautiful mosaics and icons. I took my time in the *Capella St Paolina*. There hangs a beautiful icon of the Virgin Mary attributed to St Luke's hand.[33] St Luke the Apostle was a physician and artist. A group

31 It was completed in AD 432.

32 The basilica retains the original colonnaded triple nave, lined with panels of rare mosaics.

33 That is how we know what the Blessed Virgin Mary looked like.

of people had gathered there for vespers, so I sat with them and listened to the short service. When I left, it was with a certain feeling of calm that seemed to exude from St Luke's icon.

Bus routes to *Vaticano* are frequent and come from many directions. On the short walk back to my *pension,* I gazed into the shop windows and even went into a boutique still trading. It had those magic words 'Sale' plastered on the window. The garments were all such impossibly tiny sizes that I speculated whether the clothes were samples or had been worn once on the catwalk.

Further on, I saw a 'TIM' sign, where all things for mobile phones were sold. I ducked in for a SIM card but alas I had no ID; my passport was in my room.

I hurried home, grabbed the passport and returned to the shop. As I arrived, the lady was already locking the door. I pleaded and she kind-heartedly opened again to sell me a SIM card. I was extremely relieved and so grateful that I put €5 into a beggar's hat. The beggar was an old lady who'd been kneeling with her head on the ground for a long-time awaiting alms, and I had a lot to be grateful for.

On the way home, I stopped at Santa Clare's Café for a cappuccino and some pizza. My day had been enormously busy and I was dying to get back to my spartan bed where I knew I'd sleep very well indeed.

Chapter 4

Still Rome

I awoke to the pleading peal of bells from St Peter's. Seven o'clock and already the faithful were being called to prayer. I opened the window. Cool morning air, mingled with the unmistakable aroma of good coffee, streamed into my room. That made getting out of bed easier. It was my second day in Rome and a myriad of adventures awaited.

My plan for the morning was to go to *Trastevere*[34] in the old quarter of the city, also known as 'the heart of Rome'. In the afternoon I wanted to return to the Vatican museums to revisit the Sistine Chapel. This time I hoped to experience the atmosphere of the celebrated museum at leisure and not be constrained to the timetable of a tour group.

The sunny weather was perfect for my first challenge, which was to find the correct bus stop somewhere on the other side of the Vatican precinct. As I walked, I gazed in shop windows and at the goods being peddled by street hawkers. *Italy is known for stylish jewellery. I might see some nice earrings to remind me of my time here.*

Further along on the sidewalk, a man was setting up suitcases. *I should buy myself a new suitcase to replace my poor bag damaged during the flight from Australia.* He stopped for a moment to judge my readiness to buy. *This fellow has found a niche market, maybe in cahoots with the baggage handlers.* I laughed to myself at the thought. *I'll do it on my way back. I don't want to be carrying stuff.*

Up ahead a bus to Ponte Sisto was waiting at the bus shelter. I asked the driver, '*Scusi, l'autobus va Santa Maria Trastevere*?'

His animated reply in Italian sounded as if my assumption was correct, and he was going that way. With my map at the ready, I boarded and sat on the first empty seat, which happened to be near the front. *I hope the driver will tell me when it's my stop.* More people boarded, and we commenced our journey.

The scenery became more residential, less like the city proper. We travelled alongside the embankment of the Tiber River. The bus stopped at a bridge and the driver waved his hand towards the door—it was my stop.

'Ponte Garibaldi,' he said, pointing to the narrow stone bridge.

Once on the other side of the river, I was confronted by a labyrinth of cobbled alleys, with crumbling terrace houses and faded paintwork. Here and there washing was strung in the narrow lanes between buildings. In contrast, other streets had terraces with small balconies to house potted plants. Further on, I could see greenery spilling from rooftop gardens, but not a street sign in sight.

I stopped at Fior di Luna Gelato for an ice cream and to ask for directions to *Santa Maria Trastevere*. In the glass-covered display counter, an array of tempting gelato held me spellbound. The shopkeeper knew the signs. He suggested I try a strange combination of chocolate, lime and pink peppercorn. I agreed to it but was surprised to see him fill a small takeaway cup instead of a cone. *They say when in Rome…* Business was slow and the shop assistant seemed happy to chat. *If only I was a native speaker.* Then he traced the directions to the church on my trusty map.

After rounding several corners, I stumbled onto a piazza with a fountain in front of a simple, Romanesque-style church. Much to my relief, it matched the pictures I'd seen in my guidebook. I particularly remembered the stunning mosaic frieze above the colonnaded porch. I was relieved at the success of reaching my destination. I paused to admire the balustrade on the roof with its sculptures of saints, not unlike those at the Vatican.

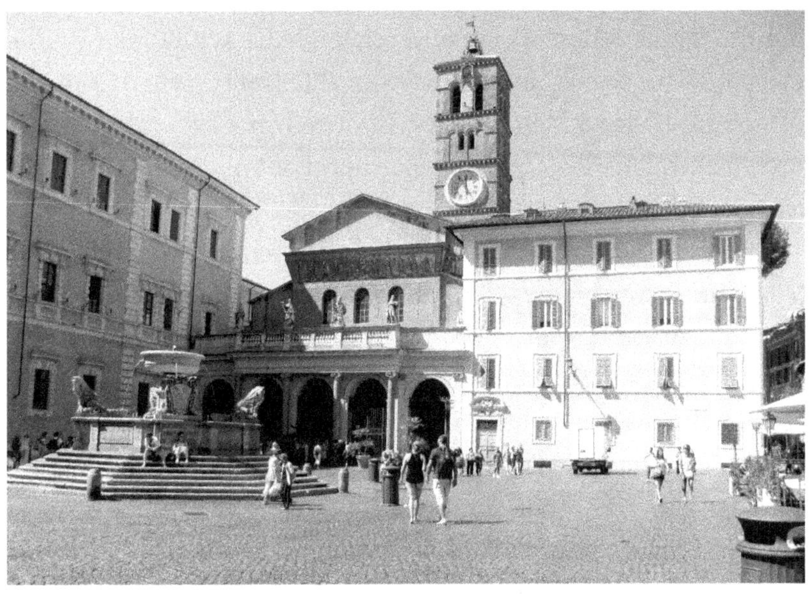

As I stood by the fountain finishing my gelato, a wedding party spilled out of the church. Confetti and the laughter of guests rained on the happy couple. Meanwhile, the photographer darted back and forth, trying to capture the moment. *What luck.* I felt privileged to arrive on a Saturday and be like a little mouse in the shadows peeking at the jubilant gathering as they celebrated an important part of their everyday cycle of local life.

After the wedding party had left, I entered the church. My guidebook said this is the oldest basilica in Rome. It was founded in AD 221. Unlike architecture in the city proper, I thought the exterior was plain.

Inside, 22 granite columns with ionic capitals, divide the nave from the side aisles. The mosaics and frescoes were not added until refurbishment in the 12th century. The apse is lined with mesmerising mosaics. The brightly coloured figures, which are depicted on a shimmering gold background, are intended to convey the glory of Heaven. At the peak of the triumphal arch are the Greek letters alpha and omega—the symbols of divine eternity. The scenes in the mosaics illustrate events from the life of the Blessed Virgin Mary. I noticed that several included architectural features in the background of the scene. To me, this added depth to the composition.[35]

I visited various side chapels in search of the 7th-century Byzantine icon of the *Madonna di Clemenza*. I found it above the altar in the Capella Altemps chapel. Sadly, it was in poor condition. *It's very dark, due to time and smoke from candles. It needs a clean.* Then I noticed the canvas. It too was damaged. *It must be ancient; I wonder if it can be restored.* There was something poignant about it that compelled me to light a candle. I was surprised to see t-lights had replaced tapers—a modernisation and dare I say, cost-effective measure.

Outside in the dazzling daylight, I became confused, unsure of my way. I was overawed, as can happen in such special places. All the shops were now closed for siesta and there was no one to ask for help. I wandered the streets until I came to a bridge,

35 Discovery of linear perspective is attributed to the Italian Renaissance artist Brunelleschi, although attempts at perspective can be seen since 5 BC in the theatrical backdrops used in ancient Greece and Pompeii.

though not the same one I'd crossed earlier. Nevertheless, I marched across, knowing that it would take me in the right direction, which was on the other side of the river. As I sauntered along the footpath, several buses with *Vaticano* across their destination board whizzed by.

All was quiet along the Tiber. Double-storey houseboats moored on the river exposed an alternative lifestyle. After some distance, I came upon a marked bus stop. Several buses passed by before one stopped to let a person off. I didn't wait for an invitation but grabbed the handrail and scrambled aboard.

Back in my room, I ate the ham and cheese roll I'd smuggled from breakfast. It went down well with the bottle of Arancino—a soft drink made from blood oranges, which I'd bought on my way home. After a short rest, I resumed my well-trodden path to the Vatican. All the shops had remained closed because of half-day trading. *If I'd known about this custom I might have done some shopping earlier. I guess I was not meant to buy those things I'd earmarked.*

At the entrance to the Vatican Museums, I was surprised to see no queue. I walked straight in and bought a ticket to take me to all the museums, including the Sistine Chapel.

The most important exhibition on my list was the Egyptian acquisition.[36] I'd read that outside of Cairo and the British Museum, the Vatican boasted the best collection. I was not disappointed; the layout and quality of the artifacts were truly exceptional. I'd hoped to see the Book of the Dead, but it alluded me. There was a uniformed man sitting by the door, so I asked him where I could find it.

'Not here, Madam,' was his reply.

---

36 Fr Ungarelli, a 19th century Egyptologist, founded and developed the Egyptian Museum.

'In that case, can you tell me if the Etruscan Museum[37] is open?'

'Yes, it will be open after one hour.'

I thanked him and went back to viewing the Egyptian antiquities, assured that I had at least an hour at my disposal.

For me, the highlights of the Egyptian display were several elaborately decorated mummy cases. The one I particularly revered was the sarcophagus of the mistress of the house of Hetepheres from the fourth dynasty. Then there was the unforgettable gilded, marble mask. Its black onyx eyes followed me around the room. A wooden box with alabaster canopic jars caught my attention with its distinctive decorations. Anubis, the black jackal god of the underworld, was propped next to a hollow bronze cast of a cat—the god Bastet. *I wonder if this bundle was a beloved pet or was the cat already deified during its lifetime?*

Another room held a plethora of alabaster figurines, amulets and pottery shards, whole wall friezes and reliefs of battle scenes from Assyria and Palmyra. Throughout the rooms, granite and limestone statues of pharaohs and gods stood sentinel. Further on, I saw a fragment of limestone with a portrait of a handsome young Etruscan man. The inscription read: Black Etruscan from Fayum[38], one of Egypt's oldest cities, located southwest of Cairo. Further along were statues of baboons. They reminded me of a lady I'd met on my Egyptian trip who'd experienced premonitions in her dreams. One night she'd dreamt of baboons and the very

37 The Etruscans predated Romans in Italy. Their capital was Rome. Evidence shows that they also lived in the South of Italy and Pompeii.

38 These stylised portraits were copied from the Greek and Roman ones, then transported to Egypt during the Ptolemaic period.

next day, we saw those same baboons painted on the wall of a tomb. The memory of her telling us still gives me goosebumps.

Though an hour had passed, I'd not yet seen any papyrus scrolls. *I'll try to come back to that after seeing the Etruscan collection. It should be opening about now.*

I hurried along, but there was a barricade in front of the closed door. Nearby, a guard sat on a high stool.

'Will the Etruscan rooms be open soon?' I asked.

'No, madam,' he replied. 'They are closed for refurbishment.'

Had I misunderstood the other man or had something been lost in the translation? I moved on to the next set of rooms, which happened to be the Profane Museum. Once again, a guard sat in front of closed doors.

'What time do the doors open?' I asked.

'This salon is closed today. It is open only two or three times a year,' the young man responded in what sounded close to a scripted spiel.

'I've come a long way, from Australia,' I said. 'And this is the second museum with closed doors. I feel very unhappy. I'll never have another opportunity during my lifetime to come here again.' As he listened to my impassioned tale, his expression became sorrowful and I hoped sympathetic to my plight. I took a deep breath. 'Even the Book of the Dead in the Egyptian Museum, which I'd come specially from Australia to see, I'm now told it's not open.'

'Oh, I am so sorry.' The guard's demeanour changed. 'It's long way. My cousin, he live in Sydney.' He smiled, waiting for my reply. 'You know Sydney?'

'What a coincidence. I live there,' I replied.

'Oh! I do not believe in coincidence. We meet for reason.'

'I agree. Have you read the Celestine Prophecy?'

'No, I believe it up to us to use opportunity or not. What is your work? You must be teacher?'

'No, I used to work in business management and yes, we ran education, but for adults, not for children.'

'I want work—teach children. You know Montessori?'

'Yes. My children went to a Montessori school when they were little.'

He looked at his watch. 'I am happy to meet you. We talk. You wait *una momento.* I speak with boss.'

He hurried along a private little hallway. I stood there, pondering what on earth was going on. *He seems harmless enough, but I wouldn't expect a museum worker, a stranger, to take such an interest. How long will he be? I should get going, there's so much more I want to see.*

Just then, the fellow returned, accompanied by another man. who proceeded to sit on the vacated chair. The young fellow opened the door to the Profane Museum[39] and invited me to follow him inside.

It appeared as if there were several rooms, all filled with statues. *Here I am, alone with a stranger in a lonely place, looking at vulgar, irreverent things.* I grappled with my conflicting thoughts as I gingerly followed him into the darkened room. *It's an adventure. I won't think about it anymore. But I wonder why it's called profane. I hope it's not too suggestive or indecent.*

As I stepped into the darkened room, he turned on the lights. The first bust we paused to look at was of Thalia, a

39 The Profane Museum was one of the first two areas in the Vatican opened as a museum rather than a private collection. The sculptures inside are from Greek and Roman antiquity.

beautiful young woman—the muse of comedy and poetry. I thought the sculptor had successfully captured her lyrical purity and innocence. Another memorable bust was that of a young warrior with coal-black eyes. I felt them stare fiercely at me. *I wonder why my guide has forged ahead.* He turned back to me with a pleased look on his face. No need for a drum-roll or introduction. His gleeful demeanour was enough. He stretched his arm towards his quarry. I recognised her by the blunt-cut hair-do, and the wide-set eyes, heavy with kohl. It was the incomparable Cleopatra. *I think she's a favourite with most tourists and he expected I'd be thrilled to see her, particularly as I'd come straight from the Egyptology collection. That was his clue.*

Then he led me to another room with larger-than-life statues. One was in lustrous porphyry and another in red granite. It captured my attention. *I've seen pictures of a similarly dressed man with the same hair. I wonder if this might be a Varangian.*[40] The inscription on the accompanying plaque read, 'Barbarian'. I tried to ask the guide if they were the same, but his explanation was lost, either due to his lack of English or my lack of Italian. So apart from what I gleaned from the plaques, my visit to the Profane Collection matched that of a blind person with only his seeing-eye dog acting as guide. On one hand, it was a comical experience, however, on the other, it was a privilege to receive the private tour and to see so many marvellous works of art.

Of the many beautifully executed reliefs on decorative panels, stele and friezes, I particularly loved one of a young woman who offered food to a toddler. She stood under some kind of fruit tree. *I wonder if it's a fig tree,* I pondered. Behind

40 During the 10th century, they were bodyguards to the Byzantine emperors along the important trade route connecting the Baltic to the Caspian Sea.

the tree the figure of Pan loitered. He spied on the pair while holding his reedpipes in his hand.

The Egyptian artifacts were from the Ptolemaic period. I marvelled at the sculptor's ability to chisel so much detail, particularly evident in the variety of hairstyles and curly beards. But it was the fine draping of the garments worn[41] by both male and female forms that left me in awe.

As my guide didn't seem to be in any hurry, I allowed myself the luxury of taking many more photos than I'd do normally. I think he was enjoying the break from 'playing statue' on the chair by the museum door. When we finally left, I tried to give him a tip, but he refused to take any money. He put his hand on his heart and bowed sagely several times while saying, 'You welcome.' He kissed my hand in the old European fashion and said, 'Ciao, bella.' I'll never forget the kindness and empathy he'd shown me.

I returned for one last look at the Egyptian Museum and was excited to find an exceptionally long papyrus in a display case attached to the wall. The little sign at one end read *Book of the Dead*. Being prose, the scroll had few illustrations. *I wish I could read those hieroglyphs*, I thought, as I meandered back through to the galleries.

I found the Pinacoteca Gallery.[42] The first two rooms were filled with altarpieces and other medieval art, mostly tempera, painted directly onto wood panels. I couldn't take my eyes

41 The headless Nicobide Chiaramonti female figure is well known for the way the drapery of her tunic is being blown in the breeze. It is a notable example of movement and of the body under the tunic.

42 There are 460 works of art here, including those from Giotto, Fra Angelico, Raphael, Caravaggio, Leonardo da Vinci and many other equally renowned artists.

off Giotto's *Stefaneschi* triptych. The central panel portrayed Christ enthroned. The side panels were of St Peter's and St Paul's martyrdom. It came from the original 4th century St Peter's Cathedral, the colours as vivid as if they'd been painted yesterday.

My plan was to exit via the Sistine Chapel and then go onto St Peter's Cathedral. Back at the Sistine, Michelangelo's awe-inspiring ceiling—his crowning glory[43], was a dizzying sight. Looking up at the ceiling made it impossible to examine each panel at any length. He used the architectural features of the building—beams and cross-members—as part of his *tromp l'oeil,* to achieve even more realism in his work.

The Sistine Chapel is also used for the conclave of cardinals to elect a new pope. *I hope the* Last Judgment, *positioned at eye level behind the altar, inspires the cardinals to make an honest and fair choice.* I smiled to myself.

When I stepped inside St Peter's Cathedral[44], I was overwhelmed by the voluminous expanse above me. I felt small. Insignificant. Like Jonah, when the whale swallowed him. As my eyes adjusted to the more subdued light, I noticed Michelangelo's *Pieta,* a poignant marble statue of the lifeless body of Christ in his Mother's arms. I could see several people dabbing their eyes. The juxtaposition of youth with death and beauty with grief made my emotions also rise.

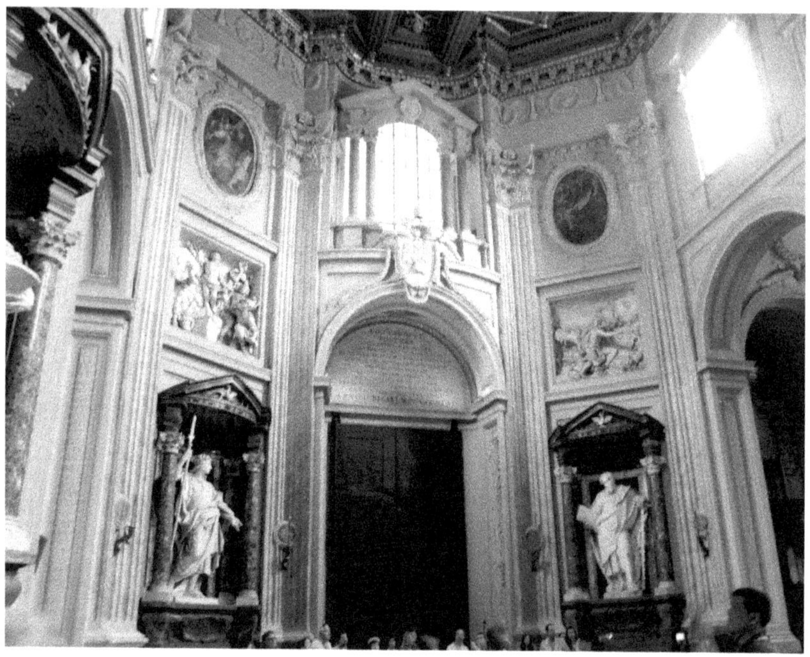

A tour group stood near enough for me to listen to their guide, so I resolved to remain at close quarters.

'Here you see,' said the young guide, 'the large central nave is divided by four aisles formed by giant Corinthian pilasters. These are attached to the vast piers that support the structure.' He pointed up at the enormous central dome.[45]

He's young. Looks as if he's come straight out of the seminary. I suppose guiding must be a part of his training.

'The dome is considered an architectural feat. See how it bathes the nave with natural light? It streams through 16 windows placed in the drum and the same number in the lantern.'

Wow! Though it's so far above us, it bathes the whole church in natural light.

He motioned the group to follow him. 'Come forward to see the mosaic in the centre of the dome.' They gathered in a huddle to peer at it. 'This structure with gilded bronze twisted columns is the centrepiece of the church. Called a baldachin, it is the papal altar and is built over the very tomb of the Apostle Peter.'

Those gathered moved forward and I followed—an interloper on the periphery. Suddenly the troop came to a stop at one of four semi-circular niches.

'These niches support the dome,' the guide explained. 'And they house larger-than-life statues. Each of these four figures relates to the Passion of Christ. This one is St Helena, holding the True Cross.'

Such a classic Roman beauty, standing there triumphant as she supports the weight of the enormous cross. I could hardly tear myself away from admiring the drapery of her raiment. Somehow, the sculptor had instilled movement and life into the marble. I recalled that St Helena was the mother of Constantine the Great. He was the first Roman emperor to convert to Christianity.

The group moved over to the opposite niche. 'This is St Veronica holding her veil[46], which she provided to Jesus to wipe His face when He stumbled along the road to Calvary. The imprint of his features remains visible on the veil.'

The surprised look on some of the people around me made it clear that few had known of this interesting story. The image on the veil is sometimes referred to as the first icon.

'Over there,' the guide pointed to the statue of a soldier, 'is Longinus, who was instantly converted when he pierced Christ's side. The last is St Andrew. The *loggias* above each hold their relics.'

46 In Greek, *vera icona* means true image and this forms the name Veronica. The veil of Veronica is kept in a church in Manopello, a small town in the region of Abruzzio.

The crowd moved towards Bernini's[47] bronze statue of St Peter, where a constant stream of visitors filed by. Some stopped to say a quick prayer while others posed for a photo. Still more paused to touch his foot. This ritual touching, over time, polished the statue so much that the toes are no longer discernible.

'It's a superstition,' said the guide, 'equal to throwing coins into the *Trevi* fountain or putting your hand into the bas relief known as the *Mouth of Truth*.'[48]

I'd intended to have some quiet time for rest and contemplation, but of course, the masses of ever-present tourists were difficult to avoid. They were heading in one direction and I was swept along in their wake to one of the larger chapels where chairs were positioned in neat rows.

One of the uniformed attendants asked, 'Are you here for Mass?'

The chairs look so inviting. In my best Italian accent, I replied, '*Si, si*.'

He ushered me through. No sooner had I sat down when the Mass commenced. I couldn't understand a word, although the singing was lovely so it didn't matter. Not knowing the order of service, I copied the other people when they stood and sat. The service was short; hardly time for me to rest my feet. Behind me, the ushers had begun clearing the chairs, so I took my cue to leave. I strolled back home, only stopping briefly for some pizza and a bottle of Peroni.

---

47 Bernini was the chief architect of St Peter's for 50 years.

48 A large mask in the portico at the church of Santa Maria Cosmedin said to bite off the hand of liars.

On Sunday morning, I headed off in the opposite direction from my usual forays. My destination was *Santa Caterina d'Alessandria, Chiesa Russo* for the liturgy.

After five steady but unhurried minutes of walking, I arrived at St Peter's train station. I could see on the other side of the railway the distinctive tent-style bell tower, topped with a small golden cupola. It dominated the skyline.[49] The newly built church had been consecrated a mere three years earlier.

I think the wide set of stone stairs leading to the main entry porch took me longer to ascend than the actual walk from my hostel. *How on earth do the elderly train travellers manage?* When I reached the top, I noticed it was not the main entrance. That was nearer the parking lot, where several late-model cars were already parked. We were up high enough to enjoy the city skyline—a panorama of terracotta roofs dominated by the familiar Dome of St Peter's.

Although there are Russian Orthodox churches in all the major cities of Italy, I thought it unusual to have a non-Catholic church built so close to the Vatican.[50] Inside, the church is plain. Icons hang on the walls but otherwise, it is unadorned. Scaffolding stood against one side wall, I assumed, in preparation for frescoes. *If I return in five years' time, the church will be spectacular.*

I perused the parishioners as they arrived. *The majority look like young families with only a few old expats. I guess the young are most likely here on secondment, working in IT or other specialised fields. Perhaps some are migrants.* In the city, I successfully blended into the crowd, but here I was the odd one out. I knew no one,

49 A contrast to the classical Baroque style architecture typical in Rome.

50 The plan to build a Russian church in Rome dated back to the late 19th century but was delayed due to the Russian Revolution and two world wars. In 2001, approval was granted to build in the grounds of the Russian Embassy on Gianicolo Hill.

whereas the regulars exchanged friendly nods or greetings. The priest was young and in the style of Fr Andrei in Bari, so unlike the stereotyped old monks with flowing beards.

Liturgy commenced at 10 o'clock—an hour later than I'd expected. I had to leave before the end because I didn't want to be late for the pope's blessing at midday in St Peter's Square. I was torn between two events.

By the time I arrived at St Peter's Square tourists were already gathered, but we were to be disappointed. The pope was away, so his blessing was by way of video beamed onto screens positioned around the piazza. People snapped photos in all directions but as soon as he'd raised his hand in blessing, the multitude vanished.

A bit disappointed at the non-event, I settled on wandering through the city and stopping for lunch at an alfresco café. In truth, the attraction was the free Wi-Fi. I wanted to phone my family. The internet in the hostel was problematic, but here, I had a better opportunity to connect. I settled in and ordered their speciality—arancini with a ragu sauce and with it, a glass of local wine.

The few people wandering nearby were all tourists, except for two bare-headed young priests. Their heavy brown cassocks swished as they passed by. The city was dead and I was tired, so I wandered back home to pack for my early start the following morning.

Chapter 5
Southern Sunshine

All too soon, my three days in Rome were over. Though I was sad at the thought of leaving Rome, an effervescent flutter pervaded my body in anticipation of what lay ahead. With those thoughts, I made my way to Roma Termini—the main railway station and interchange for long-distance journeys.

After so much ancient architecture during my past three days, it was a surprise to walk into a modern building bustling with eateries, escalators and a tourist information counter close to the entry. I stood in the queue to get directions to my platform when a young dark-haired man came up to me.

'*Senora*, you want buy ticket. I get for you,' he said, tugging at my elbow.

'*Gracias*, no. I already have my ticket.'

Unfazed, he approached another person in the line. Our luggage was a dead giveaway. We didn't need a flashing light or a sign with 'tourist' written on our foreheads. The voice of the hotel receptionist, still fresh in my mind, had warned me to look out for scammers, touts and pickpockets at all the major tourist hubs, but especially the railway stations.

The signage at the bank of ticket machines was only in Italian. Automatic machines and me are a bad combination at the best of times but in another language, forget it. Thank goodness I had a pre-booked ticket. The information clerk told me that long-distance trains operated from the upper level and to hurry as there was not much leeway between arrival and departure.

As soon as I stepped through the gates and onto the long platform, a sleek, silver python of a train glided into position. From under its round black nose, a red streak like a moustache wrapped itself along the body of the carriages. I hurried along, peering at the numbers on the cars. Finally, I found mine, but the platform was much lower than the train door. By this time, I was hot and flustered. I glanced around for platform staff, but there was no one around. Instead of steps, I had to negotiate a couple of precarious metal rungs attached to the base of the carriage doorway then lever my heavy luggage through the narrow opening.

I'm misplaced in this modern age.

An image flashed through my mind—*me in an Edwardian-style travelling outfit complete with a perky feathered hat, my hands warm in a soft fur muff. Porters manoeuvred my travelling cases into the carriage of the Orient Express. A uniformed guard positioned a set of wooden steps and held out his hand to guide me up. We exchanged pleasantries. Inside, another attendant escorted me to my compartment, while a third stowed my baggage.*

I snapped out of my reverie when I heard a young, able-looking woman address me from inside the carriage. She'd seen my plight.

'My name's Leonie,' she said with a ready smile and an extended hand. 'Where are you going? Are you travelling alone? Let me help you.'

'Yes. I'm on my way to Sorrento via Naples,' I replied. Leonie's kind expression made me feel comfortable.

'I'm taking a small group to Pompeii today.' She chuckled. 'Come and join us.'

'Are you? My plan is to visit Pompeii and Herculaneum tomorrow.'

Leonie explained that her business was to lead small groups of women from South Africa on tours. This time, they were enjoying a couple of weeks in Italy. Judging by their banter, they were mostly middle-aged and seemed to be old friends. They chattered and giggled all the way, akin to a pack of school kids, only much older.

Leonie was a feisty woman, solid and I estimated in her 30s. She constantly told jokes and passed around a bag of lollies. The group took me under their wing as if I were an honorary member of their collective. Leonie gave me her card and invited me to tour South America with them.

When we arrived in Naples, I bade them farewell and once again, Leonie helped me off the train. I had to accept that train travel was no longer as easy for me as it used to be. So I changed my mind about getting the bus from Naples to Sorrento in favour of a taxi. Somewhere I'd heard that the museum in Naples owned an exceptional amassment of all things Egyptian and Pompeiian. *I'd love to look around Naples, the birthplace of Sophia Loren. But I'm a bit scared to wander around by myself in what is supposed to be the crime capital of Italy.*

There were plenty of taxis at the rank. I bartered exceptionally hard with the driver and managed to get him down to a flat €120. He refused to budge any further.

'Alternatively, I can use the meter,' he said in a brusque tone. 'Then I must double the total to get me back here to Naples.'

I should walk away, but he's the next cab in the rank so the others won't take me. Awful price, I ruminated, *but worth it to save the hassle with my bags.*

The trip was a good 50 km and took a little over an hour. I still felt ripped off, so when we arrived and the driver unloaded my bags, I paid him the agreed price but didn't give him a tip. He was not happy. But then, neither was I. He began to berate me so I quickly stepped into the safety of the hotel.

From the outside, I thought the hotel modest, but inside it seemed cosy enough.

The young man at reception greeted me. 'Welcome, my name is Carlo. Please sign the registration book.' While I did that, he snapped his fingers for the bellboy to carry my luggage to the lift.

Once in my room, the porter showed me where each thing was located then drew back the curtains to reveal a stunning water view.

'Come, next door.' He motioned me to follow. 'We have rooftop bar, open from five in the afternoon till midnight.'

We strode onto the terrace. Outdoors, the sight was enough to render me speechless.

'This Bay of Naples,' he said with a sweeping flourish of his arm. 'And over there is Capri.' He smiled from ear to ear with pleasure as if he'd presented me with a gift. Then he left me to soak up the panorama. The sparkling water melded seamlessly with the cloudless sky while yachts, their sails billowing, bobbed around like corks in a barrel.

On the deck, comfortable cane armchairs were positioned around low tables interspersed with potted palm trees. I imagine they'd provide a calm ambience for private tête-à-têtes. Garden beds hugged the low walls of the terrace and in one corner stood the shuttered bar. High stools awaited guests for pre-dinner drinks. I was tempted to relax with a book, but I didn't come all this way to laze about when Sorrento and the Amalfi Coast awaited. *I must have a look at the town and find the Circumvesuviana train station for my big expedition to Pompeii in the morning.*

Carlo was still at reception. I asked him the way.

'When you step outside, turn left and look for the main street on your right. It will take you to all the shops and the interchange for trains and buses,' he said. 'I recommend you take the bus to see the Amalfi Coast but sit on the right-hand side.'

When I arrived, I saw people getting onto a public bus that was bound for Amalfi. I could ride all day for €7 round trip. *That's a cheap excursion.* I sat on the right-hand side, as Carlo advised.

'You will never forget this trip,' he had told me. I was puzzled by the strange look that swept over his face. 'Also for the breathtaking vista,' he quickly added.

Am I imagining it or he is alluding to something? It made me feel a little uneasy but I swept the thought away.

The road traversed lush countryside—vineyards on one side and olive groves on the other. Several long tunnels were cut right through the mountains and in between, bright sunlight streamed through the bus windows, directing my gaze back to the Mediterranean.

After a while, I noticed that the road had narrowed considerably. It hugged the edge of the cliff beyond which was a sheer drop. My heart lodged in my throat. It became even more terrifying when the bus driver negotiated precarious hairpin bends as we skirted the southern flank of Sorrento's peninsular. Then I noticed—there were no guardrails!

Traffic, including buses as big as ours, travelled in the opposite direction. *I don't know how the drivers manage to pass each other. They must have nerves of steel and years of experience to do this run*. Then I saw the tell-tale scrapes along the bodywork of the buses travelling in the opposite direction. What a hair-raising experience. I said a silent prayer[51] and wondered why Carlo hadn't advised me to take the ferry.

My focus was recaptured by the dark blue water, which glistened in the sunlight. Sailing boats and ferries drew closer to their destinations. The little village of Positano—the preferred holiday destination for the jet set—was simply an assembly of pretty villas that spilled down an almost vertical slope to the Gulf of Salerno. Down there the hydrofoil to Capri—a known tourist trap—leaves regularly from the dock below.

Two hours later we stopped at Amalfi, the largest coastal town, being the last stop on this route. This was where some of the passengers changed to another bus, which continued to Ravello and Salerno.[52] These local buses are smaller and travel less frequently along a more hazardous road.

I'd have enjoyed travelling with them to visit the church of San Pantaleon. The Orthodox know him as St Panteleimon.[53] However, that would mean I'd be late getting back before the last bus from Amalfi to Sorrento along the same perilous road less travelled, and I'd certainly not do it at night.

Our driver was on a break, and I had almost 20 minutes to wander around. An ice cream van was doing a good trade and

51 There is a ferry service available around the Amalfi Coast, servicing the waterside villages and resorts.

52 The views from Villa Rufolo are the best on the coast and are said to have inspired Wagner when composing his operas.

53 St Panteleimon was a medical doctor and great healer. Miracles attributed to his intercession are recorded.

I joined the queue for a gelato. Further along stood a prickly pear[54] vendor wearing what looked like gardening gloves. He was busy peeling the spikey fruit ready for sale.

Wide stairs, facing the sea, led to the 9th-century Cathedral[55] of St Andrew the Apostle, which has been built and rebuilt several time over the centuries, each time in the architectural style of the era. This is where the relics of St Andrew have been interred. However, there was no time for me to visit that day. I heard the bus driver calling out, 'Bus to Sorrento now boarding.' Those words could not be ignored. To my relief, I found travelling in the opposite direction was not as scary because we were buffered by the side of the mountain.

While walking from the bus interchange to the hotel, I stopped at the *supermercato*, where I bought provisions for the following day's trip to Pompeii and Herculaneum.

Back at the hotel, I proceeded to the rooftop, where a few people were relaxing and enjoying a pre-dinner drink. I bought a Campari and tonic and sat at a small table, where I could gaze out across the bay.

Downstairs, the dining room offered a choice between *table d'hôte* or a la carte. I'd been looking forward to some fish but there was none on the menu. The waiter was most apologetic and promised to get some for the following evening. I agreed to the set menu, then enquired about wine.

54 Prickly pear is a popular fruit in all countries around the Mediterranean and Central America, yet it is banned in Australia. Imported in 1788 for its red dye used on soldiers' coats, it became prolific and hard to eradicate and was banned in Australia.

55 A cathedral is the principal church of a diocese and is run by a bishop. It is his cathedra or seat.

'Madam, I recommend you try the Lacrima Christi[56], a popular local wine. It's from the slopes of Vesuvius,' the *maître de* told me.

'Do you have a half bottle? I couldn't drink a whole one all by myself.'

'Don't worry.' He smiled. 'We'll keep the cork to ensure it stays fresh for you to finish tomorrow.'

'Oh, what a good idea. In that case, I'll try the Lacrima. Thank you.'

After dinner, I returned to the rooftop terrace for coffee and Amaretto. The lights of the city, like sparkling jewels on the dark velvet, stretched out into the distance. I gazed at the view while reflecting on my wonderful day, then caught up with the important task of writing my journal. Each day I saw astonishing things I might never again see in my life. I wanted to remember them.

Another perfect morning greeted me when I awoke. Breakfast was a la carte, so there was no opportunity to make a snack to take away with me. I was glad I'd had the foresight to shop yesterday for the trip to Pompeii and Herculaneum[57]; Ercolano, as the locals pronounce it.

When I arrived at the station there were already many travellers waiting on the platform. I overheard some people next to me speaking in English. I turned to them to ask if the next train was stopping at both Pompeii and Ercolano.

56 Translates as Tears of Christ.

57 An earthquake in AD 62, followed by the devastating eruption of Mt Vesuvius in AD 79, obliterated all forms of life in its path. The city of Pompeii was swallowed up by the lava before it flowed on to Ercolano and the coastal towns of Oplontis and Stabiae.

'The local trains stop all stations,' replied a sunburnt man in shorts and a t-shirt. 'We were at Pompeii yesterday and today we're off to Ercolano.'

'That's where I'm going,' I said.

'I detect an Aussie accent,' he said.

Before I could answer, two ladies—I assumed their wives—joined us. 'Hello,' said one lady. 'Sounds like you're a fellow traveller.'

The man in shorts interrupted. 'My name's Ron.' He gestured towards the lady who was wearing sunglasses and a hat. 'That's my wife, Sheila, and with us is Nigel and his wife, Jill.'

'Nice to meet you all,' I said. 'Do you mind if I travel with you to Ercolano, then?'

'Of course, it's a long way. Roughly 50 minutes,' said Sheila.

During our conversation, I learned that the two fellows were both on annual leave from the British navy. Nigel, who'd served for 25 years, was a cook and had travelled all over the world during his career. I discovered both Ron and Nigel had fought in the Falklands and in the Gulf War.

We arrived at our destination, Ercolano Scavi, which is what the excavation site is called opposed to the township, which is just called Ercolano. Tour guides held signs aloft to gather their pre-scheduled tour groups. Taxi drivers stalked the crowded station exit, touting for business.

'*Signore e signori taxi agli*, long way, taxi,' they cajoled.

Nigel sniggered under his breath. 'Not too many fools this trainload. The site is only 500 metres away and it's all downhill.'

Ron interrupted, 'They're offering to go the scenic route, Ha, ha.' He laughed.

'Did you see the sign advertising bus tours to Mt Vesuvius?' asked Sheila. 'We should do that. You know it has been quiet for centuries, so the locals have covered the slopes with vineyards.'

'Could it still be active?' asked Jill. 'Sounds exciting.'

The banter continued as we strode purposefully to the entrance of the archaeological site. My new companions already had tickets, so I bade them farewell and proceeded to the counter. There, I was offered a complimentary map of the site and a choice of a single ticket or a discounted ticket that included a visit to either of two other sites—Oplontis[58] or Pompeii. However, the ticket was valid only for the day of issue. *I don't know anything concerning Oplontis. But I've wanted to see Pompeii since my school days. In the 1960s I heard that you had to be 21 years or older to enter the site because of the lewd paintings on the walls of the brothels and other areas.*

The people queueing around me were family groups, teenagers. *We were so naïve then. Perhaps the titillating stories were untrue.*

Through the turnstile and along a cobbled path, I descended into a labyrinth of ruins. It felt as if I was venturing straight into the annals of history. The streets were narrow and apple trees now grew amongst the buildings. I'd allowed myself only two hours of sightseeing and hoped that the self-tour map would assure me of the most suitable route.

The tour notes indicated that Ercolano was a smaller but more prosperous resort compared to Pompeii and had been favoured by the wealthier Romans. The place was sufficiently far away from the epicentre of the volcanic eruption to allow

58 Oplontis was a luxury village on the coast, about 4.4 kms south of Pompeii. It is best known today for the sumptuous Roman Villa Poppaea, which is open to visitors. Stabiae township, also on the coast, was five km north of Pompeii. All three were obliterated by the eruption. Stabiae had the largest concentration of luxury seaside villas in the entire Roman world. They were positioned on a 50-metre-high headland overlooking the Gulf of Naples.

the populace to evacuate. They thought valiantly that it was just another false alarm, ever hopeful of being spared.

Three days of noxious gases were followed by a sea of six pyroclastic flows that immediately, upon contact, solidified everything in their path. That explained the reason houses with their beautiful frescoes and everyday household items, as well as graffiti on walls, were so well-preserved. These remnants provide us with remarkable insight into many aspects of their lives. *Like being in a movie.* It felt surreal trespassing in the homes of those unfortunates.

I passed by a row of dark, overgrown barrel arches with a sunken area that had once been a beach. The eerily desolate site intrigued me. When I read my notes, I understood the horror of what had taken place in these boathouses. Although most of the city was evacuated before the eruption of Vesuvius, the remaining residents sheltered under the arches of the boathouses as they awaited rescue from the sea. Sadly, help didn't arrive in time. In the 1980s, around 300 human skeletons were discovered there, together with items of jewellery, coins, keys to houses and work tools. *Hard to imagine the horror. Those poor unfortunates waiting in vain.* I shuddered. *What a choice—drown in the sea or burn in the lava.* The caption on the notes indicated that the temperature increased upward of 500°C. Nowhere other than the boathouses is the horror of the Vesuvius eruption captured so dramatically.

I continued up the ramp, where a small group of people were entering a two-story dwelling. When they stopped, I remained at the edge of the crowd so I could hear their guide.

'The House of the Deer is one of the most luxurious villas of this ancient city. It was named after the white marble statue of a deer hunted down by four dogs, found here.'

That's not the sort of sculpture I'd want to possess, even if it is nature.

The guide continued, 'Imagine the owners standing on their large terrace to enjoy unsurpassed views over the Bay of Naples. Like most of the local dwellings, it too was built around a central courtyard.'

I loitered within earshot, photographing the marble-paved corridors, while I strained to catch the commentary.

'Note the walls adorned with vivid black and red wall decorations.'

The group moved from the corral of that room into the next.

'Instead of a welcome doormat, there is a special mosaic at the entry door.'

The listeners moved to look. When they left, I ventured over to examine the decal and was most impressed with the attractive arrangement of cobalt-blue glass chips designed to represent cherubs riding sea creatures. The colours appealed to me but being obsessed with safety, I thought the stones would be slippery, particularly when wet.

On my own, I wandered out to the large, private garden where stone furniture remained positioned alongside marble statues. The casual setting made it easy for me to imagine the occupants' lifestyle, so eerily like our own.

A little further up the road, I came upon another two-storey residence called Trellis House. My notes indicated that the name referred to the balcony rails. It was a boarding house for lower socio-economic people. The accommodation was over a ground-floor shop and was divided into family units, each with separate entrances. Carbonised remains of wooden furniture and even a portrait were found there.

Further on, I entered the House of Telephus, which was constructed on three levels with panoramic views across the sea. A larger tour group were on my heels and had gathered outside the front door. I was trapped inside.

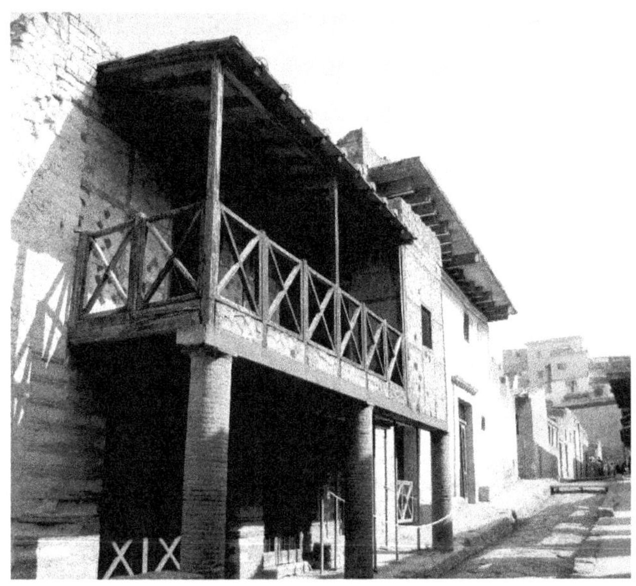

'This is the second largest house in the city,' their guide said, 'and is one of the major highlights we'll see today. It is so-called because a relief portraying Telephus[59] adorns one of the main reception rooms.'

Someone in the group asked, 'What is the purpose of those discs hanging between the columns of the portico?'

'Those masks have a Dionysian theme and are hung between the columns to ward off evil spirits,' the guide replied. 'Villas like this give us an accurate impression of the high standard of living enjoyed by the citizens and give us a glimpse into their customs.'

As the mob moved indoors, I squeezed out of the building and onto the street. The direction I took led to the Palestra, which is a huge sporting complex. This was a popular destination for

59 Telephus was the son of Hercules, founder of the city of Herculaneum.

residents to pass their leisure time, playing ball games and wrestling. *I'm glad these Roman stadiums weren't only for war and gladiators.* From the outside, I thought it a hodgepodge of ruins laid out on the floor of two colonnaded terraces. The description on my map noted that there was a niche set aside for religious rites. *Indeed, every culture has some sort of belief in a higher being.*

Further on, I came across a stone bench with several round holes set in a neat row. I thought it could have been a communal latrine, a bit like ones I'd seen years ago in Ephesus, but it turned out to be a shop counter. Amphoras of beer and other refreshments fitted into the depressions, which kept the drinks cold for the shopkeeper to dispense. There were several of these arrangements throughout the city. Most businesses had a dwelling upstairs where the owners lived, not unlike what we see in our own cities and towns.

My next port of call was at the house of Neptune and Amphitrite. I stood patiently while listening to the commentary of yet another tour group.

'This villa is considered one of the most beautiful homes to see in Ercolano,' the guide said. 'It was thought to be the home of an affluent, art-loving merchant and takes its name from the well-preserved wall mosaic adorning the dining room.'

I could see the mosaic and wondered who the figures could be and what they were doing.

'This mythological scene shows Neptune, the ancient sea god, with Amphitrite, his nymph bride. Note the decorative use of shells and the theatrical masks above,' said the guide.

Having managed to extricate myself from the tour group, I retreated up the road to the delightful Samnite House.[60] To the left of the entrance was a courtyard. On the boundary wall, a

60 Around 5 BC, the first inhabitants of the area were the Samnites, who spoke Oscan, followed by the Etruscans, Pelasgians and the last were the Romans.

large fresco of an arbour gave the illusion of a larger yard. I was intrigued. *Did the artists of the time also know about trompe-l'oeil?*

The stately House of the Mosaic Atrium takes its name from the large atrium decorated with black-and-white checkerboard mosaics. The clever use of architectural space ensured an abundance of natural light, making the rooms seem even larger. I took note of the lovely, coffered ceiling in the vestibule.

In the garden stood a well-preserved marble fountain sheltered on three sides by columned porticos. *These most likely saved the fountain from obliteration.*

My next stop was at the House of the Wooden Partition. There was a noise behind me. I turned around. A group of students were gaining on me.

I heard their teacher remark, 'The name of this villa is derived from the folding wooden partition. You could call it a gate. They would have used it for privacy between the reception and the office when conducting business meetings. The wooden structure has supports for hanging oil lamps.'

Unabashed, I followed them out to the atrium. 'The floor here is white marble and dates back to the time the house was first built, while the wall paintings and floor mosaics are from later restorations.'

One of the students asked, 'Professor, was that after the earthquake?'

'Most likely,' the teacher replied. 'All for nought, it seems, only to be wiped out soon after by the eruption of Vesuvius.'

So there was a previous disaster. An earthquake, then followed sometime later by the volcanic eruption.

I moved with them to the Hall of the Augustales.[61]

61 The Augustales sect was an order of priests from the cult that worshipped Augustus, the then emperor of the Roman Empire.

'This house once belonged to an association of freed slaves working together to ascend the ladder of Roman society,' continued the teacher.

Freed slaves? I pondered. *All cultures throughout the ages have had a pecking order. Some rich, others poor, rulers and subjects, some masters, others slaves.*

Most of the students listened politely but a few on the periphery pushed and whispered. I smiled to myself at their antics. *Children, pupils, regardless of country, all behave the same.*

'Come this way to see some of the best-preserved frescoes in Ercolano.'

I tagged along.

The professor pointed to one of the better-preserved examples. 'This beautiful work of art represents Hercules about to enter Mount Olympus, accompanied by the Roman goddesses Juno and Minerva.'

The kids were getting restless, jostling and pinching each other as the teacher continued to regale those who listened to his tale.

'The fresco directly opposite alludes to the battle between Hercules and the Etruscan god, Achelous.' The teacher paused for questions, but there were none. 'In the rear, is the caretaker's room, where a body was found on the bed.'

This captured the students' attention once more.

'Sir,' said one of the boys. 'Was it all contorted like the ones in the museum?'

Some of the kids were horrified, others pushed each other and sniggered, yet others raised their hands in zombie depiction and made baying sounds. They enjoyed every bit of gory detail.

Discoveries continue daily.[62] One day, I could return to have a closer look.

I had to move on. I knew my time was limited. *I'm pushing it. Trying to see as much as humanly possible in the brief time I've allowed.* I consulted the train timetable Ron had given me earlier in the day. *It would be good to catch a taxi up the hill.* I looked around, but sadly, there were none. *I'll have to run if I'm to catch the next train.*

Chapter 6
Pompeii

The distance from Ercolano Scavi to Pompeii Scavi was only 15 minutes but it served as a good enough break to refresh my brain from my morning's viewings. After all, the main course was Pompeii. Ercolano was merely the appetiser.

There were plenty of vacant seats on the train. I chose a compartment with two long benches facing each other. Some people chatted; others read the newspaper. The train made its smooth trajectory. All was quiet except for the soft burr of wheels and, if I had allowed myself, I'd have easily been lulled to sleep.

A sudden noise jolted me into the present. A raucous band of gypsies descended upon us through the interconnecting doors. The young men were dressed in black shirts that were unbuttoned to mid-chest, displaying their thick gold necklaces. I gasped, unsure if they'd be friend or foe until two squealing women wearing flamboyant red flounced skirts commenced an energetic jig. The troupe created a mood of revelry that filled the carriage.

One of the fellows began to play an accordion while another strummed a popular tune on his guitar. The ladies sang and danced in time to the music. Along with some foot-stomping tourists, I joined in by clapping to the beat. Doubtless, this encouraged the ensemble further. *I want to dance. Where's my dance partner when I need him?* After a couple of songs, one of the men passed a hat around for contributions. I gladly paid for the unexpected diversion. Not so the locals, who *tsk, tsked* and gave nothing. Someone muttered, 'Don't encourage them.'

As the train slowed, I realised we'd already arrived at Pompeii Scavi.[63] Most of the passengers alighted. I followed in their wake. This time, a different breed of touts accosted us outside the station with offers of cheap guided tours. Some included secret, never-previously-seen artifacts. Others offered express tours for time-strapped travellers. *I loathe these aggressive gauntlets in any country.* I put my head down and hurried along, avoiding all eye contact.

As I strode through the entry gate, I noticed the exorbitant price of admission and thought it would surely keep touts out. Not so. They were replaced by other less aggressive and better-dressed 'guides', who spread an invisible spider's web to catch us. The tours they offered were even more expensive.

I hurried away in disgust. But in my haste, I forgot to invest in an audio device or even a map. When I reconsidered and asked one of these 'guides', he quoted me a ridiculous price. I laughed. *What a shameless vagabond. Does he think I'm a fool?* His mouth curved in an arrogant half-smile to add insult to injury. There was no point in arguing with him. I just pursed my lips in response.

'The price is based on my hourly rate,' he explained in excellent English, 'and it matters not if there be one or ten people on the tour.'

63 Twice as large as Herculaneum, the area excavated in Pompeii is around 50 hectares.

I stalked off in the direction of the steady stream of tourists. When they stopped to look at something, I did too. I regretted not having a map. I noticed a group of stragglers and asked them if I could take a quick look at theirs.

One of the girls took pity. 'We have a spare one. You can keep this,' she said, handing me an A4 sheet of paper.

'Thank you so much. You have rescued me.' I was touched by their kindness.

Ahead of me was a set of stairs leading to the portico of a dilapidated villa. I thought it a good spot to sit uninterrupted and eat my lunch while I studied the map. I need some food to revive me. I retrieved the cheese roll I packed earlier, along with the biggest, juiciest pink-fleshed peach. It was unlike any peach I had ever eaten. In fact, I don't recall ever having heard of pink-fleshed peaches.

Once my hunger was sated and a route mapped, my mood improved. I headed to the Temple of Apollo[64], located in the forum. Many fluted columns with ionic capitals stood in what I thought looked like random fashion. They must have originally supported a sizeable building, now reduced to a mound of rubble.[65] I paused to look at a bronze statue of Apollo. A more mature couple followed me into the clearing. I overheard them discussing a basilica somewhere in the southern part of the forum.

'It's the oldest and most important public building in the city,' said the man.

'You can tell by its size,' agreed his companion. 'Built with five naves. Imagine how magnificent it must have looked.'

They noticed me eavesdropping. We made eye contact. They smiled at me and I smiled back.

---

64 Apollo was the son of Jupiter.

65 In Pompeii, the weight of burning ash and pumice that rained down relentlessly for two days, caused roofs to cave in and buildings to collapse, covering the town in debris. In 2021, a four-wheeled chariot was found under 6 metres of rock.

'Could I impose on you to take my photo in front of those columns?' I asked. 'I'd be happy to take yours in return.' I thought it a fair exchange.

'No problems,' said the man. 'Those columns are all that's left of the Temple of Jupiter, Pompeii's largest and most important place of worship.'

His partner joined in. 'My notes say that a double set of stairs led to the columned vestibule reserved for priests. There were niches there that contained statues of the three main gods—Juno, Jupiter and Minerva.'

'The temple appears to have sustained severe damage during the eruption,' I ventured.

'No, no,' the man corrected. 'It happened during the earthquake in AD 62 and was still being rebuilt when Vesuvius decimated Pompeii.'

After that congenial exchange, my stride became more confident. I headed past the tribunal and other municipal buildings, then continued to the Temple of Vespasian. The area around the temple was surrounded by a wall elaborately decorated in stucco. In pride of place, I saw a marble bench. *I presume it was used as an altar.* A bas-relief decoration on the side panels depicted the sacrifice of a bull. *That confirms my assumption.*

Back along the main street—Via Dell'Abbondanza—I continued to the House of Menander. The information plaque indicated Menander had been a wealthy Greek poet and a relative of Emperor Nero's second wife, Poppaea Sabina. The house contained a large peristyle hall[66], servants' quarters, a stable and a large atrium. Traces of wall paintings were still evident throughout.

66 A peristyle hall is a continuous porch formed by a row of columns surrounding the perimeter of a building or a courtyard.

I entered the dwelling to see the artwork. Scenes in the atrium suggested hunting trips. The other rooms were decorated with mythological themes. Elaborate floor mosaics featured fauna and flora from the Nile Delta. *I wonder how they knew about camels and palm trees.* There was no one to ask.

Further along, I came upon the two-storey house of Paquius Proculus. A distinctive mosaic pavement led me from the road to the entrance of the house. In the vestibule, I was greeted by a beautifully executed mosaic of a crouching dog. Signs of pets in a household always made me think the owners were nice people. This area led to the atrium, where the rooms were similarly 'carpeted' in intricate mosaics reminiscent of the Nile region. To me, this was clearly indicative that some of the people enjoyed extensive travel.[67]

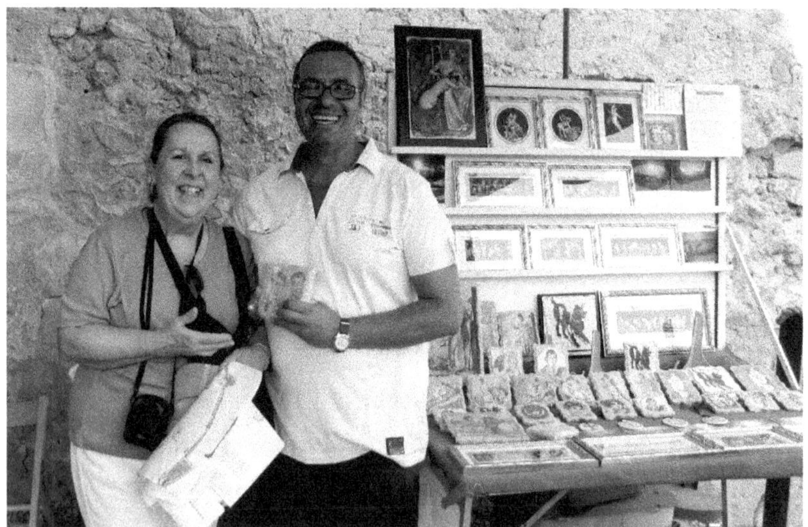

By way of contrast, colourful medallions with mythological scenes decorated the corners of the floor. The backyard held more surprises. *Wow, this looks like the perfect place for BBQs or dinner parties. The Pompeiian lifestyle seems to have been not dissimilar to our own.*

Near the boundary wall, I was astonished to see a beach umbrella shading a small table with colourful artwork. The vendors stood nearby. My eyes were drawn to a stone fragment with a beautiful portrait of a man and a woman. The man in the picture was familiar. *He's the spitting image of the Etruscan man I saw at the Vatican Museum.*

'Bella. You like?' asked the vendor.

'Yes,' I replied. 'Where is this from?'

'I make,' he replied. 'See? Here is my name. You like?'

'You made this copy,' I corrected. 'I saw the original recently in the *Museo Vaticano*.'

'This be Paquius Proculus and his wife. It found here in this villa. Original at *Museo Nationale* in *Napoli*.'

'How much?'

'This painting very important. Wife of Paquius Proculus, she 'ave the wax writing tablet in her hand. You know she look after the bakery business. Her husband, he make bread.'

Judging by their house, the bakery was a thriving business. What luck, to come upon the only souvenir seller in Pompeii.

I enjoyed the banter. I think he did too. A good little business appropriately stationed on the land of another astute business owner. I couldn't resist such a personal memento of my visit to this beautiful villa. He even asked his wife if she'd take a photo of the two of us holding his artwork. I was elated. *What a lovely exchange.*

I retraced my steps to the intersection of Vicolo dell Lupanari to find one of the 35 brothels servicing the city.[68] This one was in a prime position at the intersection of two main streets. In the 1960s, we'd heard that many lewd paintings[69] were found in the brothels of Pompeii. At that time, there were restrictions as to who could view them. I walked in. No ID required. On the ground floor of the establishment were a few small windowless cells, each furnished with a narrow stone bench.[70] *I expect it would be covered with a mattress of some sort.* On the lintel over each doorway was a pictorial depiction of different services available. There was an upper floor that was closed for refurbishment at the time.

My next destination was the House of the Faun, named after the bronze statue, found in the courtyard. This property, with all the features of an aristocratic household, was one of the largest and took up the whole block.[71] An information plaque indicated that the property was considered one of the most illustrious of the entire Roman Empire. I was excited to be there to see it for myself. The house was divided into two parts, with peristyle halls—so grand, I thought they were inspired by those in the city's forum. Both atriums had private gardens. A copy of the bronze statue of the dancing faun[72] adorned the larger of these areas.

Underfoot, mosaics of intricate floral patterns stretched out over the floors to resemble luxurious Persian rugs. At the

68 The population of Pompeii was estimated at 10,000. The brothels provided both male and female prostitutes, most of whom were enslaved.

69 These paintings have all been transferred to a special area of the museum in Naples and are easily accessible.

70 These ensured the client was not too comfortable and overstayed, thus keeping the queue moving.

71 Bound by four roads, it occupies the whole area of 40 m x 110 m.

72 The original is kept safe in the museum in Naples.

entrance, a mosaic depicting two doves busy building a nest greeted all who wished to enter.

Gracing the floor of one of the main reception rooms was a reconstructed mural depicting the decisive battle between Alexander the Great and Darius, the King of Persia.[73]

I noted the considerable number and variety of businesses that lined all the main streets. This town was clearly a thriving community. In its heyday, Pompeii had an impressive aqueduct and enviable plumbing system that served the entire town. The communal baths, eateries, theatres and even private houses had underfloor heating. *I wonder if those stone benches in the brothel were similarly heated.*

An information board noted that during excavations, carbonised loaves of bread were found in the ovens at the Bakery of Modesto. Bread was the staple of the poor; eaten with vegetables and the fish they'd caught. Meat was a luxury.

Next, I visited the House of Vetti, named after the owners—two freedmen. The social system of the time enabled slaves to work elsewhere in their spare time. Their earnings had allowed them to buy out of their bond and to become independent. Some, like the Vetti brothers, even progressed to a much higher status.

A large tour group had already entered the premises, so I shadowed them. This house was another grand aristocratic home with colonnades and an atrium. Though the architectural features that brought light and space into the villa were

73 The murals give us an idea of the culture and lifestyle led by the inhabitants before the eruption.

something to behold, I was fascinated with the grandiose murals that decorated every room.

'Spend some time looking at the enthralling frescoes throughout this villa,' said the guide to the group. 'You'll see deities like Dionysus or Bacchus, the god of wine, and other mythological creatures. The scenes represent legends that the population held most dear.'

'Those brothers must have been rich,' said a tall man standing in front of me.

'Yes, it's evident that the owners spent vast sums of money decorating their home,' the guide replied.

'Who is that confronting person at the entry?' asked a gentleman with flushed cheeks. Everyone turned to view the statue. A few awkward giggles ran through the crowd. I understood why the man was flushed. He was either blushing with embarrassment or titillation.

'Priapus, the god of fertility, as can be seen by the size of his phallus. His job was to ward off the "evil eye",' said the guide.

As the guide spoke, he glanced around at the familiar faces of his group. Our eyes met when the tall man stepped away leaving me in full view. *He is giving me the evil eye. I'm sure he suspects that I'm a 'ring-in'.*

I moved away from the crowd and into another room. Various culinary utensils were strewn around the spacious interior and I was surprised to see a cauldron still hanging over the fireplace. I peered in, curious about what may have been cooking on the day when all hell erupted. *A pork stew or their favourite vegetable—purple cauliflower.*

When the group entered the kitchen, I caught the guide's familiar voice. 'The ultra-rich served exotic meals, including sea urchin or giraffe, to their guests.'

I shuddered at the thought.

Fountains and statues positioned in the courtyard had once augmented the garden but now were sadly in ruin. The group followed me out and I heard the guide once more.

'The lead pipes that fed the fountains are still in working order. Take note of the decorations and statues of cupids and satyrs.'

Indeed, the bas-relief decorations were elaborate and at times erotic.

I soon realised I'd not done myself justice by touring both excavation sites in one day. My energy was flagging. Even though I'd only seen a fraction, I felt tired. However, there was one more house I absolutely had to see—*Villa Misteri*—the Villa of Mysteries. This was located outside of the city walls and promised to be the climax of my whole trip, so I'd left it until last. In retrospect, it would have been smarter to see it earlier when I was feeling fresher. I'd thought that, like drinking wine, I should start with the lesser and end with the best.

The grandiose mansion, surrounded by lush greenery, was positioned to overlook the sea. I was particularly taken by the hanging gardens cascading around the portico at the front of the building. In the middle of this private territory stood a rotunda. Beyond were a couple of reception rooms that led to an expansive central atrium encircled by a peristyle hall. Many rooms radiated from the expanse of this atrium.

With each refurbishment, the house was enlarged. Colonnades, porticos, decorative cornices and corbels were added. I was astounded to find that the excavation of the building had not yet been completed. Archaeologists believe a magnificent *porte-cochere* entry, large enough to accommodate horse-drawn carriages, still lies hidden beneath the pumice, all waiting to be found.

Villa Misteri is considered the *pièce de résistance* of Pompeii because of the quality of its frescoes. The most intact and important artworks are painted on a rich burgundy background and are found in the atrium guest hall. The most mysterious mural is one that spills over two rooms. The subject is a sequence from the Dionysiac cycle. I stood for a long time, transfixed, enjoying the beauty of the figures, while I tried to work out the meaning of the scene.

I concluded that Hercules, Juno and Minerva were formal gods. They gave structure and law to the populace, whereas Dionysus, also known as Bacchus, along with Pan and Priapus, were central to the Pompeiian lifestyle of fun and debauchery, of wine, sex, music and food. The artwork, with 29 life-sized figures, portrays the solemn rite of passage into adulthood. As I followed the central character, the mural seemed to take on a life of its own. In a series of vignettes, it showed the progress of a young woman as she was initiated into the mysterious cult.[74]

The last owners of the property had grown fruit and cultivated vineyards. I assumed their lavish lifestyle was the result of their labour. *As well as producing wine, they most likely ran a tavern. This mansion reflects their success in business.*

I arrived back at my hotel exhausted. What I needed was a refreshing Campari and tonic from the rooftop bar. Finally, with drink in hand, I sat gazing across the calm emerald grotto of the bay. I could have stayed there all night, but my stomach grumbled for lack of attention. I made my way to the dining room.

74 The cult of Dionysus was strongly associated with satyrs, centaurs and sileni, and its characteristic symbols were the bull, the serpent, tigers/leopards, ivy wreaths and wine.

The waiter had my bottle of wine ready from the previous night and said it would go particularly well with the suggested menu.

'For *prendo,* I recommend the *Gnocchi Sorrentino*—a typical local dish—gnocchi in a tomato *passata.*' He smiled before continuing. 'For *secondo,* chef has prepared fish specially for you—cod with roasted onion and artichoke. It is his specialty. Then, for *dolci,* I recommend the classic *sfogliatelle,* which is a many-layered Neapolitan pastry with a sweet ricotta filling.' He wore a satisfied smile. 'I think you will enjoy what we have prepared for you.'

I was taken aback by this unexpected gesture. 'Please thank chef. It sounds delicious. I-I'm looking forward to it,' I stammered.

He made me feel special and he was right—it was a delectable meal. Most of all, I was impressed that they'd gone out of their way to provide me with the fish I'd previously requested.

I wonder if the residents of Villa Misteri *were as well cared for by their staff as I was this evening.*

I was feeling very satisfied with my side trip to Sorrento and because it was my last night, I allowed myself a final nightcap. Out on the terrace, a soft warm breeze wafted in from the bejewelled night sky. I sat sipping a creamy Frangelico and listened to the background music coming from the bar audio system. '*Torna a Sorrento*', sung by none other than Dean Martin[75] in his native Italian. His relaxed manner and velvety baritone were as creamy as my liqueur.

'Come Back to Sorrento'. As if I needed encouragement to return to Sorrento. Perhaps I will… one day.

Chapter 7
Calabria

At the ungodly hour of 5:30 in the morning, a minibus loaded with 15 equally sleepy travellers arrived at my hotel for the next phase of my adventure. Davide, the young tour leader, stowed my luggage while I stumbled onto the bus. Surprisingly, the group were all Australians. Most had an Italian background. We catnapped all the way to Naples, where we stopped at a bistro for a hearty breakfast.

A group of Spanish speakers, along with their guide, Kareena, joined us. Now that our group comprised 43 people, we transferred to a larger coach for our journey through Southern Italy and Sicily. Our driver, Mauro, a cheery, middle-aged Italian, made each of us welcome as we climbed onto his gleaming coach.

'You are in the hands of a professional driver,' announced Davide. 'He's no slow coach.' A stifled giggle arose from the passengers. 'We have a tight schedule to maintain. You will need to listen carefully each time we stop and be sure to return on time.'

I sat next to Lucia, whose two friends sat behind us. Lucia was my age; a motherly person handing out sweets and biscuits to her companions. A bit chubby but not fat, her light brown curly hair bounced around as she entertained us with little jokes. Sophia, the elder of her two companions, had the alluring eyes and wide smile of her namesake, Sophia Loren, though her demeanour was more subdued. The third member of the party was Sophia's daughter, Rosa, who'd recently graduated from law school. Lucia referred to her as, 'my niece—the judge', which made poor Rosa blush.

Davide handed out itineraries and maps for the tour. The long drive was an opportunity for the group to discuss activities for the next four days and for the guides to gauge our common interests.

'We won't reach our first stop, Paestum, for a while,' he said. 'So I'll pass the microphone around. 'Tell us your name, which country you come from and what you hope to see on this tour.'

Our new associates were from various South American countries including Argentina, Brazil and Uruguay. As people introduced themselves, I noted various commonalities within the group and made a mental note of people I'd like to get to know better. They were a diverse bunch—different ages, occupations and backgrounds. Several people had similar interests to me—some history, others archaeology and art. The week ahead was shaping up to be both interesting and a lot of fun.

Laura, a doctor, and her tall husband, Salvatore, sat across the aisle from me. They were both blonde so I assumed they were from Northern Italy. He preferred to be called Sal. Their friends sat behind them. As we'd all stayed in Sorrento, we began to compare our travel experiences. Sal and Laura had not been happy with their hotel. Others from their group who heard our conversation added their complaints; the usual sort of things: rooms smaller than expected, boring meals, poor cleanliness and even outright rudeness. Although only three stars, my hotel in Sorrento[76] exceeded my expectations for locality, spectacular views, cleanliness and exceptional service. Staff had displayed a desire to assist in any way they could, not to mention my unforgettable chef-inspired dinner on my last night. *Without a doubt, I would return there.* My fellow travellers listened to my story with envy. We had successfully broken the ice.

Buses tend to lull me to sleep, especially when I've had an inordinately early start to the day. The blur of the lush countryside, the low hum of the engine and the gentle rocking motion of the vehicle as it responded to the curvature of the road, must have simulated a return to the womb, and I soon surrendered to sleep.

Davide's voice broke my siesta. 'We'll arrive in Paestum in 10 minutes. Our local guide will meet us at the Greek Archaeological Park.'

I noticed travellers in nearby seats were also rubbing their eyes, yawning and stretching their limbs. Kareena rose from her seat, microphone in hand, ready to speak when a young Aussie voice interjected.

'We're still in Italy. So why is this place Greek?' The owner of the voice was a teenager travelling with his parents. 'I'm Joe, by the way, from Leichhardt in Sydney,' he added.

'The Greeks colonised this land before the Romans arrived,' responded Kareena. 'When we get to Sicily tomorrow, you'll see many more examples of Greek architecture. Greece is but a short distance across the Ionian Sea, so naturally, its influence is evident throughout southern Italy.'

76 Tirrenia Hotel, Sorrento.

Joe's parents, Tony and Angela, were busy whispering in his ear and I thought they were a bit embarrassed by their son's lack of Italian history.

Kareena continued. 'Paestum, founded in 600 BC, was a major Greek city on the coast of the Tyrrhenian Sea in Magna Graecia.[77] The Greek colonists called it Posidonia, after Poseidon—deity of the sea.'

We drove through the gates of the park, where our specialist guide, Paula, waited. She was a small woman in her forties and wore a wide-brimmed hat and big sunglasses. *She reminds me of Audrey Hepburn in the movie* Breakfast at Tiffany's. Armed with a bright orange umbrella, she was ready for all contingencies. I was pleased to see Kareena and Davide open a couple of deck chairs and settle themselves with a thermos under the nearest sprawling olive tree.

Paula's orange umbrella was like a beacon. Her no-nonsense strides had us scurrying after her as she made her way towards the impressive Greek temple positioned to advantage on a nearby hill. As the stragglers caught up, she began her talk.

'*Allora*! Archaeological evidence shows us that the city grew quickly, with roads and public buildings decorated with works of art. Like other Greek colonies, the settlers built impressive temples and dedicated them to their gods. Coins found on this site prove that a sophisticated trade existed well beyond local market barter.'

'What is that structure?' interrupted a tall gentleman with dark, slicked-back hair. His accent had a hint of the Spanish lisp.[78] He pointed to the huge columned edifice ahead of us.

77 Many coastal townships around the south of Italy were one Greek colonies. Collectively they were known as Magna Graecia because they were culturally and linguistically Greek.

78 Castilian Spanish of the Middle Ages originally had two distinct sounds for what we now think of as the 'lisp'—the cedilla and the z, as in 'dezir'. The cedilla made a 'ts' sound and the 'z' a 'dz' sound. Both in time were simplified into the 'lisp' or what Spaniards call the '*ceceo*'.

'Sorry, I should introduce myself. My name's Alejandro, but you can call me Alex.'

'These, sir,' said Paula, 'are the three magnificent Greek edifices for which Paestum is renowned. They date back to 550 BC. They're still in a good state of preservation and are dedicated to Hera, Athena and Poseidon.' She took a breather from her story as we struggled up the slope.

Sal stepped up beside Paula to ask a question. 'I thought they had Latin names,' he quizzed.

'That's right,' Paula replied. 'During Roman rule[79], they were renamed Juno, Minerva and Neptune.'

Paula forged ahead. 'When it comes to recollection of size, our perception becomes skewed. However, I think it fair to say that at least the main temple is even larger than the Acropolis in Athens.'

I remembered the Acropolis being a huge site, but that was 30 years ago and not as well travelled. Memory can be very deceptive and at that time, I'd seen nothing with which to compare.

When all the stragglers regrouped, Paula continued, 'Following the discovery of Pompeii and Herculaneum in the 18th century, and during the construction of a new coastal road from Naples, the ruins of Paestum came to wide notice.' She scanned the group, hoping to maintain our attention. 'The whole city covers 120 hectares, but only 25 hectares have been excavated. The three main temples are located there.'

It was getting warm. Rosa and Sophia began peeling off layers of clothing. Paula noticed her discomfort. 'It always gets warmer as we near the temples,' she said. 'It's not too bad yet but wait until noon. Then it will be quite hot.' She used her hat

79 Romans ruled from AD 227 until the Muslims sacked the city in AD 871.

to fan herself. 'The glare from the stone creates another source of heat.' We quickened our pace for the last few steps to the temple.

'Temple of Hera,' introduced Paula, with a flourish of her arm. 'The oldest of the three. She was the goddess of women, marriage, family and childbirth. Noted for its wider-than-normal columns. Do take a walk inside to get a better sense of the scale and to gauge the strong curve in the design.'

We walked up the stairs towards the columns to see what Paula meant.

'An open-air altar, where people could attend rites and perform sacrifices was unearthed in front of the temple. This ensured the holiest area remained strictly for priests.' Paula motioned us to follow her. '*Andiamo*! Let's go.'

We trudged to the second temple. 'Built around 450 BC, this is the most complete of the three temples. I encourage you to walk inside.'

'Who are the altars dedicated to?' Renata asked. I remembered her sitting at the back of the bus with a distinguished-looking gentleman, whom I supposed was her husband.

'There is a bit of confusion regarding the dedication,' answered Paula. 'Statues around the larger of the altars seem to indicate Apollo as patron of the temple, but it could equally have been Hera or Poseidon.' She peered at her watch. 'Have a wander around but be back in 10 minutes.'

Everyone scooted off in different directions like ants, some taking photographs and others reading signage. I was disappointed there wasn't more to see other than a few foundation stones that outlined public buildings, roads and protective walls.

I returned to Paula, who was waiting for us under her brolly. I giggled to myself. *She's so like Mary Poppins.*

'Temple of Athena, built around 500 BC, at the highest point of the town. It is the smallest of the three temples. The architecture is Doric and only partially ionic.'

'Is it far?' asked Alex's wife, Gabriela. 'Do you mind if I wait here for you to return?'

'Don't worry, Gabriella. We won't be going there today; entry is prohibited due to the fragile state of the limestone. You will drive past it in the bus.'

I noticed how remarkably relieved Gabriella appeared. I wondered why.

The sound of Paula's voice drew our attention once more. 'The temple was later used as a Christian church,' she said. 'We know this because three Christian tombs were discovered under the floor.'

I caught sight of Davide and Kareena coming towards us.

'If you have time,' Paula added hurriedly, 'visit Paestum Museum. It's the building we passed near the entrance. There, you will find the largest collection of artefacts discovered during excavations. Unfortunately, significant pieces disappeared from the site before modern controls, and they remain to this day in a few private collections around the world.'

'Sorry, guys. No time today,' interrupted Davide.

'You must come back another time, then,' said Paula, 'to see the famous Tomb of the Diver, a fresco of a naked young man diving into the ocean. It symbolises the transition from life to death. The other scenes in the tomb are of homosexual lovers.'[80]

Renata's husband introduced himself. 'I'm Vincenzo. Please call me Vince. I'd like to know if the beaches of Paestum were

80 European intellectuals doing the Grand Tour, amazed by how well-preserved the temples were, made it their reference point for classical architecture until Athens was added to the European cultural itinerary.

also the landing place of US Infantry during the Allied invasion of Italy.'

'They were,' answered Paula. 'Three days ago was the 69th anniversary[81] of this event.'

Many people thanked Paula with tips before we boarded the bus for our drive through Campania. There was a short stop for lunch at a nondescript roadhouse, where our group were the only customers. I bought panini and coffee. At least the bread was fresh and the salami tasty.

Back on the bus, we continued through the many tunnels of the Apennine Mountain range to Reggio Calabria. There was another quick comfort stop at a roadside kiosk in a tiny spot on the map called Valentia.

'A town named after my wife,' laughed a tall fellow from the Spanish-speaking group. 'Her name is Valentina,' his deep voice bellowed. We all turned towards them.

At first, the man's wife looked a bit embarrassed to be singled out in this way. Then, sweeping her long brown hair from her face, she revealed a beautiful wide smile. 'Mateo,' she said, patting her husband's forearm. 'You must introduce our daughter.'

'Oh, yes,' He pushed forward a lovely blonde teenager. Like her mother, she too showed signs of embarrassment. 'Our daughter, Maria-Elena. We are from Brazil.'

I could see Joe and another young person on the bus gazing across at her. Rosa whispered, 'I hope the young ones find something in common.'

'Tonight, we stay at Reggio Calabria on the coast,' said Davide. 'In the morning, we catch the first ferry across the channel to Sicily.'

81 That anniversary was in 2012.

We arrived at our hotel half an hour before sunset but delayed registration in favour of a stroll along the esplanade. Many people strolled along the corniche with their dogs, while others fished from the beach. I wondered if they were locals or holidaymakers. Meanwhile, splashes of orange, pink and purple began to meld across the darkening sky.

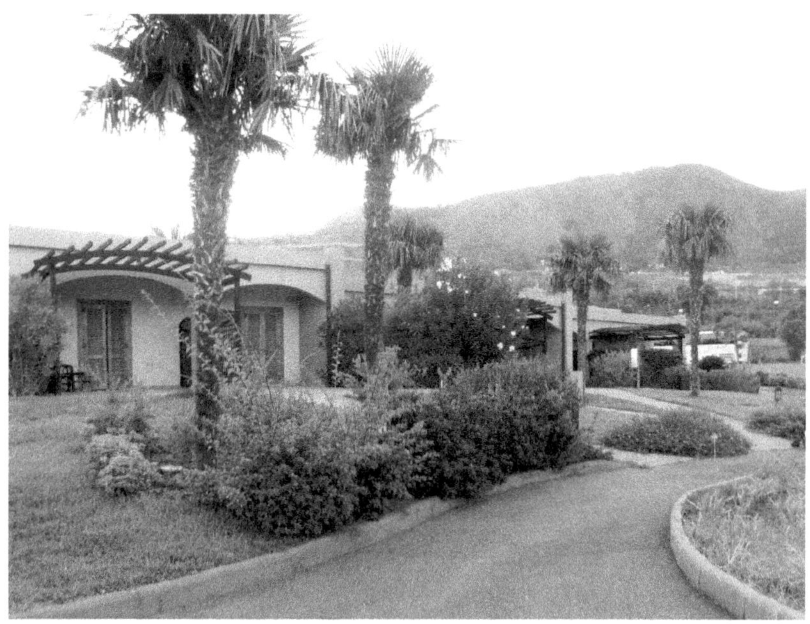

Our hotel was over-booked, so we were upgraded to the Montesano, an upmarket resort and reception venue. The complex, with illuminated paths, was a welcome contrast to its neighbours. Inside, smartly uniformed staff stood behind the reception counter. To one side of reception there was a well-stocked bar and islands of low tables which were softly lit by table lamps, ideal for quiet tête-à-têtes. This appealed to me and I resolved to return for a pre-dinner drink.

Kareena and Davide distributed the keys and we made our way to our rooms. I was surprised to be allocated a double room with a bath. Now, one thing I enjoy enormously while travelling is to soak in a bubble bath.

I examined the bottle of bubble bath perched on the shelf. It was labelled 'Ortygia', considered a luxury range, from Florence. I smelled the bar of soap while anticipating its creamy texture on my skin. The subtle floral scent was the same as the bubble bath.

Matching candles were positioned near a stack of sumptuous white towels. It was like entering my own private spa. As I drew the bath, the perfume of orange blossom, lime and pomegranate filled the air. *Shame I'm travelling solo, but what the heck. I love being pampered at any time.*

That night, dinner was silver service in the restaurant. A wedding celebration was in full swing in the ballroom next door. The music, although pleasant, made it difficult for us to converse. I ordered a glass of house red wine.[82] Our meal was from a set menu, starting with a simple onion and pecorino pasta. This was followed by a firm fillet of grilled halibut with a caper-based salsa verde on the side and a colourful accompaniment of grilled zucchini and red bell peppers. A delicious *zabaglione,* with freshly picked local berries rounded off our meal.

Gabriela was still feeling fragile so she and her husband were the first to retire.

In the morning, the group was abuzz. Dr Laura had called in on them. She suspected arrhythmia and insisted Gabriella immediately consult with a cardiologist at the hospital. Although both Gabriella and Alex spoke excellent Italian, Davide accompanied them.

82 By 2012 standards, it wasn't cheap at €5.

Chapter 8

Sicily

At breakfast, we learned that Davide, Gabriella and her husband, Alex, hadn't returned from the hospital until 5:30 am. They were tired. However, we were booked on the early morning ferry to Messina, so sleep would have to wait. The ferry, a huge whale of a ship, took some time to load. We pulled out a little after eight. I didn't know what to expect.

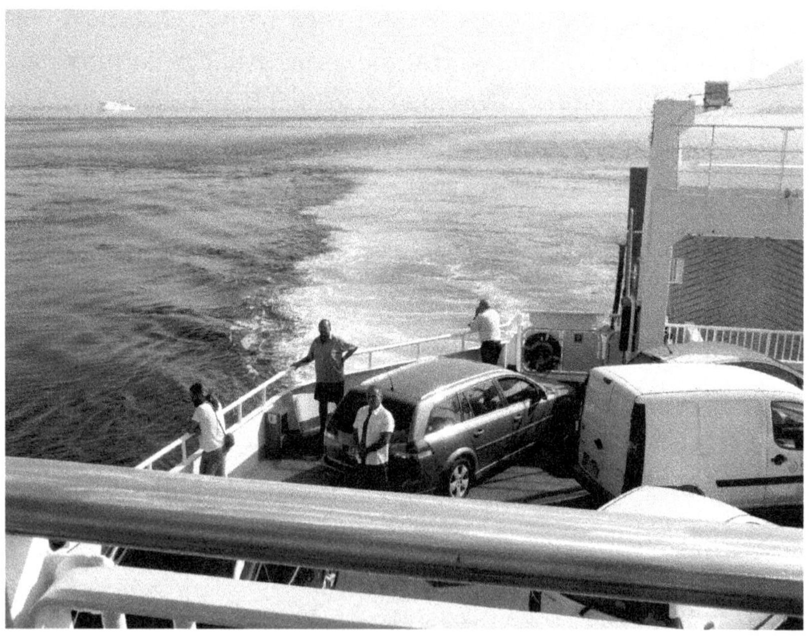

There were many cars, trucks and buses belching out fumes while waiting to board. I worried about overloading and felt uneasy when our bus drove into the hull with all of us on board. It was a relief to alight and scramble up a narrow stairwell to the deck, where we regrouped. We could sit outside for the 30-minute crossing or stay in the lounge, where drinks were available.

'I know some of you might have a Sicilian background,' Davide said. 'So you may sleep while Kareena tells the rest of us a bit about the island nation of Sicily.'

Kareena took the microphone. 'Sicily is a land of history, myth and legend. Its origins now lost in the mists of time[83],' she said. 'Evidence has been found to indicate settlement since at least the Palaeolithic era, after which, many different nations have occupied the land.'

'Mostly Greeks,' said Pedro, who'd teamed up with young Joe. I thought Pedro might be Greek, though he travelled with the Spanish speakers.

'Yes, they were attracted to its strategic trading position and to the fertile volcanic soil,' Kareena said. 'The city of Syracuse was the most important Greek colony. It had enjoyed a long-held peace during the Byzantine era,' she added. 'The Greeks expressed their power and might through the magnificent cities and temples that they built. The buildings were covered with stucco made of marble dust, which dazzled in the sun.'

'What an amazing sight it would have been,' said Lucia, who was sitting alongside Rosa and Sophia.

'Indeed, that was the purpose—to lure trading ships to Sicilian shores. Like advertising today.' Kareena laughed at her little analogy.

83 It is the largest island in the Mediterranean Sea.

'I thought Palermo was the capital,' said Vince.

'It was never a Greek colony. Various nations dominated it,' said Kareena. 'In AD 948, when Arabs encroached Sicilian territory, they made Palermo their capital. It remained the centre for Asian and European trade until Norman Crusaders invaded in 1061.'

As we neared the wharf, she handed the microphone over to Davide.

'As you see, we have arrived in Messina.'[84]

'My ancestors came from Messina,' announced Dr Laura. 'I remember visiting my grandparents, who lived in this charming town. We rode our bikes by the water and peered at the men fishing. Now the walkways are wide and paved for the increasing number of tourists to enjoy the coastal views.'

The bus slowed to a stop. Mauro parked in the special coach zone. From there, we walked the short distance to the town centre. I was glad to get a bit of exercise.

We gathered around an impressively large marble fountain in the piazza. Kareena told us that it was dedicated to the mythical founder, Orion.

'I always think of Messina as a beautiful little tourist trap,' she said. 'The *duomo* cathedral[85],' she pointed to the church across the square, 'was severely damaged during the 1908 earthquake, then further destroyed during World War II by subsequent bombings. Now it has been fully rebuilt with a tall bell tower or *campanile,* as the Italians call it.'

We moved inside, where my gaze was drawn to the barrel-vaulted ceiling above the long narrow nave. It made me feel

84 Messina was founded in 358 BC by Greeks from Naxos.

85 *Duomo* is the traditional name for the principal or main church or cathedral in each town.

as if I was walking through a tunnel. We stood back and craned our necks to appreciate the beauty of the stained-glass windows.

Back outside, Davide told us more regarding the bell tower. 'In 1933, an astronomical clock was installed into the tower. As you can see, the clock is decorated with religious and civil figures. Beautifully gilded, the figures come out each day at noon. Unfortunately, we're too early to see the spectacle and we've no time to wait. We have a lot of territory to cover. However, we do have time to stop for a drink from a little kiosk I know just around the corner.'

Laura told us the region was famous for granitas so I ordered a coffee-flavoured one, expecting it to be like iced coffee. I watched as the shopkeeper poured half a cup of black coffee into a glass filled with shaved ice. The finishing touches were a dollop of cream on top. Far too much ice for my liking, but I could see the younger members of our group enjoying their fruit-flavoured varieties. We found benches in a shady spot, where we could perch with our refreshments.

'Tonight, we'll be staying in Syracuse, which is the largest city in Sicily,' said Davide. 'Tomorrow, we head to Taormina[86], the second largest city. It's on the east coast of Sicily and is close to Mount Etna, Europe's most active volcano. There are trails for volcanologists and hikers that lead to the summit. Unaccompanied people are allowed to ascend only partway. Small eruptions are frequent, making it too dangerous to go without expert guidance.'

This information didn't instil a lot of confidence in me.

86 Taormina is popular with Italian visitors for water sports and caving, while its tourists prefer history and archaeology.

'But for now, relax. It will take us roughly 45 minutes to get there,' he said.

I'd privately dubbed him the master of 40 winks so was not surprised to see him settle into his seat and immediately close his eyes. I noticed several other people follow suit. I rested my eyes too.

Kareena's voice woke me with a start. 'Here we are,' she announced. 'The best way to visit Taormina is on foot. Mauro will leave the bus in the special parking area while we wander into town. All the buses look the same *en masse* so be sure to write down the number of our bus so you don't get lost later.'

Lucia and I scrambled for pens and paper. Others prodded at their smartphones.

'First up, we'll visit Chiesa San Nicolo di Bari. Second, the Teatro Greco, followed by free time for shopping,' said Kareena. 'That means a late lunch at Mt Etna.'

A labyrinth of alleys and cobbled streets radiated from the town centre. We made our way across the piazza to the church, pausing briefly to admire the Tauro fountain, named after the bi-ped marble statue of a female centaur—the queen of Taormina. With a six-pointed crown on her head, she held a sceptre in one hand and a globe in the other and was the unofficial city emblem. It made me think of the Queen Victoria statue outside of the QVB and the town hall back home in Sydney.

Kareena motioned the group to follow her into the church. 'As we enter, note the decorative portal above the doors and the Renaissance-style rose window surmounting it.'

Remembering my special time in Bari a fortnight earlier, I was heartened to see yet another church in honour of St Nicholas. I told Kareena that I hadn't expected this saint to be so revered by both Catholic and Orthodox churches.

'There are at least 14 churches[87] in Sicily dedicated to St Nicholas of Bari,' she said. 'This one has been remodelled several times over the centuries. Built by Normans during their occupation of Sicily, the austere appearance—all bare stone, utilitarian, with no embellishments—is typical of Norman[88] architecture.'

We made our way to the main attraction—Taormina's ancient *Teatro Greco*. The elevated position is the perfect setting for the theatre. Clambering up the stepped seating was a bit of an effort. Some of the older people in the group were puffing and panting. I loved the airiness and gentle breeze on my cheeks as I stood gazing at the Calabrian coastline.

'The Greeks loved to construct their buildings in beautiful scenic locations,' said Davide. 'Here, we face the stupendous view of Naxos Bay and in the distance, the forbidding south face of Mt Etna.'

I wish my friend Marina were here. She'd take photos that would do the scene justice. Perhaps she'd even set up her easel to paint the fabulous view. I can't wait to see her in Paris.

'The theatre is deemed to have pitch-perfect acoustics.' Kareena interrupted my thoughts. 'It's especially popular during the high season in summer. You must book well in advance for opera, orchestral concerts and plays. As you can imagine, many a Greek tragedy has been performed here over the centuries.'

Salvatore, at the urging of Davide, went around to the other side of the theatre, where Sal broke out into a stirring rendition of '*Nessun Dorma*', from Puccini's *Turandot*. Though

87 The Chiesa di San Nicolo in Messina appears in the movie *The Godfather*.

88 The cathedral was built by the Normans in 1197.

he sang softly, his voice filled the entire theatre. 'The reason for the amplification,' explained Kareena, 'is in the shape of the amphitheatre. It creates a soundbox making it easy to be heard no matter where you are sitting.'

'Beyond the theatre,' continued Kareena, 'the cliffs drop down to the sandy beaches of the sea coves. A narrow stretch of sand connects to *Isola Bella*, which is a tiny island and nature reserve.'

Our little tour ended when Davide and Sal returned. We were given an hour to wander around the narrow streets filled with the scent of flowers cascading from terracotta pots. Plants lined the buildings and spilled out onto the sidewalk. Brightly coloured geraniums decorated window ledges and filled Juliette balconies. Elaborate entrance portals gave further character to the ancient houses.

I felt I was in a close-knit village that had developed over the centuries with residences and businesses growing alongside each other. In amongst it all was the church of St Catherine of Alexandria, where Arab, Norman and Greek styles converged. Catherine of Alexandria is another saint common to both Eastern and Western churches. My mind flashed back 20 years. I recalled my visit to St Catherine's Monastery deep in the Sinai desert—it's the site of the burning bush and Moses receiving the Ten Commandments.

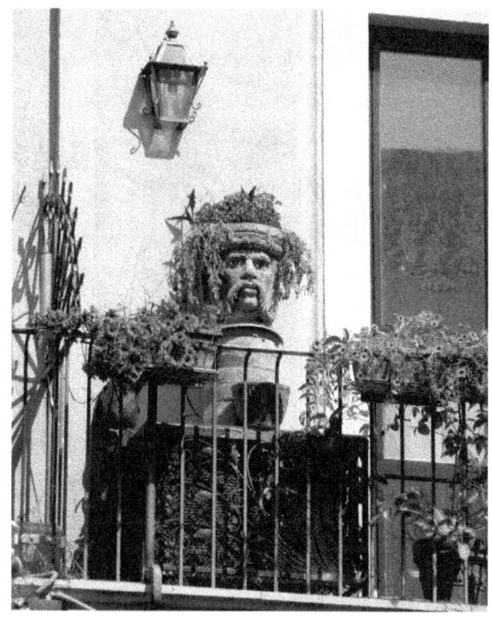

We walked and talked. A variety of goods were on offer in the gift shops. Taormina's decorative ceramics were a popular souvenir, in particular, the brightly coloured pottery Sicilian heads. These were fashioned after a legend from the Muslim occupation. When a woman found out that her Moorish husband had taken a lover, she killed him and cut off his head, using it as a plant pot. *A grisly but captivating tale,* I mused.

Our little trio stopped at a ceramics shop. Here, Rosa bought a huge jug covered in blue, yellow and red folk art.

'What will you use it for?' Sophia asked her daughter. 'Don't you think it may be too cumbersome on the plane?'

'But ideal for serving sangria to a crowd,' Rosa cheekily replied. 'I'm already planning a party and those colours will look great.'

Meanwhile, I bought some ceramic numerals to replace my current house number. Lucia bought a dear little sugar bowl and creamer. 'If I change my mind when I get home, it could become a gift.' She laughed.

There were several alfresco eateries where people lazed in the warm sunshine. We were about to go in one when we heard the haunting sound of a piano accordion. Like the Pied Piper, it drew us into another little square where the lone busker played a familiar tango. A few tourists gathered to listen. Some stood mesmerised. Others took photos.

'Piazzolla,' Sophia whispered as she began to move to the South American beat.

'I adore his music. I love the piano accordion.' I spoke softly, leaning closer to Lucia.

'It's a bandoneon,' she whispered back. 'Smaller. No keys, all buttons.'

She's right. I remembered those gypsies in the train near Pompeii; they'd had the same instrument. A man with his guitar appeared from nowhere. He joined in, quickly picking up the tune. They must have known each other and it was all part of the act.

From the growing crowd, emerged a young couple who started to dance. When they finished to enormous applause, the audience threw money into the musician's hat. Green, blue and red notes sailed through the air, accompanied by the jingle of coins. After this surprise interlude, we felt incredibly happy and continued our shopping as we wove our way back to the coach. No one missed the bus, which I'm sure was an enormous relief for our guides.

An hour later we reached Mt Etna, which at 3300 metres, is Europe's highest volcano. We could walk the one km track to Silvestri Craters or use the cable car. We opted for the cable. I was glad I'd worn a warm jacket because it became quite cold and windy at that height.

Davide was waiting for us at the top. We rubbed our hands and made shivering sounds in greeting. 'It's not cold,' he chortled. 'Sometimes it drops to 6°C. Now that's cold!'

'Is it dangerous to be so close to the crater?' Lucia asked.

'So it's not the cold but the danger that made you shiver,' laughed Davide. 'The three most dangerous volcanos are Etna, Stromboli and Vesuvius. Are you scared?' He waited for her response.

'Yes, you cheeky boy,' she replied, wagging her finger at him in a motherly mock rebuke.

I too, was a bit apprehensive at first, but he reassured us there'd been no smoke or rumblings from Etna[89] all month. Still, the excitement of being there bubbled inside me.

89 Six months earlier, in February 2012, Mt Etna had had intensive activity and a minor eruption.

When we'd all regrouped, Kareena spoke. 'Mt Etna National Park comprises some 60,000 hectares. Founded in 1987, it is inhabited by many animals and birds.'

'You undoubtedly noticed the base was covered in orchards and vineyard,' added Davide. 'The scene at this height is different. Vegetation is sparse. As we ascend, you'll notice the landscape becomes increasingly denuded.'

'Do the vineyards produce strong wine?' asked Alex.

'Yes, there is an interesting range of liqueurs that you will be able to taste when we return,' Davide answered.

'Mt Etna is both frightening and seductive,' Kareena interrupted. 'It emits a fine volcanic dust. Tourists are fascinated by its might and beauty. However, it can flare up at a moment's notice and caldera edges are known to collapse without warning. The cable car has been obliterated several times. The last time was in 2002. When Etna spews, the temperature of the magma is approximately 1000°C. No wonder the setting for Dante's *Canto to Hell* was here.'

'I've seen photos of Etna covered in snow,' said Mateo.

Valentina gave him a quizzical look. 'Are you mistaken, *bello*?'

'Mateo's right,' replied Kareena. 'During winter, at the summit, it snows heavily, enough to even attract skiers.'

As we walked toward Silvestri, one of five craters, there was an eerie silence. People spoke in whispers as if in deference to the power of the volcano. Underfoot, loose rocks crunched. At times, the soles of my feet felt warm through my shoes as I stepped on spongy ground whereas at other times, I stubbed my toes on hardened lava. Hills were covered in sulphurous yellow, pink, green and gunmetal blue exactly as I'd imagined a moonscape. The colours reminded me of Queenstown in Tasmania, where in the early 1970s, pollution from copper mining stripped all vegetation.

As we roamed around, steam and smoke constantly emitted from the ground. The smell of rotten egg gas was inescapable.

Thankfully, the wind picked up and I realised how tired and hungry I was and that it was time to make our way back. Even though the restaurant at base camp presented an extremely limited menu, we knew they'd been waiting for us.

'I could eat a horse,' said Tony. I agreed with him, as did Joe and Pedro and most of the others.

'Not on the menu,' quipped Angela.

From the basic homestyle menu with the usual variety of dishes, I ordered *Etna Arancini,* stuffed with minced veal and pork. I found myself wondering how they'd managed to get them so crisp and crunchy on the outside while remaining soft and creamy inside.

The food arrived quickly and when I put my fork into my arancini, the sauce spurted out like lava and flowed around its perimeter to form a rich red moat of roast tomato sauce on my plate. The waiter hurried over with a bowl of grated parmesan to sprinkle onto our food.

When we'd finished eating, the waiter invited us to taste the speciality of the district—*Fuoco del Volcano Con Lava,* a concoction of herbs and rose petals infused with 70 percent proof, absolute alcohol. The colour was as intensive a red as Etna's molten lava. The black and red label indicated it to be a warming digestive. I tried a little and immediately felt its fieriness slide all the way down my throat. Not only did it warm me, but it also set my whole body on fire.

The waiter offered us a different digestive, this time made of cherries and strawberries, but he warned us this one was even stronger. 'Enough to blow your socks off,' he chortled.

I declined.

Someone had ordered coffee. The aroma was most inviting. I caught the waiter's eye. '*Mi scusi.*' I beckoned. '*Per favore, avere un caffè.*' What I needed was coffee.

Lucia and Sophia were keen to look at the souvenir shops next door. I joined them after coffee and ended up buying myself a necklace. Beads fashioned from volcanic rock and *coralina*. I guessed the term meant faux coral. The beads were interspersed with silver ones the size and shape of a five-cent coin. I don't normally wear beads, but this piece appealed to me, and I thought I might even start a new trend.

Syracuse was half an hour away, not enough time on the bus for even Davide to have a snooze. Kareena took up the mic. 'Does anyone know which famous figure was born in Syracuse?' she asked.

Alex called out from the back. 'Archimedes, mathematician and inventor of the water screw, which enables low-lying water to be drawn up.'

'Give the man a prize,' Pedro said.

We all laughed.

'Syracuse is an important historical and archaeological city,' Kareena said. 'The limestone buildings display the severe lines of medieval architecture, together with exuberant flourishes of Baroque. There are two safe harbours, pristine forests, abundant water supply and fertile volcanic soil. All are necessary elements to make this a perfect region for trade.'

There was a lot of chatter while a bag of lollies did the rounds of the bus.

Davide took the mic. 'We're going straight to the hotel. Tomorrow will be a big day. We plan to visit a little island off the coast called Ortygia to see more Greek ruins and a Norman castle.' He raised his voice slightly to garner our attention away from the sweets. 'After we register at reception, you'll have a couple of hours before dinner. Take a walk around the town or just relax. We'll meet for dinner in the hotel dining room at 7:00 pm.'

I hoped our accommodation would be as nice as Messina. The name of the hotel certainly gave the impression of a jolly place. However, it was a misnomer. Only one small lift worked and there was no Wi-Fi. I can accept most things but draw the line when I can't use the internet. I went outside for a little while in search of bottled water and fruit for the following day, then continued to walk around the block. I needed to get some air and a better sense of the place.

At seven, the group met in the dining room. We sat at four large, round tables. Dinner consisted of gnocchi, chicken schnitzel and steamed vegetables, followed by plain ice cream. I'd expected regional food so was disappointed with this meal. I sat with the Australians—Tony, Angela and Joe. We all chipped in for some wine. The red was a lovely local merlot called *Gorgio Tondi Estate*. Although the colour was lighter than our merlots, its flavour was beautifully balanced; reminiscent of succulent ripe berries and jam. Everyone liked it enough to live up to the Aussie drinking reputation by ordering more.

I imagine all slept well that night. I know I did. Thankfully, we didn't have an early start the next morning.

Chapter 9
Ancient Mosaics

I awoke later than planned. From my window, a clear cerulean sky promised another perfect day for sight-seeing.

Most of my co-travellers were already at breakfast when I entered the room. There was a huge array of food on the buffet table to tempt the most jaded palate: juices, compotes, cereals and eggs to order, a range of bread, croissants and brioche. Then there were cold meats, assorted salami, ricotta, feta and cheese slices, as well as eggplant, not to mention hot dishes; a solid foundation for travellers. The aroma of eggs and bacon was a familiar temptation. *What I really want is a good coffee, not the stewed stuff in those big urns.* I was determined to have good coffee even though it meant I'd have to wait until I could buy a takeaway.

What surprised me the most was the sight of people sitting outdoors with icy granitas and brioche for their breakfast. I thought I'd join them until I discovered they were the smokers. This habit continues to be prevalent in Europe. I sat inside. Kareena came up to each of our tables to issue a not-too-gentle reminder that we were scheduled to assemble with our luggage in half an hour at reception. I had to hurry.

On the bus, Davide announced, 'We have a very full day. Today, we must cover 153 km from Siracusa to Agrigento; a total of five hours' travel. However, we'll be stopping at Ortygia, where we'll have an early lunch. Then onwards to Armerina to enjoy the fabulous mosaics at the Villa Casale.'

'What time will we arrive at our hotel?' asked Vince.

'Not till 6:00 pm, all being well.' Vince pulled a face. 'You can have a good sleep after the mosaics.' Davide laughed with a look of commiseration at Vince's discomfort.

We arrived quite quickly at our first stop—Neapolis Archaeological Park.[90] Still early morning, we were the first tourists to arrive. Our local guide, Arturo, a history student from Siracusa Academy, was waiting for us at the entrance.

Kareena greeted him. 'Arturo, *come stai*. Sorry for the early start.'

'*Non problema*. I live here at the student accommodation,' he replied, then raised a wave and nodded in greeting to the rest of us. 'Welcome to the largest archaeological site in Italy.'

'Is it Greek or Roman?' asked Pedro.

'Both. There are two. We start at the enormous 5th century BC Greek theatre[91] positioned to take the best advantage of the view,' Arturo said, motioning us to follow him. 'Whereas the Roman amphitheatre, built in the 1st century AD, was for gladiator and animal sports.'

We clambered around the seating, being careful of any loose rocks. I wondered if Sal would again sing something, but he stayed chatting to Laura and the other Italians.

---

90 This park and the whole of Siracusa was declared a UNESCO world heritage site in 2005.

91 Its 64 rows of seating accommodates 15,000 people.

Arturo gained our attention once more. 'Carved straight into the rock, this is the largest amphitheatre in the world. Imagine attending a performance here on a magical moonlit night. You could almost pick up the voices of Agamemnon, Medea and Oedipus.'

Sitting under the stars in the moonlight appeals to me. I remember a night like that. It was the Light and Sounds show on the island of Philae in Egypt.

We did our best to keep pace with Arturo as he led us along a path to the quarries peppered with caves. He stopped at the entrance to one particularly large one called the Ear of Dionysius. With a little imagination, I could see how the entry was shaped like a human ear. There is a folk legend passed down the centuries by word of mouth. It concerns a ruler who eavesdropped on the prisoners incarcerated in the caves. Then he used the information against them.

Arturo asked half of the group to stay where they were while the remainder followed him into the tunnels, where they chatted normally. Indeed, we heard their conversation quite clearly. Then we swapped positions so everyone could experience this strange phenomenon.

When we reassembled, he said, 'The old necropolis is mostly in ruin. This is where the tomb of Archimedes can be found.' He pointed in the direction. 'You can look for it if you like.'

Davide appeared. The time had come for us to get back on the bus. Our destination this time was Ortygia.[92]

92 Settled since the Bronze Age.

Two bridges connect Ortygia to the mainland so the 15-minute drive to our destination was easy. Dotted with splendid Baroque-style buildings, it is a manicured island surrounded by crystalline waters. Boats of assorted sizes, including a huge cruise ship, were moored in the harbour.

We continued to the furthest point of the land mass to find *Castello Maniace*. This Norman fortress[93] was originally surrounded by a moat and is now filled in. During Napoleonic times, the ramparts had been equipped with cannons. The fortress remained a military base until 1970 and it continues to bear the aura of its prison past. I thought it a depressing place. The bare rock structure lacked any greenery. Not a tree in sight. Its current purpose, apart from tourism, is to function as a working lighthouse. It was a sunny spot ideal for wandering if not for an unwelcome smell carried on the breeze, akin to rotting innards left by some lazy fisherman. It cut short our enjoyment.

Although only 11:00 am, one of the seaside restaurants had opened for lunch. My mother used to always say, 'The appetite comes during the meal' and I've always maintained this to be an unequivocal truth. Several freshly made salads were displayed, cafeteria style, alongside a range of cold meats. Some of our group ordered pizza while I enjoyed a sort of antipasto platter with salami, olives, artichokes, buffalo mozzarella and fresh crusty bread, still warm from the oven. The restaurant was licensed and despite the hour, I ordered a cleansing ale.

Our bus was parked on the outskirts of the town. I thought it a bonus to stroll back through the main square—*Piazza del Duomo*—as it allowed time to admire the architecture. The square was flanked by Baroque mansions, cafés and churches. The main cathedral was built on the ruins of what once was the Temple of

Athena, now a Catholic church with three naves. Fluted Doric columns delineated the wide central nave from those at the sides. There was a peaceful and intimate atmosphere, which I think was due to the soft natural light filtering from windows set high in the walls. Both side naves led to beautiful secondary altars decorated with frescoes. Many reliquary boxes were kept there for ease of veneration.

I wandered outside. Tucked away at the back of the piazza was a little limestone church. It caught my eye with its distinctly Spanish-style architecture, a contrast to the Norman and Baroque buildings alongside. This is the church of *Santa Lucia alla Badia*, patron saint of Siracusa, and is where Caravaggio's first work[94] hangs. The floor in the entry foyer is tiled with blue and white quadrangular-shaped majolica tiles.

It was Lucia's birthday and she especially wanted to visit this church to light a candle to her patron saint.[95] When she came out, a busker was playing in the square. Davide grabbed Lucia and they danced to the music while we gathered around them, clapping in time. She was delighted with this spontaneous celebration.

Having appeased our stomachs with the early lunch, the two-hour drive to Armerina promised to be a closed-eye experience.

As we neared our destination, Kareena's voice began to wake us with a few salient points concerning our next destination.

'*Villa de Casale* is a luxurious palace in the middle of a vast estate,' she announced to her stretching, yawning audience. 'Built

94 The church proudly displayed Caravaggio's painting *St Lucia's Martyrdom*.

95 Catholics in Europe, like the Orthodox, name their children after a saint.

on four levels, it includes a spa complex with pools, gym, sauna and baths, as well as the usual accommodation. The mosaic floor in the gym is especially known for its huge chariot-racing scene.'

Salvatore raised his voice. 'I hope we don't have to rush. This villa is renowned for its many mosaics and is a UNESCO heritage listed site.'

'There's certainly much to see,' said Davide. 'We'll spend an hour there, so don't hurry. You'll have time to enjoy it. Each room is decorated with mosaic scenes covering the floors and apses.'

Kareena stepped in. 'Although the mosaics are the most celebrated aspect of the villa, there are also sensational frescoes on some of the walls inside. Even some of the exterior walls still have evidence of paint.'

In its day I imagine it to have been a stunning sight.

When Mauro had finished parking the bus, Davide had the last word. 'To maintain quiet and allow for peaceful contemplation of the artworks, we've prepared an audio presentation for you to use as you go from room to room.' He handed out the audio devices.

'Let's meet back here on the bus in one hour.'

As I walked up the path I was surprised and a little disappointed to see a temporary building site. I expected to see an unhindered view of palatial buildings with columns, porticos and pediments to reflect the status of the owners. Instead, scaffolding obstructed the exterior and workmen milled around with their wheelbarrows.

Once inside, I switched on my audio device to listen to the commentary as I walked around the site.

'Located about three kilometres from the town, this villa was thought to be the home of Emperor Maximilian. Excavations revealed

one of the richest, largest and varied accumulations of Roman mosaics in the world, a UNESCO World Heritage-listed in 1997.'

I followed the others along a boarded-up corridor that led to a specially contrived mezzanine. I felt like I was being herded and had no option but to keep up with the others all the while concentrating on the commentary.

'The mosaic floors cover some 3500 square metres and are unique for their excellent state of preservation. Over the centuries, landslides and floods hid the remains and thereby protected the colour of the tiles from the sun.'

When I reached the top landing, the wooden partition along the elevated walkway had changed to toughened glass. It acted like a balcony, enabling us to view the tiled floors without ever walking on them. Not only did this protect the mosaics, but it also afforded an excellent bird's eye view of the whole picture. I think this arrangement would have pleased the artisans.

'The layout of the complex follows an articulated plan to cater for the needs of the owners and includes thermal baths, triclinium, basilicas, halls with apses, private apartments and servants quarters. The rooms are further enriched with arcades, fountains, statues and internal gardens. The tiles used were of African origin. Hair and clothing styles pictured in the artwork reflect Algerian and Tunisian fashion of the time.'

These themes were another example of the prevalence of travel abroad, at least around the Mediterranean Sea.

The next room was an open expanse. It was difficult to make any sense of its purpose, until the audio indicated that it was the gym.

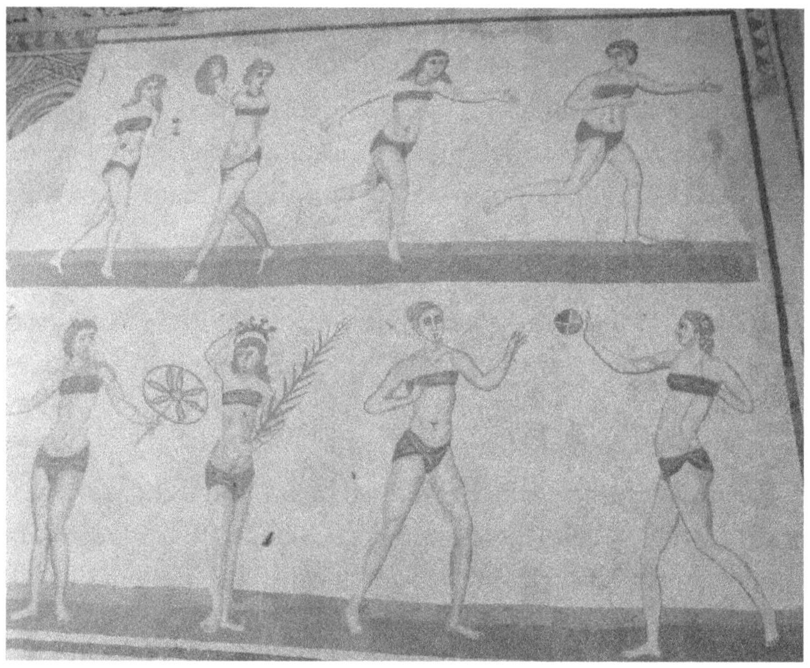

'The gymnasium floor features chariot racing at what looks like Circus Maximus in Rome. The mosaic picture known as The Bikini Girls *is also located in this room. The scene represents 10 girls wearing bikini-like garb performing gymnastics, playing ball games and competing in a race. Note the lone figure at the side holding a laurel crown ready to present to the winner.*

I'll never forget how in the late 1960s, I bought a fuchsia-coloured bikini. As far as modesty was concerned, by today's standards it was tame, but my mother was terribly upset and said that to be dressed like that was vulgar. In the 1960s, we thought we'd invented miniskirts and the bikini, which was named after the Bikini Atoll, where America conducted several nuclear explosions.[96] However, the bikini had already been invented by the Romans and worn in the 4th century AD.

96 A nuclear bomb was detonated on 1 July 1946, and again in '54, '56 and '58. The atoll is still more radioactive today than Chernobyl or Fukushima.

We moved to a long narrow room; more of a hall really, and a perfect canvas for another major work of art.

'The most spectacular decoration in the villa is the Hunting Scene. It can be found in the 65-metre-long hall. There is a tiled apse at either end. The centre of the room is occupied entirely by an African safari scene, with its elephants, camels, tigers and other birds and beasts.'

I loved all the animals and the sailing ships, feluccas and barges. The men sported what I'd call a 'basin cut' hairstyle. They stood by their craft, holding oars. The colour of the tiles was particularly bright as if the work had just been completed. Unfortunately, we were only able to gaze at it for a few minutes due to another large busload of visitors who'd arrived and who were pressing us at the rear.

'This room leads to the Basilica, which is the largest room in the house and is decorated with glass tiles. It is accessed through a monumental entrance divided by two columns of pink Egyptian granite from Aswan. The exceptionally elaborate floor at the entrance consists of marble derived from all parts of the Mediterranean and is the richest decoration in the villa. The type of tile used was the most prestigious in the Roman world.'

It was September—early autumn in the northern hemisphere—and there was a nip in the air. I wondered how the Roman owners had managed to keep these large rooms warm. I heard a couple behind me discussing this problem. Their guide said, 'Hot air was circulated into the cavity between the walls and under the floor for the comfort of the residents.'

I wondered at the veracity of the explanation. How could they blow hot air without electricity to power a blower?

'Reception rooms feature grand peristyle halls with Corinthian columns. You are now in the main visitors' area, which is called a triclinium. It has three atriums, where mosaic decoration depicts the

12 mythological labours of Hercules. The bedrooms are off to the right and are decorated with erotic scenes. We hope you've enjoyed your visit to the villa. It is the most important Roman monument in Sicily.'

I stepped out of the exit and onto the street. There'd been a lot to take in and I was mentally weary. I was glad for some takeaway coffee and chocolates from a pop-up kiosk, before boarding the bus for our three-hour-long trip to Agrigento for the night.

'Before you doze off,' said Davide, 'let me tell you briefly about where we are staying tonight. Agrigento, which dates to the Bronze Age, is a small town with many churches. As we approach, those awake will see its pretty coastline with sandy beaches and palm-lined corniches. It is a popular place for locals to stroll on a balmy evening.'

'Most famous for its folkloric Almond Blossom Festival,' interrupted Maria-Elena. 'We were here two years ago for the festival.'

Her mother, Valentina, appeared pleased with her daughter's comment.

The thought of the festival intrigued me and I made a mental note of it in case I ever returned.

'Yes,' said Kareena. 'It's a lovely time to visit. It marks the beginning of Spring when there are parades and people singing and dancing in the streets. Pink and white almond blossom petals like confetti cover the whole town.'

'The festival draws dancers and musicians to the town. Residents dress in sumptuous costumes for the occasion,' Davide added. 'The celebration begins with the lighting of the torch at the Valley of the Temples. Later, prizes are awarded for the best traditional dress, best singer, best orchestra and even the best-decorated balcony in the town. We'll take the time to visit the Valley of the Temples in the morning.'

'Relax for now,' said Kareena. 'We don't meet until seven o'clock for dinner in the hotel dining room.'

Our hotel was a four-star establishment that featured a modern mosaic on the wall behind reception. After seeing the brightly coloured mosaics at the villa, I thought this modern scene, all grey and pink against a metal splashback, looked insipid and out of place. I hoped the food was better than the décor.

That night was a birthday celebration for both Lucia and Renata, and we also wanted to thank Mauro and Davide, who would be leaving us after lunch the following day.

As Sicily is known for its fishing industry, fish was featured on the menu. For starters, I had *cavolfiore*—a green variety of cauliflower bathed in anchovy and garlic-flavoured melted butter. Delicious. This local vegetable is sweeter than the white cauliflower that we are familiar with, so the saltiness of the anchovy balanced the flavours. For *secondo*, some of us had tuna steaks while others had swordfish, but both were grilled and served with plump capers, also from the local region.

The birthday cake was a scrumptious Sicilian Ricotta Torte. This is a very special traditional treat. Ricotta is flavoured with orange zest, candied peel and orange liqueur and andwiched between layers of sponge finger biscuits or cake. It is then weighed down for a short while to compress the mass in a loaf mould. When sliced and served, it looks like a cassata, though unfrozen.

Chapter 10
Palermo

The last day for our congenial little group had arrived and many of us were genuinely sad at the prospect of parting. Our young local guide, Patrizia[97], a folder in one hand and the obligatory umbrella in the other, met us after breakfast in the hotel foyer. 'Call me Pat,' she said. '*Andiamo*, follow my parasol to the Valley of the Temples.'

She took off with an energetic stride in the direction of the ruins and anyone not paying attention had to run to catch up.

'By 5 BC, the complex of 10 temples was completed,' said Pat. 'They are dedicated to the various gods and goddesses.[98] This is one of the best-preserved archaeological sites of the ancient world.'

We began at the grandiose Temple of Zeus, supported by a giant, stone-like structure called a telamon. This roughly carved figure of a man with his arms raised is based on the Titian god Atlas, who tried to overthrow the king of the Olympus gods. For this, his punishment was to hold the world on his shoulders in perpetuity. The eight-metre-tall telamon might have been used to support some of the weight of the temple. It provided us with a sense of the sheer scale of the original building, now mostly in ruins. From there, I could see the remains of the other temples scattered far afield in the lush valley below.

Next, we visited the Temple of Hercules, which is thought to be the oldest temple in the complex. Although only nine columns remain today, in its heyday, it was as large as the Parthenon in Athens.[99]

From there, we made our way to the Temple of Concordia[100], one of the finest Greek temples in existence. With its thick plain columns, it is a perfect example of a Doric temple. Incidentally, it is the building used in the UNESCO logo and is the second-best preserved temple in the world.

'The temple's grand scale, spanning over 40 metres in length,' said Pat, 'remains apparent to this day. It has survived almost unscathed since its foundation in 430 BC.'

'Why is that?' asked Alex.

'One reason could be its conversion to a Christian church.[101] During reconstruction, the temple was reinforced and is therefore able to withstand the region's earthquakes.'

'What's that bit of metal? It looks like a torso, lying on its side,' interrupted Gabriella.

'The bronze nude is Icarus.[102] Take a moment to admire the striking, contemporary work, created by Igor Mitoraj, a Polish artist,' Pat replied.

---

99 The Parthenon at the centrepiece of the Acropolis in Athens stands at 31 metres high and 70 metres long.

100 Concordia means harmony.

101 Converted to the basilica of St Peter and St Paul in the 6th century.

102 In Greek mythology, Icarus forgot his father's warning and flew too close to the sun and his demise.

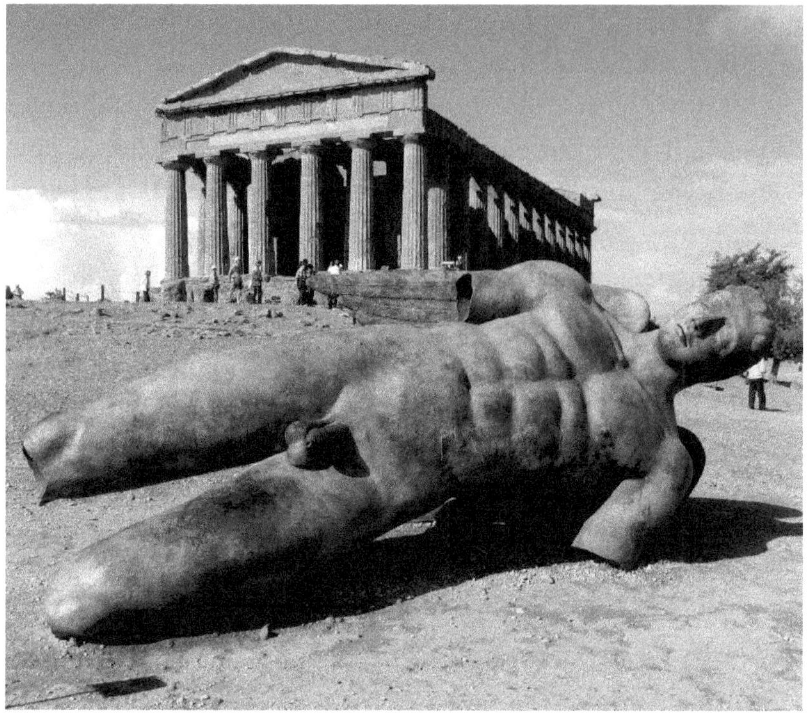

I went up to see it closer and ran my fingers over the shiny surface. The warmth of the sun radiated from the metal onto my face.

'Is the church you refer to the one through there?' asked Alex, pointing to a cross we could see in the distance.

'That's the church of St Nicholas and is a splendid testimony to the process of preservation by transformation of temple to church. Chronologically, this was the last building in the area. If you look carefully, you'll see it's slightly elevated, so its shadow dominates the Valley of the Temples. The church was constructed by *Cistercensi* monks in the 13th century, re-using material from the original temple.'

'Is that the same St Nicholas as the church we saw in Taormina?' asked Mateo.

'Yes, he is the most revered saint of the people,' Pat replied. 'The façade has remained unfinished, but the church has a characteristic pointed arch at the entry. Inside the church, various treasures have survived. Look over there.' She pointed at a tomb. 'The bas-relief on the sarcophagus portrays the myth of Phaedra and Hippolytus.[103] Phaedra's husband, Theseus, had a son, Hippolytus, from a previous marriage. She enticed Hippolytus, but he rejected her. In retaliation, Phaedra told her husband that Hippolytus tried to rape her. Theseus' revenge was to ask Poseidon to kill Hippolytus. Phaedra knew the truth would come out, so she committed suicide rather than be killed.'

We heard Davide's heavy footsteps approach. This was the signal to wrap up.

'The regional Archaeological Museum is laid out in the former Convent of St Nicholas,' added Pat, before bidding Davide goodbye.

When we'd all boarded the bus, I noticed four strangers. Patrizia had allowed four random travellers onto our bus for the remaining 132 km trip to Palermo. Unofficial passengers. *I wonder if they paid cash to our tour leader.* It reminded me of my time in Saint Petersburg in 2007, when my friend Irma and I had spent the day visiting the fabulous Peterhof Palace. She had good connections and was able to get tickets for a sold-out performance to the ballet for the same night. We didn't want to be late, so she sweet-talked a tour guide to take us on their coach into St Petersburg. I slipped the guide a US $10 note that she could change into roubles for a competitive price later. At the time, I thought it brazen of Irma, but now appreciate that it's how the world works.

103 From Greek mythology and through the plays written by Sophocles and Euripides, we meet Phaedra and Hippolytus and the spurned husband Theseus.

Out of the bus window, greenery and a decreasing number of buildings became a blur as the outskirts of the city flashed by. An all-pervading sonorous hum from the tyres speeding along the road surface—like white noise; barely perceptible—was enough to hypnotise me into sleep.

Two hours later, we arrived in Palermo. Its lofty position overlooked a splendid harbour on one side and on the other, a rich valley, called the Conca d'Oro, filled with olive, orange and almond-producing trees.

After unloading the luggage and registering at our hotel, we walked to a restaurant nearby for lunch. As we entered, we were greeted by the hearty aromas of roast meat. It spiked our appetites. They'd been expecting us. Most of the group ordered the roast. I ordered *Fritto di Paranza*, which is whitebait and scampi fried till crunchy and crisp in paper-thin batter. A fresh side salad with olives and other vegetables accompanied the seafood dish. Again, I ordered a cold, cleansing ale. I'm not normally a beer drinker, but the Italian beer was light and suited my palate. Ideal for the warm climate and a foil to the salty food.

At the end of the meal, Patrizia said, 'Anyone who comes to Palermo without seeing Monreale arrives on a donkey and leaves as an ass.' We laughed. 'It is the quintessential presentation of architectural beauty,' she added.

'It's an old Sicilian saying,' added Dr Laura.

'In the 9th century, when Palermo was dominated by Islam,' said our guide, 'the archbishop was forced to move outside of the city walls. Monreale Cathedral was built for him and the cathedra moved there. When the crusaders brought Christian control to Palermo, the seat returned once again to Palermo Cathedral.'

Mauro drove us straight to the enormous 12th-century Monreale Cathedral[104], famed for its mosaics.

'Although the architecture is from the Norman era, refurbishments have added Byzantine, Arab and Baroque elements,' said Patrizia.

Palm trees and pretty gardens decorated the Moorish-inspired cloister. We learned that the colonnade is made up of 228 richly embellished twin columns spanning the perimeter of the cathedral. I was amazed at the diversity and artistry applied to the columns. They were even more decorative than those at *Sergiev Posad,* one of the ancient Golden Ring towns out of Moscow, which I'd visited five years earlier. At Monreale, the columns were fluted, twisted and inlaid with pearlescent and shimmery quartz, mosaics and arabesques. The capitals were further enhanced with biblical scenes fashioned in stucco.

Patrizia explained that a collaboration of Byzantine and Islamic artisans was responsible for the overall richness of the complex. The interior of the cathedral was a compilation of precious images and biblical scenes executed in mosaic, which covered every surface.[105]

The gold mosaic background is a brilliant contrast to the brightly coloured garments of the figures. The image of Christ as Pantocrator making a blessing in the Orthodox manner covers the apse over the altar. And below Him is the Enthroned Virgin and Child.

Columned arches divide the three naves. The friezes are further covered in mosaic biblical scenes. In contrast, I thought the marble and stone floors were quite subdued. They feature interesting inlaid designs, including the signs of the zodiac and heraldic crests. The Cosmatesque technique of inlay includes ribbons, bands, roundels and geometric shapes. The colours are naturally derived from granite, porphyry, glass tesserae and malachite. The technique has been used to decorate many surfaces and is testament to Arabic influence in the architecture of Palermo.

What an overwhelming day. I'd seen unsurpassed examples of human creativity and artistry inspired by faith, executed with a passion and dogged will; a zealousness I liken to that of the Egyptian royal tombs.

The bus drove us back to Palermo and we alighted outside the *Capella Palatina*. All too soon, the time had arrived to say goodbye to Patrizia, Davide and Mauro. After handshakes and hugs, we parted.

Kareena led us inside. 'The Palatine Chapel is an exhilarating architectural synthesis, a fusion of Byzantine, Norman and Fatimid styles.' She pointed to the ceiling. 'The substantial use of intricate patterns in the vaulting is another sign typical of Islamic architecture.'

'The mosaics here are of unparalleled elegance,' interrupted Salvatore. 'I see the arches are an elongated shape and the columns are more slender.'

His wife Laura agreed, adding, 'The elongated proportions of the figures and clinging draperies are statuesque.'

Kareena gazed from one to the other, then said, 'They're also noted for subtle modulations of colour and luminance.'

'Are they the original tiles?' asked Pedro's mother, Manuela.

'The oldest are probably those covering the ceiling, the drum and the dome,' Kareena replied. 'The transept mosaics, dating from the 1140s, are attributed to Byzantine artists, with an illustrated scene of St John in the desert along the north wall. Below this are five saints, the Greek fathers of the church: St Gregory of Nyssa, St Gregory the Theologian, St Basil, St John Chrysostom and St Nicholas.'

Dr Laura added another snippet. 'Guy de Maupassant said the *capella* is an incomparable monument, the most surprising religious jewel ever dreamt of by man.'

'Who's this Guy?' sniggered Pedro. Manuela gave her son a disapproving look.

What a cheeky monkey, I thought. *His mother looks embarrassed.*

'Henri René Albert Guy de Maupassant was a famous French author and tireless traveller. He was the master of the short story form,' Kareena replied.

I totally agree. The mosaic scenes with their bright colours and shimmering gold background are awe-inspiring.

Sal interrupted with a bit of a chortle. 'He said he hated the Eiffel Tower, but every day ate lunch at its restaurant.' The little group around Sal and Laura shared a laugh.

'Follow me,' said Kareena. 'It's only a block back to Palermo Cathedral.'

When we arrived, she said, 'The church was built in 1190 on the site of a Byzantine basilica, destroyed and rebuilt several times over the centuries.'

'Are there more mosaics here?' asked Joe. He was unimpressed.

'None here,' she replied. 'You'll find it a complete contrast to Monreale and *Capella Palatina*. This church was built on the site of a mosque.' Kareena pointed at a column with a bas-relief inscription in Arabic. 'This Koranic verse is the only remnant of its Islamic past.'

'Tit for tat,' remarked Joe, giving the column a friendly pat.

'By comparison, the interior is subdued,' Kareena said. 'White columns, walls and marble statues. The only embellishments are a fresco over the altar and on the ceiling. The floor is granite and marble. The crypt is lined with many royal sarcophagi. You can see it at any time and there is no charge.'

Hurrah, we're not going inside. I'm going cross-eyed and need a break from too much colour and information. I noticed the look of relief on the faces of others in the group.

As the aroma of coffee wafted in the square, several of the group scrutinised the tables and chairs in front of the numerous cafés, while others headed toward carousels of postcards near shop doorways.

'You have free time now,' Kareena said. 'We'll meet in the dining room at 7:00 pm for our last dinner.'

We checked our watches to see how much time we had for relaxation.

'Most of you are leaving Sicily in the morning. For those who are staying on, hotel reception will help you with directions to explore more of Palermo. There is much to see: churches, museums, art galleries, palaces and piazzas with classic sculptures and beautiful fountains. Enjoy the afternoon. See you tonight.' And with that, she left.

Lucia, Sophia and I remained in the piazza, intending to relax and do a bit of shopping, but we were waylaid by the rich caramelly aroma of freshly brewed coffee coming from an alfresco café. We'd just managed to place our order when we heard the bells toll from the church across the square. A wedding party emerged and huddled on the steps for photos. Limousines began to arrive.

'It's another wedding party waiting to go in,' said Sophia, gesturing toward more cars drawing up in convoy.

Sure enough, it was a quick turnaround. The first party left and the second went up the wide stairs into the church. Our refreshments arrived and we relaxed enjoying the *Mazaresi* cakes recommended by Lucia. They looked like macaroons. Light-as-a-feather meringue made with ground pistachio and sandwiched together with crème fraiche, pistachio and sour cherries. We chatted about our plans for Rome.

Meanwhile, the second wedding party emerged. Pigeons were in position to dive onto the rice and rose petals traditionally thrown at the newlyweds. The air filled with joyful laughter as guests escorted the young couple into a horse-drawn carriage.

After paying for our refreshments, we were ready to leave when we noticed the piazza was filling once again, this time with uniformed men. I heard a trumpet and a tuba tuning at the other end of the square. A brass band had begun to form. I asked the waiter what was happening.

'It is a memorial service for Boris Giuliano, who was killed by the Mafia,' he replied. 'After the service, there is to be a parade.'

'Aren't people afraid of the Mafia?' I asked.

'You see there are many *carabinieri, militare, polizia* and the priest; all people respect the priest.'

'What happened to the deceased? I asked.

'In July 1979, Giuliano, who was the chief of police and head of Palermo's Flying Squad, was having his morning espresso at the Lux Bar while waiting for his driver. He'd had a bit of success investigating heroin trafficking and money laundering.'

He's got the story down pat, I thought. *We'll have to tip him for that.*

Sophia said something to the waiter in Italian. I understood the gist of it—something to do with Mafia 'business' interests.

The waiter smirked at her. 'He soon found out,' and in a lower voice said, 'The killer was Corleonesi boss Leoluca Bagarella, a well-known hitman. He shot Giuliano three times in the neck and then standing over the body, made sure he was dead with four more bullets in the back.'

Second-guessing if the Mafia would make trouble at the memorial, we decided we'd seen enough and left.

It was our last night and we exchanged emails, vowing to stay connected. Our dinner was lovely. We started with Bruschetta, which went well with the chianti; a soft red to suit all tastes. For our main, we enjoyed Pasta Norma—another classic of the region, made with eggplant, tomato and rigatoni pasta. They say that after the first taste of this dish, the playwright Nino Martoglio exclaimed, '*Chista è na vera Norma*! This is a true Norma!' after Bellini's lead character in the opera. It must have struck a high note. I could almost hear Maria Callas sing '*Casta Diva*', a haunting prayer to the goddess for victory over the Romans. It went well with another Italian classic—a salad of rocket leaves and shaved parmesan. For dessert, we had honey-roasted figs with limoncello gelato. I love fresh figs and the gelato was tangy, but not too sharp.

Several people had early morning flights, so they retired straight after the meal, while the Australian hardcore remained to enjoy something more pungent like a good Cabernet. Besides, there was no Wi-Fi, so no reason to leave.

The taxi driver and I chatted all the way to the airport. It cost me €50 but I didn't mind because the service was exceptional. He carried my luggage right up to check-in and checked the departures board to confirm my 11:00 am flight to Rome was on time.

In the departure lounge, I was surprised to see the gang: Kareena, Renata with Vince, Valentina, Mateo and Marie-Elena, Angela, Tony and their son, Joe. They'd left ahead of me on the shuttle. Dr Laura and husband, Sal, were on the same flight home to Milan, but they flew business class.

The flight was smooth and there was a shuttle from the airport to Rome Termini, the central train station, where we finally went our separate ways. The Australians were looking forward to staying with their Italian families. Arrivederci and safe travels.

Chapter 11
The Eternal City

I dragged my luggage behind me on the short walk from the station to my *pension*. My case clattered along the cobblestone footpaths, past homeless gypsies and drunks sprawled in every alcove along the path.

I turned into my street, which was flanked by commercial buildings. There was no sign of shops, cafés or hotels and it was not what I expected. I started to think I might be lost. I searched for street numbers, which were not immediately obvious. Finally, I stopped in a driveway. The number matched that in my itinerary, but the entry was blocked by imposing black-painted double doors. They were wide enough for a small Italian car to drive through. Next to the door was a polished brass entablature with the words 'Everest Inn' engraved in bold capitals. Below the smooth brass plate, I could see a keypad with a button labelled '*Entrata*'. I felt like Alice must have when confronted by the tiny door. There I stood poised outside a not-so-tiny but equally mysterious door.

I pressed the button. It buzzed once… twice… then a voice said, '*Allora.*'

'*Equesto*, Everest Hotel,' I asked, and cynically thought, *might be easier to climb Mt Everest*. There was no reply, but the sound of the door clicked. My reflexes were fine-tuned and I pushed the heavy door open before it had a chance to lock me out.

Inside, I expected to see a hotel foyer, a reception desk with smiling staff to welcome and assist me with my luggage to a bank of lifts with shiny chrome doors. However, this was not the scene that confronted me. Instead, I stood in a cold, dark atrium, with four buildings clearly marked A, B, C and D. *Have I stepped through a wormhole into a parallel world?* I consulted my itinerary once more. There was a 'B' next to the street number on my itinerary. With trepidation, I moved toward the door marked 'B' and wondered what lay ahead. In front of me was an old lift. I drew a deep breath. *My next little adventure.*

The lift resembled some ancient capsule for one person with luggage or two people without. The metal concertina doors, which had to be opened and shut manually, were quite heavy. I took another deep breath. The lift bounced a little as I stepped in with my heavy bags. As soon as I closed both doors securely, it took off, even though I'd not selected my floor. Quickly, I jabbed at the third-floor button. The lift continued its upward trajectory, creaking and shuddering, its gears grinding, and I seriously worried I'd not survive the journey.

Finally, it stopped. I opened the doors and slid my luggage out. No sooner had I stepped out and closed the doors when the lift took off just as abruptly as before.

I stood in a tiny foyer barely larger than the lift. The desk was unattended. I was about to ring the bell at the counter when a young clean-cut and bespectacled fellow walked in.

'Good morning,' he said. 'Could I have your passport, please?'

I was reassured when I saw the words 'Everest Inn' embroidered on the pocket of his maroon jacket. I'd found my hotel.

After the ritual of registration, he picked up my bag and showed me to my room. It too was not made for the proverbial cat. Sparsely furnished with a narrow single bed, which doubled as a sofa to watch the TV screen that was attached to the wall. Below the TV was a shelf and chair. I walked across to the shuttered window and opened the curtains, wanting to see the view, only to find opaque glass. When I opened the window, I was aghast to find myself looking into a common shaft, where services for all four buildings converged. The whole lot was covered with a thick blanket of black soot. All the aircon units were attached to the walls. *I'll only be here to sleep and it's only for two nights. I'll be out every day,* I told myself.

I hand-washed my 'smalls' in the ensuite and hung them on my stretchy, pegless washing[106] line; an indispensable travel aid. I always manage to find somewhere to attach it, preferably in the bathroom. The washing dried while I was away on my first excursion.

If you ask most people what you should see in Rome, they'll invariably say, 'The Sistine Chapel, St Peters, the Colosseum and possibly the Vatican Museum.' These are all on the tourist trail. For me, the real gems are further afield. Of course, they're never part of a tour, so you need to have enough time to be able to reach them using public transport. One such gem, quite close to the centre of Rome, is the Villa Borghese Pinciana.[107] The surrounding parkland also houses the zoo.

106 I wouldn't leave home without it. Laundrettes are not easy to find in strange cities and the hotel takes too long.

107 The museum was established in the 20th century.

I walked through the grand gates to the two-story mansion. There were no crowds and I looked forward to sauntering around the property. However, inside I was surprised to find that entry was dependent on a time-restricted ticket.

To preserve the amazing artworks in the Galleria Borghese, the number of visitors in each room at any one time is regulated. I had 45 minutes to wait before being able to enter. It wasn't enough time to wander through the gardens so I had no choice but to sit and wait at the entry with my brochure. Small groups of four or five began to gather, congregating around the door to the museum and gallery. Judging by their conversation, I think the visitors were Russian. A lady sitting alongside me said she comes to Rome three times per year and each time she visits this villa. She never tires of it.

The Villa Borghese Pinciana has been the seat of the Borghese family since 1580. In 1605, Cardinal Scipione Borghese, the nephew of Pope Paul V, began to develop his grand plan for the family holding—a chateau to house his amazingly rich acquisition of art and sculpture. It was a two-storey mansion with 20 rooms on each floor, the upper housed the paintings, while the lower contained the sculpture.

The gardens were designed to be the finest and most elaborate since antiquity. They are better described as a park because they include a lake and several allegorical follies. The setting is so grand that the annual open-air opera season is conducted here.

At last, a guide welcomed our group and allowed us to enter the gallery, but first, she told us the house rules. 'No photos, not even without the flash,' she said. 'This is extremely strict. You will be asked to leave if you violate this rule.'

When I stepped into the first room, I immediately understood the reason for such rigid restrictions. The interior was so unexpectedly lavish—on a par with any of the large European palaces of the time. We stood in the main salon, frozen, our mouths gaping at this masterpiece of Baroque décor. The beauty was so overwhelming I didn't know where to look.

The smooth granite floors, inlaid with elegant patterns and colours, were polished to gleam like ice. Walls and doors were hung with panels embellished with moiré silk and outlined in gilded moulding. The ceilings were a work of art. Some of the walls were covered in silk, others in richly patterned wallpaper. These are merely a backdrop to the richly framed paintings, sculptures and items of furniture, which are further enhanced with precious *objets d'art*.

Imposing corbelled ceilings vied for our attention. In some rooms, the frescoes were held in a central lozenge but in other rooms, the entire ceiling became a fiesta of colour. The *tromp l'œil* designs were dizzying in their 3D imagery, the most stunning example being in the main salon where a fresco called *Marcus Fighting the Gauls* dominated the room. The colours and movement in the figures can only be appreciated from a central position, preferably lying on the ground. Craning my neck, I gazed intently and for too long. It made the room spin.

Life-sized sculptures of velvety marble, shiny bronze and lustrous granite enthralled us. Cardinal Scipio was a generous patron of Bernini, whom he said had the ability to put life into marble and to unite painting and sculpture to the architecture. In one of the rooms, there was a whole assembly of Bernini's busts. Of his larger work, my favourite was Apollo and Daphne. Also popular was Canova's controversial[108] *Venus Victorious*, said to be Napoleon's sister, Pauline, reclining naked on a chaise. The most highly regarded composition is *The Rape of Proserpina*.

108 Too lifelike, the nude was relegated to a private room for restricted viewing.

I think the paintings on the second floor are equal to those found in any of the world's major art galleries. I was particularly taken by *Self Portrait as Bacchus*, painted by the young Michelangelo in 1593.

Cavalieri d'Arpinpo's *Flight into Egypt of the Holy Family* was particularly lauded for the expressive faces of the family. Many other beautiful works included Titian's *Sacred and Profane Love* and Caravaggio's *St Jerome*. I was taken by the poignant depiction of *Christ's Deposition* by Raphael. Some of the art I remembered from school days, but there were other works I'd never seen, including several Botticelli, Veronese and particularly Rubens.[109]

After spending an hour and a half there, the group were ushered out. In terms of beauty, if not fame, I believe this museum to be a serious rival to the Sistine Chapel. I was on such a high I needed to ground myself with an aimless walk in the park. A little while later, I had difficulty finding my way back to the bus stop. A Japanese lady, who said she was a long-time resident in Rome, suggested I accompany her on the bus to the Spanish Steps.

'They say all roads lead to Rome, but they should also say, many roads converge at the Spanish Steps. Don't worry, it's not far.'

We travelled along the Via Veneto, home to many luxury hotels, boutiques and Belle Epoque cafés.

We alighted at the *Piazza di Spagna*. I thanked her and she walked away in the direction of the Metro. The large square was filled with people strolling around, shopping or resting on benches. This piazza was a popular gathering place for tourists to watch buskers or sit on the wide stairs eating ice cream cones. The plants in the middle of the 137 steps added a blaze

109 Rubens *Susanna and the Elders* 1608 is likely to be the most valuable.

of colour; the perfect spot for a selfie. To the right, I noticed a plaque on the building indicating it to be the Keats-Shelley Memorial House. This was the place where they gathered with other writers, artists and intellectuals. At the time, Keats was extremely ill with tuberculosis and died there in 1821.

On the left-hand side was an unassuming building with a cat logo on the windows. The cat intrigued me and I walked over to explore. The signage said Babington's Tea Rooms. In the 19th century, English aristocrats flocked to Italy on their Grand Tour and especially to the preferred destination of Rome. The area around both the top and the bottom of the Spanish Steps was *the* place to be seen—shopping in exclusive boutiques or relaxing in the fashionable cafés. Two enterprising spinsters, Isabella Cargill and Anna Babington, decided in 1893 to open a tearoom for the many English travellers unaccustomed to coffee drinking. Isabella was the granddaughter of Captain William Cargill founder of the city of Dunedin in New Zealand.

There's always been a resident cat, which brought them enough luck to continue the business through two world wars. Regulations no longer allow the moggies free rein, so the cat was replaced by the logo. There are real cats at Babington's but they must stay out in the back garden. The current owners are Isabella's grandchildren.

My plan was to splurge on High Tea at Babington's.[110] I ordered a glass of champagne to sip while I waited for the food. Presently, an overloaded cake stand arrived with all the accoutrements—finger sandwiches with an array of fillings and petit fours. These days the menu is more extensive: eggs, salads, burgers, curries, cakes and pancakes. Not to forget tea, all sorts of tea: green or black, floral, herbal or iced and there is coffee, though tea is a

110 They're open from noon until 11:00 pm, except Tuesdays.

serious matter here. I tossed up between Assam from the top-producing region of Halmari in India, and Miss Babington's Tea, scented with Australian rose, vanilla and myrtle. I settled for the Assam; always a favourite of mine, but this one was so delicious I bought four packets to take home as gifts.

The direct route back to my hotel was via the Metro, but the ticket machine wasn't working so I thought I'd walk back but was too bamboozled to work out which street to take. It was safer and less stressful to get a taxi, even though I knew he'd drive the long way around and overcharge me. I was too weary to care. I'd seen too many impressive sights and was awash with information. It had truly been a day filled with highlights.

Back in my shoebox at the Everest, while changing into my PJs, I noticed my legs were swollen and there was a red rash on the calves. I thought it might be cellulitis, but I had no time for medical issues. So a positive attitude, a long shower and an early night were the only other remedy.

Chapter 12

Three Coins in the Fountain

Next morning at breakfast, I made a salami and cheese sandwich and placed it into the fridge in my room alongside a piece of fruit in readiness for lunch. Then off I went to Termini Interchange to pick up the 9:00 am Red Bus, which I could ride all day. Lo and behold, standing there also waiting for the bus, were Vince and Valentina. We sat upstairs enjoying the wind ruffling our hair. They were heading to the Colosseum. I intended to do the round trip for general orientation before deciding where to alight.

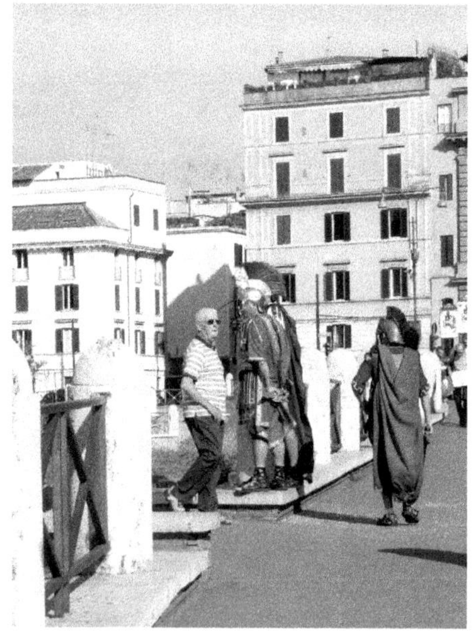

As I bade them farewell, the Colosseum loomed over us. I thought it was much smaller and dirtier than portrayed in my brochures.

Men sporting red tunics, armour chest plates with exaggerated six-packs and Roman helmets with bright red brushes strutted on the footpath. They were ready to pose with the tourists who wanted happy snaps. We drove past Circus Maximus, which is a huge archaeological site. I decided to give it a miss because it really needed a guide to make the visit to the ruins meaningful. I was not going to make the same mistake I'd made in Pompeii.

I could see the Pantheon on Capitoline Hill and resolved to make it my first stop. If buildings could have gender, I'd call the Pantheon with its imposing Greek pediment and thick Doric[111]columns male. This main building in the piazza was augmented with an impressive fountain with sculpted figures. The edge of the basin provided seating for small children. While there, the nutty aroma of good coffee beckoned from the open doors of cafés.

In front of me, a crowd gathered. Flag bearers milled in the forecourt, while a few people holding megaphones ascended the steps of the Pantheon. People waved placards and banners in protest regarding the EU financial Crisis[112] and the overwhelming number of African refugee arrivals. The Pantheon looked old and forlorn, as if it wanted some peaceful tourists instead of the infernal noise coming from the revved-up crowd.

With my trusty map firmly in hand, I skirted around the edge of the protesting crowd to the back of the Pantheon. From there, I continued down via *Della Minerva* to the peace and quiet of the *Chiesa Santa Maria Sopra Minerva*, one of the main churches of the Dominican Order. This is the only example of Gothic architecture in Rome. The deceptively plain façade belies

111 The thicker, heavier columns reflect strength, power and masculinity.

112 Standard and Poors had downgraded all the Euro zone countries. There was a high level of debt in Italy and unemployment was rising. It was a fiasco. There were anti-Islam protests in Australia.

the jaw-dropping beauty of its interior. The vaulted ceiling is painted an intense blue with contrasting gold ribbing. The panels between the ribs display alternating frescoes of cupids and putti with stars. The walls, arches, friezes and surfaces around the splendid stained-glass windows are covered in frescoes. Cobalt and gold-painted pilasters delineate the main nave from the sides. I paused to take in the fresco in the Carafa Chapel, which was painted by Filippo Lippi.

I studied the small brochure I'd picked up at the entrance. It indicated where the Egyptian obelisks were found buried in the yard. They were presumed to be associated with a previous pagan temple on the site dedicated to a goddess, some say Isis, others say Minerva.

To the left of the main altar is a beautiful marble statue of *Christ Carrying the Cross of Redemption* sculpted by Michelangelo. Apart from several popes, the main tombs in the crypt include those of St Catherine of Siena and the artist, Fra Angelico. I'd already seen so many churches, yet all of them paled in comparison with this gem, which I found off the beaten track.

I stumbled from the church into the sunlight feeling a bit humbled by the colour and artistry attributed to some of the most famous Renaissance artists. By way of contrast, a marble elephant carrying a red granite obelisk graced the centre of the piazza. The obelisk had been brought out of Egypt in the 1st century to decorate the Temple of Isis being built on this site. Bernini's unusual composition of an elephant carrying the obelisk is popular with photographers. I couldn't resist taking a selfie.

Rather than go back and be caught up in the rally, I preferred to wander along some narrow alleys in the direction of the Trevi Fountain, the largest fountain in Rome. This fountain became famous after it was featured in the 1953 film *Roman Holiday* with Audrey Hepburn and Gregory Peck, where they threw coins into the fountain. I remember being enamoured with avant-garde films in the 1960s. A scene from Federico Fellini's film *La Dolce Vita* with Anita Ekberg and heartthrob Marcello Mastroianni was set at the Trevi fountain.

Along the way, I was easily diverted by the magic word 'Sale' splashed across a shoe shop window. Inside the shop was a cornucopia of Italian designs made from the softest leather using an artist's vast palate of colours not imagined back home. The hardest decision was to restrict myself to only one pair of shoes. The place for leather is Florence but that destination was still a couple of days away, then Spain and France; I knew I had to pace myself.

Artists at *plein air* easels sat with watercolours, pastels, even oils, sketching and painting memorable glimpses of domes and cupolas framed by the alleys where they sat. I couldn't resist and bought a couple of small watercolour and pen sketches of charming street scenes. Once framed they'd look very nice, even too nice to give away.

At the *Piazza Trevi*, there were many tourists perched on the steps that surrounded the fountain. In the water, I could see many coins. How could I not do the tourist thing and throw coins into the fountain, the largest in Rome? The fountain ensemble comprised a central niche, carved into one side of the Baroque palace where an enormous statue of Neptune stands in a chariot drawn by two tritons. It was impossible to get a photo of the fountain without a myriad of tourists' heads, but I wandered around looking for a vantage point. Nearby, a young couple were speaking in Russian.

'Misha, you take my photo and then I'll take yours,' she said to him.

I decided to introduce myself and offer to take their photo together. They were delighted and surprised that I spoke the language. I was pleased to have surprised them too.

'I'm Michael and here is my wife, Natasha,' he said. 'But call me Misha; everybody does.' Of course, they reciprocated with an offer to take my photo too.

We sat on the steps for a bit of a chat. They were on their honeymoon from Chelyabinsk in Middle Russia near the Ural Mountains. I told them that five years earlier, I'd spent a couple of weeks in Ekaterinburg, which is approximately 200 km north of Chelyabinsk, and I told them how much I thought the country had improved since my first visit in 1993. They agreed that much work had been done to improve infrastructure, roads, transport and housing. The country was experiencing a renaissance. There was continual restoration and reinstatement of ancient churches and monasteries to their former glory. They said both were incredibly positive regarding the future.

'Anyone willing to work hard can make a good life,' Misha said.

They were surprised to hear of Russians living in Australia and had never heard of Russians who'd fled to China after the Russian Revolution during the civil war. Nor did they know of the consortium formed in the 19th century to build the Chinese spur of the Trans-Siberian Railway—Russian engineers and Chinese labour. This gap in their knowledge was due to the suppression of information during the Soviet period and it is most likely Natasha and Michael's parents didn't talk openly about such things. To change the subject, I said I was surprised by the number of Russians presently holidaying in Italy.

'Yes,' said Natasha. 'This is our first trip, but since 1991, my parents and their friends travel regularly to Egypt, Turkey and all over Europe.'

I could have ridden the red bus all day long. This time I went in the opposite direction back to the hotel for a break and to have the sandwich I'd prepared earlier before returning to my wanderings around Rome. My next destination was the Colosseum. I was told that you couldn't visit Rome and not see it.

There was a long queue at the ticket counter. Entry to museums and places of interest for EU residents was free and most places extended this courtesy to seniors from Australia, but not so at the Colosseum. I bought an audio guide but had to leave my passport at the counter, held as security.

'Where do I go?' I asked the cashier.

'Upstairs!' She waved me off rudely without even looking at me. 'Next,' I heard her say. Obviously, her job was selling audio, not giving directions.

Armed with my ticket and a small brochure, I approached the stairs. I could feel my leg playing up but pushed through the discomfort. At the top of the steep staircase, I saw metal doors open and people stepped out from a lift!

There was no 'start' sign to indicate where to commence the audio tour. I decided to turn it on anyway with the thought that I'd get the hang of it. The audio didn't work. I asked a young person to help. He managed to get it going but five minutes later, it went dead. I wasn't about to tackle the stairs and face the rude woman again, so I clung onto the coattails of the group ahead of me.

I snapped a few photos. My brochure indicated the arena had been used as an entertainment centre for gladiator contests, games, executions, mock battles, including sea battles, and animal hunts. Gladiators were armed warriors usually, slaves who entertained the blood lust of Roman audiences by fighting in the arena. *What a depressing place.*

I continued to walk around the perimeter until I completed the circuit. When I returned the defective audio and tried to complain, the person at the collecting point wasn't interested and put it into the same pile as all the returns. I imagine that's how I received a defective one and now some other poor visitor would too. At least I retrieved my passport.

As I approached the exit gate, I saw a man sitting there reading a newspaper. I asked him if they had any feedback forms. He said there were none. I asked where I could lodge a complaint, but he merely shrugged his shoulders, unperturbed. I couldn't get out of there fast enough, away from all the tourists who wandered along happily like a herd of sheep. It was a mistake. One should only go there in a group with a guide.

Once again, with my trusty map, I left the tourist trail to find the church of St Clemente where the brother-saints, Cyril and Methodius, are buried. St Clemente was the third successor to St Peter the Apostle. He was the disciple of St Cyril and St Methodius. They were all from Macedonia. In the 9th century, Cyril and Methodius created the precursor to the Cyrillic alphabet.[113] All three saints are commemorated by the Eastern Orthodox, Catholic and Anglican churches.

Rebuilt in the 12th century on the ruins of an earlier Norman church, the Basilica of St Clemente is one of the oldest and most interesting churches in Rome. It was not far away, just two blocks. I arrived at the sight of a high cement-rendered wall, which enclosed the bell tower. Except for a colonnaded porch[114] and fountain, the exterior is unadorned.

113 Creation of the Cyrillic alphabet is attributed to St Cyril and St Methodius and is therefore named Cyrillic, after St Cyril. However, Cyril and Methodius created the Glagolitic alphabet on which the Cyrillic is closely based.

114 The portico is preserved from the original church.

The interior of the church exudes a serene beauty. The subdued colour of the marble and stone floor complements the geometric design of triangles and squares. The nave is bound by Roman columns. A central aisle leads to the altar, which is surmounted by an apse covered in a mosaic pattern. A life-sized fresco of saints covers the wall behind the altar.

I gazed up to the heavily coffered and gilded ceiling where a central lozenge featured a bright and busy fresco of the Glory of St Clement. This is the only evidence of Baroque decoration still evident in the church. I noted the austere baldachin over the altar, its pediment adorned with one lone anchor in memory of St Clemente's martyrdom. He was beaten then weighed down with an anchor around his neck, to drown.[115]

A young couple waited by the notice on the front door indicating the possibility of a visit to the crypt. Wishing to do the same, I paid at the office. Presently, a guide led us down some stairs into a dark maze of tunnels and doors under the church. A mosaic depicting Saints Cyril and Methodius with St Clemente was illuminated. The guide pointed at the floor to alert us to be careful as there were rocks protruding from the bare ground. I'm not sure if he could speak or if his sign language was due to the language barrier. My brochure indicated that the basilica was built over an ancient church, which was constructed over a previous temple to the pagan god, Mithras. With each rebuilding, material was recycled from the previous structure.

115 According to St Cyril's own report, in AD 861, he recovered the body of St Clement in the Crimea, together with the anchor. The body was solemnly escorted to be interred in the Basilica San Clemente. A year later, St Cyril died in Rome. St Methodius asked for permission to take the body back to Greece. When the pope and people of Rome refused to allow it, St Methodius requested that he be buried in San Clemente Basilica together with Cyril and Clement.

I noted original brickwork, with traces of frescoes from hundreds of years back. The best preserved one is of St Clement's body being taken from the Vatican to the church of St Clemente. Remnants of bas reliefs and bases of columns jutted out in a higgledy-piggledy fashion. The guide used a torch to show the way. He pointed to a flat rectangular area on the ground. This is where the saints are buried. We reached a dead end where a simple stone table abutted the wall. A mosaic icon and a couple of bas reliefs of the saints adorned the wall. One of these commemorated 1000 years of Orthodoxy in Russia—988 to 1988. The table is used occasionally as an altar for memorial services. The atmosphere was dense and dank, indicating a lack of oxygen because we were a long way below ground.

The visit was steeped in history and meaning. The brave martyrdom was inspirational. I left St Clemente church with a light step and a feeling of peace and calm.

On my way back to the bus stop, I happened upon a pharmacy where I tried to buy a pencil sharpener for my lip liner and eyeliner. I didn't know the Italian words, so I resorted to sign language. The assistant was mystified and called upon the pharmacist for help. Again, I made my left hand into a fist and inserted the pointer finger from my right hand into my left fist making a slight turning movement. The poor chemist gave me a strange look and waved his hand at me to vamoose out of the door. Now I was the one who was left mystified. Out in the sunlight it dawned on me what he must have thought.

I boarded the red bus and made my way back to Termini then strode along the familiar path to my hotel. I passed by another pharmacy where I tried my luck once more. A carousel of eye makeup and other accessories greeted me at the door. I scanned the items displayed and soon found a pencil sharpener amongst other items hanging there. I was thrilled. *Success at last!*

I was two doors from the entrance to my hotel when I noticed that the unobtrusive little restaurant[116], the one I'd passed so many times previously, was already open for dinner. Though it was early, I went in and made myself comfortable. The menu appeared most appetising and proved to be the best food I'd eaten during my whole time in Rome.

For *primo*, I ordered *Carciofi alla Romana*, which is artichoke braised lightly in white wine and garlic; a Roman speciality. For *secondo*, I chose *Sauté di Cozzi e Vongole*, which is a dish of mussels and clams cooked in white wine, garlic and tomato and served in the same broth. The waiter recommended *Bruschetta Crema Tartufo* to soak up the lovely juices from the mussels. This turned out to be an unforgettably delicious dish. The bread slices were topped with a creamy concoction of chopped mushroom, ricotta and truffle. I ordered a glass of Matheus Rosé. The waiter poured it from the familiar round bottle I remembered from way back in the late 1960s when it was quite the fashion. Although I'd had quite sufficient to eat and lingered with my second glass of rosé, the waiter tempted me with Sicilian Cassata for *dolci*.

Coffee was complimentary. I sat reflecting on my five days and nights in Rome. Never enough time, but I was satisfied with what I'd seen and done. I'd thrown my coins into the Trevi Fountain. Who knows? One day maybe I'll come back to explore the National Museum and the Ethnographic Museum,

116 The Il Barocco Ristorante on via Napoli, Rome, is a moderately priced café.

both of which trace the richness of Roman history and customs throughout the ages.

My evening meal at Il Barocco had been an unforgettable way to spend my last evening in the Eternal City.

Arrivederci, Roma.

Chapter 13
IL Bella Nord

The beauty of northern Italy awaited as did the drive through the classic Tuscan landscape to our destination of Florence. I anticipated amazing architecture and artworks like Michaelangelo's *David* in the flesh, so to speak, and possibly to touch his marble foot.

Milan, Turin, Lake Como and Venice would follow. I planned to sit in Hemingway's favourite corner of Harry's Bar in Venice and sip an iconic Bellini. Even though terribly touristy, I vowed to take a gondola ride through the narrow canals and make a wish under the Bridge of Sighs.

I don't enjoy early mornings but somehow I managed to be outside my hotel by seven o'clock. *Just as well I'd settled my bill last night and confirmed my pickup,* I thought as I searched for my tour group.

A coach was parked a little way down the street. I hurried towards it, my luggage creating an embarrassing racket on the cobblestones. A man stood next to the coach's open luggage compartment. He grabbed my suitcase and in one seamless motion, stowed it in the hold. He scanned the list for my name, but it wasn't there. Clearly, this was not my bus. He retrieved my luggage and I stood bewildered on the pavement. An involuntary shiver passed through me. Was it nerves or the gentle breeze?

Another bus pulled up in front of me. This too was not my bus.

A taxi pulled up at the curb and after the customary pleasantries, he stowed my luggage in the boot and opened the front passenger side door for me to get in. *That's more like it,* I thought. Then I proffered my travel voucher, but he barely glanced at it and proceeded to ask me where I'd like to go! That's when I twigged. He hadn't been sent by my tour company. This was not my cab. He unloaded my luggage and I stood on the curb once more, feeling dejected and foolish.

I could feel my blood pressure rising. I was in a pickle. Did I misunderstand or had I been misunderstood? I asked myself what had gone wrong with the confirmation call I'd made the previous evening and how would I connect with my tour.

Meanwhile, another bus pulled up. I peered at the destination board. It read: *IL NORD*—North. Some people began to board. I walked over, unsure if this was my coach or another that happened to also be going north. The guide scrutinised her long list for my name while my nervousness mounted. When she finally found my name at the bottom of the list, I became instantly relieved and clambered on board. The compartment was already half-full but I found an empty window seat at the back and made myself comfortable.

At last, I could put aside my false start and begin my next adventure. The bus rounded a few corners before coming to a stop in Esquolina Square. Here, a whole group of noisy travellers filled the remaining empty seats. They were all from Australia and New Zealand and I knew I'd been married up with a band of compatriots.

The tour leader was a blonde-haired, blue-eyed South African called Nora and the bus driver was called Mario. Although born and bred in Kenya, Nora had lived in the UK for three years, then Italy for ten. Short and slim, Nora's size belied her formidable presence and ability to keep our group of 30 in tow. Nora chatted to Mario as the engine of the bus warmed up.

We introduced ourselves to those nearby and began to chat. They had started their tour three days previously and had been to Sorrento, Pompeii and the Amalfi Coast. Funny thing, they too were unhappy with their accommodation in Sorrento. Their grand hotel had promised views of Mt Vesuvius but was far from grand unless that was a prefix for grand-fiasco, we joked. My fellow travellers complained of leaking ceilings, mildew and decrepit fixtures. They said that their dining experience had been planned to process diners quickly to enable the staff to finish sooner. They said they were served a bland and boring set menu with no choices.

As we left the bustle of the city, Nora took up her microphone to welcome everyone on board and give us an idea of our first day together.

'Mario says we'll be in Assisi for morning tea. It's roughly two and a half hours' drive, depending on road building works. Then we'll drive to Siena where we're booked in for lunch, shopping and sight-seeing before arriving in Florence.'

We checked our watches and made ourselves comfortable for the long drive. As we left the city and suburban sprawl, we entered Umbria—the green heart of Italy—where undulating plains abound in tall avenues of cypress amidst olive groves.

As we drove through Spoletto, Nora mentioned the annual summer arts festival held in June and July. I was surprised to learn it featured a vast array of concerts, opera, dance, drama and visual arts, as well as roundtable discussions.

Soon, my early morning start and the soft buzz of chatting voices sent me into a light doze. When Nora's voice brought me back to the present, I gazed out the window where I could see we were crawling through massive road works.

'The government is constructing a new ring road from Rome to Milan, in preparation for the 2015 Milan Expo.[117] It's an important event with many international guests expected to attend.'

Nora gave some general information and encouraged us to carry our passports at the ready for random security checks. 'It is an accepted procedure all over Europe,' she said. 'Incidentally, it's common for people in Italy to also carry their log book when driving.'

The faces of the people across the aisle didn't look convinced. Meanwhile, one of the men was darting around spare seats to take photos of the roadworks. His constant pacing was distracting.

'If you're going to Morocco or South Africa,' Nora continued, 'get your passport scanned and have a couple of copies laminated because everywhere you go it will be required for ID checks, but you may come across some people who demand a $100 bribe to return it. If it's a copy, you can walk away unperturbed.

'Our first stop, Assisi, in the province of Perugia, is the land of St Francis,' said Nora. 'Do you all know this saint?' she asked.

A child's voice with a New Zealand accent called out from the back of the bus. 'He's the saint who cared for the animals and preached to the birds.' We all turned around to see who was speaking. It was a young dark-haired boy sitting with a girl who could have been his twin sister. I estimated they must have

117 The theme for 2015 was sustainability, feeding the planet.

been nine or ten years old and I wondered why they were here and not at school.

'That's true,' said Nora, cutting into my thoughts. 'St Francis became a monk only after his wife died. He was rich but gave away all his possessions to live a chaste and simple life dedicated to God. A following developed around him and in time, it became known as the Franciscan Order of Friars. The monastery gets a vast number of pilgrims and the campus dominates the town.'

We parked in the piazza and walked to the basilica. Assisi is a pretty town with narrow, cobbled streets complete with baskets of hanging geraniums. We found a little coffee shop, called Café Anna, for our morning tea break. I felt rejuvenated after sitting outside in the fresh air with a coffee and listening to the splashing of the fountain in the middle of the piazza. I bought a little pack of my favourite chocolates—Baci from Perugia.[118] We were so near the factory but had no time in our busy schedule to visit. Instead, we followed Nora to the church.

'The Basilica of St Francis is a synthesis of Romanesque and Gothic architecture,' she said as we stood admiring the exterior. 'The church has two levels and is known for beautiful frescoes attributed to Giotto, Cimabue, Lorenzetti and Martini, which record the life of St Francis. The most famous is the Cimabue portrait of St Francis in his diaconal habit, which clearly reflects his humility.'

Inside the upper church, I was struck by the soaring height of the ceiling and impressive ribbed vaulting over the central

118 In 1987, Nestlé bought the company and continues to make the Baci—kisses, as per the original recipe.

nave. It looked like a long gallery. The cross above the altar was the work of Giotto and was one of the most artistic treasures of the basilica. The three Franciscan religious vows are: poverty, chastity and obedience.

She went on to say that the frescoes had shocked the people with their dramatic break from the stylised Byzantine paintings, which they were used to seeing. These showed recognisable scenes from everyday life without the use of gold, fixed images or symbols. The church also has a large collection of medieval stained glass windows of which the oldest are found in the lower church where side chapels were added to accommodate the growing number of pilgrims. These include chapels dedicated to St Nicholas of Bari, St Anthony of Padua and Mary Magdelene. St Francis's tomb has also been placed in the crypt.

Nora managed to tear the avid photographer, James, away from the many angles he needed to shoot and to get back onto the bus where the rest of us waited to get on our way to Siena. He sauntered down the aisle mumbling something about getting locations for his next movie. He asked Nora if he could have the skylight open for a few panoramic shots of the city. She spoke briefly to the bus driver. Mario turned his head towards the aisle and loudly proclaimed, just one word—'No!'

Unfazed, James lay down in the aisle and began taking photos aimed through the windscreen.

'*Stai scherzando,*' Mario said with a wave of his hand. Without knowing what that meant, we all understood what was meant. As we pulled away from the kerb, the bus did a kangaroo hop, dislodging our intrepid photographer.

We soon reached the rolling hills and cypress trees of the Tuscan countryside. An hour later, we were in Siena. A maze of narrow streets and alleys radiated from the fan-shaped *Piazza del Compo,* a grand medieval square in the middle of town, where we parked. Siena is one of the prettiest medieval towns in Italy. The contest for supremacy between the pope and the Holy Roman Emperor occurred during the time of the Medici family's supremacy. Rivalry between Florence and Siena is historic. It started during their rule and now includes art, warfare and football.

Lunch was in a large trattoire with both indoor and outdoor seating. Sheila, Simy and I settled for a table outdoors under a huge awning.

Simy, with her long dark hair tied back and big dark eyes, seemed to be a gentle soul, quiet and respectful of others. I think she was my daughter's age, a single lady with a Middle-Eastern background. She was vegetarian but this posed no problem in any of the places where we ate. She worked as an interpreter in a law firm in Iran. Sheila, who sported a blonde page-boy hairstyle, was from the UK. She was quietly spoken and undemonstrative. She enjoyed watching the passing parade but said she was not impressed with James's antics.

At lunch, some of the group ordered pizza. We shared a bruschetta with tomato and truffle, which was as delicious as the one I'd eaten in Rome. The girls liked it too. Simy ordered a dish called *malfatti,* which is a spinach gnocchi served on a lake of tomato sauce and torn basil. Spinach is a popular ingredient in Tuscany. Sheila and I opted for *Paglia e Fieno,* a spinach fettuccini in a white sauce topped with the regional pecorino cheese. We couldn't eat any more but bought a slice of *Panaforte di Siena* for later. Siena is known the world over for this sweet meat. Panforte is a medley of dried fruit, nuts and spices, including cardamon, cinnamon, cloves and honey. It dates back to the 13th century.

Fed and rested, Nora led us to the *duomo*, in the centre of town. This was my introduction to the distinctive architecture of the north. Tuscan Romanesque, the *duomo* is dominated by its marvellous 13th-century dome attributed to Bernini. The *campanile* has six bells. I admired the slender, fluted, Corinthian columns and rose windows with intricate designs in stained glass. The gargoyles and abundance of bas-relief sculpture added to the external decoration. The façade, deemed to be the most impressive in the whole of Italy, marks each of the four cardinal points and adds to the status of the church.

Inside, alternating stripes of white and greenish-black cover the marble pillars, reflecting a Moorish influence. These are surmounted by huge fresco-covered friezes designed to support the vaulted ceiling. Sapphire blue panels between the ribs, like a tapestry resembling the night sky, were studded with golden stars of every shape and size.

We saw so many statues by famous artists, which included Michaelangelo's St Paul, Donatello's St John the Baptist and Bernini's St Jerome. They take pride of place in the side chapels. The intricately decorated, Carrera marble pulpit is concerned with the doctrine of The Last Judgement and Salvation. It has seven panels illustrating the life of Christ, sculpted by Nicola Pisano.

Pinturicchio's frescoes in the Piccolomini library covered the walls in brightly coloured family crests and biblical scenes. Beautiful, illuminated pages of ancient manuscripts are displayed in temperature-controlled cabinets. Siena's meticulous archival recording has preserved much detailed knowledge of the past. The cathedral is said to outclass the *Duomo* of Florence.

I particularly liked the ornate marble mosaic floor that covers the whole cathedral. The 56 inlaid panels feature scenes from the Old Testament. These are usually kept covered but we were lucky to be visiting in September when they are on view. It's difficult to appreciate each work when there are so many brilliant examples vying for attention. In the end, they all begin to look the same. However, some scenes were memorable for their subject matter: Misericordia, Ruoto della Fortuna, Slaughter of the Innocents. They symbolise the four virtues—wisdom, temperance, courage and justice.

St Catherine of Siena is the patron saint. She is remembered for her work fighting corruption in the church and for convincing the pope, who was seated in Avignon, to restore the papal seat to Rome. Unfortunately, the group walked past St Catherine's basilica, where her head and a finger are kept for veneration. We were overwhelmed with admiration for the *Duomo di Siena* but needed to break for lunch. Those who wanted to could visit the relics in the basilica during this free time.

For much-needed light relief, we headed to the *Loggia della Mercanzia*. Undisputed as the retail market since medieval times, the area is a maze of boutiques, quaint cafés and artisan workshops. Some of our group went shopping, others headed straight for coffee.

A carousel filled with postcards caught my eye. It stood at the entrance of a ceramics and souvenir shop. The cards were all drawings of cats dressed in bright folk costumes, dress uniforms, medieval and ecclesiastical clothing. I couldn't resist. Unsure of what I would do with them, I chose five designs that appealed to me. When I brought them home they sat in a drawer for eight years, and then out of the blue, my first grandchild was born. The parents called her Siena and I recalled the postcards, which, when framed, were ideal for the nursery wall. It made a lovely first birthday gift.

I caught up with Simy and Sheila for coffee. We rushed to be on time for the bus. Then I had that sinking feeling when I couldn't find my purse. Where had I left it? Had I been pickpocketed? In a bit of a panic now, I quickly retraced my steps. When I'd checked everywhere I'd been and not found the purse, I was convinced it had been stolen. *How could it have happened?* I questioned myself. My jacket was a special travel vest with only inside pockets that were firmly zipped up, and the vest itself zipped up, so it was impossible to access valuables without first removing the vest. What of my passport? I put my hand inside to check the pocket dedicated to the document when I felt a familiar lump. It was my purse! I'd put it into the wrong pocket. Hurrah! All was well and I hurried back to the bus, where everyone was waiting.

Florence was only an hour's drive away. As we neared our destination, it became increasingly misty and our arrival was to drizzling rain, the first I'd seen since I'd arrived two weeks earlier.

Our hotel was on the outskirts of the central tourist district, ten minutes' walk from the cathedral which is known as *Duomo di Firenze* or *Santa Maria del Fiore* or simply the Duomo. Located right next door to our hotel was a launderette—an essential feature for travellers. The hotel dinner booking was only an hour and a half away so I opted to get my laundry done. Yes, I was in Florence—the city of Michelangelo—and I was doing the laundry. When such a rare opportunity comes up to get my larger items laundered, it becomes a priority.

Meanwhile, the heavens had opened up and I didn't fancy walking around in the rain, so returned to my room for a relaxing bubble bath before dinner. I had the luxury of time. I would be returning to Florence at the end of this tour for a few more days on my own to discover all those other gems not generally found on the tourist trail.

Simy, Sheila and I met in the restaurant. We sat chatting when shock, horror, Kim and James were shown to our table. Although we already knew their names, Kim did the introductions.

'Hello, I'm Kim and this is my husband, James,' she said, leaning across to shake our hands.

Her husband followed suit. 'James, 007,' he quipped.

Kim said she was having trouble with her legs. They looked similar to mine, so we decided the culprit must be long-haul travel. They'd flown from New York, where James was a film producer. He began to tell us all about his exciting lifestyle when the lady with the two kids joined us. We soon learned she was called Marion and was from the Adelaide Hills. The children with her were Sophie and Oliver. They'd recently moved from New Zealand to Marion's house after a tragic car accident in which their parents had died. Their mother had been Marion's sister. *What a sad story. That explains why the children are out of school and are so subdued.*

Our dinner was delicious. We started with minestrone, followed by *Bisteca Florentina* and a Chianti from the region. Simy had a vegetable risotto instead of the meat. The children were happy with spaghetti Bolognese.

'Did you know this dish comes from Bologna?'[119] Kim asked the kids. They didn't know.

'In an Australian survey,' said Marion, 'children's favourite dish was found to be spaghetti Bolognese or spag Bol, as we call it.'

119 Bologna University is the oldest university in Europe.

I recalled that survey and if I remember correctly, spag Bol was the favourite followed closely by hamburgers, then fish and chips. Apart from ice cream for dessert, kids loved tiramisu.

'This is all likely due to the huge post-war migration from Italy to Melbourne and Sydney,' I said, expanding the story for the benefit of our English and American friends. 'Post-World War II saw an influx of European migrants who sought a better life. With hard work as market gardeners, greengrocers and restauranters, they helped to change our bland cuisine.'

'And coffee,' said Marion. 'They transformed a tea-drinking colony into coffee lovers.'

'Yes, real coffee, not the synthetic essence and turpentine chicory that was used in those early days,' I said. 'Ivan Repin, a Russian who arrived in Sydney in 1925, opened the first coffee shop. It was in King Street Sydney. The business grew to become a chain of bistros. The Russian word for "quick" is *bistro*. Later, the business was sold and became Cahills Brasserie.'

The children, bored with this adult conversation, asked to be excused to return to their room where they could watch TV. After they left, I continued my story.

'Concurrently, Café Florentina in Melbourne imported the first coffee machine, starting the Australian coffee culture. I remember in the 1950s going to Leichhardt with my parents, aunt, uncle and cousins to a coffee shop for a new hot drink called cappuccino.'

The waiter must have overheard us, because he returned with coffee and a plate with small slices of chestnut cake and *zuccotto*, which is an almond and chocolate confection. He said the chestnuts are ground into flour, then used to make this cake, which is a speciality of the region.

Chapter 14
Michelangelo

Although we were early, a queue had already formed outside the Accademia. Our local guide, Santina, was waiting for us. She said to call her Tina. While we waited, she told us the Accademia was the first school of fine arts to teach painting, sculpture and drawing.

'Is the famous statue of David the one we saw out in the square?' Kim asked.

'The one outside is an amazing copy,' she replied. 'The real one is inside the gallery. Tourists can't resist but take selfies with David. The statue in the piazza is your opportunity to do this. Inside, it is a strictly no photos policy.' James didn't seem to be listening. Tina walked over to him and said, 'If you take a photo inside, they will escort you out immediately. No second chance. OK?'

James looked affronted but quickly recovered. She turned to the rest of us. 'Actually, the original *David* was moved from the piazza into the gallery for safe-keeping.'

The line surged forward, through the gauntlet of security where bags were x-rayed. The crowd then moved swiftly down the long galley towards the light at the end of the corridor. They didn't stop to look at paintings on the walls but headed straight to the familiar shape of *David*.

People moved slowly around the statue, looking adoringly at each curve of his body. David stared back at them with intent. I was riveted by his large hand, which held the stone he was about to throw. I could almost see the blood coursing through his pronounced veins. His head a mass of luxuriant curls, sensual lips and a straight Roman nose belied the action he was about to perform.

'It's smaller than what I expected,' I said.

'Yes,' said Tina, as we gathered around her. 'The first thing people notice is the size of the original[120] compared to the larger one outside.'

Out of the corner of my eye, I could see Kim shadowing James, who I thought was itching to take a photo.

Tina continued, 'Michelangelo was 29 when he was commissioned to sculpt *David*. As a result of this work, his future was immediately assured.'

I gazed at David. The nobility of his stance, his determined profile, youthful body and the accentuated collarbone from which rippled a perfect muscular torso, all were hallmarks of a young hero. I could have stood there all day but for the pressing tourists. Like us, they too were mesmerised and wanted to pay homage.

For me, it was an emotional experience. I sidled up to Tina, who was standing at the edge of the group and said, 'I feel as if I'm drunk on this art.'

She gave me an understanding smile. 'I feel like this every day I come here.'

120 The original statue is 5.2 metres.

Tina motioned us to move away from *David* and back into the hall where more statues stood between the paintings on the walls. 'These incomplete statues are also the work of Michelangelo,' she said. 'They're referred to as the slaves or prisoners.'

In the half-finished figures, I saw every notch and groove executed by the master himself. After only ever seeing photographs of his work, to stand so close was sublime. I felt as if I stood in his presence.

'They look as if they're trying to escape,' Andrew said. He was travelling with his mother, Carmela, both from Melbourne but visiting family in Italy.

'Good observation,' Tina replied. 'Michelangelo sculpted freehand. It is more conventional to develop a cast and map out the shape on the block of marble to know where to chisel. Michelangelo didn't do that. It is said he gently scraped at the block to liberate the figures imprisoned in the marble.'

'Is that why they're called "prisoners"?' Andrew asked.

'They say he chose the marble from the quarries himself as if he was looking for something within. He saw the figures in the block of stone. When he chipped and scraped, he released them.'

From this hall, we proceeded to the other rooms where rich displays of paintings from the 14th century, like the *Coronation of the Virgin* and *Escape into Egypt*, graced the walls. Works by other Renaissance artists included Filippo Lippi, Bartolomeo and others. I particularly liked Sandro Botticelli's *Madonna of the Sea* for its gentle and contemplative depictions of the Blessed Virgin and Child.

'The ruling Medici family were boundless patrons of the arts, music and theatre,' said Tina. 'So vast was their amassment that many other important galleries in Florence were recipients of items they commissioned.'

One of the rooms we visited had an exhibition of tapestries. In another room was a series of musical instruments: Stradivarius-created cellos, violins, violas and a sort of keyboard. These were selectively acquired by the wealthy banker, Federico di Medici.

After the Accademia, we followed Tina outside to the Palazzo Vecchio to see the church, belltower and baptistery, all fine examples of Florentine Civic Architecture. The Tuscan-Gothic cathedral dedicated to Santa Maria Fiore took 140 years to build and is the third largest of its kind in the world. The three arched doors at the entry were surmounted by frescoes.

We stepped inside the church, onto the intricately inlaid marble floor, which Tina described as simplicity personified. It certainly appeared to be a contrast to the exterior. Marble reliefs decorated the walls. On display was a painting of Dante explaining his *Divine Comedy*.

Architect Arnulfo di Cambio designed the cathedral. When he died, other architects continued the work. They include Brunelleschi, Talenti and Rossellini. When Giotto took over the construction, he added the 82-ft *campanile*. Neo-Gothic, the bell tower is covered in an elegant and restrained façade of green, pink and white marble.

Tina told us the Romanesque Baptistery is the oldest building in Florence. It is said Dante was baptised here in the font. The building has four distinctive bronze doors corresponding to the four cardinal points. Michelangelo dubbed them the *Gates of Paradise*. The eastern door is the work of Lorenzo Ghiberti.

Inside, slender Corinthian columns with gilded capitals stand sentinel. Overhead, I could see the huge apse lined with magnificent Byzantine mosaic. I thought the depiction of the Last Judgement to be the most fearsome.

Tina told us the terracotta-covered dome was added later by Brunelleschi. This landmark rises high over the heart of the city. 'If you take the time to climb to the top you'll be rewarded with spectacular views across Florence.' She suggested we could ascend the dome in our own time. 'This morning,' she said, 'you have seen the two most famous symbols of Florence—the *duomo* and the statue of David at the Accademia.'

A murmur of concurrence passed over the group; somewhat subdued, as we were becoming a little wilted. Fortunately, the ten-minute walk to the Basilica of Santa Croce served to re-energise us.

Santa Croce mirrors the Tuscan Gothic façade of the *duomo* cathedral. Inside, the use of white marble affords an air of calmness and simplicity, which is one of the Franciscan tenets. The magnificent marble pulpit is decorated with bas-relief scenes from the life of St Francis. Giotto's frescoes are to the main altar in the *Cappella Bardi*. The most famous one portrays the death of St Francis.

The tombs of famous people, including those of Galileo, Machiavelli and Michelangelo, are located in the crypt. Visari decorated Michelangelo's resting place with images that reflect architecture, sculpture and painting, to represent the artist's lifework.

Tina said, 'In 1966, a flood-damaged many of the irreplaceable artworks, including Giotto's frescoes, and Cimabue's *Crucifix*, which was painted on wood in the Orthodox manner—with four nails—one in each hand and one in each foot. Fortunately, it was possible to restore all the works.'

'I know the reason,' said Marion. 'If one foot is on top of the other you'd need an exceptionally long nail to go through them both.'

'I don't know,' Tina said. 'We know that in the 4th century, Helena, the mother of Emperor Constantine, made a pilgrimage to the Holy Land. She returned with several precious items, including the True Cross and nails used to crucify Christ. Several miracles occurred proving the authenticity of these items.'

Andrew interrupted. 'So were there four nails?'

'Legend says that during the return voyage, there was a terrible storm. Helena threw one of the nails overboard to quell the sea. Her prayers were answered, however, it meant she would bring home only three nails. After Christendom split into East and West, some ideas changed and in time this story was forgotten.'

'It's not something I've ever given much thought,' said Marion.

'You need two nails for the hands,' rationalised young Andrew. 'So if only one nail remains then the feet had to be crossed to drive the last nail through them. The problem is that all the revered nails are the same length.'

The coach drew up and those going on the half-day tour to Pisa climbed on board. A handful stayed behind including Simy, Sheila and me.

It had begun raining. We followed the aroma of roasting coffee beans to a modest café nearby and shared a pizza for lunch while we waited for the downpour to cease.

After lunch, we wandered around the streets avoiding puddles and pausing under awnings. The buildings were old and the rain made them appear more forlorn. A staircase across the pavement caught my eye and I thought it would make a nice photo. As we approached, a door opened and someone came out. We were near enough and brazen enough to go in.

Inside, the guard was asleep in his chair by the door. Without missing a step, we immediately mingled with other people examining the exhibits. I picked up a brochure. We were on the first floor of the *Museo Nationale Bargello*.[121] There were many rooms, one of which was dedicated to the sculptures of Michaelangelo and another to Donatello. The focal point in the middle of this room was Donatello's bronze-cast *David*. I'd only ever seen photographs, where the sculpture appears cold and foreboding. In real life, I found the face surprisingly more expressive. Donatello's statue of St George stood nearby. It is the epitome of youth and courage.

On the second floor, a range of applied arts made a welcome contrast to the paintings and sculptures we'd seen earlier. There were marvellous rugs, colourful ceramic vases, silverware and other *objets d'art*. By the time we arrived at the ground floor, our way was barred by a large group of tourists.

We heard their guide say, 'The Bargello is the second-ranking museum in Florence after the *Uffizi*.' I made a mental note to see the *Uffizi* on my next visit. 'The Bargello started out as the town hall, but was subsequently converted to a prison, hence the name,' the guide explained. 'There are three floors exhibiting a melange of artworks.'

We looked at each other, hoping they'd soon move.

'When we exit, it will be into the courtyard, where executions were held.' The group followed their guide into another room, but we'd had enough and left through the same door we'd entered without disturbing the guard.

---

121 In the 16th century, it was the residence of the bargello, that is of the head of the police. It became a prison in 18th century and a museum in the 19th century.

Outside, the sun was trying to break through the gentle drizzle. When it had subsided sufficiently, we made our way to the leather market. Simy bought a handbag for her sister and another for her niece. I saw a 'bucket style' bag in an unusual warm terracotta colour with a tan trim. Ideal, I thought, as hand luggage. We headed in the direction of our hotel but paused along the way at a dear little boutique. Simy bought herself a new suitcase with matching hand luggage and yet another handbag. Just as well our hotel was only 10 minutes away because we'd accumulated so many shopping bags it made it hard to negotiate our way over the puddles.

Sheila was tired but after changing into dry clothes, Simy and I went out again to claim the tax refund on her purchases. That was when we discovered the gold market at the Ponte Vecchio, which is the famous covered bridge across the River Arno. I was sorely tempted by a pair of gold and enamel earrings but at $445 after the tax refund, it really was too much of a splurge. Not even halfway through my trip, I had to be sensible. What surprised me was the number of shops with handwritten signs in Cyrillic script announcing that Russian was spoken and roubles accepted.

Rejecting the earrings made me itch to buy something else. A specialist glove shop caught my eye and I bought myself two pairs of leather gloves, one pair black and the other a shade of clotted cream. The shop assistant fitted me, just as they used to do in the 1960s to ensure a perfect fit. I still love those gloves and often wear the black, but rarely the cream, since I no longer have as many dressy occasions.

Dinner was at *Trattoria da Giorgi*, a mere five minutes' walk from our hotel. The relaxed atmosphere gave us the opportunity to compare our afternoons. The people who'd taken the afternoon tour to the Leaning Tower of Pisa raved about it. I made a mental note to visit it when I returned for my independent time in Florence at the end of the tour.

A three-course set menu with a vegetarian alternative was offered. We started with a share plate of sharp cheeses and smoky salamis on the antipasto platter and a serving of bruschetta laden with fresh chopped tomato. This was followed by a comforting pasta called *Casarecce con Chianina Ragu*. It is a typical Tuscan dish of fettuccine with a rich meat sauce, made with Chianina. This is a local breed of cattle. Simy had a meatless dish a bit like haloumi of pungent fried mozzarella with tomato and basil. For sweets, we could choose between tiramisu or panna cotta with strawberries. The food was delicious and part of the tour but coffee and wine were extra.

I sat between John, a sheep farmer from Queensland, and Dave, a kiwi fruit orchardist from New Zealand.

'A Kiwi growing kiwis,' I blurted without thinking. I couldn't help it; it must have been the wine. Though well-intended, my pun did not go down well. He must have been sick of people responding in that way. I realised my *faux pas* too late. That put a stop to my getting to know him better. Though he did say he was trying to diversify into the truffle industry.

After dinner, the group returned to the hotel. Some went straight to their rooms but, as it often happens, a few of us remained at the bar drinking tea or wine.

The next day we headed to the old university town of Padua. I thought it a charming little backwater. When originally planning my trip, I'd read that there were two outstanding landmarks not to be missed—Basilica di Sant'Antonio and the Capella Scrovegni. The latter was built by Enrico Scrovegni in 1303. He commissioned Giotto to cover the walls in the most evocative frescoes illustrating the life of Christ.

When we arrived in Padua, Nora explained, 'St Anthony is the patron saint of the city. As you can see, the basilica is an exotic building. The exterior is Romanesque.'

'Are those towers minarets?' Kim asked.

'The architecture is somewhat eclectic. Originally Romanesque, later additions included Byzantine and Gothic elements. The slender bell towers are decorated with features reminiscent of Turkish minarets,' Nora replied. 'The domes are similar to those in Venice, which you'll see when we visit St Mark's Square. The interior, however, is with Baroque enhancements.'

We entered the dark and austere church. The sculptures were mostly by Donatello, as were many of the bas-reliefs. These decorated the church walls and were of scenes from the life of St Anthony.

'Follow me to the tomb,' said Nora. We followed her to a more ornate section of the church where brown-veined, marble walls provided a contrast to the white bas-reliefs and marble statues. 'This church was specially built as the last resting place of their revered patron saint and ensured his tomb would always remain in his beloved Padua.'

Some people paused in contemplation while others lit candles. After a few minutes of reflection, Nora interrupted once more. 'You may write an invocation to St Anthony. It is said he is generous in fulfilling requests, especially those for healing. As you exit, your notes may be deposited into a box provided by the door. The friars will take up the requests and pray for your sake.'

Nora suggested a kiosk in the square where we could buy lunch or otherwise go to the little café next door. Simy, Sheila and I bought panini and a takeaway coffee from the kiosk, which we consumed in the square. I asked Nora when we'd see Scrovegni Chapel.

She looked a bit non-plussed. 'You'll have to come back to do that,' she said.

'But isn't it the reason for visiting Padua?' I blurted, crestfallen. 'Could the three of us scoot over and do it now, during this lunch break?'

'Unfortunately, the only way to do this is to pre-book a date and time. The chapel is small and the number of people allowed inside at any one time is limited. Before entry, visitors must attend a 15-minute multimedia presentation. Only then may the chapel frescoes be viewed. The timed visit is for a further maximum of 15 minutes.'

I was clearly disappointed there was not enough time to see the chapel.

'Most people come here to see the basilica. St Anthony is a very popular saint,' Nora said. 'Did you not enjoy it?' she asked, sensing our disappointment.

This is the very reason I include individual time pre and post-tour. I understand they must cater to the majority but my interests are different from most tourists. I grumbled a bit but had no option other than to accept it. However, along with a few of the other folk, I felt we were being herded like sheep from one spot to another simply to shop.

I was also tetchy because I needed a rest from all the experiences of my previous two weeks of touring. It was my fault; I always try to do too much because I know I'll never have the opportunity to return.

Chapter 15
Harry's Bar

We covered the 39 kilometres between Padua and Venice quite quickly. Our first distant glimpses of Venice were of tall spires and domes. *Which one is St Mark's?* I wondered. A conspicuous feeling of excitement emanated from the group.

Our bus stopped in *Piazzale Roma,* a huge square that is the informal interchange and end of the road for vehicles. We gathered on the wharf. Many vessels crowded the harbour, including a luxury cruise liner, the *Crown Princess.* There was a gentle breeze, which carried the intoxicating smell of the sea.

Here we farewelled our bus driver and transferred with our luggage to a *vaporetto*—a water bus. We'd come to the end of the road beyond which there are no cars because there are no roads in Venice. Travel is by foot or by boat. So we were in for an unexpected 30-minute cruise to Piazza San Marco.

On the deck, seating was limited but inside we sat comfortably alongside our luggage. I enjoyed the view through the open windows. Meanwhile, the *vaporetto* plied further along the waterway. The sound of its engine was too loud for Nora to speak to us except to say, 'Relax and enjoy the sunshine.'

Our mooring was a short distance from St Mark's Square. We followed other travellers along a curious wooden ramp, which covered the wide footpath. Nora must have noticed our dismay as we battled with the din from the wheels of our suitcases.

She paused to address us. 'Don't worry about the clattering noise. It's just a short distance,' she said. 'Venice is called the city of water not only because of the canals but also due to the frequent heavy rain, which often floods the city. The locals wear gumboots. You probably didn't pack any. So these ramps were built to assist tourists to get around.'

We arrived at St Mark's where a pretty young lady sporting a smart bob waved at us as we approached. She held a colourful umbrella in one hand and a folder in the other—the trappings of a local guide. Nora introduced Francesca to the group then left us in her capable hands.

'Did you know Venice is a chain of islands?' Francesca asked. 'The main island, where we are standing, is divided in two by the Grand Canal.'

We followed her into the centre of the wide quadrangle. Meanwhile, birds swooped in search of crumbs or perched on ledges and lamp posts. James busied himself photographing them.

There was a sign stating *Do Not Feed Birds*. Dave laughed. 'What's the point of those signs? The birds are not easily discouraged.'

'The signs warn tourists,' Francesca replied. 'We want to discourage the birds because their droppings eat into the stonework and the noise and mess is unsustainable.'

They were a distraction, but Francesca soon brought our attention back to the introductory information she was obliged to give. 'Settlement goes back 1200 years,' she said. 'Venice was the most independent state in Italy, governed by the Doge and his Great Council. The town prospered because of the lucrative trade in fine silks and spices from China and the Middle East.'

'I thought Marco Polo brought them to Italy,' said young Oliver.

'You're right, young man,' Francesca replied. 'In 1221, one of the most celebrated Venetians, Marco Polo, travelled with his father to China where they stayed for 17 years in the court of Kublai Khan. He was the first European to travel to Southeast Asia and opened the lucrative trade along the fabled Silk Route.

What a clever lad, I thought. *I give Oliver full marks for paying attention.*

Just then the clock on the tall tower boomed. We spun around to see where the sound had come from.

'The astronomical clock, which strikes every hour, was commissioned by the Doge in 1493. Look at the top.' Francesca pointed with her trusty umbrella.

We gazed at the bronze ensemble—two figures striking a bell. The beautiful clock face was cobalt blue enamel with golden signs of the zodiac. The clock face was housed inside a fixed circle of marble decorated with bas-relief numerals. We turned back to our guide.

'We are in the centre of the city,' she said, 'surrounded by St Mark's Cathedral, The Doge Palace, the Marciano Library, the Correr Museum, the Archaeological Museum and this magnificent clock tower, as well as the many shops and cafés.'

James darted with his camera, snapping in every direction. *Is he seeking the perfect angle,* I wondered, *or putting on a show? Look at me, look at me.*

'Will we go into St Mark's Cathedral now?' John asked.

'No, we'll go there tomorrow,' Francesca replied. 'To understand the city better you need to know the greatest period of flowering was the Renaissance in the 15th century. Families like the Medici's ensured the rebirth of artistic endeavour. They became patrons of renowned artists like Leonardo da Vinci, Raphael and Michelangelo.'

'Is *Carnivale* the peak time for tourists to Venice?' asked Kim.

'*Carnivale* is a time of feasting before Great Lent. In the 17th and 18th centuries, people doing the Grand Tour endeavoured to be in Venice for *Carnivale* and to spend Holy Week in Rome.[122] Venice is known for its fabulous revelry, decorative masks and costumes. There are several shops specialising in masks,' she said.

'Cakes are especially popular during *Carnivale*,' added Carmel.

'Why do some of the cakes have an Austrian influence?' asked Sheila.

'Austria shares a border with Venice. In 1792, Napoleon ceded Venice to Austria, where it remained until Garibaldi's unification of the Italian states in 1866.'

On cue, Nora arrived with her list. 'There's been some mix-up,' she said. 'The hotel has overbooked. I'll read out the names of the people who will accompany Francesca to the hotel and the rest of you will come with me.'

Carmel, Andrew, John, Dave, Simy, Sheila and I remained with Nora, while Kim, James, Marion and the kids followed Francesca back along the path. Nora then led us to the water taxi jetty to take us directly across the canal to the island of San Clemente.

On board for the short crossing, Nora had time to give us some background. 'The island is named after St Clement. In 1131, the island became a monastic settlement church and for

122 The Grand Tour, a sort of finishing school, often continued for more than 12 months. Italy was especially seen as the crossroads of the ancient Christian worlds. In the 19th century, Madrid, Seville, Vienna (for music), St Petersburg (Russia), Jerusalem and Egypt were also added to the itinerary.

centuries it functioned as a monastery[123] with an adjoining hospice for pilgrims travelling to the Holy Land. Later, it became an asylum and remained so until 1992. After extensive redevelopment and renovation in 2003, it became San Clemente Palace[124], a luxury resort away from the bustle of the city, offering peace and tranquillity.'

Bound by spectacular gardens, our five-star hotel was magnificently decorated in a soothing palate of taupe and gold with antique and reproduction furnishings. The entry looked across the water to St Mark's Square. At the rear of the property, there was a large swimming pool, tennis courts, gym, day spa and conference centre.

My room was so large I thought I could raise an echo off the walls. In the marble bathroom, a fluffy white robe lay draped on the bathtub. An assortment of Salvatore Ferragamo toiletries was displayed on the vanity. Their luscious fragrance filled the room.

That night we joined the rest of the group in a cosy homestyle ristorante located in one of the myriads of alleys radiating from St Mark's. It specialised in regional dishes.[125] For starters, we shared an antipasto platter. This was followed by *Valdostana*—veal stuffed with spinach, onion, mozzarella, and prosciutto, served with a gorgonzola-laced sauce. The

123 During French and Austrian occupation monasteries were outlawed. So in 1810, Napoleon turned the island into an army garrison.

124 In 2016, it was bought by the Kempinski group and redeveloped into a luxury hotel. It has become a member of the exclusive Leading Hotels of the World group and rebranded to be known as St Clemente Kempinski Palace. It also caters for wedding receptions.

125 Spinach, asparagus and onions are gown on the outskirts of Venice.

vegetarian option was *Frittata alla Verdua*, a vegetable frittata. For *dolci*, creamy vanilla panna cotta with fresh strawberries rounded off the meal.

After dinner, we cruised on the Grand Canal. This gave us a better sense of the size of Venice and was a welcome chance to enjoy the city by night. Then back on the water taxi to our island paradise for a nightcap or two at the magnificently mirrored *Arte-Deco*-styled bar. We sat in sumptuous leather armchairs pretending we were used to this lifestyle.

It was late and I felt very tired when I retired to my room. I don't remember anything after my head sank into the huge cloud-like pillow where I was out for the count until morning.

After a leisurely shower, I went down to breakfast. Three large rooms were set up for the many guests. Our group was scattered at small tables, but I found a vacant seat next to Carmel and Andrew. The buffet was laden with every food you could ever imagine, catering for an international clientele. I headed straight for the juice, then ordered Eggs Benedict as a treat, but couldn't resist a croissant with an almond and *crème patisserie* filling.

As soon as I'd sat down, the waiter materialised to take my coffee order. '*Café con latte per favore*,' I said in my best Italian. Black coffee arrived with a little jug of hot milk. I said to Carmel, 'I used to order Americano, but it's like cheap instant with too much milk. Now I order black with milk on the side. But why do they always serve boiled milk? I hate when it has the skin on top.'

She looked at me quizzically. 'What do you order back home?' she asked.

'Flat white. I don't order cappuccino because there's too much milk and the coffee under the foam is scalding.'

'What you should ask for is *café con latte freddo a parte,*' she said with a bemused smile at my naiveté. I made a mental note.

Our first excursion was a boat ride to the island of Murano where the famous decorative glass is made. It was fascinating watching a demonstration of glass blowing and moulding. The demonstrator made a lovely ornamental horse. Then he asked young Sophie if she'd like to try. She was too shy, but Oliver gave it a go. It was challenging work for a young kid.

I spent in the vicinity of €80 on half a dozen gifts, including a *Mille Fiori*[126] paperweight, a pendant and a thimble. I couldn't resist a pair of dangly earrings for myself.

We were offered a side trip to the islands of Burano[127] and Torcello, where Hemingway was a guest of the Cipriani family.[128] In 1948, he stayed for the whole of winter, writing *Across the Water and Into the Trees*. It is a poignant story about an old soldier reminiscing to a beautiful young girl as they sat in Harry's Bar, Florian's café and made love at the Hotel Gritti. The critics panned the book for being too emotional, but I loved it.

Tourists to Torcello usually visit the Cathedral of the Assumption[129] to see Byzantine mosaics, which date back to the early 12th century.

The group didn't look excited so Francesca said, 'Alternatively, we can return to St Mark's Square to see the five-domed St Mark's Cathedral, then go shopping.'

---

126 A distinctive pattern like a million flowers encased in clear crystal. An intricate process developed in the 15th century in Murano.

127 Burano Island is a small archipelago with five islands connected through bridges. In 1872, it established the first school of lacemaking.

128 The Cipriani Inn still operates as a hotel.

129 Founded in AD 689.

The group consensus was to return to St Mark's. When we arrived in the crowded square, Francesca drew our attention to some interesting things concerning the exterior decoration.

'Built in the 11th century, it is the greatest example of Byzantine architecture in Italy. Thought to be inspired by the Hagia Sophia in Constantinople, now called Istanbul.' she said. 'The great central dome in St Mark's Cathedral is called the Ascension Dome. The inside surface of the dome is lined with rich gilded mosaics. When we get inside, you'll see in the centre of the dome, the image of Christ the Pantocrator. The other domes are for the four Evangelists.'

James was weaving in and out of the tourist throng to get more interesting shots. The crowd shuffled like a herd of cows, clogging his way.

'At the entrance, look up to see the Romanesque carvings adorning the main portal.' Francesca pointed to them. 'Above the balcony are the four bronze horsemen and at the top you'll notice the central arch of the upper loggia.' We strained to follow her direction. 'See how it's crowned with a beautiful façade of blue? The golden lion symbolises St Mark but his statue is at the top.'

The stunning interior of St Mark's Cathedral had us straining our necks while inching along with the masses of tourists, in awe of the size and decoration of the church. Once we passed through the bottleneck at the entry it became less cramped and we could appreciate the interior. The mosaics set in a gilded[130] background are made of marble and *tesserae*[131] from Murano.

130 This tile is made with gold and silver leaf sandwiched between two layers of glass and fired twice in the kiln to embed the metal.

131 Opaque glass fired in large slabs in a kiln is then hand cut with a hammer and chisel into small cubes. Their irregular finish makes them a wonderful reflector of light.

The scenes were a reproduction of the work of Titian, Tintoretto and Veronese.

The relics of the Evangelist Mark are located here. Many of the most precious artefacts displayed were plundered from Constantinople and brought here during the Fourth Crusade, the most notable being the ancient icon, *Madonna Nicopeia,* which was the city's most precious item.

After spending a good hour inside, we were ready for a break. A few of us wanted to take a gondola ride along the maze of canals to have a glimpse of Venice's unique lifestyle. There was an extra charge for the excursion. Simy and Sheila opted out.

Up to six passengers were allowed per gondola. I climbed in with Carmel, Andrew, Marion, Sophie and Oliver. Before we cast off, a photographer appeared out of nowhere and offered to take photos. He promised to have them ready upon our return. Some grumbled at the €5 price. *What value do you place on a memory?* I thought. *Something to look back on and remember the magic.*

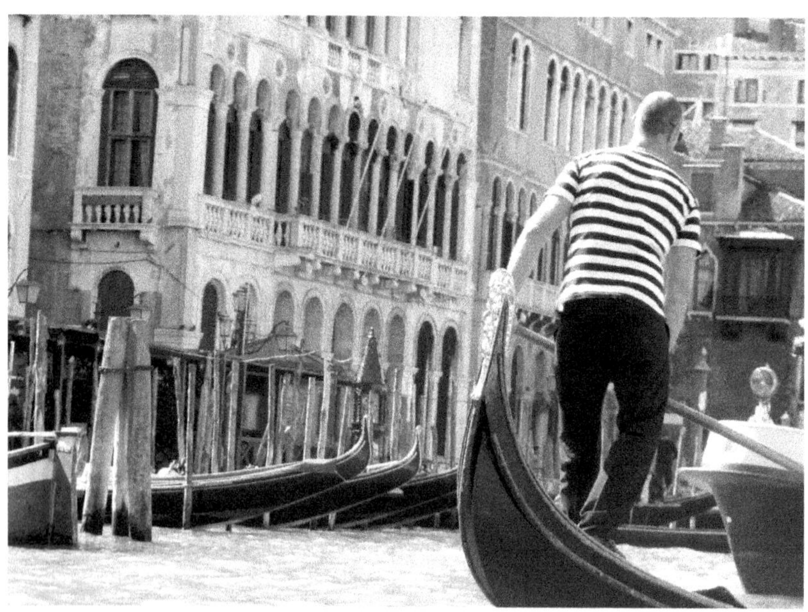

The day was warm and sunny, ideal for floating along the maze of canals and under the bridges. Tightly crammed buildings lined the edge of the canals. Flowers in boxes spilled from balconies and windows. Here and there, tiny boutiques managed a display in a doorway or a window, indicating what was on sale. One even had a mannequin on the landing steps.

We headed towards the most famous edifice—the Bridge of Sighs. It is the only fully enclosed limestone bridge. It has two barred windows and connects the Doge Palace to the prisons. The name of the bridge refers to the sighs made by prisoners at their last sight of freedom as they were led in shackles from the court to the prison across the canal. Superstition has it that if a couple kisses while passing underneath this bridge in a gondola, they will enjoy eternal love.

After our gondola ride, I met Simy and Sheena for a bit of shopping. It's easy to get lost inside this labyrinth of narrow alleyways jam-packed with gift, fashion and shoe shops, albeit with expensive price tags. I bought a new pair of sunglasses but lost the girls in the interim.

I wasn't interested in shopping, I wanted to find Harry's Bar. I made my way back to the square. There, I bumped into Carmel and Andrew. What luck. They were heading to Harry's and what's more, they knew the way. The exterior of the café is nondescript; a perfect place for clandestine assignations. The Cipriani family has owned it for decades.

Inside, was like stepping back into the 1930s. Little tables with bentwood chairs and high stools surround the bar. I felt as if I'd stepped straight into the film set of *Casablanca*. The head waiter, who even looked a bit like Humphrey Bogart, had worked there for a long time. He was most welcoming and told us the history of the place.

'Since 1931, this was a haunt for the literati, intellectuals and eccentric aristocrats.' He handed us menus. 'Many a drunken evening was enjoyed.' He laughed.

'Ernest Hemingway…' I interrupted.

'*Si,* Ernesto was a regular patron.[132] He ate here every day. It was like his second home. He and his wife Mary lived at the Gritti Palace Hotel, which is not far from here.'

'Can we sit at his table?' asked Carmel.

'No. I'm sorry, but his favourite table, in the corner, is constantly booked.' A fleeting look of satisfaction crossed the waiter's face. 'But you'll have a better view of it from your table. Let me take your photo,' he said, reaching for Andrew's camera.

Andrew chatted with him in Italian. His mum added something, then turned to me, 'I've ordered Bellinis. Is that OK with you?'

'It's a touristy thing but you have to do it,' I replied, tongue in cheek. *It's the very thing I hoped to do.*

'Of course. They have a machine now to make batches of it because it's so popular,' said Andrew. 'The owner, Giuseppe Cipriani, invented the cocktail—Prosecco over the juice of pink peaches.'

'Those peaches are amazing. I bought some in Sorrento,' I declared, the memory of their taste returning to my palate.

When it arrived, the drink was a beautiful pale pink. The taste was sweet but at the same time tangy and the bubbles gently prickled my tongue. I was excited about our visit and began to liberally sprinkle my conversation with a few Italian phrases to impress the waiter.

Andrew said, 'You're funny, but be careful what you say "*si*" to. Italian is not English with a funny accent.' We laughed.

Being lunchtime, Andrew ordered *Tramezzini*—finger sandwiches filled with chopped egg and anchovy laced mayonnaise. Carmel thought we should also share a plate of *Beef Carpaccio.*[133] This traditional Italian dish of worldwide fame is typically served as an appetizer and consists of paper-thin slices of raw fish or cured beef served on a plate with olive oil, cheese shavings and lemon. Sublime. I had it again 12 years later while on a cruise and the vivid memories of my first time flooded back.

The waiter told us that in 1959, Carpaccio was also created by the owner, Giuseppe Cipriani, especially for Countess Amalia Nani Maceio, whose doctors had recommended she eat raw meat.

We were lucky because it wasn't busy and the waiter had time to regale us with these stories. After a couple of Bellinis, we were fully relaxed and laughed a lot at our own jokes.

Carmel and Andrew headed back to the hotel. We parted at the water taxi jetty. In the square, I found Sheila and Simy having a hot chocolate at Florian's, another of Hemingway's favourite spots. The girls insisted I order one too because it's their speciality. I'm glad I did. It turned out to be so thick I didn't know whether I should drink it or eat it. I've never had such a delicious hot chocolate before or since.

Afterwards, Simy went to pick up something she'd bought while Sheila and I checked out the boutiques lining the square. We found a lovely linen and lace shop. I was in the market for a lace mantilla, but they had none. Sheila bought a gift for her sister. Then I spied some linen guest towels embroidered in taupe-coloured thread. I thought they'd make a nice gift for a friend but in retrospect, I ended up keeping them for myself.

133 A speciality, this dish is traditionally paper-thin slices of raw lean beef or tuna or salmon with rocket, capers and a mayonnaise made with egg yolk, Dijon mustard, olive oil, lemon juice and thick cream. So delicious.

The island shuttle boat was at the jetty in time for us to return home, where we were blessed with space—an exceedingly rare commodity in Venice. I spent a leisurely couple of hours exploring the hotel and surrounding gardens where a substantial number of fluffy white bunnies were busy nibbling at the lawns. They didn't even look up at me.

A large, old church stood near the jetty. The interior was in a sad state of disrepair. I wandered around looking for faded remnants of frescoes and imagining how it must have been when new.

I had free time but deemed it sacrilegious to do my laundry in such a high-class hotel. So I opted to wallow in the bathtub. I used those expensive toiletries to fill the tub with fragrant bubbles. When I finally climbed out, my body felt silky and pampered. I sat cocooned in the soft towelling robe, manicuring my nails.

Dinner was back on the mainland. *I imagine the hotel restaurant here on the island is too expensive for the likes of us.* Our group met at the hotel jetty where pre-dinner drinks were being served. Sitting there in a sublime state of timelessness, I gazed at the last vestiges of orange and purple sky as the sun set over the glistening water. Not wanting to break the magic, we sipped Prosecco in silence while waiting for the shuttle boat to arrive. I decided I could easily get used to this way of life but had yet to meet someone who'd fund it. I mean enjoy it with me, of course.

Before dinner, we had a Spritz, which is Prosecco with a slosh of Campari. *Yum, I'll order this again.* The set menu offered a choice between two regional dishes. One was the *Sardi en Soar,* fresh sardines pan-fried with onions, raisins and pine nuts in its own *jus.* Simy had *Fagioli All'Uccelletto,* a casserole of vegetables and broad beans. Polenta, which I'm not used to, is a staple of the region and was served on the side. For dessert, we were served *Fritole Venessiane*—doughnut balls filled with custard; a special dish, traditionally served at Easter time. The waiter offered *café corretto*, which is black coffee with a slosh of Grappa. Grappa is a potent little liqueur produced in the nearby town of Vicenza. It instantly warmed me.

Sadly, it was our last night at St Clemente Palace. Before retiring to my room, I noticed the business centre was still open so popped in to use the computers. I had a few emails with news from home. I was alarmed to hear there'd been civil disruption in Sydney and in Paris.

In Paris, the Charlie Hebdo cartoons sparked a couple of days of rioting. Posters appeared everywhere that read, *Behead all those who insult the Prophet* and *Behead those who insult Islam*, an ideology we were not familiar with. This was a shocking portent of what was to come. I was due to visit Paris in two weeks' time. The family was naturally worried for my safety.

We'd never had riots back home. The world was changing and the couple of names that were featured on the front pages of our tabloids we would hear many times in the future. Born and bred in Australia, these two fellows, who were childhood friends[134], had aligned themselves with the outlawed organisation called ISIS.

Curiously, every time I go overseas, some sort of disaster happens. This time I was concerned for my daughter who was living in the inner city, but she assured me all was well and not to judge a community by the acts of a couple of radicals.

I joined the others at the bar for one last drink. How lucky we'd been for this quirk of fate to experience this incomparable hotel.

---

134 Sharrouf and Elomar went on to Syria followed by their families. On Facebook, we saw one of the sons holding up a severed head.

As I climbed into bed, I wondered if divine intervention after my visit to St Clément's relics in Rome had brought me here to the island of St Clemente.

Our bags were deposited in the lobby before breakfast. I sat together with Carmel and Andrew in the dining room. They preferred boiled eggs, salami and bread rather than cereals and yoghurt. They encouraged me to try the Italian bread. There was a large assortment of different shapes and sizes on offer as well as sweet rolls. The waiter came around for our tea and coffee order.

I smiled and said, '*Café con latte freddo, a parte. Per favore.*'

Andrew gave me a little clap. 'Well done,' he said. 'Coffee with cold milk on the side.'

Chapter 16
Torino

Bittersweet—I was sorry to leave Venice and our island paradise, yet excited for what lay ahead. The morning was bright and sunny, with the slightest nip in the air. Our boat delivered us and our luggage for the last time to the wharf where Mario and the rest of our group waited. As soon as both groups were settled in the coach, we forged further north.

As we travelled, the countryside became more rural. Our destination was Verona, an hour and a half away. The two groups chatted and compared notes while James darted around with his camera. Upon arrival, Mario delivered us to the main piazza to wander around while he met with other drivers in the parking lot.

Although still early, the town was already buzzing with tourists, buskers, mime artistes and assorted street theatre. I thought I heard someone yell out, 'I love you' in a strange high-pitched voice. The crowd moved towards the sound. A man sat in a pram, dressed like a baby, all in pink, wearing a bonnet and sucking away on a big dummy. Nearby, a Statue of Liberty impersonator covered from head to toe in silver paint stood in a state of frozen anticipation. I was used to seeing this type of entertainment in Sydney but hadn't expected to see it here.

A guitarist ambled along the alleyway to claim a position in the square. I couldn't believe my eyes when a character with three heads came towards us.

The buskers posed for photos and created a colourful spectacle. There was an air of joviality and excitement in the square. The tourists generously supported their efforts. Sheila and Simy stood either side of the pram draped with a pink rug to hide the man's feet, while I took photos. There was plenty to amuse us.

I thought it a lovely, atmospheric village with its narrow, cobbled streets that were flanked with boutiques, cafés, souvenir and gift shops. A pair of Birkenstock crocs caught my eye. Half a cat was painted on one shoe and the other half on the corresponding shoe. It captured my imagination, but there was no time for shoe-shopping. Nora, with umbrella aloft, was making her way briskly down one of the alleys while we scurried after her.

It surprised and disappointed me to see the grotty walls of these narrow passageways heavily covered in bits of paper and graffiti. I expected something romantic—bougainvillea or jasmine-laden pergolas to lead to the famous balcony. Nora must have seen the look of aversion on my face as I paused, confounded by the scene.

'What is all this?' I asked.

Nora explained. 'These are messages of undying love. As you know, Verona is the location of Shakespeare's play *Romeo and Juliet*, the young lovers from rival warring families, their passion and their fate,' she said hurriedly, before signalling for us to follow.

We traversed this rabbit warren into a small courtyard with a balcony. There was nothing else there apart from the balcony. Behind us another throng of tourists neared.

Nora spoke quickly before she was drowned out by the crowd. 'Verona is known for many romantic tragedies and the story of Romeo and Julietta was written in 1512 by *Luigi da Porto* in Vincenza.'

'But at school, the teacher said the play was written by Shakespeare,' said young Sophie, her face contorted in confusion.

'Luigi's story is considered the source of Shakespeare's play, which was written in 1591. Many tourists come here to see Juliette's balcony and to enact Romeo's lines.'

'Is this the balcony from the play?' asked wide-eyed Oliver.

Nora smiled. 'Of course, Juliet was a fictional character who didn't exist. She never lived in this house, nor heard Romeo delivering his speech of undying love. But who cares? We all want a little romance to reflect upon, to imagine and inspire us.'

Some of our group appeared disappointed, while others were amused by the tale that had captured our imagination for so long. Indeed, it is simply a fairy tale.

'Why were all those bits of paper stuck on the walls?' I asked.

'Notes with messages of undying love are stuck to the walls of the street leading to this balcony.' Nora laughed. 'You decide—is it romantic or a truly bizarre custom?'

'Is it similar to the padlocks lovers put on bridges, which I've seen throughout Europe?' asked Sheila.

'Yes,' Nora replied. 'You can also write letters to Juliet seeking advice for your love problems. A team of workers will answer the letters. A bit like writing to Dorothy Dix. Letters to Juliet receive a handwritten personalised reply. The answers are meant to be inspirational, something like, "Love is always worth fighting for; take the risk. The last thing you want is to be full of what-ifs",' she said.

I've followed that mantra all my life, but I have one lingering 'what if'. I wonder, if I'd not turned tail when my first love slighted me, whether my life would have turned out differently? Maybe, maybe not. You can't escape your fate. With that thought, I turned and followed Nora onto the bus. Our next destination was the lake district.

The three main lakes in Italy are Garda, Como and Maggiore. Our bus headed to the largest in Italy—*Largo di Garda*, situated an hour away.

'Our destination, Sirmione, is on the southern bank of Lake Garda,' Nora explained. 'It's located in the shadow of *Castello Rocca Scaligera*—a medieval castle. The township is famous for its thermal baths and spas.'

A takeaway kiosk in the town was doing a roaring trade. We grabbed refreshments before boarding one of the boats moored in the harbour.

The summer heat had ended, but the air was warm enough for a sleeveless top; perfect weather for cruising. The steel blue mountains loomed against an ultramarine sky and the crystaline water lapped gently on the sides of our boat. I felt every muscle relax as we glided on the lake. Occasional bubbles from ancient geysers gurgled up to break the surface of the water.

The crenelated walls of the castle and its majestic turreted watchtowers dominated the town. Gesturing toward the castle, Nora said, 'Well preserved, even though *Castello Scaligera* was built in the 13th century for the rulers of Verona.'

'The castle appears to be on an island surrounded by the lake,' said Kim.

'It occupies the narrowest point of the peninsula; this Roman fortress was designed to protect the township. The only way to enter was to cross the moat, which was secured with two still working drawbridges. These still lead to the city gate.'

John, Dave and Andrew joined James in photographing the spectacular sight.

'Lake Garda,' said Nora, 'is a place for recreation and healing with its many spas and holiday resorts. This area is known for the curative powers derived from mineralised thermal springs.'

'What minerals are found here?' asked Sheila.

'Sulphur, sodium and iodine,' Nora replied. 'Did you know that warming, soothing baths ease respiratory problems, rheumatism and various skin disorders?'

As we travelled further north, I gazed across to the shore where red-roofed villas nestled amongst evergreens. Nature's autumnal palette with its splashes of orange, brown and the red of the maples and chestnuts completed the striking picture.

Nora pointed out to a yellow three-storey villa directly ahead of us. Purple bougainvillea covered the balconies. 'Over there is the *Villa di Maria,* which was the former home of Maria Callas. Most of the villas here belong to celebrities.'

'Are any of them open for inspection?' asked Dave.

'Are you thinking of relocating?' taunted John.

'When my truffle business takes off,' quipped Dave. 'I can dream.'

'Yes.' Nora giggled at the boys' competitive jibes. 'There are several homes open to visitors. *Villa Desanzano del Garda* is one such home set on a hectare of parkland.'

'What's that?' Andrew pointed at ruins on the headland.

'That is an archaeological site called *Grotte di Catullo,*' Nora replied. 'This was once a magnificent Roman villa surrounded by olive trees. The site encompasses the ruins, and a small museum has been assembled there. It's worth a visit to see the mosaic floors and marvel at the ingenious redirection of hot water from the lake to provide underfloor heating.'

'They were a clever bunch, those Romans,' quipped Carmel, patting herself on her back.

We arrived back in the harbour for lunch. My stomach grumbled noisily. Sheila, Simy and I decided to share a pizza and then followed it with gelato. Back on the warm and cosy bus with full bellies, the three of us instantly dozed off.

Two hours later, we awoke in Lake Como, surrounded by limestone and granite mountains. It is an idyllic position at the foothills of the Swiss Alps. The wishbone-shaped lake has been popular with aristocrats and the wealthy since Roman times. Como is reputed to be the playground of not only the rich and famous, but the infamous too.

Different-sized boats, hydrofoils and ferries littered the harbour. Mario took charge of the luggage on land while we boarded yet another boat. This one was a modest one-level vessel with a canvas roof to provide shade over the simple bench seating for the passengers. An enclosed cabin at the front of the boat was exclusively for the driver.

Captain Guido's enthusiastic manner was most welcoming, and we settled in for our scheduled tour of the lake. The captain was blessed with the voice of a professional spruiker. He was a local and knew the area like his own backyard. In fact, he insisted that it was his yard. An operatic aria, possibly Maria Callas, played softly in the background while he rattled off many famous names and pointed out villas, even adding little snippets of gossip to amuse and amaze.

'*Villa d'Este* in Cernobbio is one of Italy's most iconic properties. It occupies an enviable position on the lake, amid

25 acres of luxurious landscaped parkland. The villa, formerly home to Gianni Versace, is now a luxury hotel. You can stay there for €5,000 per night.' [135]

We chuckled at the idea and checked our euros. 'In 1948, it was the scene of the celebrated murder of the wealthy silk manufacturer Carlo Sacchi, shot dead by his lover, Countess Bellentani, with her husband's automatic pistol.'

Our eyes lit up as the charismatic captain shared his secrets with us.

'Over there,' he pointed to another grand mansion, '*Villa Balbianello*, featured in the Bond film *Casino Royale*. Did you see it?'

He knew the group was mostly Australian, so pointed out a villa belonging to Rupert Murdoch and another to Kerry Packer. Our avid photographers were snapping at a frenetic pace. I wondered if they'd remember who owned each of these grand villas.

Further along, a waterfront property covered in scaffolding came into view. Capitan Guido told us it belonged to the Russian owner of an English football club and his Italian girlfriend. Not unique in the area for being involved with 'creative' enterprises, he'd been shot. If not to make him suffer for the rest of his life, then why else would someone want to shoot him in the legs? Now that he was wheelchair-bound, the urgency of the recent renovation was to install mobility ramps.

'Do you know George Clooney?' Guido asked. He knew that would ensure our attention. '*Villa Oleandra* is one of two

135 The price has moved up and down over the years and the price will vary dependant on the type of accommodation.

villas Clooney owns.' Guido pointed across to another mansion, saying, '*Villa Gastel* was owned by Luchino Visconti[136] and was the venue for many parties attended by the celebrated stars of the film world with celebrities like Coco Chanel and Maria Callas.'

When we reached the headland, we turned around. Guido pointed out a few more villas and their biographies.

'There on the point is the *Villa Melzi,* a white three-storey building set in parkland. Nearby, is the *Villa Serbelloni,* where Franz Liszt wrote the 'Dante Sonata', and it is now part of the Rockefeller Foundation.'

Kim asked, 'Is it true that Madonna had a villa here too?'

'Yes, of course. Madonna, Sylvester Stallone and Sophia Loren all have villas here, Richard Branson owns the *Villa la Casinella* and Arkady Novikov, a "flamboyant" billionaire, bought *Villa Fontanelle,* which was owned by Gianni Versace until his murder in 1997. The restaurateur Novikov is affectionately known as the "Blini Baron". To conclude, let me remind you many of these villas are open to visitors.' We loved his intimate tales and he chatted casually to those around him.

Sailing while gazing at a lifestyle we could only imagine was a relaxing way to spend our afternoon. The sun began to set, and Captain Guido pointed out several more villas as we headed back.

'The four-storey white building is *Villa Carlotta*.' He pointed to a huge mansion set in magnificent parklands. 'It is known for its magnificent display of azaleas.'

136 A neorealist director, Visconti was one of the greatest international film directors who emerged from the post–war Italian cinema industry. He directed *Death in Venice,* one of my favourite movies. Mahler's haunting 'Symphony No. 5' features in the unforgettable opening and closing scenes.

When we landed back in Como, we thanked the captain, with tips, for a very entertaining afternoon.

After all the sitting, I was relieved to stroll the short distance to our hotel. We passed by clothing and shoe shops, but they were already closing. Colourful Prada outfits and Jimmy Choo stilettos adorned the window of a corner store. Hotels, restaurants and cafés, which lined Como's streets, were now coming to life. Nearby, a shaded courtyard café beckoned us to duck in with the promise of a cool glass of Prosecco. We continued along the narrow-cobbled alleys and admired the buildings. Iron fences enclosed beautifully landscaped estates, many dating back to the Middle Ages.

In contrast, our hotel was modern and comfortable. After registration, I was most grateful to find my luggage already in my room. From my window, the view of the Alpine foothills topped with the last remnants of snow was breathtaking. After a long soak in warm fragrant bubbles, I dressed warmly for dinner. The temperature had plummeted to a not unusual 14°C.

Sheila and Simy saved me a seat at their table for dinner. With us were a nice couple who were from Sydney—Antonella and Giorgio Brindisi, who were in the interior design business and were visiting family in the port town of Brindisi near Bari, where I'd started my trip one month ago.

Como in the region of Lombardy is renowned for cheese, meat, polenta and rice. Upon Giorgio and Antonella's recommendation, we started with *Bitto and Bresaolo*—cheese and dried beef, to share with our red wine.

For *secondo*, I had *Rissotto all'amarone*, a meaty risotto with an auburn tinge derived from the use of red wine instead of white. Sheila ordered *Rissotto pesci* with shellfish. Simy settled for a vegetarian risotto with porcini mushrooms. The girls ordered strawberries and gelato for dessert, but Giorgio and I had Monte Veronese cheese, which we enjoyed with a little sambuca. The food was regional and delicious, as was the wine.

Being our last night of the tour, the group was more relaxed and sat chatting and drinking a bit longer than usual. When we eventually disbanded, I was so tired I didn't bother to change or draw the blinds. Surrounded by a cocoon of mountains under the moon's protective gaze, I sank into the deepest sleep.

In the morning, remarkably refreshed and not particularly hungry, I wandered out to the breakfast room. Sheila was sitting alone. Simy wasn't there. She'd gone for a walk. It would be rude to leave Sheila on her own so I helped myself to some yoghurt and berries. We chatted over a pot of tea and exchanged email addresses. Sheila was staying on for another week using Como as a base to explore the local villages before returning home.

Simy and I boarded the bus for the 40 km trip to Milan where our tour would end. Her holiday was over and she needed to return to work. As we approached the outskirts of the city, the roads filled with traffic and footpaths crowded with a sea of people heading in the same direction as us. Nora announced a change of plan.

'We had intended to visit the *Duomo di Milano* this morning but the city is closed to traffic due to the Formula One Grand Prix. There are many more people in town because of the race, not to mention it also being fashion week. If Mario takes the back streets, we can deliver you to Termini Centrale. It's easy to travel around town and make your connections from that central spot.'

The location suited me perfectly since my hotel was only a short walk from the station. We said our goodbyes and made our way in different directions.

I left my bag in the hotel luggage room and headed back to the railway for a train to Torino, in Piedmont. It is home to Fiat Motors, Olivetti and the Juventus football club as well as the Shroud of Turin. A few familiar faces were queueing for tickets.

I struggled a little with the ticket machine, but a man offered to help me. I'd been warned to beware of scammers and pickpockets lurking around bus and train stations and anywhere there's a crowd. He was dressed neatly in a suit and his shoes were clean. He spoke passable English in a bright and reassuring tone and sounded genuine enough. It was a snap decision to allow him to assist me and I even tipped him for his trouble.

Getting onto the platform was a little tricky because the ticket machine was playing up or was my ticket a 'dud'? I didn't want to miss my train, which was due at any moment, so I hurried through without proper validation. When my train arrived the carriage door was a metre higher than the platform. No porters. No one to help. I was so glad I only had hand luggage for my two days in Turin.

After all the wonderous sights I'd seen in those past few weeks, the two-hour train trip to Turin through flat undulating plains seemed uninspiring. I read a little but sudoku proved to be a better diversion. A food trolley appeared. I bought a panini with salami and cheese and a black coffee. Black is the safest when you can't be sure of the quality.

Upon arrival at Porta Nuova, the central station of Turin, I purchased a map from the Tourist Information Bureau near the railway and discovered my hotel was on the next street. Once settled, I went off to explore. The trouble with touring on your own in a foreign country is language, time and direction. I found the *Palazzo Reale,* near the main square, but the palace was closed. *I might have time to see it tomorrow,* I consoled myself.

The Renaissance-style Cathedral of Turin, located in the same precinct as my hotel, was where the Shroud of Turin has been kept since 1578. The church was open but curiously desolate. I strode down the main aisle, which was bordered by two side aisles, with 13 small chapels.

I expected a long queue and a crowd of pilgrims. Instead, I was alone. The aisle led to a showcase where a framed photo of the cloth that covered the face of Christ was exhibited.[137] A small sign indicated the shroud was exhibited[138] only on rare occasions. Pilgrims were encouraged to pause in prayer or light a candle. I helped myself to a brochure from a stack near the candles.

The brochure noted some unique features concerning the image imprinted on the cloth. In 1532, the Holy Shroud was threatened several times by fire and was partly damaged while in Chambery, France. For this reason, it is kept in an extended and horizontal position in a hermetic shrine, created using innovative technology from the aerospace industry.

Not seeing the actual relic left me most disappointed. I wandered aimlessly down the street. Without intending, I

137 This burial cloth with the superimposed positive image of Christ, when overlaid on the negative image of the Shroud of Turin is identical. John 20 refers to a cloth covering the face of Jesus in the tomb.

138 The last time it was displayed was two years earlier, in 2010. Some investigations were being conducted and the next time for display was 2015.

happened upon *Chiesa Santo Sudario*[139] where a sign with a picture of the shroud and an arrow pointed in the direction of a doorway. Inside, a mature lady stood behind a poorly lit counter. She said something to me in Italian. I didn't understand but smiled at her. I said, '*Si, si,*' and nodded. She came up to me and led me by the elbow along a corridor and into a darkened room.

It was so dark, I couldn't tell where I was standing, or the size of the room. She indicated for me to remain where I stood. After walking several paces, she turned on a light. The contrast was dazzling. Without another word, she stepped from the room. My cheeks became hot. I was short of breath. My knees buckled beneath me. I knelt without intending to, as if an unseen force had brought me to the floor. Tears flowed involuntarily, which they'd not done for many years. I managed to hold onto a rail in front of me.

I was drawn to the source of light. Before me, a horizontal, framed[140] image of the Shroud of Turin hung over an altar. Above it was a large, beautifully framed painting of the Resurrection. To my left was a smaller image—the imprinted face cover of Christ.

Except for one small light, everything else remained in darkness. I stayed a few minutes praying, then left. The caretaker spoke gently to me at the exit, but I was bereft of words. I motioned to give her money, but she waved me away.[141] I hurried out. I needed air.

Awestruck, I'd been momentarily elevated to another plane. Now I was emotionally exhausted. The only other time I'd felt

---

139 A photographic copy of the shroud, placed in the same frame as the expositions of 1931 and 1933, is located at the back of the presbytery of this church.

140 The simple frame here is the original one that held the Holy Shroud when it was kept in France. The display case at Turin Cathedral is atmosphere-controlled to help preserve the actual shroud from deterioration.

141 She suggested I visit the attached museum, but I was well beyond that.

this way was at the Holy Sepulchre in Jerusalem. Intellectually, I knew the image in this church was a framed facsimile, but some things and some places exert a unique energy. It's as if they're infused with a subconscious inner knowing; a memory that somehow transfers the power of the original into the copy. This enables the copy to exude an equal energy.

Human intellect is unable to understand what is beyond knowledge. You can only accept or not accept. I know I had experienced a strange force of power. It struck me without warning.

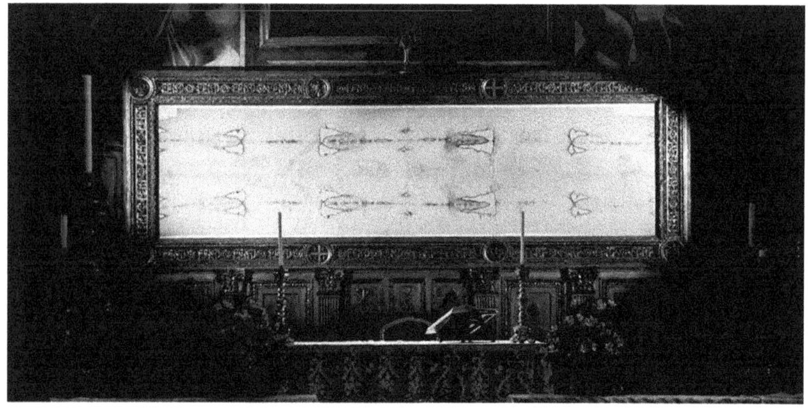

Outside, after several minutes, I regained my equilibrium. The afternoon was balmy, and I mingled with families who were walking around the plaza enjoying the sunshine as if they could store it up before winter arrived.

I stopped at a kiosk for a coffee and found myself standing near the *Museo Egzio*, the Egyptian museum.[142] Fortunately, it

142 This is a highly recommended museum. The quality and quantity of the items was overwhelming.

was open till late, so I could wander at leisure. The entry ticket included a short brochure with a diagram indicating the layout of the museum. The exhibition represented the period from the Palaeolithic to the Coptic era. The museum is said to have an accumulation of the most important Egyptian artifacts, second only to the Cairo Museum of Antiquity.

I saw magnificent limestone statues of pharaohs, sarcophagi and mummy cases beautifully decorated in colours so bright I thought they could have been painted yesterday. Each case featured the stylised face of the incumbent staring eternally back at us. An array of animal mummies, including baboon, ibis and cat, together with all sorts of wrapped and unwrapped examples, filled many of the showcases.

Steles covered in hieroglyphics, decorated boxes, carved alabaster canopic jars, gold jewellery encrusted with lapis, turquoise and carnelian, pottery jars, linens, statuettes depicting an array of gods, leather sandals and all manner of funerary objects, vied for my attention. I was both exhilarated and exhausted by the quantity of artifacts on show.

What I really wanted to see was the immense collection of papyri. Of particular importance was the Turin Royal Canon, also known as the Book of the Dead, which provided scholars with the first complete list of pharaohs in the order of their reign.

The Coptic Codex, which is the most important Coptic literary document in the world, is housed here. The canon was used by Champollion to decipher the Rosetta Stone. Another unique acquisition was the contents of Kha Merit's tomb, discovered by Schiaparelli. The whole tomb had been transported to the museum. I was glad I had my iPad with me because photography was not limited. I was able to take some impressive close-up shots of the most comprehensive illustrated hieroglyphic account of ancient Egyptian life.

From the museum, I cut across the huge quadrangle of *Piazza San Carlo*, lined with beautiful Baroque buildings. The twin churches of *Chiesa San Carlo* and *Chiesa San Christina* stood opposite each other but were both closed. In the centre of the square, taking pride of place, was a bronze statue of Emmanuel Philibert Duke of Saxony in his feathered helmet, astride a prancing horse. The inscription celebrates the duke's many successes in battle, and for the return of French-held territory, including the Duchy of Saxony and Turin.[143]

Music wafted from the portico near the historic Café San Carlo, where people sat at marble-topped tables enjoying their drinks. A sign on the shop awning indicated it had been established in 1822. Famous patrons included Cavour, Dumas, Puccini, Picasso and Hemingway.

An orchestra of buskers were gathered to entertain the people strolling around the square. The ever-popular piano accordion was being played by the lead musician. He was accompanied by a guitarist, a banjo and conga drums. They belted out a familiar Latin song. Couples began to dance, others clapped to the rhythm. I enjoyed the festive atmosphere.

143 Emmanuel Philibert was born in Chambrey, where the shroud was kept. During his reign, he regained Saxon territory, including that of Turin, which was held by France. The shroud was taken to Turin Cathedral. Emmanuel died in Turin and is buried in the Chapel of the Holy Shroud.

I listened for a while before stepping inside. The chandelier-lit *Caffe San Carlo* is one of Turin's top spots for *bicerin* and the Piedmontese *Amaretti Bonet,* which is a chocolate mousse. Its name means bonnet or chef's hat. It was on my list to visit because I'm a chocoholic.

Invented here, the *bicerin* is a hot beverage of chocolate mixed with strong coffee and cream. The menu postscript noted that the author Alexandre Dumas described it as 'unforgettable'. The tantalising aroma of cacao pervaded the room. I ordered one, determined to compare it to the *bicerin* I'd had at Florian's at St Mark's Square in Venice. This was a rich and rather thick hot chocolate drink made with cream. You had to eat it with a spoon. I didn't detect any coffee in their recipe. They were not the same, but I couldn't vote one way or the other as both were delicious. You might have to see for yourself.

Back at the hotel, I read up on the shroud. It had such an impact on me. It is a length of linen bearing the negative image[144] of a man with wounds consistent with crucifixion and mirrors the Gospel texts. It is known to have converted doubters to believers.

The controversy around its authenticity is due to its sketchy provenance that dates to the crucifixion of Christ in AD 30 or 33. Documentation confirms the cloth had been transported later, to both Edessa and Constantinople. When in 1204, the crusaders sacked Constantinople, the capital of the Byzantine Empire, they looted and brutalised the population and stole the shroud. The whereabouts of the shroud between 1204 and 1353, when it reappeared in France, is uncertain. It was damaged, during a fire in 1532 at the Chapel of Chambery in France. In 1534[145], the

144 In 1898, when photographed for the first time, the imprint behaved like a negative.
145 The shroud was brought to Turin in 1534 for veneration to end the Black Plague.

Poor Clare Sisters patched over the 22 scorched holes. Following this, repairs have been undertaken many times.

In 1988, scientists used radiocarbon dating to authenticate the cloth. This investigation confirmed the cloth to be from the medieval era, around 1260–1390. The threads analysed were from the patches made by the nuns during repairs, which would be consistent with the radiocarbon findings. However, some of the fold marks predate those examined by carbon dating.

The question remains, is it an icon or a relic? In 2002, a team of conservators stated, 'We are not conserving a cloth but conserving an image on a cloth.' A member of the conservation team, Dr Alan Adler, notes the gospels of Matthew, Mark and Luke refer to a piece of linen cloth, whereas John refers to strips of linen. Regardless, it doesn't detract from the facts of what happened, rather, the shroud brings to life the event that had so profound an effect on me. Mind you, science cannot explain the negative versus positive markings on the linen.

The next morning, I had enough time to retrace my steps to view the Baroque palace of the House of Savoy. UNESCO heritage listed in 1997, it is the size of Buckingham Palace with an expansive forecourt and is open to the public.

Inside, the rooms of the palace reflected the same level of wealth and grandeur as that of many other European palaces. I thought the decor in the succession of rooms was more Rococo than Baroque in style. The parquet floors are laid in elaborate designs. Lush rural scenes and serious portraits hung on silk-covered walls, while frescoes adorned the ceilings. There was so much detail vying for our attention. The sumptuous chandeliers provided additional light to that filtering through the windows, which were covered in exquisite drapery behind ornate pelmets, fringed swags and tails; a standard comparable to any grand theatre curtain. Antique vases and other ceramics and *objets d'art* were positioned with meticulous order among the gilded Louis XV furniture.

The armoury had a vast amassment of weaponry including armour for both horse and rider and taxidermy of falcons and horses, which I passed by quite quickly. Falcons regaled in metal helmets really freaked me out. In the last room of this section, helmets, chainmail, swords and guns with associated paraphernalia were displayed. They had been accumulated over many generations. Judging by the number of people examining the array of armoury, I'd say it was a popular exhibit.

My hotel was within easy walking distance of all the sites I'd planned to see, and I was satisfied I'd achieved everything possible in the limited time I had. I collected my luggage and made my way to the station for my train back to Milan—the seat of the Italian stock exchange and headquarters for numerous multinational companies.

Chapter 17
La Scala

Alighting from the train, I tripped over my own feet. My knees and left palm endured the bulk of my clumsiness. No one bothered to stop; they hurried by. I don't know if I was more upset by the lack of compassion shown by fellow travellers or my undignified arrival in sophisticated Milan, the global nerve centre of fashion and design.

Customer service at the hotel was casual. I'd expected more formality from the Milanese, but they were not so inclined in this establishment. They'd asked for payment up front for my two-night stay, a policy I'd not encountered anywhere else. Was I dishevelled? Did they think I was a vagabond? Perhaps they thought I was a 'hot pillow' customer. I had a little laugh at the thought.

My room was basic but clean. I unpacked, showered and applied lots of cold water to my injuries. From the window, I could see heavy storm clouds threatening to engulf the city. Suddenly, it pelted down. While I waited for the rain to abate, I did a bit of laundry and ate the fruit I'd taken at breakfast.

A shower and a half-hour rest was enough for me to regain confidence before I made my way downstairs once again. The young gentleman at reception, whose name was Guido, was friendly and helpful. He showed me how to find the *duomo* and *La Scala* on the Metro. He even offered to obtain tickets for me to the theatre, but I already had my reservation.

Ten minutes later, I was at Milan Cathedral. A magnificent Gothic and Renaissance church, its size second only to St Peters in Rome, the façade was covered in statues and bas-reliefs. I couldn't believe the veritable forest of capped pinnacles and spires on the roof. It struck me as unusual because I'd not seen anything quite like it anywhere else in Italy. The cathedral is dedicated to the Nativity of the Blessed Virgin Mary and is the seat of the Bishop of Milan and symbol of the city.

The grey stone church spire rises 108 metres to a gilded and copper statue of the Madonna. The church is further decorated with gargoyles, turrets, buttresses and parapets. A signboard indicated it had taken three centuries to build.

Inside, an extensive number of thick pink and white marble columns rise to the lofty, ribbed ceiling. Pews to accommodate 40,000 people covered the boldly patterned mosaic floor. Light sparkled through arched and rose-shaped windows. The stained glass made a dazzling display of the countless biblical scenes. An enormous reed organ near the main altar next captured my attention. As I stood there wondering what it must sound like, my reverie was broken with the sudden approach of four people.

'Hello, *come esta*?' asked a familiar voice. It was Carmel and Andrew with their relatives. 'Have you been down to the crypt?' Andrew asked.

'Not yet. Is it worth going there?'

'Of course,' Carmel replied. 'We were there a moment ago and are on our way to the roof to enjoy the panoramic view of the city. If you want to follow, the lift near the entry will take you up, but your return is by way of the stairs.'

After parting company, I made my way to the crypt. The low, corbelled ceiling made the room feel oppressive. It only seemed that way because the main level of the church had extremely lofty ceilings. The intricate decoration on the thick columns made them seem heavier, stumpier and added to the feeling of closeness. This optical illusion made me feel sandwiched between the ceiling and the intricately patterned floor. I didn't stay long and sadly forgot about the tapestries.

Outside on the steps, using the church as a backdrop, a photographer was taking advantage of the setting to capture a hijab-clad bride with her beaming groom. A stretch limo waited for them in the forecourt. It seemed everywhere I went there were weddings.

Pedestrians traversed the square between the *duomo,* Galleria, *Palazzo Reale* and the Metro. I admired the elegant, Neoclassical buildings around the boundary of the piazza and was finally drawn to the magnificent bronze equestrian statue. I knew the statue was important because of its size and prominent position. The plaque identified the uniformed rider as Viktor Emmanuel II, the first king of united Italy, leading his troops at the Battle of Solferino.[146]

I enjoyed mingling with the locals who were going about their normal lives. Guido had told me about a short-cut to *La Scala* through the Galleria Viktor Emmanuel II, which is the oldest shopping centre in Italy; great when raining. The original idea was to provide a covered passage between the *Duomo di Milano* and *La Scala*. The Galleria is an arcade, decorated with caryatids, pilasters, arched windows and balconies—places to

146 Jean-Henri Durant, witness to the 1859 battle, was so horrified by the suffering he saw there that it inspired him to commence the writing of the Geneva Convention and to begin the formation of the Red Cross organisation.

stop for an aperitif or a nightcap after the opera at Camparino.[147] I'd have loved a Campari and tonic but sadly this day there was no time.

The entry to the arcade is through an imposing arch reminiscent of the Arc d'Triomphe in Paris. As I stepped inside the Neoclassic mall, I was surprised at the airiness. It was filled with natural light that streamed down from the splendid glass and iron roof—a feature which became popular in the 19th century. The Galleria was built in 1877 and was larger than the Burlington in London[148], St Hubert's in Brussels and the Passage in St Petersburg.

The Galleria Viktor Emmanuel exuded an air of unmistakable elegance and luxury. It was 'the' meeting place for the Milanese bourgeoise during the *Belle Époque*[149] and is still considered one of the ritziest spots in the city.

Referred to as the Salon of Milan, it is home to some of the city's oldest and most prestigious boutiques and restaurants, including Biffi Caffè, founded in 1867 by Paolo Biffi, pastry chef to the monarch. Across the aisle from Prada is the Michelin star Cracco, reputed to be one of the 50 best restaurants in the world. It offers a range of eating and drinking experiences on five levels. I wished I could have gone there, if not to eat, then at least to see the hand-painted wallpaper and antique mirrors. Again, time was against me. I passed by the Savini, which was the favourite restaurant of artists like, Maria Callas, Toscanini, Verdi and Puccini, who went there to unwind after their performances. Even today you'll find a refined, sophisticated atmosphere, complete with live music.

147 A trendy cocktail bar serving drinks based on Campari.

148 London 1818, Brussels 1847, Passage 1848.

149 The period between 1871–1914.

I was mesmerised by the *haute couture* labels in the boutiques. They were out of my reach and included Prado, Versace, Armani and Luisa Spagnoli, Borsalino hats, Church's shoes, Vacheron Constantine watches and Dolce Gabbana and Bulgari jewellery. Town House Galleria, the prestigious seven-star hotel, is situated here too. Gazing into shopfronts delayed my progress and all that window shopping caused a yearning for coffee and something sweet.

There was a distinct aroma of roasting coffee beans in the air. I followed my nose and was surprised to find the aroma coming from McDonald's. What was it doing amongst these top-end boutiques? Though this Macca's was unlike any I'd seen.[150] It was beautifully appointed with black columns decorated in gold to blend with the ambiance of the centre. The menu had an Italian slant. I ordered a Focaccia with mayo, tomato, ham and lettuce for €2.40. Then, intrigued by its name, I ordered the latte and gelato confection to accompany my coffee. It consisted of a chocolate biscuit tube like a brandy snap, filled with delicious vanilla ice cream for €1.90.

Later, I was shocked to learn that on 16 October 2012, McDonald's was forced to close their doors. After a 20-year tenancy, management pronounced that the eatery was not in keeping with the overall culture of the arcade. During the last few hours of operation, McDonald's gave away 5000 free meals.

At the exit from the arcade, I admired a highly polished granite and marble floor inlaid with heraldic and cosmic symbols. To my surprise, a young couple stood on the bull's head and twirled around three times.

A man alongside me laughed. 'You can always tell the tourists,' he said under his breath. He turned to see my reaction.

150 An upmarket slant on the old McCafé.

'There is a superstition that continues to inspire them to pirouette three times on the head of the bull. They look so silly but they do it for good luck.'

'I don't go in for these superstitions,' I said. 'I expect someone to jump out from a secret alcove and shout, "Smile, you're on Candid Camera!" We both laughed. I turned to the exit and made my way out.

A footpath led me through a lovely rose patch to *Teatro alla Scala*, where most of the great Italian operas were premiered. Adjoining the theatre was a museum with a display of posters, photos, sketches and memorabilia. I waited for a small group tour of the theatre and museum to gather. In the theatre shop, I bought a couple of souvenir mouse pads decorated with the program cover from the 1955 performance of *Carmen*, conducted by the renowned Herbert von Karajan.

The guide arrived and we followed her up some steps, along a narrow, dimly-lit staircase. The carpet muffled our footfalls as we entered the box. She hushed us when she realised there was a rehearsal taking place. The music was calming and the voices pitch perfect. Even though the performers were not in costume, this unscheduled performance whet our appetites and I longed to attend a performance.

In the museum, I saw an old black-and-white photograph of a good-looking gentleman. His name was Ignazio Marini. Born in 1811 in Bergamo, Italy, he died in 1873 in Milan. He was a basso cantante and principal artiste at *La Scala*, where his wife was a mezzo-soprano. He starred in many Donizetti and Verdi operas and toured overseas to New York, London, Mexico, Cairo and St Petersburg in Russia.[151] He may be the grandfather of my own maternal grandmother, Louisa Marini.

151 He was in St Petersburg from 1856 to 1863.

They married young in those days probably because there was no contraception.

Back through the Galleria and across the square, I made my way to the *Palazzo Reale*.[152] Inside, all the embellishments had been removed, which was a great pity. Was this the price of progress or was it a case of it being too expensive to preserve the old dinosaur? Despite all the trappings being gone, the large space is suitable for exhibitions.

A collection of 250 works by the Spanish born artist, Pablo Picasso, shipped from the *Nationale* Picasso Museum in Paris, was on show. Several rarely seen paintings from his rose, blue and columbine periods were on show. This was an exceptional treat for me; something I'd not expected. I particularly liked one of a child called Paul as Harlequin.

Picasso's style changed in the 1920s as he experimented with cubism. An example from that period was *Les Demoiselles d'Avignon*. Although he lived much of his life in Paris, his roots were Spanish. After he had experienced the horrors of the Spanish Civil War, he painted his famous *Guernica*. The war had a profound effect on him, after which his style became increasingly geometric and surrealist.

This exposition proved to be a taster for my planned visit to the *Museu Picasso* in Barcelona in a week's time.

I was surprised so few people were riding the Metro. Was I foolishly brave? It was quite late by the time I stopped at the charming little *Ristorante Lepitit* near my hotel where I ordered *Milanese Cotletta*, which turned out to be Veal Schnitzel.

---

152 The royal palace.

Each day is an adventure and now that I've mastered the Metro, even changing lines, I'm looking forward to navigating my day of discovery like a local. First up, I had to tackle the problem my travel agent had created when he'd prebooked my ticket to see Leonardo da Vinci's *Last Supper*. I made my way to the church of *Santa Maria della Grazie*, where it is kept.

'I have no cancellations for today,' said the lady at the counter.

I was crestfallen.

'Why didn't you phone yesterday?' she asked.

I was kicking myself. *Why indeed? I didn't think I'd need to. I thought I could talk my way in.*

She continued to explain. 'The room where the painting is kept is humidity-controlled with a special filtering system to ensure preservation. The number of people in the room at any one time must therefore be limited.

I was extremely disappointed. *Of course. I understand. How stupid of me not to think of it.*

'Would you like me to put you on the cancellation list for tomorrow?' she asked, handing me a brochure.

'Thank you, but unfortunately, tomorrow I will be leaving Milan for Florence,' I replied.

'If you wish to see more of Leonardo's work, I recommend you go to the *Pinacoteca Ambrosio*. Meanwhile, have a look at the church and the cloisters here. There is no charge for that.'

The Renaissance church of *Santa Maria della Grazie*[153], a terracotta, gabled building with a plain façade, was originally a

153 UNESCO heritage listed in 1980.

convent, built around three courtyards with beautiful cloisters. Bramante's refurbishment added a Baroque-inspired semi-circular extension with apses and a dome, supported by a colonnaded loggia. Whilst incorporating the need to house important ancient relics, the style of the architecture reflected the era.

Inside, the church was unapologetically Gothic. Slender, Corinthian-capped columns reached up to the ribbed vaults of the high ceiling. The inside, painted in dove grey with white and gold decorative features, resulted in a calming and peace-filled space. In the original 15th century church, the walls had been covered in frescoes but were discarded during the 19th century refurbishment.

The Last Supper[154] hangs appropriately in the refractory so that the diners may reflect on the event as described in the Bible.[155] The Last Supper was like the beginning of the last chapter of the chronicle of Christ's time on earth. The event, as portrayed in the Gospel, is the subject of Leonardo da Vinci's painting. The final gathering of the apostles was the culmination of Jesus's previous 30 years and His final goodbye. The epilogue takes place 40 days later, during Ascension and ends on the 50th day with Pentecost.

Placement of the figures and clever use of perspective, draws our attention to the central figure of Jesus. Abandoning the usual fresco methodology on wet plaster, he elected to use tempera[156] to achieve a more spectacular effect. This technique lifts the stress of deadlines because the paint uses a binder and

154 Painted in 1490.

155 Matthew 26:17–30, Mark 14:12, Luke 22:14–16 and John 13:21.

156 The powdered pigment is mixed with a fixative of egg yolk, water and glue to make an emulsion. and is applied to a dry wall whereas fresco is applied to a wet wall which takes longer to dry so it saves time to use tempera.

is applied to a dry plaster wall. Its placement in the refractory where steam, smoke and dirt filled the air caused irreparable damage to the artwork. To add to the problems of the tempera issue, during World War II in August 1943, the Allies bombed the building and the refractory was razed to the ground. It had to be a miracle that the only wall left standing was the one with *The Last Supper*. Since the restoration of 1978–1999, conservationists placed the painting in a sealed climate-controlled environment, to delay losing the painting.

In search of the *Pinacoteca,* I happened upon a little gem called San Maurizio. Entry was free, so I wandered in. It was once a Benedictine monastery, a cloister for the wealthy maidens before they entered marriage. Now it is an archaeological museum. Its austere, even shabby neo-medieval exterior belies the magnificence of the interior decorated in the Renaissance style. The complex is divided into two sections—church and monastery. The church boasts eight beautifully decorated chapels.

My eyes darted from one wall to another. Each surface was covered in framed frescoes of saints and bible scenes. Even the arches were a mass of heraldic ribbons and flags. Such an amazing find took me by surprise and I wondered how many others I'd walked by without realising.

Like *Santa Maria della Grazie,* Bramante was commissioned to do San Maurizio's restorations. The barrel-vaulted ceiling of the nave was intricately decorated between the false ribs. Rosettes and lunettes situated high on the walls provided the interior with soft light. Everywhere, beautiful frescoes grace the walls. The most important period of painting being from the 16th century. On the vaulted ceiling of the monastery is a fresco of a starry night, with God placed in the centre with the four

Evangelists. All are surrounded by angels. In 1557, the sisters commissioned the building of an organ like the one seen in *Duomo di Milan*, and had it installed in the convent hall.

As I walked around, I noticed bare patches where paintings were missing. I was told this was due to the rising damp caused by the Niron, a subterranean river. It generates a high degree of humidity. In 1964, the frescoes most in danger of ruin by the moisture were detached and remounted elsewhere.

The most important frescoes in the church are by Bernadino Luini. I particularly liked the painting called *Holy Family* for the tender expression on the face of the Blessed Virgin Mary. Joseph looks on in a fatherly fashion as the Baby Jesus blesses the infant St John the Baptist as John's mother, St Elizabeth looks on. The group appear relaxed, their skin tones are luminous and the vibrant reds and blues of their clothes contrast with the dark background. Much of this art has been dismantled and lost, so it's only here that we are able to appreciate the tender expressions of his subjects and the true nature of his art.

A short way up the road I found the Library *Pinacoteca Ambrosiana*. The gallery, on three levels, is named after St Ambrose, the patron saint of Milan. In 1607, Cardinal Borromeo commissioned the building of a large public library[157] to house his vast assembly of books. This is reputed to be one of the most important libraries in the world.

Its collection numbers more than a million printed volumes, of which 40,000 are manuscripts in Italian, Latin, Greek, Arabic, Syriac and Ethiopic.[158] There are 12,000 drawings, among them works by Raphael, Pisanello, Leonardo and other masters. Not

157 Built in 1609, the Pinacoteca Ambrosiana, was one of the earliest libraries to grant public access.

158 An ancient language used by the kings of the Axumite empire and still used in most Christian Abyssinian literature and in their liturgy.

to forget 22,000 engravings and other unique rarities such as old maps, musical manuscripts, illuminations, parchments and papyri. Even though I couldn't flip through the pages held in the display cabinets, I felt inspired by the magnitude of my surroundings. It was as if I were having an audience with the great masters themselves.

The most precious artifact is the *Codex Atlanticus,* a 12-volume set of writings and drawings by Leonardo da Vinci. I also saw works by many other authors and artists, including a first edition of Dante's *Divine Comedy.*

My favourite painting was Veronese's *Sacred Family, with the addition of St John the Baptist, St Tobias and Archangel Gabriel.* I couldn't take my eyes off Joseph's face. His expression so tender and so loving as he gazed upon the Baby Jesus. Upstairs was a beautiful marble statue of St Anna and her child, the Blessed Mary, by Benzonni. I'd not seen the two of them characterised in this way before. Presentation of the Virgin Mary into the Temple is the usual depiction of Mary as a child.

Another room exhibited more recent work from the 19th century. My favourite was a painting by Emilio Longoni labelled *Chiusi Fuori Scuola.* It means locked out of school and was a delightful study of two little children on their way to school. The older child, shy and unsure, is holding the hand of a younger sibling, who is full of mischief and beams cheekily.

There were so many works of art from the Renaissance. Botticelli's *Madonna del Padiglione,* meaning Madonna of the Pavilion, was stunning for its bright colours. The next room was filled with paintings by Leonardo da Vinci. There on the wall, I saw the largest copy of *The Last Supper.* It made up for my disappointing start to the day.

Then it was back to the main square and the Metro. I had lunch at Café Panzera, near my hotel. I ordered grilled Atlantic salmon with roasted pine nuts on a bed of scalloped potato slices. It had been a busy and wondrous day. Over coffee, I made extensive notes in my journal to ensure all was not simply left to memory. The beauty and talent I'd witnessed had far exceeded my expectations.

Back in my room, as I packed my bags, I tried to push away the dreaded thought of boarding and disembarking with all my luggage on the early morning train to Florence. A bubble bath was a superb solution to help lighten my mood. I rested, washed my hair and manicured my nails as I prepared for my big night out.

As a lover of music, ballet and opera, I could barely contain my excitement. I possessed a ticket to the hallowed ground of *La Scala*. Some of the worlds most renowned operas were premiered in this theatre: Bellini's *Norma,* Donizetti's *Lucrezia Borgia,* Verdi's *Othello* and Puccini's *Turandot* but there were more. Reputed to have perfect acoustics, the theatre became home to the crème de la crème of the music world. Over the years, principal conductors included: Toscanini and Barenboim, Bernstein and von Karajan. How I would have loved to have been there then. Of course, I have videos but it's not the same.

In the foyer of the theatre, I bought a program and a glass of champagne then propped myself at a high counter to observe other patrons gathering. *I hope I'm dressed in line with local custom. Milan is the centre of fashion and I don't want to look like orphan Annie.*

The season opens each year on 7 December, which is the feast day of St Ambrose. My September visit was not optimal because the opera and ballet had finished months earlier. The concert season was already in its last days before recess, but I had exceptional seats—four rows from the front in the stalls and near the aisle. They were expensive by our standards. The conundrum is always price versus value.

The program I'd purchased was unfamiliar, but it didn't matter because the experience was what mattered most. I'd bought the tickets online, well ahead of time. Inside the theatre, my eye went straight to the stage curtain, which was resplendent in burgundy velvet, fringed in gold. My seat was surrounded by six tiers of loge, their gilded balconies a statement of opulence in an otherwise understated auditorium.

In front of me sat a middle-aged couple. He was immaculately groomed and wore a dark, well-cut suit. His younger partner, her smooth blonde hair cut in a bob, wore a classic navy-blue sheath. It was the perfect background to highlight her lustrous, drop earrings and opera-length string of plump, creamy pearls. I wondered if they were Paspaley pearls from Broome. Then again, they too might be fakes. They were seated in the third row, which was cheaper because it's too close to the stage to enjoy the panorama of the set.

As soon as I heard her ask her partner, in French, to photograph her, I knew they were visitors like me. I offered to take one of them together. I relished the chance to practice my French in preparation for my visit there in a couple of weeks' time. They were delighted with my offer and insisted on reciprocating. He said they were in Milan for a few days on business. She didn't say anything and so I thought they were most likely colleagues. The lights began to dim, which brought our conversation to a close.

The Philharmonic[159] Orchestral Concert featured Schumann's *Symphony No. 4 in D Minor*, a light and transparent score to set the tone. After the interval we were enthralled by the boldness and drama of Brahms' *Symphony No. 1 in C Minor*. The brass, tempered by the string section, was longer and meatier. Although Schumann and Brahms are often paired, it's usual for the performance of corresponding symphonies to be performed. Schumann is normally scheduled as the curtain raiser before the exuberant Brahms. However, this program, while not as scintillating, proved to be uplifting and inspiring. What a sensational way to end my stay in Milan. I left on a high note.

Chapter 18
Florence Again

My trial by train started early at the main railway centre. Like our own central station, it had more than one level and many entrances. Since all notices were in Italian, I went to the information desk for help. The queue was long but my time was short. The lady scrutinised my ticket and pointed up, which I think meant for me to go upstairs for the intercity trains.

Indeed, a row of platforms, some with trains already alongside, were waiting to depart. My documentation said platform seven, car eleven, seat eight. A uniformed man stood at the entry to the platform. He said I had to verify my voucher in the ticket machine before I could board. The machine wouldn't cooperate.

The train engine began to hum. The uniformed assistant blurted out something like '*Gusto*', and waved his hand, indicating I should hurry. The machine refused to work. I ran past him, scanning the carriage numbers, and quickly found the door to my car. I struggled to climb onto the train, but the assistant ignored me. A lady in the doorway gave me a hand. The luggage bay was full and the aisle too narrow to accommodate baggage. Someone moved a smaller bag to an overhead rack to make room for my big case.

Perspiring with the effort, I looked for my seat, hoping it would be vacant and that I was in the right compartment and on the correct train. The seat was unoccupied, and I hoped this was a turning point for the rest of my arrangements to follow smoothly. The less than gallant individuals I'd encountered that morning reflected poorly on my overall impressions. I was hot and cranky.

Modern train travel had lost the romanticism of bygone days. I fantasised about the 19th century when luggage was wheeled on trolleys by uniformed porters and assistants who were positioned at each doorway to help the fashionably dressed passengers board. Friends and family graciously farewelled the travellers and wished them a safe and happy journey.

I brushed my disappointment aside and reminded myself that I'd soon be in beautiful Florence to do the things not offered on my previous tour.

The same nightmare welcomed us on our arrival in Florence. Struggling women, possibly Amazonian descendants, helped each other to disembark with our heavy luggage. At least there was no rush because we were at the end of the line.

I took the next available taxi. My hotel was another quaint little *pension* situated at the opposite end of town from where the tour group had previously stayed. The *pension* was run by Leonardo and Ricardo, who I thought were brothers. I'd arrived earlier than they expected. Ricardo sent me to the lounge and fetched me coffee while I waited for my room to be cleaned. It didn't take long. He escorted me to the third floor in yet another funny old lift. It reminded me of a glass cage and I felt hemmed in.

My room was spacious and had a lovely view across a sea of terracotta roofs and domes towards the Arno. I settled in quickly and had reception confirm my tour for the following day to Pisa. The rest of the day I planned to spend exploring the *Uffizi*, Italy's most important art gallery.

Not originally intended to be a museum, *Cosimo de' Medici*[160], called upon the architect, Giorgio Vasari, to design a grandiose U-shaped building with porticos positioned in the centre of town to become the administrative and judiciary offices of Florence. In Italian, the word *uffizi* means offices. Construction began in 1560 and was completed in 1580, while the Medici hegemony was still secure over Florence.

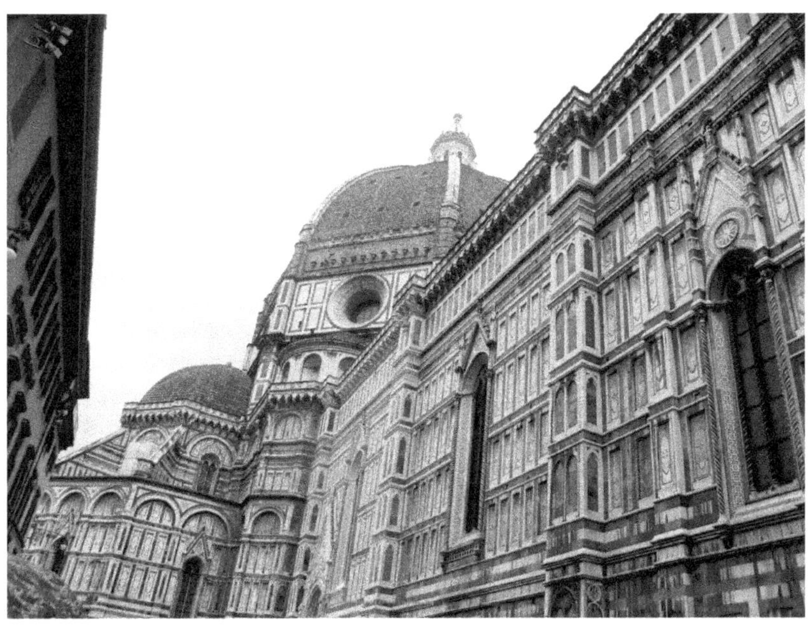

Vasari also built the Secret Corridor, which joins the *Uffizi*[161] to the Pitti Palace. Anna Maria Luisa was the last lineal descendant of the main Medici line. Her husband had syphilis so there were no children. She retired to the Pitti Palace, where she died in 1743, leaving her priceless art acquisitions to the city of Florence.

The Medici acquisition takes up two whole floors. In the 19th century during refurbishment, most of the ancient artifacts were rehoused in the Bargello Museum[162], leaving a wealth of paintings and sculptures dating from the 13th to the 18th century. The rooms are joined in chronological order. In room two was a crucifix by Maestro della Croce using four nails—two in the hands and one in each foot.

Of the 13th century masterpieces, some of the most important paintings were tempera on wood. *Madonna Ognissanti* is an example of innovation and development of technique. Giotto broke with the Byzantine two-dimensional and implemented a three-dimensional style. He suggested perspective through his use of light and additional architectural elements. A fine example of Cimabue's love for bold colour could be seen in the *Madonna Enthroned*.

Room three contained many icons, including several of St Nicholas of Bari. I particularly admired the depiction of the saint in a central lozenge surrounded by vignettes of his life and miracles. The vignettes showed the saint as a real person brought to life.

From the period of the Renaissance, I was drawn to Leonardo da Vinci's painting of the Annunciation, which is said to be his earliest work. Another one I revered was Filippo Lippi's *Madonna*

161 The Uffizi became a public gallery in 1865.

162 The Bargello was the museum Simy, Shirley and I sneaked into while the guard slept.

and Child with St John as a babe. This is his masterpiece. For me, the subjects exuded a calm serenity. I thought close friendship was already evident between the babes and foreshadowed the future event of Christ's baptism.[163]

Most famous, but in a style not to my liking, were the portraits by della Francesca of the Duke of Urbino in red cap and gown and his demure wife. In profile, as was the fashion of the time, it suited the duke to show his best side as his other was disfigured. With a grey complexion, a hooked nose and half-closed eyes, he reminded me of a snake. His features were hard and his demeanour appeared unforgiving.

Most spectacular were the Botticelli rooms. *Primavera,* also known as *Allegory of Spring,* is light and airy; full of hope. However, *Birth of Venus* is the better known. She is the goddess of beauty who emerges fully formed from the sea, her golden tresses falling gently over her naked breasts. Zephyr, the god of wind, blows her gently to shore while Flora looks on.

In a special cabinet I saw Caravaggio's 16th century shield with the head of Medusa, who looked to be a very fierce but impressive creature. Some say the face is a self-portrait of the artist when he was younger. The Medici family used it as their symbol of power. It also inspired the Versace emblem. I thought it curious that this deranged image was displayed alongside the Madonnas and saints.

One of the most beautiful paintings is Raphael's *Madonna of the Goldfinch*. There is an angelic expression on the Madonna's face as she gazes lovingly at the two babes, who reflect her own calm beauty.

---

163 St John was six months older than Jesus. Their mothers, Elizabeth and Mary, were relatives (Luke 1:39–45). John the Baptist was so-called because he baptised Christ (Matthew 3:13–17).

An early painting by Michelangelo of young Bacchus sitting by a fruit bowl and raising a glass of red wine was said to be of the artist himself, whereas his composition of the Holy Family from the 16th century might have been a cartoon for a sculpture. The placement of the figures seemed set to fit into a block of marble. Yet the subjects are full of life and energy. The colours of their garments dominate the painting and, contrasted with the background of nudes, they fade into oblivion.

At the time it was painted, Titian's *Venus of Urbino* created an enormous controversy. Mark Twain labelled it, 'the foulest, vilest obscene picture.' I particularly loved the warmth and luminosity of Venus's skin and the use of chiaroscuro[164] to make the subject dominant. Mark Twain and others who proclaimed a negative critique were affronted by the frontal view, whereas Annibale Carracci's 19th century painting, *Bacchante*, shows us the back view of a similar reclining nude. However, *Bacchante* is not that pure because she faces a dark, devilish Bacchus, who leers at her with lust. We can't see her response to his lecherous stare. I love the angle of Carracci's figure. It reminded me of a classic Picasso nude from his Blue Period.

By the time people get this far, most of them are ready to leave but the exit is through a long sculpture gallery. The black and white granite floors are a perfect foil to the silken white marble forms. The ceiling of the gallery is divided into sections by decorative beams and each panel covered in frescoes. Natural light streams from a wall of sash windows.

Beyond this space was a café with a sizable terrace from which I enjoyed the panorama of the city, Ponte Vecchio, and

164 Chiaroscuro is the use of contrast, light and dark elements in a picture to create drama and the illusion of three-dimensional volume on a flat surface. Rembrandt and artists of the Flemish school frequently used the technique.

the Arno beyond. I rested there for almost 20 minutes with a cool drink. My head was full of so many images, I wanted to clear my thoughts before I returned to the exhibitions.

The remainder of the display included Rubens, Rembrandt, Van Dyke, El Greco and Goya. A whole room was dedicated to the Rembrandts, which I think ought to be a priority for any visitor. The main attraction for me were Rembrandt's portraits from the 17th century. As well, there were drawings, sketches and busts. I studied the portraits for some time. These included a rabbi and a self-portrait from 1669. Another was of a bearded old man, which was Rembrandt's last self-portrait. The man was a morose old fellow with puffy eyes, but on closer examination, I saw in his eyes a profound and inconsolable understanding of his life. It is said that the portrait expresses feelings Rembrandt could never put into words.

It's hard to have a favourite Rembrandt, but a particular highlight for me was the 1634 *Portrait of a Young Man.* He was clean-shaven, had reddish brown hair and was wearing a mahogany brown cloak and black velvet beret. There was something about his expression—something spellbinding, familiar and empathic. I knew him, from long ago, perhaps from another life.

I left the gallery on a high, full of emotion, as if walking on clouds, my head filled with the wonderment of what I'd seen. I ambled without need of destination across the city and over Ponte Vecchio until the colours and all the gold in the shop windows became a blur.

A magic sign snapped me out of my reverie. A large sign that read 'SALE' was splashed across a shoe shop window. It reeled me in through its doors to join other like-minded women. I could have bought a dozen pairs in gelato colours and the softest of leathers. These shoes were top quality Italian footwear. I settled on a pair of mushroom-coloured toe-peepers.

As I scanned the shop, I saw in a discreet corner, the new season stock. A pair of black, ankle-high boots with Cuban heels; timeless classics. They enticed me. *Should I get a bargain or yield to the shiny presence of those timeless boots? I have a high arch, which I know will be hard to fit.*

I tried them on. The soft leather enveloped my foot, there were no gaps. I knew they'd been made for me. I had to have them, regardless of the price. In fact, I bought both pairs. With a satisfied grin across my face, I strolled out wearing the boots while carrying my own shoes together with the bargain priced toe-peepers, all secured in the store's bag.

On my way back to the hotel, I bought an ice cream and some nuts. I tried to watch the TV news but there was nothing in English. The *Uffizi* had filled me with thought-provoking artistry, so I was satiated and had no desire for anything other than sleep. I slept for nine hours.

Chapter 19
A Feast Day

There's nothing nicer than the smell of genuine leather, and I had new boots. I thought their softness and the way they caressed the arch of my foot was the mark of a well-cut last, unlike the footwear back home. When I was a child any new clothing or shoes were first worn to church, and here in Florence, on a high day, I planned to wear the boots.

The Exaltation of the Cross is an important feast day in the Anglican, Catholic and Orthodox calendars. It celebrates the finding of the True Cross by St Helena, the mother of the Byzantine Emperor Constantine.[165] Many miracles had occurred after petitions were made to that Cross, thus authenticating it. This finding also confirmed the location of Golgotha. Most importantly, this feast day celebrated how an instrument of shame was used to overcome death and bring believers to salvation and eternal life.

Perfect weather made for a pleasant 10-minute stroll from my hotel to the church. No need for a map to find the church. Its five cupolas, covered with multi-chromatic ceramic tiles, were a beacon above the terracotta roofs. A veritable arabesque of colours, it reminded me of St Basil's in Moscow. However, this church was taller and more magnificent than I expected.

Built in the Moscow Baroque style[166], the upper-level church is known as the Church of the Nativity and the lower-level church is dedicated to St Nicholas of Bari.[167] As I drew nearer, my heart sank. Scaffolding was wrapped around the building. I hoped it was not closed for restoration.

The gates, a crochet of black iron lace, were open. I strolled through to the gardens. A well-trodden path led to the vestibule of the church. There, I spoke to a young lady at the candle desk.

'Welcome. You are early,' she said. 'The choir is still setting up and the liturgy will commence at ten o'clock.'

That was an hour later than I expected. I should have consulted the internet instead of assuming the services began at the same time throughout the world. The sound of my Cuban heels echoed in the huge empty space, so I tip-toed around examining the icons and frescoed walls and ceiling before returning to the candle desk. The lady was busy replenishing supplies as I waited to buy candles.

'The iconostasis is unusual,' I said. 'It reminds me of the 1888 Church of Mary Magdalene in Jerusalem.'[168]

---

166 Muscovite Baroque of the 17th century differed from the Western Baroque and was based on traditional Russian architecture. The layout was a Greek cross and it incorporated five cupolas, the larger in the centre, with four smaller ones on each side. During the 18th century reign of Peter the Great, a Western-influenced Baroque was used. The Latin cross layout came into being for churches and the French Baroque features graced palaces. Interiors and exteriors were highly ornamented and bold colours used. Peter's daughter Elizabeth brought Italian architects to work in the major cities of Moscow, Kiev and St Petersburg. The best-known architect of the time was Francesco Bartolomeo Rastrelli.

167 In 1873, Nicholas I's daughter Maria was an exceptional supporter and collector of the arts. She conceived the idea to build the church for the many Russians visiting and living in Florence.

168 In the crypt of Mary Magdalene church in Jerusalem are the remains of Prince Philip's mother, Princess Alice of Greece, alongside her aunt, Grand Duchess Elizabeth of Russia and Elizabeth's sister, Barbara.

'They are similar in style, both inside and out,' she said. 'Our church was built around the same time. The iconostasis was paid for by the tsar from his own purse.'[169]

The iconostasis in each of these two churches is identical. The contrast between the marble and wooden frames around prominent icons is a distinctive feature. I've not seen the like anywhere else.

The church filled and the Liturgy began on time. As we were all leaving, I introduced myself to the priest and praised the wonderful choir. He was pleased to see an Australian visitor and asked me to pass on his regards to Fr George in Sydney. At first, I was surprised but now I understand many of them had met and formed friendships while they'd studied at the seminary in New York.

I felt elated as I walked back to my hotel. After a quick change into more casual attire and a bite to eat, I returned to the city, intent on visiting the Pitti Palace. My route took me over the famous Ponte Vecchio, to the other side of the Arno River. This precinct had become familiar territory and I traversed it like a local, buzzing around confidently, as I would while shopping back at home.

Ponte Vecchio, as the name suggests, is the oldest bridge in Florence. Designed by Giotto and his pupil, Gaddi. The shopping strip is known for its goldsmiths, jewellers and purveyors of priceless antiques. This was the only bridge not damaged during World War II.

A bust of the famous goldsmith, Cellini, graces the centre of the bridge. A fence was erected around the statue for couples

169 Not much is written in the West about the charitable works he did, quietly and without fanfare. The West prefers to parrot the Soviet misinformation even though they no longer exist.

in love to attach a small padlock, with or without their initials, then throw the key into the Arno. Urban legend has it that this gesture will ensure their love will last unto eternity.

A secret royal passageway called the *Corridorio Vasariano*[170], was built for the exclusive use of the Medici family. The double-tiered bridge runs for one kilometre above the Ponte Vecchio to the church of Santa Felicita. The construction allowed the family to move between the Pitti Palace and the Palazzo Vecchio above the dirty streets, far away from the bawdy throng.

The Medici family were wealthy bankers, talented merchants and the most powerful family doing business in Venice, Florence and Milan during the 15th and 16th centuries. Their patronage allowed the growth and flowering of art and culture during the Renaissance. They accumulated such an enormous collection of artworks that they had to build new palaces to exhibit them. Financial patronage was not merely a benevolent venture, rather an astute investment as it is with our big corporates displaying significant artworks in their foyers. They assisted trade between cities, states and countries. Our modern banking is fashioned upon the Medici financial dealings as money lenders and currency exchangers.

I continued in the direction of the Pitti Palace, past the shoe shop where I'd bought my boots. Travel guides say the rustic stonework of the palace gives it a serene appearance. To me, the dirty-brown-coloured bricks were ugly and the design of the three-storey building, without any embellishment, seemed plain when compared to all the magnificent architecture I'd seen throughout the rest of the city.

170 Visitor access to the corridor was possible until 2021, when the fire department suspended tours along the route due to security and non-compliance with the new fire ordinance.

The palace, although designed by Brunelleschi and built in the 15th century, was commissioned by Luca Pitti, a rich banker who was in competition with the Medici. Ironically, the expense incurred in construction and decoration bankrupted Pitti. Cosimo de' Medici purchased the Pitti Palace and after Vasari enlarged the building, it became their main residence. When the Médicis died out, the palace acquired several new owners, including the Dukes of Tuscany and those from the Austrian House of Lorraine. During Napoleon's reign it was used as his headquarters.

A pretty courtyard behind the palace opened onto the Boboli Gardens. This expansive park, punctuated with follies, grottos, fountains and obelisks, provided the palace with a beautiful leafy outlook. The formally laid-out gardens reminded me of other grand palaces I'd seen like Schönbrunn[171], Versailles[172] and Peterhof.[173]

Inside the grounds are several museums. I visited the Costume Museum, with over 6000 items. It comprises the history of European fashion from the 16th to the 19th centuries and includes some elaborate theatrical costumes. Garment design was only one aspect of interest. I also enjoyed surveying the variety of cloth used, from satins to taffetas, wispy voiles and delicate laces, all with intricate designs woven into the cloth.

I spent a long time at the Porcelain Museum inspecting the glassware and dinner services, where fine examples of Meissen and Sevres that the Medici had used were on display. I

171 The Schönbrunn Palace in Vienna was the home of the Hapsburgs. Its present form reflects the remodelling done during the 1740–50s in the reign of Maria Theresa.

172 Versailles, built in 1623, was remodelled and became the de facto capital for King Louis XIV.

173 Peterhof Palace built during 1747–1756 by Peter the Great. Peterhof was modelled on and subsequently surpassed the splendour of Versailles.

particularly admired a Meissen setting with an olive green and gold border enclosing a central hand-painted still-life. Sevres, on the other hand, is often more ornate and tends to incorporate a lot of gold embellishment. There was one exception—a pristine white service with a wide navy and gold border. It took my imagination straight to the long table it must have graced during fabulous state dinners and celebrations.

On the ground floor, the Silver Museum held other contemplative groupings. There were the usual household flatware and silverware, which I didn't spend much time examining. However, the stylish jewellery, elaborately decorated caskets, enamelled snuff boxes and cigar cases had me mesmerised. As well there was an exhibit of *objets d'art* featuring rock crystal, amber and ivory.

Of all these museums, the Palatine Gallery with countless treasures displayed across the 28 royal apartments is the most famous. The rooms don't follow a chronological order, they suggest more decorative intentions. Over 500 masterpieces, examples from the greatest artists of every epoch, were acquired by successive generations of the family. The Palatine collection is an irrevocable statement of the Medici's wealth. I'm glad I allowed plenty of time to wander around this not-to-be-missed museum.

The rooms themselves were grandiose, both in size and decoration, with frescoed ceilings, sparkling chandeliers, rich wallpapers and even inlaid parquetry floors. These rooms were mere vessels built to host magnificent French tapestries, rococo furniture and ancient sculptures. They stand sentinel to the gawking stares of visitors, who seem only to care for the paintings on the walls.

My attention was drawn to a 15th-century painting by Filippo Lippi of the Holy Family with St John and St Margaret.

The round shape of the artwork amongst rectangular works was what first attracted me. It was painted in tempera on wood, rather than canvas. Architectural motifs in the background indicate the artist's ability to portray perspective.

The 16th century masterpieces here included the largest assembly in the world of Raphael's work. His *Madonna del Granduca* is a gentle yet formal rendition of the Holy Theotokos, veiled and dressed in red and navy. Her expression is serene and majestic as she gazes at her Baby, whereas with the *Madonna della Seggiola,* Raphael created a more casual family portrait with the Madonna cradling Baby Jesus just as you'd see any loving mother and child. I couldn't stop admiring her unusual headgear—a fine sage and cream fabric, wound round her head in turban style, with its ends hanging loose. Standing apart, a young St John observes the group.

From the humility of the Blessed Virgin and Holy Family, I saw Titian's contemporary portrait of the proud and handsome Isabella d'Este, regaled in a sumptuous navy blue and gold dress. Her wealth and status are evident, as is her beauty. I recalled seeing her palatial property on Lake Como during my recent group tour. These two portraits were beautiful, albeit worlds apart.[174] I thought they needed to be hung more distant from each other.

I was captivated by Veronese's 1560s *Portrait of A Young Man Wearing a Lynx Fur*. This particularly handsome man, possibly of Moorish descent, sported a trimmed beard and short, dark hair. He stared back at me, his stance self-assured, even arrogant. The lynx was a trophy. I'd say the archaeological features in the background suggest the man was well-travelled.

174 Matthew 19:24: 'It is easier for a camel to go through the eye of a needle than for a rich man to enter the kingdom of God.'

The 17th-century painting of the Holy Family with St John and his mother, St Elizabeth, characterises a Rubenesque vision of the Madonna. In the foreground, a wicker cradle seemed an unusual addition to the scene. I overheard someone near me say it was typical of Flemish art of the time. Next, I came upon another Rubens painting, *The Four Philosophers*, which I remembered liking from school days. Four men seated around a table with Peter Paul Rubens himself at the far left and next to him, his brother Philip, who died later that same year. In the background, looking down on the group was a bust of Seneca.[175] What I prized most about the painting was the beautiful red Persian rug used to cover the table.

Exhibitions the world over always lead viewers through a maze of counters displaying a myriad of souvenirs for sale before the visitor is allowed to exit. As expected, this museum's shop area was strewn with appealing mementos. I'm not averse to this practice, as the souvenirs are usually of superior quality. I picked up a couple of postcards and was ready to pay when I caught sight of some pretty enamelled drop earrings in a locked cabinet that sat at eye level on the counter.

The assistant looked bored. I asked him if I could take a closer look. He unlocked the stand and gave them to me. I held one up to my ear, trying to catch my reflection. He assumed a mummified stance and gazed over my head as if expecting someone. I asked him for a mirror. He reluctantly found one. The earrings were gorgeous, and I hoped to negotiate a better price from the €98 ticket but the shopkeeper became distracted by a young lady who'd appeared at the counter. I waited with my purse in hand but the two of them ignored me. Judging by

175 Lucius Seneca was a Roman Stoic philosopher, statesman and dramatist from the post-Augustan age of Latin literature.

her coy smile and batting eyelashes, they were in an animated discussion meant only for two. I returned the earrings by placing them on the counter in front of him and without a word walked away.

There was a little supermarket across the road. I bought a sandwich, a beer and fruit for lunch. I wanted to buy a packet of nuts but didn't know the Italian word. Remembering my failed attempts at communication in the chemist shop in Rome, I felt it best to look up the word for nuts on my iPhone. The young fellow at the checkout watched on, smiling. I thought he was impressed, but when he showed me his Samsung, I understood he thought his phone was better than mine.

We chatted a bit. He was surprised I'd been travelling around Italy for so long and suggested I should consider staying. How I'd love to. I have a friend who, in the 1960s, did exactly that. She fell in love and stayed for a several years, returning to Sydney when the relationship ended. But of course, at my age, it's all too late.

My plan was to see the Medici Capella, but I couldn't find the place. So I decided to visit the enigmatic *duomo* complex. The distinctive dome of the Cathedral of Santa Maria del Fiore rises above the skyline, making the cathedral the city's most iconic landmark. Created by goldsmith and architect Filippo Brunelleschi in the 15th century, the vast cupola comprises both an inner and an outer shell. Engineers believe it is the structure's precise herringbone brickwork that cleverly takes the load. Built without flying buttresses or scaffolding, the architectural marvel has left architects and historians puzzling over its construction.

Architect Massimo Ricci dedicated much of his life to the quandary of the cupola's creation and may well have uncovered the answer. By carefully mapping the dome and building scale models to evaluate his theories, Ricci arrived at the most likely explanation. According to his calculations, a complex system of chains, hooks and ropes allowed the careful construction of the breathtaking octagonal space.

Outside it had started to drizzle. I headed to the leather market. Stalls were shielded with patio umbrellas. They were colourful and added to the ambience. I bought a large handbag that I planned to fill with my bits and pieces to carry aboard the plane. As the rain became heavier, I ducked into a chemist for a few toiletries. Having used all my cash, I had none to purchase a cheap umbrella along the sidewalk. Dodging the rain as best I could, I made my way back to the hotel and arrived wet through.

After a hot shower, dry clothes and a little rest, I asked Leonardo where I could get a meal. He advised me to try the Antica Trattoria da Tito. 'It's only a short walk from here,' he said. 'They've been in business a long time, since 1913.'

I knew I'd come to the right place when I read the sign scrawled on the door. *We don't sell well-done meat here.* However, I was early and the doors were closed, so I roamed around the block for 10 minutes, waiting for them to open.

When I returned, there was one table not yet booked for the first sitting. The interior of the restaurant resembled a small but cosy cave where the tables were covered in the ubiquitous red checked cloths with a starched white topper. Mismatched chairs were in accord with the white-washed walls covered in scrawled compliments from the clientele. This eclecticism added to the atmosphere. A younger couple at the table next to mine grappled with the menu. They spoke Russian. I offered to help them order and ended up sitting with them.

They were in their mid-forties and already grandparents. Sergei said they didn't travel very often, only twice per year. Since the lifting of the Iron Curtain, people were free to travel anywhere they chose. France, Egypt, Greece, Turkey, the Greek Islands and all around the Mediterranean were popular destinations for the well-heeled and adventurous Russians.

The menu was concise, making it hard to decide between *Osso Bucco alla Florentine* and the steak, which was the trattoria's signature fare. I ordered a grilled sirloin of milk veal. Olga settled for sirloin of beef with braised artichokes and Sergei ordered eye fillet.

For starters, we shared a platter of marinated anchovy bruschetta and *Crostone,* which was served with blue cheese and a chestnut-flavoured jelly. This complimented the robust red wine Sergei had ordered. The main meal arrived with a side of roast potatoes and a mixed green salad. This was the best food I'd eaten anywhere.

I told them that many Russians had migrated to Australia since *perestroika,* especially those working in IT, whose expertise was in demand.

Olga smiled. 'Yes, economic migrants.'

'But now our country is experiencing a Renaissance,' said Sergei proudly. 'There is much rebuilding and refurbishment going on. Not to mention the enormous change from state to private ownership. That's why we choose to stay put.' He raised his glass for a toast. 'To our unexpected meeting. We hope you will visit us.'

'Not just hope,' said Olga. 'We insist. You must visit. We have plenty of room and can show you around.'

I said I'd noticed a great deal of change in Russia between my first trip in 1993 and the last in 2007. 'Change takes time. When we consider the implementation of new systems, policies, standards, and particularly the culture of self-determination, one must understand this doesn't happen overnight.'

'We expected it to happen sooner. Some people think the delay is too long and doubt change will ever happen,' said Sergei. 'We're losing young, talented people. They emigrate.'

'New saddle, but same donkey,' quipped Olga.

'That is a tragedy,' I said. 'It took the West a long time to achieve what we have today and you expect to achieve the same in 20 years?'

The waiter arrived with the bill and surprised us with complimentary Limoncellos. What a fine end to an unexpectedly pleasant evening. Sergei wouldn't allow me to pay for my share—it was on them. We exchanged email addresses before parting company.

Indeed, we wrote to each other for some time, but gradually, the emails were further apart in time until they ceased altogether.

Chapter 20

All Good Things Must End

Humidity set in, exactly as it had when I'd been in Florence the previous week, and I wondered if more rain would follow. My plan was to spend the morning nearer my *pension* in the area around the main railway station until the time to join my day tour to Pisa.

I eagerly awaited seeing not only the fantastic array of Romanesque, Medieval and Early Renaissance art and architecture but also the iconic leaning tower. If time permitted, exploration of the *Camposanto Monumentale di Pisa* cemetery, dating back to the 12th century.

Before the tour commenced, I used the morning to visit the 12th-century church of Santa Maria Novella. Its link to the Dominican order is in the same manner as Santa Croce is linked to the Franciscans.

Architect Leon Battista Alberti remodelled this Romanesque building in the 15th century by adding a Gothic interior. He went on to transform the ancient external brickwork using the latest two-toned marble façade in the distinctive style of Santa Croce and the *duomo*. Somehow, he managed to maintain absolute harmony between these two disparate styles.

The first thing I noticed was the smoothness of the columns, which form an arcade on either side of the nave. At the same time, they function as support piers for the striped voussoirs[176] and the cross vaults in the high ceiling. The columns are purposely closer to each other at the altar end, to give the illusion of a much longer centre aisle. This is an architectural example of experimentation with the principles of perspective. The frescoed walls feature buildings and columns in the background to give the illusion of a three-dimensional scene.

The chancel contains a series of famous frescoes representing the life of the Blessed Virgin Mary. Another series is dedicated to the life of John the Baptist. Both were painted by Domenico Ghirlandaio, whose apprentice and assistant was the young Michelangelo. As can be expected, the scenes contain portraits of several members of important Florentine families who had commissioned the work.

The roundels within the vaults have icons of the four Evangelists. Paintings on the rear wall show Saint Dominic burning heretical books. Nearby were Saint Peter's Martyrdom, the Annunciation, and Saint John as a desert-dweller.

I made time to stop for lunch. A kiosk catering to the lunchtime workers was doing a steady trade; a sure sign of quality and freshness. A stack of paninis with crunchy-looking crusts and an abundant choice of fillings burgeoning from them—salami, ham or cheese with pieces of marinated artichoke on a layer of rocket turned out to be quite delicious. Takeaway coffee and a bottle of water for the journey readied me for the Pisa tour. Of course, we were behind schedule and I worried we'd be rushed around the site. I wondered if I'd made a mistake by not booking for a full-day tour.

Pisa is only an hour away from Florence. Most of the group slept peacefully as we traversed the rolling hills of Tuscany. Our tour leader was a young fellow called Lorenzo. *I wonder if he's a student,* I mused. He alerted us as we approached Pisa. An excited buzz rose in the coach as we caught our first glimpses of the white limestone and marble tower. There are few structures more instantly recognisable. As expected, it was off-kilter.

Other Romanesque buildings came into view. We passed a statue lying on the grassy verge of the *Campo dei Miracoli.* It reminded me of the Icarus statue I'd admired in Palermo's archaeological park.

The compound, one of the world's most recognised ecclesiastical landscapes, was like a green canvas on which the baptistry, *duomo* and leaning tower complex were positioned. These UNESCO heritage buildings looked strangely contrived, as if they'd been picked up from other locations and plopped onto this allotment. The lack of trees and gardens—those simple elements of nature—was what bothered me the most.

Lorenzo led us straight to the tower, where a steady stream of people were lining up for photographs. Other people were wandering aimlessly around the complex. A conspicuous young lady holding an orange-coloured umbrella waved at Lorenzo. She was the local guide, Antonella, who was assigned to show us around the site.

'In front of us is the famous eight-storey, 60-metre-high tower, which was originally built as the *campanile* or bell tower for the seven bells belonging to the *duomo* cathedral.'

'The way that the creamy marble colonnades and arches around the tower's girth are stacked give it the appearance of a very tall wedding cake,' commented someone behind me.

Antonella agreed. She said, 'Tiers of fine columns interspersed with rounded arches and marble arcading seem to wrap around the empty central core. They certainly give that appearance.' Muffled laughter wafted from the group.

I asked Antonella what had caused the tower to lean. The man next to me interrupted, 'Was it the recurring earthquakes?'

'The design and engineering of the tower were inappropriate for the mushy clay site selected for the project,' she replied. 'Construction of the bell tower began in 1153. By 1178, it had already started to lean and continues to do so, despite many interventions.'

'How does this impact on the other buildings in this vicinity?'

'The tower is leaning but the cathedral and baptistry are sinking into the clay,' Antonella replied. 'According to engineers from the University of Bristol, the secret lies in the ground. The soft foundation soil is what causes the tower's tilt though it is also responsible for protecting the tower from earthquakes. The tower's height, combined with the stiffness of the marble and the soft soil, ensures vibrations are absorbed. This is what has allowed the historic phenomena to remain standing for all this time.'

Someone else asked if they could climb the tower.

'Yes, you can climb the cavernous stone structure via a steep spiral staircase. There are 296 steps to the top. The steps are often slippery, heavily eroded and irregular. You will need to be very fit and have more time than we have today to complete the climb. It's worth coming back to do it because the view from the top is spectacular.'

A deep low-pitched voice from the edge of the group commanded Antonella's attention. A mature man dressed in a tweed jacket asked if Allied bombing during World War II had had much effect on Pisa.

Antonella said 48% of Pisa had been destroyed by the bombing, after which many churches and their precious frescoes suffered during the subsequent artillery attacks. 'Fortunately, the 10-degree tilt of the *campanile* was spared.' She turned and motioned us to follow.

We ambled away from the tower towards the large church called the *Duomo di Pisa*. This was the first building constructed on the site. On the way, we passed by an elongated cloister enclosing the cemetery. Local legend tells us that during the crusades, soil was brought there from Golgotha to enable leading Pisan families to rest on holy ground. I loved walking around cemeteries and reading all the plaques; they filled the gaps left in history. Sadly, there was no time for that sort of thing on a tour.

The *duomo* dedicated to *Santa Maria Assunta* reminded me of those churches I'd seen in Florence. The exquisite marble used on the exterior and Islamic-styled arches with such fine piercings and reliefs bore a resemblance to embroidery. In the 17th century, Florentine artists constructed the bronze doors to replace those damaged in the fire of 1595.

Our guide told us the interior had been extensively restored after the fire, which damaged the roof, floor and walls with all the artworks of the church. Restoration conserved the Moorish influences, particularly the striped columns along the side aisles. These fine columns were brought from Sardinia. Byzantine mosaics including Cimabue's *Christ in Majesty* dominate the golden ceiling. One of the most famous pieces here is Giovanni Pisano's marble pulpit.

Our guide told us that the movement of the cathedral's chandelier inspired a 19-year-old Galileo to develop his theory of isochronism of small oscillations. Another snippet of legend that intrigued me was Galileo's penchant for climbing to the top of the bell tower to conduct his experiments regarding the velocity of falling objects.

We followed Antonella to a conical-shaped building called the Baptistery of St John. It is Italy's largest baptistery. The exterior is covered in delicate bas-reliefs so ornate the building looked to be dripping in lace. Four creamy marble colonnades with blind arcades and the bronze doors are similarly covered. The focal point indoors is the full immersion baptismal font.

'Galileo Galilei[177] was born in Pisa and was baptised in this font,' said Antonella. 'The acoustics beneath the 75-metre cupola are so perfect that it must be either a remarkable coincidence or the work of genius.'

'Is the baptistery used for any concerts or performances?' asked a lady in dark sunglasses whom I'd not noticed before. I decided she was an interloper.

'It has been used occasionally for concerts, but for a small tip, the guards will usually sing to demonstrate the reverberating sounds.'

Right on cue, a family ahead of us requested a demonstration. The acoustics were stunning. Although only one man performed, it sounded more like a duet. New notes harmonised with the previous still reverberating remnants of the last.

'The key to these remarkable acoustics,' said Antonella, 'is the lack of soft material to absorb the sound. Consequently, notes rattle around the space for a long time—some say for over 12 seconds—before the sound dies away and becomes inaudible.'

We stood, mouths gaping, trying to understand the science behind the engineering feat. The gentleman in the tweed jacket said, 'The building could be called an extraordinary musical instrument.'

We returned in the early evening. I had a short stroll to get back to my *pension*. Along the way, I heard water from a fountain

177 He referred to himself simply by his given name, Galileo. He became an astronomer, scientist and mathematician. Albert Einstein called him the father of modern science. Later, Stephen Hawkins said Galileo contributed more to the birth of modern science than anyone else.

set in a leafy patch at the entry of the Atheneum Hotel. On the wall by the entrance, a menu for their *Ristorante Riflessi* caught my eye. The food was more varied than I'd seen all month and the prices were reasonable, but best of all, it was next to my *pension*.

The waiter led me through to a leafy courtyard set around another water feature festooned with tiny lights. There was a party atmosphere, but I was the only patron since diners still considered it a little too early. I ordered ricotta and spinach quenelles. They were served on a bed of chopped and heated tomato garnished with fragrant basil leaves. These little dumplings were the shape of gnocchi but not as dense and were light and tasty; ideal as a first course.

As guests began to arrive, so did my main course. It was Friday; grilled swordfish sounded nice. It arrived with a lettuce, avocado and tomato garnish, decorated with juicy black olives and plump capers. Toasty golden potato balls and chopped spinach were served in a separate dish. Florence and spinach are inseparable. The house white was a local pinot grigio. The waiter advised it to be perfect with the fish. He wasn't wrong. The wine was crisp, not too acidy, mildly fruity but not sweet, and a very pale colour. It had not been aged in oak.

With the chatter of other diners, I felt less alone. After my delicious repast, I felt mellow and took the time to sit reflecting on the variety and richness of the many things I'd experienced during the past month in Italy. My diligent waiter approached with the dessert menu. I held it in guilt-ridden fashion. '*Mia colpo*,' I said with a shudder. '*Solo tè*.' Just tea.

He gave me an amused smile. I thought it an appropriate comment and hoped this was all that I had said. He reluctantly took the unopened menu from me and said, 'Senora, *cannoli unico*.' So your tea is not lonely.

How could I resist him? 'OK. But only if it's a small one with Assam tea and a little cold milk on the side.'

His demeanour brightened. 'You want vanilla or chocolate cannoli?'

I chose vanilla. What a delightful evening. I left a good tip for the attentive waiter. He'd done his best to compensate me for my lack of dinner companion.

My last 24 hours in Florence began leisurely. I stepped outside to inhale the cool morning air and feel the embrace of the historic buildings surrounding me. I tried to commit to memory my last sights and sounds of this iconic city of art and history.

I retraced my route to the Church of the Nativity to take more photos of the building, so different from other architecture in Florence. This district was originally considered to be on the outskirts of the city and served as stables and barracks. The Medici menagerie of lions, elephants and giraffes was once situated somewhere in this vicinity.

Then I happened upon a nice little park with benches under trees, near walkways and garden beds. It was pleasant watching the birds squabble over crumbs as I ate the fruit I'd taken from the breakfast buffet for my lunch. I knew of nothing exceptional to see there; it was a random place to stop. Across the road stood a modest little church. I noticed people popping in for short visits and I thought I'd investigate.

The architecture of *Chiesa San Marco* and its adjoining convent was quite humble. But when I looked more closely, I could appreciate the Baroque architecture even though the embellishments were restrained.

After taking a few photos, I entered the church. Though thoroughly 'churched out', I was pleasantly surprised to find a collection of frescoes by Fra Angelico, including the *Annunciation*, which I remembered from art classes at school. Here, the Angel Gabriel converses with the Blessed Virgin Mary. The colours selected are soft pastels, muted to convey a gentleness to the scene. I thought Fra Angelico had used this palette to soften the astonishing news brought by the Archangel Gabriel. The scene is set in a cloister and demonstrates the artist's ability to portray perspective.

Not stopping for a last cup of coffee, I collected my luggage and said my goodbyes to Ricardo and Leonardo, then made my way to the airport for my flight to Spain.

Chapter 21
Madrid España

The flight to Madrid was delayed due to a bad storm in Marseilles. Herded into a lounge far from any cafés or shops, we waited and waited for departure. If they'd passed around a bag of lollies, it might not have been quite so bad. I thought of the coffee I'd missed at the *pension* but consoled myself with thoughts of the refreshments we'd receive on the plane.

The airline was Vueling; a cheaper carrier. I'd not heard of them before and didn't know you had to pay even for a cup of stewed coffee. My purse was in the overhead locker and I couldn't be bothered getting up to pay for the undrinkable.

The torture was short-lived. I landed in Madrid and made my way straight to the hotel. Dinner was being served and I was famished. I didn't freshen up, electing to go straight to the dining room. The waiter at the door asked for my room number before I was seated. There were few other people dining. I wondered if they were booked on my tour.

The set menu must have been waiting for our arrival. Though served quite quickly, it was lukewarm. The waiter plonked it unceremoniously in front of me then returned with a glass of house red. I checked the name of the hotel on the menu card. No, this wasn't Fawlty Towers but it sure felt like it. I ate and when I was gathering up my things to leave, I overheard the couple at the next table, who'd arrived before me, complain that they were still waiting for their first course.

Back in my room, I found a blonde lady of similar age to me unpacking. I'd known I would be sharing a room for this part of the tour. Her name was Barbara, and we would be sharing accommodation during the tour. Our interests were similar: art, architecture, history and Spanish music. Both of us were newly retired and enjoyed mixing individual travel with group tours.

Softly spoken, Barbara told me she'd arrived earlier and had spent the day exploring the city. I was surprised when she said there'd been a big protest rally. She was not sure if the rally was for the ongoing Catalonian issue or the recent immigration crisis, which had swelled the population five-fold. Mostly unskilled, these young men now accounted for nine percent of Spain's population.

My feet went cold as I listened to her. I didn't feel fear, just a mild uneasiness, and hoped the disquiet would not impact my long-awaited but short stay. She noticed me go quiet, which is something I tend to do when my plans are under threat of change.

'True to form, rallies are often timed to coincide with a general election,' she added, matter-of-factly.

'Is there an election?' I asked.

'Yes, Spain is due to go to the polls in about a week.'

Next morning at breakfast, we met our tour leader, Beatriz. I don't know why all our guides were so young. *They look younger because of their smooth skin protected from the sun that we in Australia tend to worship.* With long dark hair and no makeup, Beatriz was a natural beauty. Though her clothes were uninspiring, they were functional, suitable for work. When she said her name, it sounded more like '*bare-tres*'.

'Please be careful,' she said in a cheerful but serious tone. I detected what I thought was a Mediterranean accent. 'After our city orientation tour this morning, we will drop you off in town. We must warn you, though, there have been protests, even riots, and the police were firing rubber bullets at both left- and right-wing protesters.' Beatriz spoke in Spanish to the group from the Philippines. 'So keep away from all large gatherings.'

The first stop was *Las Ventas*, at the Plaza de Toros, home to the largest bullfighting ring in Spain. The stadium, a Moorish-style building, was also used for large concerts like Kylie Minogue and Coldplay, going back to Diana Ross and in the 1960s, the Beatles.

It made me think of the Colosseum, where animals tore humans apart. In this bullring, humans taunted and killed the bulls slowly with their swords. I abhor all cruel, blood-letting enterprises. I don't know why it is called a 'sport' because there's nothing sporting about it—a sad pastime and I was glad we didn't go inside. However, I wouldn't have turned down meeting some of the bullfighters rigged out in their figure-hugging outfits. I said as much to Barbara and the lady standing next to her, who was rolling a cigarette. Her name was Delia and she was a Queenslander like Barbara. They sat together in the seat behind me on the bus.

We drove around the beautifully clean city with its fine Baroque architecture, fountains and huge green parks. I was impressed with all I saw until we arrived at the Cervantes monument where revellers from the previous night had defaced the iconic statue of Don Quixote with graffiti during their drunken escapades. Further along was the Royal Palace, also surrounded by immaculately tended floral arrangements. A mounted regiment filed by and I caught the eye of a very handsome man on his Chestnut Bay with its plaited black tail—the horse, not the man!

Back at the hotel, Barbara joined a small group heading to Toledo, while I returned to our room to eat my fruit and do a quick bit of laundry. Barbara was not expected to be back until later in the evening and my plan was to spend the rest of the day at the Prado Museum.

The mild sunny day was perfect for my short walk from the hotel to the museum in the centre of the city. Families dressed in their Sunday-best pushed prams and piggy-backed youngsters as they took advantage of the mild weather to stroll through the city parks and to visit the botanical gardens that surrounded the Prado. After the gloomy cautions we'd received from Beatriz to stay out of the city, I was impressed to see another side of Spanish culture. The happy family groups lifted my spirits as I anticipated my afternoon of art.

I knew the museum's reputation was world renowned, but I didn't appreciate how large the place was until I arrived. I hoped I'd left enough time to see most of the art on display. The gallery, officially known as *Museo Nacional del Prado,* was built in the Neoclassical style. A huge, paved forecourt with decorative lampposts and a bronze statue of the artist Francisco de Goya faced the crowds, who ascended the left or right staircases to the entry.

It's widely considered to house one of the world's finest collections of European art, dating from the 12th to the early 20th centuries. Initially based on the substantial former Spanish royal acquisitions, 120 rooms are now filled with artworks. The museum is reputed to house the single best compilation of Spanish art.

The interior of the gallery was modern, spacious and well-lit. I picked up a brochure with mapped routes recommended for a one, two or three-hour duration and bought my ticket together with an audio device from the desk. There were remarkably few tourists. I imagined most had visited the gallery in the morning and had now left for lunch. The brochure described the venue as a monumental urban space and although I'd just arrived, I knew this description would be correct.

I decided to try the three-hour tour. The most famous and controversial painting owned by the Prado is *La Gioconda del Prado,* a painting from the workshop of Leonardo da Vinci. It portrays the same subject and composition as Leonardo's better-known *Mona Lisa,* which is housed at the Louvre, in Paris. The Prado Mona Lisa has been in the Madrid collection since 1819.

Following the museums refurbishment in 2012, the Prado's painting was deemed to be the earliest known studio copy of Leonardo's masterpiece. Scholars suggest the likelihood of a favoured student of Leonardo to have painted simultaneously with da Vinci in the same studio when the master created his own Mona Lisa. Until the restorers completed their work on the painting, no landscape was evident in the background. This feature was hidden under a layer of dark paint and only found after restoration.

The wide use of chiaroscuro in that era resulted in an unintended uniformity of style to the exhibition. This was especially evident in the portraits selected. I believe this method may be attributed to the influence of Caravaggio.

Diego Velasquez was a master of light and shadow. One of his most recognised works, *Las Meninas,* painted in 1656, is a wonderful example. Here, the royal family appears in light clothing against the dark background of the room. Velasquez employed an optical illusion with this work, to cause the viewer to imagine they are being drawn into the painting. The father of Mannerism, Edouard Manet, said that the Velasquez room alone was worth the trip to the Prado.

Velasquez employs chiaroscuro in the *Adoration of the Magi* and in his many portraits, but less so in his equestrian-themed scenes. There were so many astonishing paintings I'd have liked to examine at length were it not for my limited time. One I did scrutinise was *Christ Crucified*, painted in 1632. It shows the use of four nails.[178] Velázquez followed the accepted iconography of the 17th century, as did his teacher, Francisco Pacheco.

Goya's Christ is shown on the cross over a black background that resembles a void. Again, we see the use of four nails. A trilingual inscription in Greek, Latin and Hebrew at the top of the cross, declares—*This is Jesus, king of the Jews*.[179]

By complying with the status quo, Goya diminished the emphasis on blood and gore to concentrate on the painting's soft modelling. Created with loose and vibrant brushwork, Christ's head is lifted and leaning to the left, dramatically

---

178 A nail in each foot was first seen in the 5th century wooden doors of Santa Sabina in Rome. The same depiction is seen in the Syriac Gospel book. In 381 Egeria, a nun from Spain, documented St Helena finding the True Cross and four nails in Jerusalem. One nail was lost during her return trip home. The Great Schism between East and West happened in 1054. However, in 1303 Giotto continued to paint the crucifixion with four nails as seen in Scrovegni Chapel, Padua. Various other artists including Velasquez in 1632 and Goya in 1780 also used four nails, but in 1596 El Greco depicted three nails.

179 Matthew 27:37, Mark 15:26, Luke 23:38 and John 19:19–20.

looking upwards, in representation of a gesture of ecstasy, as he said, 'My God, My God, why have You forsaken Me?'[180]

Of the 160 Goya artworks held by the Prado, two have caused much controversy. They are the *Naked Maja* and *The Third of May*. The nude work was painted in 1805. The figure's eyes stare straight at the viewer. They reflect an attitude of powerful confidence. I view this painting as the initial rumblings towards women standing up for their rights.

The subject of his other painting was of an event that took place on the second and third of May 1808, when the citizens of Madrid revolted against the French invaders. On the following day, however, they received barbarous retribution.

On the left of the painting, a group of unarmed civilians kneel in a pool of blood amongst dead bodies. They are backed against a mound and face a firing squad. Members of the squad aim while a group of spectators witness the event. The dark sky reflects the terror, while in the background, a sad building fades into the ominous gloom. The only illumination in the painting comes from a lantern at the feet of the soldiers. Initial observation arouses sympathy for the helpless men facing death—or are they facing justice?

Although from a different period, critics often draw comparisons between this painting and Picasso's *Guernica*. Both have connections to the horrors of war. Both illustrate events in Spain, and both are painted by Spanish artists.

After three hours of intensive viewing, my blood sugar was critically low and I was ready to collapse. Time to have a break.

180 Matthew 27:46, Mark 15:3.

I found a quiet table in the large cafeteria on the lower level. There were few patrons because it was well past the normal lunchtime. This suited me very well. Hot coffee and an open sandwich were enough to keep me going. There was so much more I wanted to see.

When refreshed, I embarked on the two-hour route. It began with lighter, brighter paintings. There were amazing works by Tintoretto, Botticelli and Rubens, where scenes were filled with flesh and gaiety, splashed in the foreground of rich, leafy-green meadows and parks. Ruben's voluptuous *Three Graces* shows skin so soft and inviting. It made me think of well-risen dough waiting to be kneaded. Of course, in Baroque art, figures were plus sized. Today, we'd say generous. As I compare body size and shape it appears that figures become slimmer as time goes by.

Portraits generally appear to revert to a preference for the use of chiaroscuro, as in Titian's portrait of a distinctive, bearded Charles V. He's dressed in the fashionable attire of the time. With him is a large grey dog, possibly a Weimaraner, a beautiful animal with big soulful eyes.

One of the most popular Baroque artists in Spain was Bartolome Murillo. He is best known for his religious paintings and realistic pictures of everyday life. His subjects were often groups of children playing, or flower sellers and other market vendors. His religious-themed paintings portrayed family scenes instead of suffering saints.

I stood for a few minutes looking at *The Virgin of The Rosary* and was especially taken by the mother's gentle gaze and her closeness to the child. I imagine the models were a mother and her own child. She was dressed in a cherry red tunic with a bright blue mantle and a soft, translucent head cover, barely draped over her head. The child who is Jesus holds a rosary with a beaded cross. However, the cross is the symbol of the crucifixion of Jesus, an event yet to happen thirty years later. It was painted in Seville in 1640, just as the country was emerging from an outbreak of the plague. This was a time when devotion to the rosary was encouraged.

Although El Greco was Greek, he is still considered one of the most important Spanish artists. His elongated figures are distinctive and are a unique feature of his work. He was a couple of hundred years ahead of his time. Several impressionists briefly dabbled in the style before returning to what they were used to. The elongated figures were not in favour until the turn of the century, when an Italian artist, Amedeo Modigliani, embraced the style as his trademark. The work of both of those artists appeal to me.

The El Greco room housed the largest accumulation of his work I'd ever seen. Unlike other artists of the time, he altered his style to distinguish it from his contemporaries. Although he used dark colours, the focus was on his agile elongated figures and clever use of vibrant atmospheric light, which was a focal point of each painting. An example that I found most disquieting was called *Resurrection*. Painted in 1597, it depicted a group of figures in awkward angular poses with a bright white Christ hovering over them, while in the background, a frightening storm brews.

Of all his portraits, I particularly favoured one of a distinguished man with a ruffle collar whose intense stare was hard to avoid. He stands, hand on chest, exposing the white lace at his cuff, while his other hand rests on the hilt of his fine golden sword.

Along with portraits of dignitaries in fine attire, there were also many paintings of saints on their way to martyrdom. I was drawn to St Andrew dressed in an emerald-green garment holding his cross that resembled an x. St Francis was instantly recognisable in his hooded sackcloth. He was striding alongside St John the Evangelist, who holds a Gospel. In each scene an angry sky looms while ominous clouds rage overhead.

Overwhelmed, but satisfied, I left by the Velasquez gate.

In the evening, our group assembled for a night tour of the city, followed by a tapas supper. Barbara was meeting friends so Delia and I teamed up.

That evening, of the 12 gathered, most were Spanish speakers. Jose and Carmen were from Manilla. Jose was a short, wiry kind of guy, always on the move, whereas his wife Carmen was plump and motherly, looking after her friends, Carlos and Sofia, with whom they were holidaying. Carlos was a tall and contemplative fellow, but he spoke in a commanding tone. He reminded me of a giraffe. His big sad eyes looked down over the heads of his three friends. His stride was understandably long while his wife Sofia, who looked younger, scurried along, trying to keep pace with him.

The most popular tourist hangout in the city is the *Plaza Mayor*[181], and is the throbbing heart of Old Madrid. The square is lined with restaurants, cafés, cocktail bars and *jamon* outlets. These delights dealt with the belly, while street theatre and buskers provided entertainment for eyes and ears. The plaza served as a popular venue for Christmas and Easter parades and countless market stalls.

181 For centuries, the square has hosted countless important public events such as bull fights, beatifications, crowning ceremonies, trials and even public executions. The equestrian statue in the middle of the piazza is of the monarch, Philip III, under whose reign the area was first established in 1580.

Our minibus dropped us at the edge of the busy precinct to wander along the main boulevard or detour along narrow alleys, absorbing the night culture of Madrid. Beatriz kept the group together and we made our way straight to the *Museo de Jamon*.[182] It's not at all a museum, more like a deli but one where they only sell *jamon*, which is Spanish for ham. Every imaginable style of cured and smoked ham was on offer. What immediately struck me was the innumerable whole hams dangling from the ceiling. Display cases filled with an enormous array of artistically placed, paper-thin slices of pancetta, prosciutto, chorizo and salami enticed us. Even though our mouths were watering, there was little reason to buy anything since we knew we'd soon be enjoying a typical Spanish meal.

Our destination, a cosy tapas bar, was nearby. We had a reservation. The waiter led us to a long table close to the tapas bar. He handed out illustrated menus with concise descriptions of the food awaiting our choice. Cool jugs of tangy sangria arrived at our table and we had a drink while we scrutinised the menu.

This was our first social occasion as a group, so we started by introducing ourselves— our names, country and occupation. They clapped when I referred to myself as 'an independent woman'. I am not sure how they interpreted that statement, but what I meant was financially independent or retired—able to call my own shots.

The four friends from Manila stayed together at one end of the long table and the rest of us filed in to fill the remaining chairs. Couples were split up, making it necessary to communicate

182 The shop was made famous after it appeared in Pedro Almodóvar's 1997 film *Live Flesh*.

with people we didn't know. Delia and I sat opposite each other and could at least bounce our reactions off each other with body language. Next to her sat Luis and Adriana. They were from Argentina so had a different accent from the Filipinos. They appeared well-heeled and well-travelled and were comfortable with both languages.

Next to me sat their fellow Argentinian, Juan. He was a single, retired stockbroker and although he'd not met Luis and Adriana before, they had a lot in common. We got to talking about travel, as one does with fellow travellers. Juan had visited Madrid several times and been to the Prado. He said there were only three El Greco paintings at the National Museum in Buenos Aries but the Prado held the largest collection in the world. I think Juan's mother, who was Greek, may have inspired his admiration for El Greco.

The waiter reappeared and motioned for us to choose our food from the array of dishes on the buffet. Beatriz said they had several sittings and we should not delay.

The variety was enormous and included the *jamon* slices we'd seen earlier. I realised how easy it would be to overindulge. But each little dish was so inviting.

Delia, who looked to have the metabolism of a greyhound, had a healthy appetite. Amongst other dishes she chose *croquettes de patatas y jamon* – chopped ham encased in mashed potato, then breadcrumbed and lightly fried. Others in our group indulged in croquettes with a runny brie centre, cauliflower fritters, tortilla and eggplant. The men were drawn to the *empanadas,* which are little pastries stuffed with chicken or beef.

I tried the sweet potato wedges with hot chilli sauce, stuffed mushrooms, calamari rings and garlic prawns. The prawns brought back memories of the 1960s and '70s when we haunted tiny Spanish restaurants in the back alleys and basements of the city in Sydney and paid for the experience the next day, not just for the red wine, but also the garlic prawns.

Karolina was a very elegant lady from Prague. I estimated she'd be in her fifties, a bit taller than me but slender with long blonde hair that she wore plaited in a crown on the top of her head. It tended to give her extra height and make her look slenderer. She reminded me of another dear friend who had the same ability to move the food around on her plate in a clearly articulate fashion without ever overindulging. Beautiful manners, she ate like a little canary, while conversing with the single gentleman who was sitting next to her—Andreas, from Baden.[183] He was the part owner of a boutique-style wellness spa. A businessman, he looked polished and I thought an acceptable match for Karolina.

Cindy sat on the other side of Andreas. She was a young American lady of Asian or Polynesian descent. Her wavy long hair framed her face in a lionesque sort of way. She chatted to the Filipinos and seemed to understand Jose's jokes better than most of us.

The waiter came with dessert menus and an offer for tea or coffee. Amadeo and Angelina, who'd kept to themselves, were a young couple on their honeymoon. They lived somewhere in Puglia, near to Bari. They ordered *Imperial Técula Mécula*[184]—a special tart with a filling of almonds, lemon, butter, yolks and sugar. In Arabic the name means 'for you and for me'—a treat

183 Karlovy Vary is a famous spa outside of Prague and sister town to Baden. During the whimsical era of the *Belle Epoch*, curative spas were popular with artists, royalty and gentry. Tolstoy, Dostoevsky and Turgenev were all inspired to write of their visits to spa towns, including Baden. Beethoven, Chopin and Brahms, Marlene Dietrich and many other wealthy people came to relax and enjoy the casino and all that Baden and other spa towns had to offer.

184 Favourite dessert of Charles V. The sweet is a reminder of Spain's Moorish past.

for lovers to share. It arrived with a dollop of whipped cream, a sprinkle of Frangelico and two spoons.

'We enjoy something sweet in the evening,' Amadeo said and gave Angelina's hand a squeeze. She gave her husband a coy look and giggled.

I don't know how we managed to fit in dessert. Some ordered the *Crema Catalana*, which was like a *crème brûlée*. Others chose churros, a sort of pastry tube fried and rolled in cinnamon and sugar, like donuts but with lighter pastry, less dense.

We strolled back to the hotel, enjoying the lights, the buskers and the laughter of partying people. Barbara was already asleep when I arrived back so I crept silently into my bed and slept until morning.

Chapter 22
Barcelona

Soft chatter from my fellow travellers melded into a general low hum. This, together with the rocking motion of the coach, which seemed like a huge cradle, soon lulled me into the Land of Nod.

Three hours and 318 km later, I awoke in the ancient town of Zaragoza, which is the capital of Spain's north-eastern region of Aragon. Old Town in the centre of the city is home to two grand cathedrals: the iconic *Basilica de Nuestra Senora del Pilar,* on the banks of the Erbo River with its distinctive Moorish-style towers and domes, and the *Catedral del Salvador de Zaragoza* also known as *La Seo.*[185] We stopped long enough to visit these two churches and to grab something light for lunch.

Beatriz gave us a potted background. She said that in 24 BC, the Roman Emperor Caesar Augusta named the outpost Zaragoza. In AD 714, the Moors conquered the land. They ruled it for some 300 years. Their greatest legacy was the turreted *Aljaferia* Palace, which is now the parliament house. Notably, the venue was also used by Verdi as the setting for his opera *Il Trovatore*—the troubadour.

Crusaders arrived in 1118, bringing Christianity to the region. According to tradition, St James travelled to Spain in the 1st century to evangelise but had little success. Greatly discouraged, he sat on the banks of the river, weeping. He was at his lowest when the Blessed Virgin appeared to him. She stood on a pillar surrounded by angels. This vision brought him enormous consolation.

To commemorate this event, the crusaders converted the main mosque into a cathedral, the *Basilica de Nuestra Senora del Pilar*, known colloquially as Our Lady of the Pilar. The most treasured relic in the church is a small and simple statue of Our Lady, crowned with an intricate gold halo made to resemble the rays of the sun. Reputed to have taken 44 days to make, it is encrusted with triangular cut diamonds, emeralds, rubies, sapphires and water pearls. This, together with Goya's[186] frescoes lining the domes, is reason enough to visit this church.

To further mark the event, a fiesta is held, lasting nine days. The main day of the celebration is the 12 October. Coincidently, this date is also attributed to the first sighting of the Americas by Christopher Columbus. It is double the reason for celebration and is the biggest annual event. The festival is marked with parades, offerings of flowers, many open-air concerts and street theatre. Unfortunately, we were 11 days too early.

The architecture of *Catedral del Salvador de Zaragoza* or *La Seo* Cathedral is a combination of Baroque, Romanesque and intricate Mudéjar styles and is dedicated to The Saviour. It reflects the faith, history and art of Aragon. Originally, this was the site of a Roman forum, before becoming a mosque. After reconstruction, the old minaret became the church tower.

186 Goya was born in 1746 in a little village near Zaragoza.

The size of the interior of the church was overwhelming. The combination of artistic and architectural trends throughout its five naves are somehow seamlessly brought together. Even the high altar was more ornate than I'd seen anywhere else.

La Seo is the repository for an enormous collection of French and Flemish tapestries[187], which are the most important of their kind in the world. There were 11 huge tapestries on show, dating from the 14th to 17th centuries. These were displayed together with interesting metalwork, religious ornaments and reliquary busts.

Beatriz said tapestries were originally hung on the stone walls of castles to help keep the rooms warm[188], all the while portraying images that narrated stories. They were also an indisputable symbol of wealth and power. The main centres for manufacturing tapestries were Brussels and Bruges.

I was in awe of the size of the tapestries, which were woven in rich reds, deep blues, black, white, a skin colour and teal. The subjects of the work were important celebrations and historical events. The scenes were filled with people and horses going about their business in cities and parks, or events on sea-going vessels. Some folk were dressed in armour and brandished weaponry. The scenes portrayed a chronology not only of the subject matter but of the clothing and headwear too. The detail was enormous. I thought the tapestries were more beautiful than those I'd seen at the Vatican.

After our visit there was only enough time to buy coffee or hot chocolate. The Aussie trio, as the others called us, settled for

187 There are 63 tapestries dating from Medieval times and six pieces of heraldic embroidery in the collection.

188 As a teenager, I was intrigued by the Persian rugs on the walls of the family home of my first love. It may have been a habit brought to Australia from the northern climes.

the hot chocolate, which was so thick we had to use a spoon. I would have liked some free time to visit the Goya Museum. There was not enough time as we still had a long way to travel if we were to reach Barcelona before nightfall.

'Don't be disappointed,' consoled Beatriz. 'Although the Goya Museum is a lovely building, it has only14 of his paintings on show. Most of his work hangs in the Prado in Madrid.'

As we drove away from Zaragoza, we passed by a church dedicated to St Nicholas of Bari. *Even here the saint is revered,* I thought as I remembered my time in Bari. It seemed so long ago.

We passed by a forest of energy-producing turbines, their shiny rotor blades humming in the wind.

'These wind farms you see are covered in turbine generators,' said Beatriz. 'Spain is the world's fifth largest producer of wind power generated from renewable sources.'

'Do they also use solar power?' asked Barbara.

'Yes, but wind power is the major source. In Barcelona, Madrid, Cadiz and Zaragoza, renewable energy accounts for 100 percent of street lighting and public buildings.'

A laudable achievement, I thought, as a buzz of remarks drifted through the coach. I nodded off for the rest of the journey. When I awoke, we were on the outskirts of the port city of Barcelona.[189] It is the second largest city in Spain after Madrid.

Our hotel was most pleasant, the staff courteous and efficient. I'd left my carry-on case on the pavement and one of the staff diligently retrieved it, telling me to be careful of safety everywhere in the city, especially in the evening. After settling into our room, Barbara and I went down to meet the others for dinner.

189 Barcelona is the capital of the region known as Catalonia.

We were pleasantly surprised to find dinner was buffet style. There was plenty of variety: salads, vegetables, lentil dishes, spaghetti with meat sauce, soup, chicken and fish. I chose a fish dish with tiny onions. It came with sweet potato wedges and fresh asparagus, blanched but still crisp. We enjoyed the house red served in carafes for the table to share and later we were offered tea, coffee and cake or a vanilla mousse for dessert.

By then, we were getting to be more comfortable with each other and were comparing travel stories, both recent and past. Our Spanish-speaking quartet continued to stay in their little group. Although Jose did regale us with some jokes, they were likely to have sounded a lot funnier before translation. The young honeymooners disappeared straight after the meal while the others gravitated toward the lounge for drinks.

Delia ordered beer. The Argentinians insisted on a good cognac, while Barbara and I settled for Campari. I enjoy it more with tonic. Barbara preferred hers with soda. I noticed fancy cocktails arriving for the quartet, who sat at a low coffee table in the lounge area. Karolina and Andreas were drinking shots at the bar. After a while, we called it a night.

There was disarray at breakfast. Our group and others had arrived half an hour before the kitchen expected us. Consequently, they were in a tailspin. Many items were missing particularly hot foods, and we had to make do with what was there: juice, yoghurt, fruit, croissants and more *jamon*. Considering the amount of food we'd consumed the previous evening, it was sensible to have a lighter start to the day.

We started with a city tour. I was keen to do this because it helped me orientate during free time and the commentary gave me a sense of the history and culture of the place.

There were so many distinctive styles of architecture to see, particularly the Gaudi-inspired condominiums in the *La Pedrera* sector. Beatriz told us there was once a bullring, but it had closed in 1970 due to lack of patronage. Transformed in the years that followed, it became a large shopping mall.

We drove through the *Passeig de Gràcia*. This boulevard is likened to the *Champs Elysée* in Paris. The most exclusive and most expensive boutiques, hotels and restaurants are located there. This wide-open street with magnificent buildings on either side is home to the famous *La Predera*[190] and *Casa Mila* buildings, both created by Gaudi. The undulating lines of their rooftops, Juliette balconies in black wrought iron and intricately decorated window frames were pure fantasy. Some of the most outlandish of his architectural features were regarded as ground-breaking for their time. *Casa Mila* is particularly notable for the strange sculptures that sit like boulders on the rooftop. Seven of Gaudi's buildings, including these two, are UNESCO listed.

We skimmed past paved pedestrian squares and peered into treelined arcades, where people mingled with cyclists, free from the worry of traffic. Super-blocks of high-rise enclosed restful squares with fountains and benches invited people to pause. Cafés with outdoor seating did a brisk trade as their patrons gazed at passers-by. Every high-end brand of apparel was carried in the boutiques that lined the high streets.

---

190 Built 1906–1910, after which Gaudi devoted himself entirely to Familia Sagrada. A Gaudi museum and an apartment based here may be visited.

Developed in 1929 for the World Expo Exhibition, *España* Square is the main hub of the city. Wrought iron streetlights from the *Belle Epoch* punctuated footpaths amid manicured gardens, adding to the picture of elegance and unhurried pace. I wouldn't have thought it possible but what we saw was even more beautiful than Madrid.

The main attraction of the city was the still unfinished *Familia Sagrada* or Sacred Family Cathedral, with its eight spires piercing the skyline. The overall form was beyond description. At this time, visitors could only observe the construction of the unique edifice in progress. Sculptors dangled from spires while cranes and scaffolding littered the site. I was curious about the interior. Sadly, at that time there was no entry.

There was considerable symbolism attached to the extensive quantity of detail. To see it and understand it would take many more visits just for the exterior, let alone even going inside. The scant period our tour had allocated was less than a morsel. I felt as if I was a child looking into a baker's window at the mouth-watering array of cakes but never being allowed to go inside to taste one. At least we could tick the box to say we'd been there.

Antonio Gaudi, a Catalan architect, sculptor and metalsmith, was born in 1852. He was a leading figure of the Art Nouveau period also known in Spain as the *Modernismo Movement.*[191]. Gaudi was not the initial architect of this project but the second. Like our own Sydney Opera House, the artist who significantly altered and completed the work, Jørn Utzon, was the second architect, and similarly made alterations to the original plan.

Familia Sagrada was designed by Francisco de Paula del Villar as a grand neo-Gothic structure. A disagreement following a significant cost blow-out saw the project awarded

191 Modernism period was around 1880 until World War I.

in 1883 to the up-and-coming sculptor and architect, Antonio Gaudi. The church was nowhere near completion in 1926 when Gaudi died as a result of a tram accident. The work continues true to the detailed sketches left by the artist and it is hoped to be completed in 2026 for the centenary of Gaudi's death.[192] He is buried in the crypt.

While scanning the detailed decoration of the exterior, I noticed St Veronica holding a cloth with the imprint of Christ's face.[193] The name Veronica is made up of two Greek words—*vera* or faith and *icona* or image. I was puzzled when I noticed her face had no features, it remained blank. Was it to emphasise the miraculous face of Jesus transposed to the cloth? Or was it something else altogether, something to do with St Veronica. Had she lost face?

Amongst the myriad of vignettes, I saw a lovely nativity scene where dozens of animals and plant species were sculpted into the background as testament to Gaudi's immense love of nature. Everything else, although fantastic, melded into a jumbled blur.

Beatriz said there was a cryptogram around the Passion of Christ, where all the numbers add up to Christ's age when he was crucified.

---

192 A long time to build but not unique as Notre-Dame Cathedral in Paris, which took 182 years to complete building. It too is intricately embellished; however nothing is as ornate as *Familia Sagrada*.

193 This is also referred to as the icon or image of Christ, not made by human hands. Veronica was the woman who wiped Christ's face as He carried His Cross along the Via Dolorosa. The cloth was returned with the imprint of His face. This became the template for following depictions. That is how we know what He looked like. Regarding the Blessed Virgin Mary, St Luke is said to have painted her portrait, which is the template used for following depictions.

After driving along some equally beautiful streets, our tour ended at the Barcelona Cathedral[194], dedicated to the Holy Cross and St Eulalia—patron saint of Barcelona. It is intricately decorated in a lace cover of arabesques and floral motif reliefs. Animal gargoyles are staged strategically around the edge of the roof. From its Gothic cloister to its Baroque chapels, the exterior is an amalgam of architectural styles. The façade, remodelled in the 19th century, features twin towers and stained-glass windows.[195]

The size of Barcelona Cathedral is massive. However, after seeing *Sagrada Familia*, all things tend to pale in size and decoration. There are five aisles and 47 chapels. The nave is supported by soaring Gothic buttresses. It really deserves more time than we devoted to seeing it.

Outside, I noticed a sign indicating the date and program for the next choral and organ recital. These were held monthly on the last Saturday, yet another reason for a more extensive individual stay or a return trip.

Barbara, Delia and I stayed in the city to wander around and find something to eat. What I wanted was to buy a mantilla. Delia needed to buy a new memory card for her camera, whereas Barbara was tempted to buy a disposable camera.

In the labyrinth of alleyways, we found an intriguing shop, *Magatzems del Pilar*. Though dimly lit, we could see the old store fittings and hoped the staff could help in my quest.

The shopkeeper stood behind a big display cabinet. Upon closer inspection, we saw pretty fans, castanets and mantillas displayed. The image of a flamenco show flashed in my mind. I

194 It was built in 1298 on a 6th century Roman baptistry and later replaced by an 11th century Romanesque church.

195 It was completed in 2011.

was beside myself with delight, finding exactly what I'd hoped to buy. Though my Spanish was about non-existent, the lady behind the counter was most accommodating and with some sign language, we found a common tongue.

She retrieved lace mantillas in a variety of patterns from the bank of drawers behind her. When she began draping each veil over my head, I knew I was in experienced hands. With the aid of mirrors, she allowed me to inspect every angle to determine which one was most suitable. Without discussing the price, I bought one black and two whites, one for myself and the other for my dear friend Marina, who I'd soon be meeting.

I noticed a set of castanets in the glass cabinet—something I've always wanted to have as a souvenir. My kind sales assistant slipped them into my parcel and bade us farewell. I might have overpaid for the lace but I was delighted with my purchase of something that had illuded me for an exceptionally long time.

At last, a little kiosk caught our eye. We bought *panini fromage* and soft drink for our lunch. The shopkeeper gave us directions to the *Place Catalunya,* a sort of bus terminus where we would find the bus to Gaudi's whimsical park.

Many people boarded. People alighted at each stop. We stood alongside two youths. One looked intently at Barbara. I remembered in Egypt how the locals were attracted to a fellow tourist who had long blonde hair. I wondered if it was admiration or if our safety might be compromised. Barbara, a friendly soul, returned his interest with a smile. They started to chat. Still teenagers, the boys had fled worn-torn Libya. One was an amputee and the other had sustained head wounds when a mine exploded, causing him to lose one eye. We felt significant compassion for their plight as refugees and their ongoing hardships.

As we approached their stop, Barbara pulled out a gold coin—an Australian one dollar. She gave it to the youth, explaining that the picture of the kangaroo on the coin would remind him of our chance meeting from such a far-flung corner of the world.

The bus continued in a north-westerly direction. *Parc Güell,* located high above the city, was the end of the route. Upon alighting, our mouths gaped at the sight that greeted us. Even though my daughter had told me to expect an Art Nouveau extravaganza, nothing could have prepared me for what I beheld. Strange buildings, pagodas and random benches were covered in intricate mosaics. The scene reminded me of looking through a kaleidoscope where the colours and shapes danced in crazy patterns.

We followed a path under bridges and through shelters. These led to vantage points, where we paused to enjoy the stunning views across the city and on to the Mediterranean beyond. In the end we were so *Gaudied* out, we could no longer discern what we were seeing and knew the time had come to go home.

Chapter 23
Flamenco

Back at the hotel, there was no time to rest. I went quickly to the computer room to check my emails before joining the group.

Our evening entertainment was a *Flamenco Tablao* along the famous La Rambla boulevard. Beatriz told us that flamenco originated in the Moorish region of Andalusia in southern Spain. The flamenco culture emerged from the Roma Gypsies who migrated before the 14th century and are known as *Gitanos*.

The venue we selected was one of the most highly regarded in the area. It boasts of being a mecca for regional food and the iconic flamenco. We entered a cavernous hall, where the artists performed without microphones to produce a pure and unadulterated sound.

I sat next to an Indian man, Viraj, and his Japanese wife, Miko. They'd kept to themselves and I'd not previously spoken to them. They too were from Australia and lived near to the prep school that my godson attended. Viraj was a doctor and Miko worked at Macquarie University in the Japanese faculty.

Not long after we sat down, dishes of nibblies arrived, accompanied by carafes of Sangria. These were followed closely by *paella*, a traditional rice dish served on a large platter with mussels, chicken, prawns, octopus, fish and vegetables. The platter was made to be shared. We dug in. Soon after, *churros* with vanilla filling appeared for dessert. I thought the service was a bit fast but when the lights lit up the stage, I understood the meal was timed around the main event, which was the flamenco show.

On the stage, three men occupied well-spaced chairs. They strummed their guitars while scanning the room. In the background, others watched while clapping to the beat. I couldn't take my eyes off the Antonio Banderas look-alike.

Four ladies strode onto the stage, their dark hair identically parted in the middle and pulled back smoothly into a chignon, red flowers behind their ears. They stood decoratively at the sides of the stage, clapping to the beat.

One of the female dancers moved centre stage. She threw back her head to command attention and stamped her feet at an incredibly fast pace. Then she raised her hands high to punctuate the words of her song. At times, her singing was plaintive. She alternated these cries with a fuller, more passion-filled sound from deep within her diaphragm. Then, lifting her skirt to better demonstrate her fancy footwork, she flicked her flounces to encourage one of the men to join her in the dance. The others called out '*Ole*!' After his performance, he sashayed smugly back to the other men, while the girl removed the shawl from around her hips and twirled it around so quickly it became a fringed blur. The audience encouraged the performers with wolf-whistles, enthusiastic applause and shouts of '*Ole*!'

After the show, we wandered through the better-lit maze of narrow streets to get a sense of the place without necessarily entering the dangerous zones. Mostly, we stayed on the edges of La Rambla, one of the most colourful promenades in the city.

Beatriz cautioned us to hold our valuables close because the district is a known tourist trap and pick-pocketers' paradise.

'From the cross-streets you will plunge into a maze of dark and seedy alleyways that lead to the docks. That area is best avoided,' said Beatriz. 'Curious tourists and young backpackers tend to gravitate to this nerve centre, where some wild and risqué night spots ply their seedy trade.'

'It sounds like this area makes our own Kings Cross look like a kindergarten,' I said to Viraj, who responded with a throaty chortle, while Miko smiled demurely. After a while, most of us returned to the hotel but some stayed on to party.

Straight after an early breakfast, our group met in the foyer to embark on our trip high up in the mountains to visit Monserrat Monastery and the Benedictine Abbey.

Not only do tourists visit Montserrat[196] for its significant religious importance but for the natural beauty surrounding the monastery. We were the first tour bus to arrive at the abbey. This allowed us to park closer to the entrance, alongside several private cars. The clouds were so low and the view was further obscured by the early morning mist. Barbara remarked on the aura of peace and tranquillity she felt from being in so lofty a place.

The monastery is carved into the cliff face. Over the millennia, the escarpment had weathered into the most unusual rock formations seen anywhere in Catalonia. To me, it resembled hundreds of carved totem poles gathered in a scrum. The highest peak is St Jerome at 1236 metres above sea level. The 360° views

196 Founded in the 11th century and rebuilt between the 19th and 20th centuries, it continues to function as a monastery to this day. There are 100 monks and a 50-strong boys' choir.

were breathtaking. To one side the Pyrenees and to the other the Mediterranean. Although there is a walking trail, the funicular and the cable car provide an easier platform for viewing.

The area is popular with walking groups. Some tracks lead to the Holy Grotto, while others lead to quiet nooks decorated with memorial statues to writers, lyricists and monastics who were attached to the church. Remnants of chapels and hermitages destroyed during the Spanish and the Napoleonic wars remain alongside newer shrines. Shaded by oak and cedar trees, people strolled in contemplation while enjoying the amazing Catalonian countryside.

The basilica is the destination for people wishing to see the miracle-working statue of the Black Madonna and is a place of frequent pilgrimage by the Catalonians. A small museum attached to the complex is worth a visit not only for the religious items but also some unexpected masterpieces. Artworks by Catalan artists from the 19th and 20th centuries include Picasso, Miro, Dali and Braque as well as a few French masters. I noted a Monet, Rouault and Degas.

Beatriz told us of the fascinating history of Monserrat. In AD 880, a small group of shepherd children saw a bright light descending from the sky in the Montserrat mountains. At the same moment, they heard angelic singing. The music filled their hearts with radiant joy.

Overwhelmed and confused by what they'd experienced, the children told their parents, who went to investigate. For the whole month following the first visitation the parents also witnessed the visions and thought them a sign from God. When the local priest was brought to the scene, he too witnessed the miraculous sight.

The visions occurred in the same place in a cave on Montserrat mountain. When this cave was explored by the religious elders of the community, they found an image of the Virgin Mary in a creek bed. From that moment on, the cave became a holy sanctuary for religious pilgrims from all over the world.

A complete contrast, our next stop was at Torres Vineyard, where we enjoyed the most professionally organised winery tour, I'd seen anywhere. We climbed into miniature train carriages pulled by a copy of Thomas the Tank Engine. The driver even wore a train driver's cap and overalls.

The whole caboose trundled into the darkened warehouse along the pre-set rail line. Here we were held captive to view a 15-minute information video relating to winemaking. The following stops along the mechanised production line were complemented with the sounds and odours conducive to a winery. Coming from Australia where we have a world class wine industry and having made many trips to the Adelaide Hills, the Hunter and Margaret River, this performance became a little tedious.

Finally, we were invited in to taste either one red or one white wine of a brand chosen by the establishment. I was a bit gobsmacked. Compared with the generous wine tasting offered throughout our own industry, this seemed really mean. I did taste the red they had selected and found it to be drinkable. In fact, the wine was not only drinkable but it was exceptionally good. I bought a bottle and the second bottle I decided upon was a Californian pinot noir from Russian River in the Napa Valley. This wine was very expensive[197] but I'd heard the Napa Valley wines were up to the mark and I ear-marked it for the

197 €48, more than I'd pay for a wine back home, but this was special.

first dinner with my friend Marina in Paris. We planned to visit the Champagne region, where I was sure she'd insist on buying us a bottle of bubbly.

The afternoon was free. Barbara and Delia had shopping to do so we parted company. My plan was to see the Picasso Museum, home to the largest collection of his early work.

Philanthropist James Sabatés, who was Pablo Picasso's friend, bequeathed his own large assembly of the artist's work to the city of Barcelona. A venue to adequately display the acquisition was urgently required. As the 15th century palace, the *Palacio de Berenguer d'Aguilar*, situated in the Ribera district of Old Town, was vacant, it was acquired and opened as a museum in 1963.

Together with the Prado in Madrid and Picasso Museum in Paris, this Barcelona museum owns one of the largest collections[198] of Picasso's paintings. As the acquisitions expanded, five surrounding buildings on the *Carrer de Moncada* were bought. The way the buildings were positioned created a central courtyard. Exterior staircases provide easy access to the main floors of the various galleries.

I fell in love with Picasso's work during school art classes. Pablo spent his childhood in Malaga, where he was born in 1881, then went on to live and study in Madrid, Barcelona and Paris.

I was overwhelmed and excited with the plethora of artwork exhibited at the venue. Included were sculptures, drawings, posters, ceramics and lithographs. The paintings in this temple of art contained many of the rarely seen canvases from his formative years. This amassment of Picasso's creativity encompasses several paintings from later periods. Some works were originally held elsewhere in the city but the consensus was that the Picasso Museum was a more appropriate home.

The oldest painting was the 1896 *Portrait of Aunt Pepe,* where he used chiaroscuro, in all possibility due to being inspired by the work of Rembrandt. The other was his 1897 composition, *Science and Charity.*[199] In that painting, the doctor who tends his patient is a faithful rendition of his own father. In the background, a nun holds a child, suggesting Pablo was from a religious family. The composition reminded me of paintings by Johannes Vermeer. Picasso was influenced by many of his contemporaries until he found his own unique style.

The Rose Period[200], when he used pink and orange tones for circus performers and harlequins, was cheerful. After the death of a close friend, Pablo embarked on his Blue Period—a time of deep depression, when he was consumed with sombre blues and avoided contrast. I especially love his *Blue Nude,* painted in 1902 but unfortunately, it wasn't on show, it is privately held. There were several portraits, including one of Gertrude Stein. Another, *The Guitarist,* I'd call a study because I don't think the subject sat for it. I see it as an incredibly sad rendition of an old blind man, possibly a street busker, slumped in the gutter with his guitar.

Exposure to African sculptures led Pablo to his flirtation with Cubism. The most famous work of this period is *Les Demoiselles d'Avignon,* painted in 1907. Avignon is the name of a street in Barcelona.

This was followed by a period of Neoclassicism when his portraits were more conventional, like the *Portrait of Olga Khokhlova,* his second wife, painted in 1918 in Paris. He also took on commissions for Diaghilev's Ballet Russe. Degas probably

199 This is said to be Pablo's first publicly exhibited painting.

200 Rose Period, 1901–1904.

influenced him. This trend reflects a time in his life when he was focussed on his young family.

In the 1930s, he dabbled with Surrealism. In each painting, Picasso used a harlequin theme; it was his signature. In later paintings, he used a minotaur, which can be first seen in his famous *Guernica* and then in later work. The 1950s saw him concentrating on war, when he used gun-metal grey, as in his 1951 *Massacre in Korea*. I think grey, along with black and blue, are colours linked to despair.

The Pigeons, Cannes, is a light-hearted series of paintings the likes of which I'd not ever seen. The composition is framed by an open window, beyond which are palm trees and flowers. To me, the birds symbolised freedom, and the scene outdoors conjured up thoughts of vacations on the *Côte d'Azur*. The whole reflected a time of rest and recreation. I wondered if these paintings had been done during a 1957 holiday, but there was no one to ask.

I stood there for some time, mesmerised. This work was so different from anything I'd seen previously. I understood now how he and his fellow artists inspired each other. Particularly Henri Matisse, whom Picasso revered. Henri also painted *Open Window* in 1905 and *Blue Nude* in 1907. In the 1930s, fellow artist, Raoul Dufy painted many views of the south of France bound by his windows. Braque created several paintings with pigeons, which went on to be used as the world peace sign. Marc Chagall's stained-glass windows come to mind; their bright glass panels outlined with the heavy black iron.

George Braque, a Fauvist and exponent of Cubism, clearly led artists into modernism. Picasso's paintings became a series of overlapping shapes in beige tones. This series was closely followed by even more modern portraits, which I find grotesque. He said the use of bright colours and misshapen random features on faces was the way he expressed the multifaceted nature of the sitter. I thought he was expressing his own anger and fear of getting old and all the things still left undone.[201]

In 1957, Pablo Picasso's appreciable reverence to the most famous painting *Las Meninas* by Diego Velázquez, culminated in a series of analytical Cubist paintings. He donated the series, consisting of 48 reinterpretations, to the museum. Salvador Dali contributed a set of Pablo's engravings to be exhibited. In 1982, Picasso's wife, Jaqueline, dedicated 41 pieces of ceramics. His children and grandchildren have also contributed several works from their own private collections.

As I walked back, I passed poster stores, trendy bars, cafés and art galleries. They held little appeal because I knew there was nothing to top how I'd already spent my afternoon and I wanted to hang on to my joyfulness for a little while longer.

Dinner was a set menu at the hotel. We had two round tables and one was abuzz with a worrying story. The tale came to our table third-hand.

Juan and another fellow from the group had decided to spend their afternoon at the beach. There were quite a few people there, families and teenagers. Juan and his friend took turns to go into the water, not wanting to leave their belongings unattended. The friend sat up to watch Juan swim and didn't notice when someone swiped the bag right from behind his bottom. When Juan came out of the water, they discovered the bag gone. It contained a towel from the hotel and an expensive camera with many holiday photos. They reported it at the police station nearby, but the officer there

201 Picasso died in 1973.

merely shrugged his shoulders and said it happens all the time. They were so quick and the network so professional, there was nothing they could do.

'In future, you should sit on your belongings or hold them to your chest.'

Chapter 24
Carcassonne

Next morning, we hurried through breakfast and packed ready for our early departure to Carcassonne, 300 km away. We aimed to beat the morning commuter traffic and arrive there three hours later.

In the rush, Barbara tripped on the last stair, making an ungainly entrance into the lobby. I saw that she was in considerable pain, having twisted her ankle. Reception was on the ball and responded quickly with some ice. Thankfully, she wore surgical stockings, which supported her ankle and contained much of the swelling. Beatriz told her to sit at the back of the coach. Cindy, who all this while had sat there alone, moved over to give Barbara more room to stretch out her leg for the long journey. Beatriz sat alongside to render support.

Delia and I hoped we'd seen the last of the bad luck our little group had experienced. I gazed out the window at the mountainous landscape surrounding us. Beatriz said the area was called Costa Brava. I smiled to myself, remembering that was the exact name of the Spanish restaurant we had frequented in the early 1970s to eat something exotic and to dance.

Rolling hills and verdant valleys dotted with quaint villages and acre upon acre of grapes soon gave way to more rugged terrain as we approached the granite Pyrenees. Beatriz told us how these hills inspired Paul Cezanne. He spent most of his later life there in isolation, painting his beloved Provence. Cezanne was the artist who formed a bridge tying the late Impressionist movement to Cubism. He was highly regarded by his contemporaries, poets, writers and fellow artists. Matisse and Picasso referred to him as 'the father of us all'.

I stared out the window at the hills, their colours determined by the angle of the sun. A snow-capped massif loomed in the background. I pictured Cezanne with his easel, his beret, as always, on his head. He sat on a stool in the long grass in prayerful contemplation at these models of nature.

After two thirds of the journey, our route changed to a coastal outlook. Cindy passed a bag of lollies around the coach. I turned to the back to give her a thank you wave and noticed Barbara was asleep.

We drove below craggy reaches, past the treelined shores of the sparkling Mediterranean. Quaint fishing villages nestled around coves, where artists like Salvador Dali, Derain, Braque and Matisse found respite and inspiration.

After the long rural journey, our arrival in 12th century Carcassonne was a dramatic contrast. It felt as if we'd turned stage left, away from the coast and headlong into an enormous crenelated fortification with towers, drawbridge and battlements, all still intact.

Beatriz told us Carcassonne was the best-preserved example of medieval fortification in all Europe. The grey stone battlements loomed high over our coach.

Cobblestone pathways and narrow alleys flanked by heavy stone walls lured us into the town centre. I thought we'd arrived on a movie set and expected to see King Arthur and the Knights of the Roundtable gathering in the square. The complex was clean and bright as if they were expecting the queen. Little specialty shops and two-storey houses with geranium-filled balconies completed the tableau.

Beatriz's potted history gave us a sense of the place. What particularly resonated with me was the legend of the lady and the pig.

For five harrowing years, Charlemagne's army had besieged the fortified city of Caracas. Many died and only a handful of defenders remained. Alone, behind the rampart, Dame Carcas wielded straw mannequins and shot crossbow bolts at the besieging army. All this to make it appear as if they were still a force. She was desperate—only one small pig and a measure of wheat remained to feed the population. So Dame Carcas stuffed the pig with the remaining wheat and threw it over the rampart. On landing, the pig burst open and released a flood of grain.

Charlemagne was dumbfounded. He concluded the besieged must have so much food that the inhabitants even fed it to the swine. Deciding the raid futile, he retreated. Dame Carcas demanded Charlemagne to make peace. She sounded the trumpets. '*Carcas sonne,*' she yelled, which means, 'Carcas rings', and that's how the place got its name.

We all laughed. Beatriz shepherded us to Carcassonne Cathedral, where we had an hour of free time. The Filipino foursome, with Cindy and the honeymooners, wanted to visit the Basilica of St Nazaire and St Celese. However, most of the group opted for *Musee de la Torture,* to inspect the equipment used during the Inquisition.

Barbara, who was valiantly hobbling along, Delia and I decided to take a quick look at the cathedral before stopping for a coffee at the café next door. The church was peace-filled and we sat for a moment in contemplation. Suddenly, four black clad young men appeared in the aisle and walked calmly to the front. In brilliant *a capella*[202], their angelic voices soared into the apse. Delia and Barbara sat with their mouths gaping. It had immediately struck a chord. I'd had the same experience during my tour of the ancient Golden Ring towns outside Moscow. The surprise element and the angelic singing became etched in my memory.

The exit door led into a small vestibule, where CDs were being offered for sale. Barbara bought two different titles and I bought one. There were brochures, which we had autographed by the singers before we floated away on a cloud of elation.

Nearby, an outdoor café with no name was doing a steady trade. Locals with Pomeranians, Chihuahuas and other lap dogs sat alongside tourists with cameras. We joined them for coffee and sunshine. There was time for something small, a salad or a warmed croissant with ham and cheese, or cake from the countless array on offer to accompany our coffees. Although we wanted to stay longer, the hour of free time had passed and we reluctantly returned to the coach.

Chapter 25
Avignon

Two and a half hours later, we arrived in Avignon. Our hotel was called Cosy. It proved to be a little too cosy. The bathroom was smaller than the one I'd had in Rome. You could brush your teeth, have a shower and do your hair, all while sitting on the loo. Our beds were only 10 inches apart. Barbara was exhausted and went straight to bed.

Delia and I took a short stroll around the immediate precinct to get a sense of the place. Walking and talking is a fine way to get to know someone. Delia told me she lived on acreage in Queensland, where she kept poultry. It was her livelihood and she spent a lot of time outdoors, maintaining her property and tending the chooks. She too was an 'independent woman' and was enjoying travel now that her children were grown.

We had an early night after a lack-lustre dinner. Poor Barbara was coming down with something. She coughed all night despite the Sudafed and throat spray. Next day, she stayed in bed and missed going to Arles.

On the Rhone River, Arles is a city seven times the size of Paris and was once an important trading post. Because of the abundance of southern light, it became an enclave for many famous artists. Picasso, Gauguin with other Impressionist and Post-Impressionists, most notably Vincent Van Gogh, are remembered for the art they created in Arles. During his short stay, Van Gogh produced 300 works, including paintings and drawings.

The two-tiered Arles amphitheatre and colosseum thrived in Roman times when it hosted chariot races and blood sports. From the 5th to the 18th century, the site became a town with a population of 200 people. Since then, it's reverted to bullfighting.

Arles Cathedral, located in the centre of town, is resplendent with both obelisk and fountain. The fountain in the middle of the forecourt came from the Roman Circus. Water gushes from the mouths of bronze theatrical-styled masks into the pond. The constant sound creates a background of peace and calm.

The church and adjacent cloisters are the best examples of Romanesque building and sculpture in France. Some of the finest reliefs are to be found in the western portal. They feature the Apocalypse, Annunciation, Baptism of Christ, Adoration of the Maji and other biblical scenes. Sunlight filtering through the stained-glass windows adds to the enchantment.

On the lower level, separated by pilasters and columns, are statues of those saints who related to Arles: St Bartholomew, St James, St Philip and St Trophimus, who was the first bishop of Arles and to whom the church is dedicated. Even the bases of the columns are decorated with symbolic figures. The stained-glass windows are best seen from the inside, where I was also surprised to see tapestries.

On the other side of the square is the *hôtel de ville* or town hall. We stopped for a coffee from a kiosk nearby, before heading to the wine-country.

Away from the town, grassy paddocks and Paul Cezanne's precious mountains surrounded us with their embrace. Again, I thought of him sitting at his easel painting *au plein air*.

The vineyard with its large and small weathered sheds, was situated behind an unassuming fence. I immediately warmed to the place, which reminded me of Australian wine regions I had visited.

Different varieties of grapes are grown on this land, and we were encouraged to inspect the rows of ripe fruit waiting to be picked. Huge stainless-steel vats used for crushing and fermenting were evidence of modernisation. After fermentation, the process of ageing takes place in wooden kegs, as per the traditional manner.

An array of wines was offered for tasting. I tried four varieties but shied away from buying any because I did not want to grapple with additional weight in my suitcase when getting on and off the train to Paris. There were various knick-knacks on sale, one of which was a champagne cork disgorger. My own has become a symbol of independence and I thought it would make a nice gift.

Barbara greeted us when we returned from our excursion. She said she felt much better and asked if we had made plans for our free afternoon.

Our first activity was to visit Avignon Bridge to sing '*Sur la Pont d'Avignon*'. We were astonished at the inflated cost for entry onto the bridge. I loathe being ripped-off, so we turned away. We found a vantage point along the shore, where an outcrop provided an elevated area for us to sit. Not far away, in the background, was the bridge. We posed as if we were sitting on it. Like children, we sang the nursery rhyme and then, for good measure, followed it with '*Alouette*'. And that was before we had anything substantial to drink.

We passed by the *Palais d'Papes,* in the main square. It resembled a medieval fortification instead of a palace. A tour of the site was planned for the following day, so we restricted ourselves to a few photos of the exterior then left.

Barbara was keen to find the mural of the nine popes of Avignon. There was no signage because the mural was unofficial and off the tourist trail. We asked a lady who we thought might be a local. She accompanied us part of the way, then gave directions for the rest. Sure enough, in a quiet street of the business district, we found a building with an entire side wall covered in a mural. Nine panels, each painted with the portrait of a pope. After taking our photos, we retraced our steps into town.

Although some shops remained open, most were packing up for the day. The time had arrived for us to think of dinner. The warm evening was ideal for eating al fresco. Trees lit up with festive lights led us to a large square shared by several restaurants. Large planter pots with bright red geraniums were set amidst the tables and chairs. We perused the blackboard menus and found one with an inviting special deal—a three course dinner for €21 per person.

Wine was extra, but with four of us, it was more economical to buy a bottle. The first course was always a light dish. It made me think of the preamble or overture to a symphony—a little something to tantalise beforehand.

We were offered a terrine made of meats, which none of us recognised. The alternative was slices of smoked salmon and avocado on thinly sliced baguette covered with a bed of soft goat cheese. Not very adventurous but comforting to eat something familiar. The waiter brought us a bottle of red from Bordeaux.

For the main, Barbara and Cindy ordered *Poulet Provençale,* a rustic recipe of braised chicken thighs with tomatoes and black olives, seasoned at the last minute with chopped parsley and garlic in equal measure with a squeeze of lemon. Delia and I had slow-roasted lamb shanks with rosemary and sage. The lamb, drenched liberally with a dark *jus,* was melt-in-the-mouth tender. Roast Tomato Gratin on the side provided a tantalising contrast. The waiter arrived with a separate dish of *Pommes Dauphinoise* for us to share. The food was delicious. Since this was a free night, we wondered where the rest of our group was eating.

When we had finished, the waiter brought us a green salad dressed in a light vinaigrette, as is the French custom. Salad is always served after the main to cleanse the palate before dessert. For *dolce,* I chose white fromage with crème fraiche and wild strawberries. The small, dark red berries were allowed to ripen till the flavour became as sweet as honey and the aroma a lingering perfume.

After breakfast, I caught up on my emails. The news was not good. There had not been much rain and although it was only October, summer bushfires had started in the north of New South Wales. My family assured me they were out of harm's way and told me not to worry.

Our day began with a tour of the *Palais d'Papes,* which was a short walk away. Patrick, our local guide, told us that the palace was considered one of the largest and most important

Medieval Gothic buildings in Europe. Several of the group said it resembled a fortress because of its crenelated towers and ramparts. They visualised soldiers shooting arrows from between the crenelations.

'I expect there is an ancient town behind the walls,' said Viraj.

Patrick laughed. 'You're not the first to make that observation,' he said. 'Actually, it comprises two palaces, a huge library and a chapel, covering 15,000 square metres.'

'Was it in competition with the Vatican?' asked Sofia.

'It served as the Vatican until the 14th century,' Patrick replied. 'Six papal conclaves were held there. In 1377, the papacy returned to Rome, making it redundant.'

The group entered the citadel. There were 25 rooms open to view. They included ceremonial halls, a courtroom, the kitchen, the pope's private apartments and the chapels, all of which were covered in magnificent frescoes.

The bedroom walls were painted with grape vines, tendrils and oak leaves. Birds and squirrels completed the fanciful picture. A narrow corridor led to the study, also known as the Stag Hunt Room for its rich murals. These depicted the favourite pastimes of the gentry. Patrick drew our attention to the techniques of the time. These included hunting with decoys or with weasels and fishing in pools. The forest in the background was filled with fruit, flowers and herbs.

'Did the town make other commercial use of the premises?' asked Andreas. 'I understand it's a tourist attraction, but how do they generate enough money to maintain such an edifice?'

'In the early days people were not so commercially astute,' replied Patrick. 'The site was sacked during the Napoleonic wars after it was used as barracks and a prison.' He paused for us to digest the information. 'Now it is used as a conference centre and exhibition venue, as well as hosting large concerts and special events.'

There was scant time for lunch or souvenir shopping before we left for Paris. Barbara wanted to duck into St Peter's Basilica[203], which happened to be quite close. We stepped out from the bustle into serenity and calm. There were several painted vaults, gilded balconies for the choir, Renaissance paintings and a stone altar. The original vestments and hat of *Cardinal de Pres* were displayed in a glass cabinet on the wall.

A cat lay curled up on top of a chair by the door to the *boulangerie*. The tag on its collar read 'Pom-Pom'. I couldn't resist patting the furry ball of fluff. The cat peeped at me to see who had disturbed its sleep. After deciding I was friend not foe, it stretched before resuming its siesta.

We bought brioche, snails and croissants to have with our coffee at the tables and chairs outside. Soon the time arrived for us to assemble in the foyer of the hotel for our final transfer to the train station.

Paris is 700 km north of Avignon but on the fast TGV, we arrived in two hours. Because we were a large tour group, porters took care of our luggage. As in Italy, I noticed individual travellers had to take care of themselves as best they could.

Chapter 26
Paris

In the early evening, we arrived at our destination—*Gare de Lyon*, the main intercity train and bus terminus. As we boarded our coach, I could feel a new energy in the group, the excitement of arrival in Paris and anticipation of adventures yet to be had.

We ignored our grumbling stomachs and the heavy traffic as the coach made its way through the city and into the suburbs. Though a long way from the city centre, our hotel in the 19th arrondissement was larger and better than I expected.

Without unpacking, the group met in the lounge to decide how best to spend our first evening in the City of Lights.[204] Every evening, 300 buildings, bridges, boulevards, fountains and monuments, including the iconic Eiffel tower, are illuminated. The two couples from Manila and from Buenos Aires, along with Delia, Cindy and Karolina in tow, thought to venture into the city via the Metro for some shopping. Others of the group stayed at the hotel to eat.

Barbara and I agreed to have dinner nearby. Across the road were some atmospheric restaurants. We strolled along, taking in the sights, until we found one we liked. Called Hippopotamus, the name amused us, especially as we'd been eating so well and were no longer gazelles. Apart from the name, the offer of a special price for a three-course meal, sealed the deal.

'I'm starved,' declared Barbara upon looking at the illustrated menu.

Indeed, my appetite became more keenly aroused as I perused the menu. I ordered *Bœf Bourguignonne*, a classic casserole with *Riz Pilaf*. Barbara settled for *Roti Poulet*—chicken roasted with Cajun spices. *Salade Mediterranenne* sounded intriguing. We decided to share a serve. It turned out to be a Greek salad. The waiter recommended *Crozes Hermitage*. The wine was like our Australian shiraz. We're no longer allowed to call it Hermitage because it refers to the region in France where it's grown, whereas Shiraz is the name of the grape variety that grows in many regions around the world. This bottle of wine proved to be mellow with less tannin than I was used to but I found it most enjoyable.

As Barbara was leaving the group the next day, it was nice for this time together to just sit and chat. We exchanged addresses and promised to stay in touch. On cue, the waiter interrupted us with the dessert menu. *Abricots Confit au Miel e Romarin* sounded intriguing when compared to the other dessert options. With the apricots poached in honey and rosemary, it seemed less indulgent than the creamy flummeries and mousses. After all, apricots are just fruit.

Our first full day in Paris began with the usual morning tour of the city. The warm and sunny day was ideal for photography.

To experience the best views, we sat upstairs on the big red bus. The route passed by the Eiffel Tower, Arc de Triomphe, Notre Dame, Pantheon, Tuileries, the Louvre and the Sorbonne. We finished at the Charlemagne statue, across from the majestic

Notre-Dame Cathedral. Beatriz said it was the most visited site in all of Paris. Cameras clicked and flashed. Some of our group had very professional-looking photographic gear. Most of our companions had signed up for the optional trip to Versailles. The rest of us were set loose to enjoy Paris in whatever way we desired.

Delia, Barbara, Cindy and I joined forces with Jose, Carmen, Carlos and Sofia, who wanted to get back on the Metro to visit Sacre-Coeur and Montmartre. I suggested we stick together and begin by seeing the interior of Notre-Dame before heading to Sacre-Coeur and the Latin Quarter. Viraj and Miko joined us, so now we were a group of ten.

Viraj had a guidebook and regaled us with some interesting snippets about the church.

'Notre-Dame, a masterpiece of French Gothic architecture[205], is dedicated to the Blessed Virgin Mary,' he read. 'It is home to precious relics from the Passion of Christ, including the Holy Crown of Thorns. It is the place where Joan of Arc was beatified and where many French presidents are interred.'

'I think Napoleon's coronation was held in the cathedral,' added Delia.

'Yes,' said Barbara. 'However, the church was desecrated during the Napoleonic wars and was earmarked for demolition.'

Viraj butted in. 'The book says Victor Hugo, an ardent supporter, wrote his famous novel *The Hunchback of Notre-Dame* to raise awareness to the issue. The book was an immediate success. The populace rose up to demand authorities stop the destruction and immediately restore the church to its original beauty.'

205 In April 2019, while undergoing renovation, a fire broke out in the roof, causing enormous damage to the structure. Rebuilding is scheduled for completion in 2024.

From the front, we saw three entrances decorated with bas-relief figures. They represented the Apocalypse. Above the entry was a statue gallery of the kings of Israel and Judea. The central rose window dominated the area between the towers and was dedicated to the Madonna and Child. Above sat a gallery of slender intertwined columns. These were further topped with the gallery of chimera, behind which stood the two towers still awaiting spires. Viraj noted that the south tower had 387 steps leading to the two largest bells. The remainder hung in the north tower.

Distinctive gargoyle rainspouts divert water from the roof and away from the walls of the building while the grotesque, leering figures of the chimera monsters meditate on the destiny of the people below. They are a visual message for the illiterate worshipers, omens of the devil sent to gather those who don't follow the teachings of the church. The church is also known for its flying buttresses.[206] They are at the rear of the church.

Upon entry, I was immediately struck by the size of the church.[207] Elaborate rib vaulting spans the high ceiling from the entrance to the distant altar. Artworks from the 17th and 18th centuries decorate individual chapels beyond. This church is especially famous for its beautiful stained-glass windows with scenes from the Bible.

Carmen and Sofia were anxious to move along. We headed to the Metro *Cité*. There was a special deal. Ten return tickets bought together saved us €1 each. It sounds silly now, but at the time we were elated to have mastered an important aspect of Parisian life.

---

206 These arched exterior supports at the rear of the structure were among the first used in the world. They hold the weight of the walls.

207 Length 130 m, width 50 m and the height 35 m, the buttresses have a span of 15 m.

The day remained warm and sunny. We relied on Carmen, Sofia and their husbands to navigate our route. They had us alight at Chateau Rouge. I felt uneasy. Vagrants loitered around the dirty streets.

Our hunger was aroused by the delicious aroma of fresh-baked goodies. We made our way past *boucheries* and *fromageries* until we found the *boulangerie* where sweet rolls and bread, just out of the oven, were on display. The shopkeeper was glad to be inundated by our large group. We bought rolls and takeaway coffee. This kept us going. Along our route, the girls stopped to gaze longingly at designer handbags and gift shops. For me, the purpose of going somewhere is to reach my destination, whereas some people are easily distracted by unrelated things, like handbags.

In the distance, Sacre-Coeur awaited. It is known colloquially as the 'big meringue', which describes the shape of the huge white stone dome. Our ardent shoppers only acquiesced after I'd promised to give due attention to shopping on our way back.

When we reached our destination, we were confronted by a 270-step stairway. The options were to walk up all those steep steps or pay an exorbitant fee to use the funicular.

Sacre-Coeur, which sits on the hill of Montmartre, is a vast and impressive landmark. Completed in 1919, it is a unique combination of Romanesque and Byzantine architecture. There is something oriental about its appearance—it reminded me of the Taj Mahal. The main bell weighs a massive 19 tons, one of the biggest anywhere in the world. Equestrian statues of King Louis the Blessed and Joan of Arc flank the main entry. It is one of France's most important Roman Catholic buildings. The sweeping views of the city from this vantage point made our effort even more worthwhile.

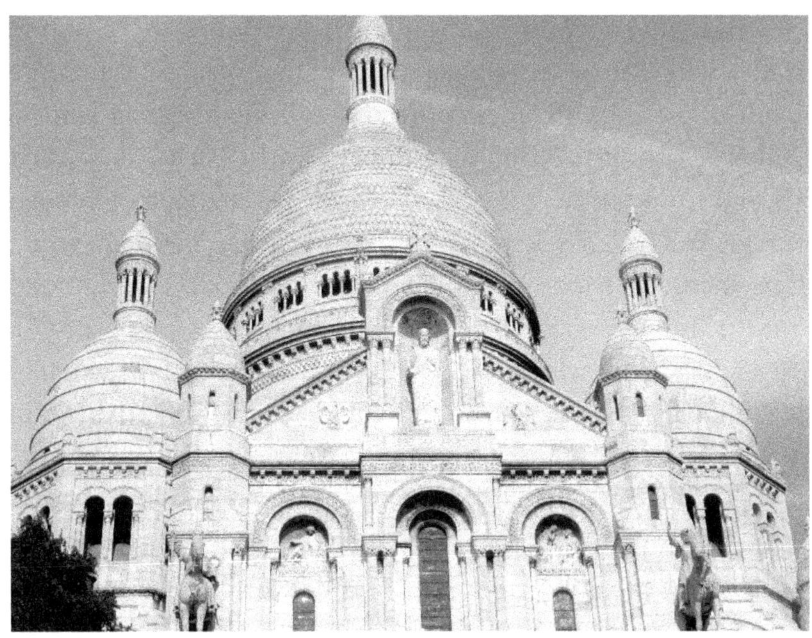

The interior decorations consist of elaborate mosaics and frescoes. The most spectacular were in the apse of the main dome. Some of our company were Roman Catholic but none so overly religious as to spend too much time in this enormous cathedral. They wanted to go there to pay their respects and to say a silent prayer before doing more shopping.

Place du Tertre, the heart of Montmartre, was close by. The square, lined with trees, is a popular outdoor atelier for local artists. Jose immediately found an illustrator to sketch his portrait. A cartoonist beckoned Viraj and Miko and they agreed to have a caricature done. Cindy loved to look at all things. She smiled a lot but didn't buy. I saw a nice little watercolour and thought it an impressive souvenir. Barbara and Delia found a kiosk serving fresh fruit juices. I enjoyed wandering around looking at the paintings for sale and observing those still being created.

Nightclubs and restaurants prepared for the evening trade, when the area comes alive with revellers. Our own models, armed with their portraits and wearing big smiles, gathered. When assured that all were present and accounted for, our little company retraced the path to the Metro Chateau Rouge.[208] The girls kept stopping to buy something, while Carlos and Jose merely smiled, said, 'Yes, dear,' and handed out the money.

Finally, we arrived at the platform. I have this habit of scanning the perimeters for exits and to see who's watching us. Our shoppers must have had a neon light on their heads flashing 'tourists'. I noticed a group of young tousled-haired kids. They appeared unkempt, streetwise and had a menacing air about them. My French was sadly lacking, even though I'd spent two terms studying French for travellers at the local community college.

I thought these little beggars were hatching a plan to divert our attention in several directions while a couple of older ones grabbed our bags and cameras. I saw red. I pointed at the group and loudly declared, 'We're not tourists, so don't think of messing with us, we'll clobber you. Piss off!' At least, that's what I'd intended to say. Perhaps I said something entirely different. However, this unexpected little outburst surprised them and they scattered in all directions to make their way to the exits.

The train arrived and we automatically piled in. Then my friends asked me what on earth the fracas was all about. I told them we were being targeted for a mugging. Carmen and

208 Years later, I read an article that described Chateau Rouge as one of the worst places for pick pocketers, scammers and muggers. It was known as crime central. We should have travelled via Metro Abbesses, which is safer and nearer Sacre-Coeur.

Sofia and their husbands thought I'd overreacted and we were lucky that the insult hadn't encouraged the kids to attack us. Well, I still disagree. I believe our group were too flashy with their display of jewellery and designer handbags thus making themselves a big target.

Back at the hotel Cindy, Barbara, Delia and I had a goodbye drink for Barbara, who was to be picked up by her friend with whom she'd stay for the rest of her trip in Paris. Later, we joined the remaining group members for the last dinner of our tour. The venue was in the Latin Quarter.

I ordered frogs legs for the first time. Others in the group tried snails. Beatriz said they were the same as chicken, but I thought the flavour was fishy, although with the quantity of garlic used, it really was hard to discern. A bit like chicken wings; not much to eat. This was followed by Duck *Confit*, prepared with a citrus *jus*, a crisp skin moistened with the citrus that cut the fatty duck perfectly. Vegetables were served separately for the table to share. Dessert of the day was *crème brûlée* or profiterole. For an extra charge we could have a cheese platter.

Pleasant background music was relaxing and helped the group enjoy each other's company. Jokes and laughter flowed as we compared notes and made suggestions for additional sightseeing. We'd have happily stayed on but our coach had arrived to take us on the final activity—a night tour of Paris.

All the major landmarks were flood-lit, fountains sparkled and streetlights flickered. We proceeded from *Les Invalides* and

Napoleon's tomb across the Seine on one of its many bridges to the *Arc de Triomphe* and the *Tour Eiffel*.[209]

Due to the large volume of traffic, we crawled along the *Champs Elysée*[210], which is the most famous street in Paris. We were dazzled by the neon signs flanking the wide boulevard: Cartier, Chanel, Dior, Versace, Armani, Hermes and other brands less familiar in our climes. Carmen and Sofia were chomping at the bit, drooling to stop and shop.

At 11:00 pm, near to the territory of *Petite Palais*, we stopped at a vantage point to see the Eiffel Tower come alive with its nightly light spectacular. Then home over the most beautiful bridge in Paris, the Pont Alexandre III, where couples, oblivious to the world, cuddled and kissed. After all, Paris is known as the city of love.

Chapter 27
Old Friends

After breakfast, the taxi delivered me to the Campanile Hotel in the Bastille arrondissement near two Metro stations, Chemin Vert[211] and Bréguet-Sabin.[212] Marina had already spent one day and night at our hotel. She'd met up with Nadia, a friend who lived in Paris with her French husband, Jacques. By sheer coincidence, our hotel was situated a block away from their apartment.

Marina and I have known each other since we were kids and have similar interests. Her parents lived on the Central Coast, where they hosted many weekend house parties. But this was the first time we had travelled together or spent more than a few consecutive days and nights in each other's company. I'm a researcher and planner, whereas Marina is happy to coast along. Her many trips abroad had been to visit family and friends. She seemed happy for me to organise our little adventure.

After making a spectacle hugging and greeting each other in the foyer, she said, in a low whisper. 'I'm a little worried you'll be disappointed with our tiny room.'

My French language teacher had warned the class that accommodation was tiny by our standards. I'd made all the bookings but had neglected to warn Marina of this aspect. She was disappointed, so I tried to console her.

'There's no point paying extra for a place we'll only use to shower and sleep. So long as it's clean and the beds are comfortable,' I told her. 'The most important thing is location; we don't want to waste too much time getting into the city centre. The Metro is near our door. I've prioritised experience over accommodation style. I'm sure we'll be fine.' Her smile of acceptance was all I needed.

Despite the drizzly rain, we went straight into town, as we were both keen to spend as much time as possible at the Louvre.[213] The gallery was closed on Tuesdays so we had to expect there'd be a lot of people, it being Monday. They patiently lined up at each entrance. Marina spied a little café across the road with wicker chairs under an ample awning. It seemed an ideal place to dust off the cobwebs with coffee and gaze at the passing parade while we worked out a strategy for the day.

A lady on her own sat at the table next to us intending, to read her newspaper. She overheard us talking and introduced herself. She was a journalist born in Moscow, now living in Paris while doing freelance work. Although Marina and I had both been to Moscow a couple of times, I'm always interested to get an insider's viewpoint, especially as this lady had grown up there during the Soviet era.

'Russian people are complex,' she said. 'They need a strong leader to keep them in place, otherwise there'd be chaos.'

We laughed at what we viewed as her truism. She was not resigned to the ongoing corruption, which is why she'd chosen to live in Paris. There'd been a purge on swindlers and

213 Built in 1200, the Louvre, Paris, exhibits 35,000 items including 5500 paintings by 1400 artists. Up to 1847 successive kings of France amassed the collection.

tax evaders, and many of the main figures had left hurriedly with their booty to safe havens overseas. *Like when Mr Skase left Australia for Majorca with his ill-gotten millions.* But she said that the country was getting matters into order.

'It all takes time,' she said. 'Ordinary people can make enough money to enjoy a satisfactory standard of life. They have the freedom to travel. You see them everywhere you go. At least, that's what it's like for folk in the cities.'

We told her of the long queues at the Louvre. She suggested we try the main entrance in the courtyard near the glass pyramid.[214]

Both of us are art lovers. As an artist, Marina had spent her life drawing and painting in various mediums, and even dabbled in sculpture and ceramics, while I was more into art history.

We meandered for three hours on the first and second floors. The work of French, Italian, Dutch and Flemish artists spanning several centuries were grouped there. The gallery exhibits most of the well-known artists through to the Renaissance period. There are also a small number of icons by *Crétois*, which were painted directly onto wood panels.

Botticelli, Titian, Tintoretto, Giotto are all there, but the highlight for the French citizens must be Delacroix's *Liberty Leading the People*. The figure of Liberty holds the unfurled French flag as she leads the band of revolutionaries over the dead beneath their feet.

214 There are five pyramids at the Louvre, erected during expansion work to cater for the growing numbers of visitors. Completed in 1989 for the bi-Centenary of the French Revolution, the main one is in the courtyard and is designed in the same proportions as the Great Pyramid of Giza.

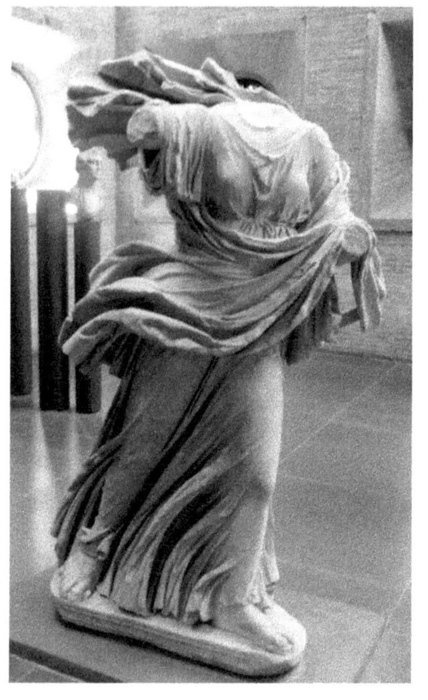

We moved on to the sculptures. I was particularly drawn to Antonio Canova's *The Three Graces*[215], who stood in their buxom little clutch, the white marble appeared plump and fleshy. The tortured expression on Michelangelo's sculpture of the *Dying Slave* was poignant, especially as he appeared to be very like the memorable *David*. Of course, *Venus de Milo* could not be overlooked, nor the *Winged Victory*, which was later used by Nike for their logo. I could almost feel the wind blowing Nike's tunic as it clung to her limbs.

The epic painting by Veronese of *The Wedding Feast at Cana* is particularly important for its use of architectural elements. These elements not only gave perspective but also formed a ring around the central tableau. The table is set with Jesus at the centre as in the *Last Supper*, but with many more figures. Regaled in colourful clothing, all appear happy and relaxed. A string trio in the foreground adds to the feeling of celebration.

I thought Vermeer's *Milk Maid* and *Lace Maker* were so like his *Girl with a Pearl Earring* and I wondered if she was the same model.

215 Several artist sculpted or painted the trio, said to be the three daughters of the god Zeus.

Ahead of us, a crowd gathered in front of a large wall, blank but for one small[216] painting—a portrait. As we drew closer, I understood the reason for all the commotion. It was Leonardo da Vinci's *Mona Lisa*. We were surprised that a painting with such a large reputation could be so small.

The slow shuffle from painting to painting had not done my circulation a favour. My feet were close to becoming blocks of ice; I couldn't feel them at all. I knew the time had come to consolidate our impressions with coffee.

There were several café options within the complex. As the rain had ceased and the sun shone, we chose *Le Mollien* Restaurant for its balcony seating, the fresh air and view over the courtyard. Marina ordered a quiche with salmon and broccoli while I settled for a baguette with ham and Emmental cheese. For a treat, we ordered Viennese coffee, which was topped with whipped cream. We shared a *Palmier*.

Feet duly thawed and circulation restored, we headed back. The Spanish collection included El Greco, Goya and Velazquez, and was where we'd left off. The first painting we saw was Goya's portrait of a *Lady with a Fan*, then *Countess del Carpio*, who wore a white mantilla decorated with a huge pink bow. It jogged my memory; I'd not yet given Marina the white mantilla I'd bought for her. Of the various other paintings, we both admired Diego Velazquez's sweet portrait of *Infanta Maria*, who takes centre stage in Diego's *Las Menignas*. Maria Margarita was the pretty blonde daughter of King Phillip IV of Spain.

The next wing featured many more portraits. In Rembrandt's *Self-portrait with Easel*, he was wearing a white head covering

216 The *Mona Lisa* is only 30 x 21 inches in size. The *Prado Mona Lisa* is slightly larger at 30 x 22 inches.

more like a handkerchief than a hat. A bemused smile spread across his face. *The man looks like a bricklayer taking a smoko.*

Caravaggio and Raphael followed, then Gainsborough's *Blue Boy*. I always remember the intense blue of his outfit. Then there was Jean Ingres's *Grand Odalisque*. The young lady reclined on a Louis XVI chaise, gazing over her shoulder. She wore nothing but the hint of an enigmatic smile. *What was she thinking?* We decided this was a memorable moment on which to end our tour.

Only one errand stood between us and dinner. That was to buy French SIM cards. We found a shop and Marina sweet-talked the shopkeeper into installing them for us. *So he should. Afterall we've spent €100.*

We ate at a little French restaurant positioned on a corner diagonally across the canal from our hotel. The menu was only in French and they spoke no English. What remarkable coincidences—first finding Nadia and Jacques near our hotel and now this restaurant, which was attached to the boutique hotel where Marina would stay for the few days while I was away at a French cooking school in Toulouse.

We sat up at the bar waiting for a table. I ordered fresh sardines *en croute* with a sort of aioli dressing. Marina chose smoked salmon with a goat cheese pâte sprinkled with chopped dill, then Duck *Confit* but I had *Beef Provençal*. We shared *Dauphinois* potatoes and a green salad. For dessert, *Fromage blanc avec compote de cerises*—sour cherries with crème fraiche. We polished off a nice bottle of *Beaujolais* before strolling back to our hotel for a good night's sleep, but not before Marina checked for emails from back home.

Chapter 28
Champagne

We had an early start for our trip to the Champagne region. Aussie accents resounded in the small breakfast room. All the tables were occupied, but we managed to squeeze in. Turns out the Chat Noir Restaurant back home in Terrigal had organised a group tour but our interest became keener when they said they'd been to Chartres and the Champagne region the previous day and had very much enjoyed the experience.

Promptly at eight, a four-wheel drive vehicle arrived for us. It seated eight people, including the driver and Valentin, our guide. First stop was the village of Reims to see the High-Gothic, cathedral dedicated to the Virgin Mary, which until 1825 was the traditional coronation place for French kings.

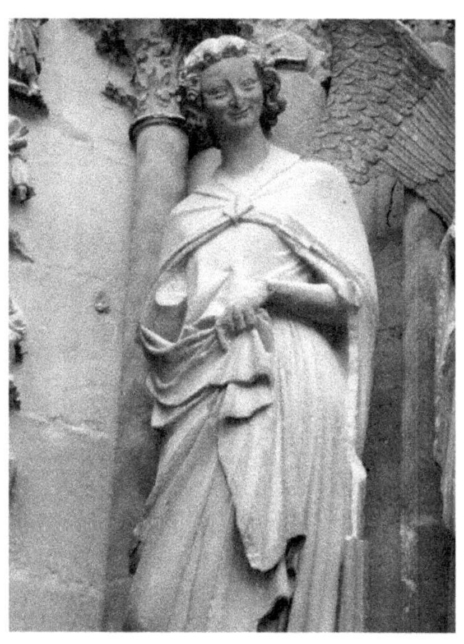

A statue of Joan of Arc mounted on a horse was erected in the courtyard in front of the church. An abundance of bas-reliefs in the embracement of the north portal included a smiling angel. I wondered if the angel's expression had been created at the whimsy of the sculptor. The north and south walls of the long nave were supported by 11 flying buttresses on each side. These counterbalanced the outward thrust of the ceiling vaults and made possible the remarkable height, thin walls and large windows.

Both village and church were completely rebuilt after World War II. I thought the cathedral was like a twin of Notre-Dame. The spires on both have never been erected atop their bell towers.

Marc Chagall created three new stained-glass windows which were installed in 1970 behind the high altar. They are a statement of beauty and serve to bring abundant light into the nave. In addition, the German artist Imi Knoebel installed nine contemporary windows reflecting the colours used in the original stained glass.

Shop windows in the high street displayed bottles of champagne. I nearly fainted when I saw the price tags. They were selling my favourite Dom Perignon for €490 but wanted €1390 for the 1975 vintage.[217]

It felt so good to stretch our legs with this short stop, but our destination was the wine country. The tranquil village of Aÿ-Champagne, surrounded by rolling hills near Epernay, is home

217 Dom Perignon is prized for its rarity, complexity and subdued flavour. Only six vintages are released in a decade and in the last 100 years only 46 vintages were released. The 1996 retails for $49,000. Another favourite is Krug, which is richer in flavour and more robust. It retails at $2500 per bottle. Owned by Remy for years, it was recently bought by the Hennessy, Vuitton conglomerate. Armand de Brignac is likely the dearest of all at $275,000 for the 2013 vintage.

to the well-known wineries of Veuve-Clicquot, Bollinger, Moet-et-Chandon and Dom Perignon.

We stopped at a quaint, Tudor-style cottage. It turned out to be the winery of Pierre LeBeouf, held in the family for many generations. After a short informative talk to introduce the art of wine-making, we were invited to stroll through to the cellar for tasting.

The tasting commenced with a First *Cru*, which was a fresh, young wine. This we compared with the *Grande Cru*, which was a combination of Pinot, Meunier and Chardonnay. Our vigneron explained why they produced this combination.

'The Pinot grape is well-suited to the local terrain,' he said. 'It produces an aroma of berries, while Meunier, being more robust, produces a rounded finish. The combination of these two varieties tend to shorten the ageing process, while the later addition of Chardonnay results in a fresh, sharp taste to the wine.'

Lunch at *Cave de Epernay* was included in the tour and we expected something simple alongside a glass of wine. The owner of the vineyard accompanied our group across the square to a small, unassuming cottage. Inside the lovely country-style dining room, a large table covered with a blue and white checked tablecloth was laid, ready for lunch.

We started with a small flute of Pierre LeBeouf Rosé as an aperitif to cleanse the palate before the meal. The set menu began with a fillet of local trout. Its pale pink flesh tasted light and fresh. This was a nice contrast to the creamy green lentils on the side. A glass of young, fruity Chardonnay was a perfect match to the trout.

That would have done, but it was only the first course. The main was *Coq au Vin*, tender chicken in a light gravy. This course was complemented by a light burgundy. It tasted like our Merlots. After a short interval, a soft custardy crème flavoured with thyme and garnished with a little biscuit called a Madeline was served for dessert. The thyme gave it a delicious tang and a distinct aroma. Tea and coffee were offered but we declined, knowing there'd be more wine tasting.

Our next winery was Dom Perignon and Moët Chandon. They are both part of the Hennessey conglomerate. Established in 1743, it is the largest and most professional winery in the region. The bronze statue of Dom Perignon, a humble monk in his Franciscan tunic tied with rope, was positioned to welcome visitors at the entrance. The foyer, unexpectedly slick, resembled an exclusive hotel rather than a factory. In the centre of the foyer stood a huge vase of purple irises. Portraits of the founders graced the walls.

Our factory guide, Camille, led us to an assembly of champagne bottles standing in line from the smallest piccolo to the largest Melchizedek.[218] She described how champagne is made.

'*Methode Champenois* is the unique double fermentation process, which results in this much-loved bubbly wine,' she said.

'Is it only made from a select few grape varieties?' asked one of the fellows in our group.

'Wine with a high acidity is used initially in the stainless-steel vats, and the sediment is siphoned off before the wine is bottled,' Camille replied. 'After fermentation, it's blended with other wine varieties, rebottled and stored inverted in specially contrived racks, then held for a period of time in cellars.'

Camille turned and we followed. 'There are 28 kilometres of cellars in our winery,' she said.

218 There are 14 sizes of bottles for champagne. From the piccolo which holds one glass to the Melchizedek which holds 40 bottles and is equivalent to 30 litres.

We saw row upon row of wooden racks designed to hold exposed individual bottles of wine. *I wonder why the bottles are stored in this manner.*

'The bottles, you see, are tapped and turned daily by hand to encourage deposits to settle into the neck. Disgorgement follows to release these deposits. The wine is sweetened before it receives its final cork and is left to age in this controlled environment.'

'Did Dom Perignon discover champagne?' asked one of the ladies.

'We believe so. It is said when Dom Perignon first discovered the bubbly wine, he exclaimed, "Come quickly, I am tasting the stars."'

Everyone giggled. What a terrific way to finish the talk. We followed Camille to the bar, where small flutes of Moët waited for us.

I slept all the way back to Paris. At the minimarket near Chemin Vert metro we bought a baguette, sliced salami, a soft blue cheese and kalamata olives. These we enjoyed with the Californian pinot noir I'd been carrying since Spain. It proved to be every bit as good as was promised. We talked for ages. I was tired but Marina was still sending emails, anxious that she'd had no reply from her family. As soon as my head hit the pillow, I was asleep.

Nadia joined us at eight for breakfast. Since Jacques always left early for work and their small apartment took no time at all to clean, it left her free for the rest of the day. Other guests had vacated the hotel and we had the place to ourselves. We talked about what we'd already done and what we hoped to do. I must have mentioned my laundry as part of the conversation. Nadia insisted I bring it over for her to do while we were out as her apartment was a mere seven-minute walk from our hotel.

I regretted imposing such a personal task on someone I'd just met but knew no way to refuse the offer with dignity. Nadia offered to accompany us to the country railway departure hub, but first she wanted us to go to the Hotel Grand[219], her favourite place for coffee. The hotel was all class, like the Savoy in London or Raffles in Singapore. Steeped in history, the Grand had hosted the *crème de la crème* of society. We sat in Chesterfield armchairs in a nook off the foyer. The leather furniture exuded an aroma of old money. A waiter brought us coffee, plain black, in fine bone china cups.

Nadia accompanied us as far as the Metro to Montparnasse, where we caught the SNCF train[220] to Chartres. An hour and a half later, having travelled through lush countryside, we arrived at our destination. An overgrown path led from the station to the cathedral. I saw something blue between the tufts of grass—a €20 note, decorated with the very windows we'd come here to see. There was no one around to claim it, so I put it in my pocket and we kept walking.

Chartres Cathedral, famed for its stained-glass windows, was even larger and more beautiful than I'd expected. Once again, the architecture was a copy of Notre-Dame, the only difference being these bell towers were complete with spires. We were surprised there were no tour buses or queues and

219 In 1862, Hausmann supervised the building of this luxury hotel located near Paris Opera Garnier. The hotel has hosted most European royalty, kings, queens, tsars and tsarinas and numerous celebrities.

220 SNCF National Society for French railroads is a nationalised service and is a quick, cheap and easy alternative for long distance travel throughout France and to neighbouring countries.

hoped it was not closed. Being a working church, its doors were always open.

Inside, we were overwhelmed by the outstanding stained-glass windows that dated back to the 12th and 13th centuries. The colour and proportions were monumental and they, along with the painted decorations, had been miraculously preserved from the ravages of humankind and time. In fact, Chartres Cathedral is one of the most admired and best-preserved examples of Gothic art in France.

I noticed a statue of our Lady of the Pillar, the same one I'd visited in Monserrat, and told Marina the story. We lit a candle for our safe journeying and for the poor person who'd dropped the €20 note.

A few people gathered for a tour of the crypt. We joined them to see the ancient frescoes, reliquaries and a precious veil said to have belonged to the Blessed Virgin Mary. We thought ourselves fortunate to come upon the group, even though we didn't understand a word because the tour was all in French. However, between the points of interest, the guide explained a little of it in English.

The train home left at six in the evening but only took an hour to reach the Metro, where we had to change to another line. Chuffed with ourselves for not getting lost, we finally arrived back at Chemin Rouge, starving. Marina insisted we eat at the nearest restaurant, which turned out to be Italian. The lasagne was nice enough and we indulged by ordering a *Kir Royale* dessert.[221] Fresh raspberries set in a *crème de cassis* jelly, it was a take on the popular cocktail of the same name. Marina was insistent on paying. This was an ongoing issue we'd had for a long time. However, this time I was firm; everything had to be halved without further discussion.

Chapter 29
Loire Valley Chateaux

At the ungodly hour of 6:30 am, Marina and I were already in the city. We joined our beret-wearing tour guide, Pierre, and 60 other tourists on the waiting coach. There were Japanese, Germans, English, Russians, Italians and Greeks. Their excited chatter hushed only when Pierre took up a microphone. He introduced himself and shared a little of what we could expect on our tour.

'Today in the Loire Valley, we will see the two most sumptuous chateaux,' he said. 'Chambord and Chenonceau, which are 237 km south-west of Paris and if there's time, Cheverny.'

'How long will it take?' asked a lady holding a sleeping baby.

'Three hours. So everyone relax. Once we're out of Paris we'll stop for refreshments,' he said. Then turned to the lady and assured her that she'd be able to get the baby's bottle warmed when we stopped.

The roadhouse petrol station turned out to be a large establishment with dining facilities for travellers. A coffee and croissant were sufficient for me. Within 20 minutes, we resumed our journey. Pierre immediately garnered our attention for some background about the chateaux.

'The reign of Francis I in the 16th century, saw an intense period of chateau-building. With the growing popularity of hunting, more lodges were required to accommodate hunters as they moved around the countryside together with their court, in search of prey.'

Someone commented loudly, 'A bit like us, they travelled between the various estates.'

Our first chateau was Chenonceau, built in the early Renaissance style with elements of late Gothic. To this day when we reminisce, Marina immediately recalls the lush European forest that surrounded the estate. In particular, the magnificent plane tree-bordered avenue, which led to the castle.

My first impression of this fairy-tale chateau was that of jaw-dropping awe. The building seemed to be suspended between air and water; its reflection mirrored in the stillness of the moat. Of course, every castle must have a moat. This one was nowhere near any water. So the builder diverted the River Cher around the castle to do the job.

After leaving the coach, Pierre gave us more information. 'Chenonceau is also known as *Château des Dames* because the estate was administered and protected by extraordinary women.'

'How did they come to own the castle?' asked one of the ladies.

'Francis I seized the estate from the original owners for non-payment of debts to the crown. After Francis died, Henry II came to the throne. He gave the palace to his favourite mistress, Diane Poitiers, who established the original flower and vegetable gardens. When Henry II died, his widow and consort, Catherine d'Medici, relocated Diane to another castle.'

Someone standing behind us said, 'It's a big castle but probably not big enough for wife and mistress at the same time.' We all laughed.

The sight of turreted pavilions, pepper pot chimneys and dormer windows captured my imagination. The fairy-tale spires reminded me of the Disney castle in Fantasyland.

We passed by two sphinxes guarding the manicured forecourt and over a bridge to the grand entrance of the three-storey limestone building.

'Catherine d'Medici installed the formal plots with fountains and a circular maze of yew trees,' said Pierre. 'In the centre of this labyrinth were bathing huts and a marble statue of Venus. Over the years much was relocated to other palaces and museums, however, Venus remains here to this day.'

We made our way through the entrance to the enormous main reception salon.

'This is where sumptuous feasts were held with much merriment provided by jesters, dwarves and minstrels playing lutes and mandolins,' said Pierre. 'Catherine decorated the castle in the Renaissance style. Many of the statues were imported from Italy, as were the tapestries and precious period furniture. All these made the chateau of Chenonceau a royal residence. Catherine d'Medici is said to have improved the library and refurbished the hunting lodge.'

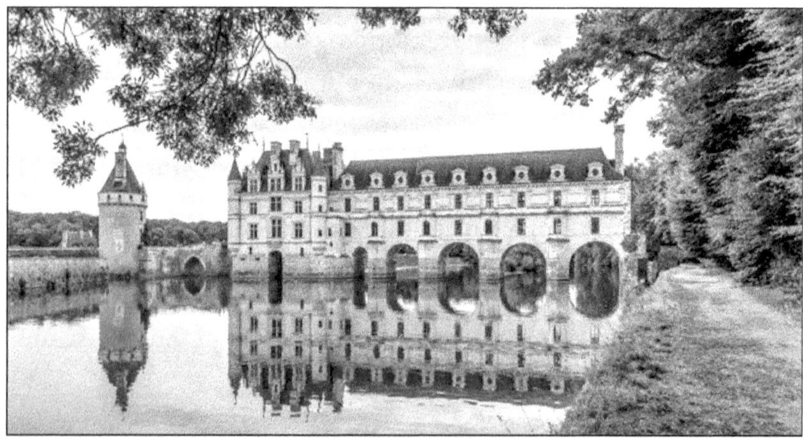

Still flabbergasted, we sauntered through to the grand gallery. There was much to admire from the vaulted ceiling high above to the black and white tiled floor under our feet.

'This large expanse was used as a hospital during World War I. It leads to the chapel. The superb stained-glass windows, lost during World War II, were painstakingly restored in the mid-1950s to their former glory.'

Pierre sounded convincing. However, Marina and I believed nothing could surpass the windows of Chartres Cathedral that we'd seen previously.

Of considerable interest in one of the smaller rooms is a 16th century tapestry inspired by Christopher Columbus's encounter[222] with the Americas. It features examples of flora and fauna from the New World territories. Upstairs, various rooms are decorated with tapestries featuring the more familiar hunting scenes. Marble sculptures of Roman emperors decorate the galleries. These were imported from Florence.

'After years of decline and numerous changes in ownership, the chateau is now owned by the Menier family. They live in one of the spare wings and keep the rest of the place for the visiting public.'

We left Chenonceau[223] on a high, I wondered how the next castle would compare.

An hour later, we were greeted by an even more remarkable sight. Up ahead was the enormous Chateau Chambord. Back-lit

222 The Eurocentric view of Christopher Columbus discovering America in 1492 persists, even though we now know that Norsemen landed in Newfoundland and settled the area in the 10th century.

223 Chambord Chateaux is 60 km away from Chenonceau, approximately one hour by coach.

by a clear, cornflower-blue sky, it resembled a medieval fantasy and reminded me of the castle in the film *Camelot*. As we drew near, we were astounded to see a veritable forest of elongated chimneypots, pointed domes, sculpted gables and graceful pinnacles amongst the roof terraces.

'Francis I,' said Pierre, 'wanted the roofline of this castle to look like the skyline of the entire city of Constantinople.' Speechless, we just stared at the sight. Pierre continued, 'Initially built as a hunting lodge, it was subsequently razed and rebuilt in 1519 to a grander scale. Chambord has 440 rooms and is surrounded by 5000 hectares of parkland. But let's see it for ourselves.'

We left the coach in the designated parking area outside the castle precinct. The walk to the iron entry gate was short, beyond which an arbour of tall trees awaited. The crunch of fallen leaves under our feet added to my anticipation of the wonders that awaited.

'Is this the place where the spiral staircase was conceived by Leonardo da Vinci?'[224] Marina asked.

'Yes, an ingenious design,' Pierre answered. 'Built to join the various levels of the castle via two flights of stairs constructed in a huge lantern-like staircase. You can ascend on one side without meeting or making eye contact with people descending on the other side.'

'Can we test it today?' asked someone else.

'Of course,' Pierre replied. 'It is the most popular feature. We'll meet on the roof, which is another favoured tourist activity.'

'What arrangements are there for lunch?' asked one of the ladies who had a couple of children in tow.

224 In 1516, Leonardo da Vinci was in the employ of Francis I. He died in the king's arms at Amboise nearby.

'We're expected in a little over an hour's time at the café in the grounds. Meanwhile, pay attention! I will raise my folder from time to time. Please keep me in sight. If you get lost, you'll have to make your own way home.'

Marina had enormous success taking photos with her new iPad. She snapped better photos than anything I managed with either my camera or phone. The place buzzed with many different languages. I juggled between staying within earshot of Pierre's commentary and tracking my dear friend. As our group ascended the double-helix staircase, she chatted to someone from another group. I rushed over and pulled her away before we both lost sight of Pierre's beret and the folder he occasionally held aloft.

The royal apartments were on the first floor. Elaborately framed portraits hung on richly papered walls. Fine furniture throughout the rooms included several beautifully carved four-poster beds. They were made up with linen and satin coverlets to match the drapes.

On the second floor, vaulted ceilings formed an elaborate sea of white and gold caissons. The chapel and oratory were on the same floor as the trophy gallery. The walls of the long room were flanked with reindeer antlers—a sight which turned my stomach. I hurried past all the gruesome taxidermy.

The stairs ascended to the great lantern tower from where the rooftop is accessed. Marina, ever keen to capture an interesting view, was first to venture out. She had a few minutes on her own to compose an interesting picture before other people encroached. When I couldn't hold the group back, they tramped past me. I followed.

I thought not everyone would be comfortable with being so high off the ground, particularly as there was little room between the turrets and spires that needed to be negotiated before reaching the roof terrace. Up close, I thought the architectural trappings even more fascinating, but the view of the vast estate below was what held both of us in awe.

On the lower level, we viewed more reception rooms and the kitchen where pots and a cauldron hung over the huge hearth. The stables and carriage room were accessed from the kitchen. Unfortunately, we didn't have time to look at them. We were due for a break, after which we still had one more chateau to see.

Lunch was in the grounds at the *Le Café d' Orléans.* We sat down to a simple set menu. There was a choice between a flan or a sandwich with either a vegetable or side salad. We both ordered Quiche Lorraine with garden salad and a glass of white wine. It was an ideal way to end our visit to Chambord.

Chateau Cheverny[225] was a mere 20 minutes away. Bathed in soft sunshine, the verdant countryside appeared especially lush. In the distance, glimpses of the white limestone chateau provided a foretaste of our destination. In comparison, I'd describe Cheverny[226] as more of a mansion than a chateau.

We strolled through the gates along a well-tended driveway where *parterre gardens* were manicured to the last leaf. Water features, topiary and velvety lawns all added to the calm and elegance of the scene.

Pierre told us Cheverny was built in 1630 as a hunting lodge. Owned by the Hurault family, it has passed down the line of heirs to the present owner, the Marquis de Vibraye.

225 Chateau Chambord is only 17 km away from Cheverny, roughly 20 minutes' drive.
226 Cheverny has been open to the public since 1922.

Charles-Antoine and his wife, Constance, live in a private wing of the chateau with their three children. Their home has been open to the public since 1922. While we were there, we met the Marquis. He showed us around the main reception room and described his relationship to the people whose portraits hung in pride of place. The painting he was most proud of was that of his children when they were toddlers. As well, there were paintings by Mignard, Titian and others from the workshop of Raffaello. Antique furniture, *objets d'art* and several 16th century Flemish tapestries were lovingly displayed.

The sumptuous apartments on the first floor were restored to convey the art of living well. An impressive example was the main bedroom. This room featured a beautifully painted ceiling by Jean Mosnier representing the story of Perseus and Andromeda. Someone commented that the bed was too small, but Pierre explained it was an illusion. However, at that time, the custom was to sleep sitting up. Lying down was for the dead.

The armoury, undoubtedly the largest room of the castle, is filled with armour and trophies. The ceiling, covered in beams and the wood panelling, is painted with floral decorations and Latin inscriptions. The main treasure is the 17th century Gobelin tapestry and a library of 2000 antique books.

Large flower and vegetable plots occupy the area behind the kitchen, with herbs in easy reach of the back door. The kennels alongside the stables can accommodate a pack of 120 hounds. Marina and I, both dog lovers, thought the dogs looked a bit like Beagles because of their characteristic tricolour coats and floppy ears. However, these hounds had longer legs. Pierre said the dogs were French Poitevins, and on occasion, the pack has been known to include English Foxhounds. Beagles and other similar dogs are descendent from the Poitevins. The pack is taken out twice weekly to hunt.

Refreshments were in the *Orangerie,* where fine dining is also available. Out of the question for us at this time, as we had a long trip back.

In Paris it had rained all day, and as we approached the city, the rain became heavier. The upside was that there were fewer cars on the roads in the city. There was still the Metro for Marina and me to negotiate. By the time we arrived at Chemin Vert, we were very tired and hungry. The lights were still burning in the little restaurant on the corner, where we'd eaten on the first night. Although expensive, the cuisine incorporated classic pork and chicken dishes. Included were seasonal vegetables enhanced with fresh herbs from the chef's own garden.

Just as well Europeans eat late, because it was nine in the evening when we sat down. It didn't seem to matter. People were still arriving and we were lucky to get a table. The menu was in French, with no English explanations, so again we fumbled with words we thought we knew and hoped we hadn't ordered tripe or some other offal.

I ordered *Porc Cassoulet*—a casserole made with pork, haricot beans and wild mushrooms. Marina ordered *Sole Meunier* and we shared some green beans and *Pommes au Gratin* with freshly baked bread and a robust red wine. This made it easy to skip dessert in favour of a small cheese platter, which we enjoyed with what was left of our wine. Well satisfied and relaxed, we stayed to enjoy a *Café au Lait.*

Back at the hotel, I sat up with my diary. Marina dispatched more emails to the family before turning to the task of culling the many photos she'd taken during the day. She called out, interrupting my train of thought.

'Come here,' she cried. 'Look at the window in this photo. What can you see? Don't you think it looks like a figure standing outside peering in at us?'

Indeed, it was a short person, perhaps a dwarf with a white forelock, wearing some sort of conical hat and a loose kaftan. He blended into the background and could easily have been overlooked if Marina hadn't pointed him out.

'You were the first on the roof,' I said. 'There was no one else there, not till our group followed us out.'

'That's right. There was no one else out there,' she confirmed.

'A reflection? Was someone behind you?'

'If it had been a reflection, then why am I not similarly reflected?' She paused. We both stared hard at her photo. 'The place is haunted. I've experienced this sort of thing before, on other trips.'

'Who knows?' I replied. 'Years ago, when I was in Jerusalem, I too had strange things happen with my camera, but never like this photo.'

Chapter 30
Impressionists

Nadia arrived early to have breakfast with us and return my washing. She'd ironed every item. That's when I realised, she didn't have a dryer and I felt doubly embarrassed for letting her do it. The climate in Paris is wetter than in London so I don't know how people live without a dryer.

Graphic design, fabrics and fashion were Nadia's artistic field of endeavour. As slender as Margot Fonteyn, Nadia carried herself with an aura of chic. That day, she wore a black fedora and sunglasses, which made her look as if she'd stepped straight out of the movie *Breakfast at Tiffany's*. A brightly patterned scarf was intricately wound around her neck. It was an eye-catching contrast to her tailored pants and blazer.

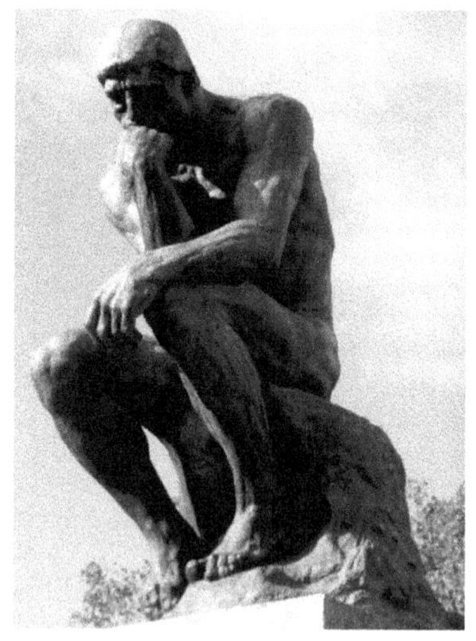

'Bags close to chests, girls,' she whispered as we boarded the train at the Metro for our short journey to Opera Garnier to see if we could buy an opera ticket for Marina to attend with me that evening. We arrived as the box office opened and were so lucky to buy her a seat near mine. Pumped with our success, we continued our excursion as planned.

The Rodin Museum, situated a few metres from the Metro, was an elegant mansion set in lush terrain. His famous bronze sculpture, *The Thinker,* greeted us in silent contemplation. We continued around to the side of the building where *The Burghers of Calais, The Gates of Hell* and the famed bust of Balzac were on display. Then we doubled back to the front door of the mansion to enjoy the interior.

Marble sculptures were set out in chronological order, but I ignored the set plan. I was extremely excited to be in the same rooms where Auguste Rodin had worked and lived—to walk on the floors he'd paced, to breathe the air he'd breathed and be bathed in the faint aroma he'd left behind. These were all part of the intangible aura of the Master. I jumped from one old favourite to another. *The Kiss* has always been my number one and here I was surrounded by several studies and sketches Rodin had made before he produced his final masterpiece.

Over the years, Marina must have sketched hundreds of figures but she was especially interested in hands. She spent a long time examining a sculpture of two hands crossed and held in prayer position. Every vein and joint was meticulously worked to be life-like.

Nadia had visited the gallery many times and guided us to a separate room where the work of Camille Claudel was kept. Claudel was Rodin's muse, his inspiration, model and lover. She was also an accomplished sculptor in her own right. There was a sepia photograph of her, which was taken by

Rodin. Photography was a new medium, which he enjoyed. I was particularly drawn to Claudel's bronze bust of August Rodin and her sculpture called *The Waltz*. I loved the way she'd captured the movement of the dancers.

On our way out to the back of the property, I noticed a few paintings along the passageway from his friends Monet, Renoir and Van Gogh.

Café L'Augustine occupied a verandah surrounded by lime and linden trees and was exactly where we needed to refresh before continuing to our next museum. Autumn leaves covered the path, adding their golden palette below the reds and pinks of the still blooming rose bushes. A coffee and croissant were enough for me and Marina. Nadia said she didn't eat during the day. *That explains how she keeps so trim, but how boring to live in a country known for its haute cuisine and resist eating.*

We returned to the Metro for the short trip to the *Musee d'Orsay*, which was built on the former train station, *Gare d'Orsay*. It is dedicated to the Impressionist era. Nadia left us there. She had things to do before Jacques came home. Besides, she'd been to the museum many, many times before.

Built on three levels, *Musée d'Orsay* is home to many artworks that were previously exhibited at the Louvre. The ground floor level is dedicated to Classicism, Symbolism and Art Nouveau, as well as the beginning stages of Impressionism.

Instantly recognisable was Ingres's painting, *The Source*. The brochure indicated that with this odalisque, Ingres had reached his peak of perfection. Further on was an early Degas. This held immense interest for me. The painting was a study of the prominent Bellini family. The girls in bright white pinafores, as was the fashion of the day, contrasted sharply with their dark toned dresses. It was the sort of fashion young girls wore to school when my mother was a child.

Next was Manet's *Olympia,* which caused a huge scandal at the time for flaunting her perfect peaches-and-cream nakedness. I loved the calm, confident expression on her face. Of course, we were also delighted to see his better-known *Picnic on the Grass.*

On the middle level were decorative arts and furniture, splendid chiffoniers, corner cabinets and *vitrine*—display cases with intricately carved decoration of the Art Nouveau style. I wanted to run my fingers over the velvety, warm glow of their polished grain. Few paintings on this level were familiar to me apart from Rousseau's naïve, dream-like jungle scenes. The sculptures included my favourites by August Rodin, Camille Claudel and Maillol.

The upper level was devoted to the Impressionist period of 1841–1919. We had to cross over a bridge in front of the enormous railway clock to get to the exhibition. I was most impressed with my surroundings and wondered if this was the setting for a movie[227] I'd seen. My camera placed the foreground into silhouette but Marina's iPad worked its magic, allowing us to photograph each other in front of the bank of windows and the clock.

Inside the enormous hall an exposition of Impressionism awaited. We were enraptured by the works of Renoir, Degas,

227 Scorsese's wonderful film, *Hugo,* was set in 1931, Paris. Hugo lived in the walls of the Gare Montparnasse train station. The cinematographer achieved a most dramatic effect with the orphaned boy, hiding behind a clock identical to the one here. The movie was based on the 2007 book, *The Invention of Hugo Cabret* by Brian Selznick.

Monet and Sisley. Post-Impressionist paintings by Picasso, Gauguin, Cezanne, Van Gogh and Lautrec all came to life before our eyes. Standing so close to them captured our imagination and held us in awe.

Auguste Renoir's composition of two girls at the piano is a favourite of mine, but I was stunned to see the same two young girls sitting together in another painting, but this time they were reading a book. I subsequently learned that Renoir often used them in his paintings. One was the daughter of fellow artist Berthe Morrisette, and the other, her cousin. This canvas was painted in 1895 and is called *The Lesson*. It made me think of my cousin and how growing up we did all things together.

His most famous scene, the joyful *Moulin de la Gallette*, was reminiscent of other busy squares in Paris where people sat at tables chatting while others danced. You could almost hear the music and laughter.

Cezanne's *Cardplayers*—not as well-known—is another favourite of mine. I love the look of concentration on the faces of the players as they smoke over their cards and their obvious dedication to the game. Edgar Degas's ballerinas is another favourite genre. I remembered when Marina and I both visited the Degas exhibition in Canberra how surprised I'd been to see his wonderful bronze sculpture of a ballerina. I'd always thought Degas only ever painted. I didn't realise he also sculpted.

We were delighted to see Van Gogh's *Self Portrait* and Gauguin's exotic island studies, the bright colours so joyful. Toulouse-Lautrec's vivid posters created for the Moulin Rouge were full of action, music, cigarette smoke and absinthe. They lured us into their *milieu*. I smiled smugly. We had tickets for the following week and would experience being there with Lautrec and the Moulin Rouge can-can dancers.

Marina and I floated out from that romantic-fantasy world, straight into the reality of the busy city. Once on the Metro, our exalted state quickly dissipated and we started to make plans for our evening activities.

Having the mini-market near our hotel was enormously convenient. We ducked in to buy a small baguette with cheese and ham to tide us over and hopefully avoid the embarrassment of tummy grumbles at the opera.[228] A quick change into our glad-rags and we were off again on the Metro. This time our destination was the Opera Garnier for the new production of *Rakes' Progress*, which is a take on *Pilgrim's Progress*.

The only way to enter these hallowed halls was with a theatre ticket.[229] Inside was like stepping into the *Belle Epoch*. The central atrium was bound by the splendid grand staircase made from solid Carrara marble. Along the walls was a sea of ornate gilt-framed mirrors that reflected the brilliance of many sparkling, crystal chandeliers. We couldn't help gawking in wonderment at the lavish interior. No matter how I tried to blend in, we were clearly tourists.

In the mezzanine, champagne was on offer. With flutes as props, we wandered nonchalantly, inspecting the stunning ballet and opera costumes displayed in glass *vitrines*. Even though the displays were changed frequently, regular theatregoers would have seen them a million times. Our behaviour exposed us as first-timers, particularly as Marina found it difficult to contain her gasps of delight. When the bells rang, we made our way to our seats.

228 The performance commences at 7:30 pm.

229 I note that since my visit, there are set tours of the theatre available during the day.

In front stalls, my seat was on the central aisle. I'd booked it before embarking on my trip to ensure an uninterrupted view. Marina's ticket had been bought at the theatre and was at the end of the row. My neighbours introduced themselves. They were Paul and Barbara from Boston. They kindly offered to move down one seat to allow Marina to sit next to me.

The theatre was stunning. The boxes were all gilt and red velvet as splendid as the *Bolshoi,* Mariinsky or *La Scala* and the extravagant stage curtain was a masterstroke to top the lot. Neither of us were disappointed by the interior. The performance was modern and included nudity and coarse language, which I thought was incongruent with our sumptuous surroundings, but my friend was completely dismayed. We agreed that Stravinsky's discordant score suited the production. Still, it's all about 'being there' and taking a tour is not the same as sitting in the audience.

After the opera, we went across the road to the *Café de la Paix,* situated on the ground floor of the Grand Hotel. We ordered *Crêpes Suzette* for our supper. To my mind, this is nothing short of ambrosia of the gods. The crêpes were flamed at our table with Grand Marnier; another recreation of the *Belle Epoch,* although if truth be known, I could have enjoyed myself just as much with a simple tuna sandwich from this restaurant because of its name. The name took me back to the best years of my youth, when my first love took me to the *Café de la Paix* in Paddington to dine and dance cheek to cheek. He's no longer with us, but the memories live on in my heart.

We splurged on a taxi home as it was unwise to take the Metro at midnight.

The next day we had a late start, taking off at 10:30 in the morning for the *Musee L'Orangerie,* positioned in the western corner of the *Jardin des Tuileries.*[230] Claude Monet designed the latest refurbishment of the gallery, where he contrived a white room as a buffer zone between the agitation of the city and his paintings.

It is the permanent home of Monet's eight water lilies murals[231], created especially for the gallery. They are exhibited as a continuum across the walls of two oval rooms. These murals were featured in Woody Allen's 2011 film, *Midnight in Paris,* a delightful fantasy, which I never tire of viewing.

L'Orangerie exhibits only Impressionist and Post-Impressionist artists. Although their styles vary, each is immediately identifiable. For example, Henri Matisse with his chunky nudes and bright-coloured backgrounds or Modigliani's elongated portraits are so different from Auguste Renoir's dreamy romantic scenes and Monet's languid lily ponds. I always think Paul Cezanne's brush strokes, particularly those used in his still-life compositions, suggest his transition to Cubism. Picasso's dreamy harlequins so different to Henri Rousseau's naïve figures amid jungle-like foliage, while Maurice Utrillo's street scenes with their precise perspective make him instantly recognisable.

What a treat to see such a vast array of Impressionism and to do it at our own pace. If only we could have stayed all day. *Perhaps there'll be time to return,* I mused. We headed back along Rue Rivoli through the drizzly rain towards *Place des Pyramides* and the Joan of Arc statue, where our day trips began and ended.

230 Napoleon III had the orangery built 1852 to protect the citrus trees.

231 Each panel is two metres high and 91 metres long.

Marina stopped to change money at a kiosk. I preferred to use an ATM inside a bank to withdraw money. They seem more discreet. But that's my careful side, whereas Marina is trusting and sees the good in everyone. The street appeared empty and, having done the exchange, we continued on our way.

A colourful window display of various accessories caught Marina's eye. There are always gifts to be bought for family members and, with that in mind, we stopped to look. A woman's voice with an Eastern European accent came from close behind us.

'You drop this, I think,' she said, holding up a plain gold band.

Marina immediately checked her own fingers, but there was no need for me to look, I boldly held her stare.

'No, not ours.'

'I find on ground, look here near you. It not mine, I not have husband,' she cajoled. 'You take.'

'No, no. We don't want it. Take it to the police station. If no one claims it, you will be able to keep it,' Marina suggested.

'I no take to police station. I 'ave no paper, no passport. You give me money. You take to police station.'

Her voice became less pleading and decidedly more demanding. I dragged Marina by the sleeve into the shop where I was sure the woman wouldn't follow. She stood in the doorway and continued to harass us. The shopkeeper told us to take our arguments out of her shop. I reached into my pocket where I had a €5 note and gave it to the scammer. But she became even more indignant.

'What this, my ring, it gold. €5 not enough money.'

I grabbed the ring out of Marina's hands and pressed it into the woman's palm, then shut the shop door in her face. We chatted to the shopkeeper, who was none too happy with us or the scammer.

'These people are everywhere,' she said. 'You must not encourage them. You must not talk with them. They come for the tourists. We must live here, you know.'

After promising not to feel sorry for beggars and street urchins and to hold onto our belongings tightly, we apologised, then left. The booking office for day tours was nearby, which was where we were originally heading to confirm our remaining excursions.

After completing the confirmations, we hopped back on the Metro to the *Musee de Cristal Baccarat* showroom and wholesaler. Located in the suburbs, the building was once a mansion, but had been converted into a factory. We walked up a steep staircase, at the top of which hung a huge crystal chandelier.

Reception resembled a miniature version of the Hall of Mirrors in Versailles. A security guard pointed to the door of the museum and handed us a brochure. Stepping through the door, I gazed up to the ceiling, which was draped in voluminous, painted parachute silk. I thought I'd entered into a fantasy world, something like the *Tales from 1,001 Nights*. The brochure indicated that the colours signified the four elements: earth, air, water and fire, which are the constituents of crystal. From the centre hung another sparkling chandelier. On either side, glass cabinets displayed antique vases.

Elevated glass cabinets held examples of prestigious stemware, which over the years, had been commissioned by monarchs, heads of state, aristocracy and captains of industry. Their guests emulated the fine designs by commissioning their own crystal and so the business grew. Today's clients include oil sheiks, maharajas, pop stars and various glitterati and want-to-be types.

The clarity of Baccarat's crystal, be it clear, rose or coloured, speaks for itself. What sets this company apart is the skill of the designers and artisans, the glass-blowers, glasscutters, engravers, embossers and gilders. On display were the easily recognisable perfume flacons made for Dior, Guerlain, Van Clef, Hennessy cognac, along with other examples of patented glassware commissioned by their loyal clientele.

In the other rooms we saw wonderful examples of more modern designs in glassware—expensive feature pieces for display. Sleeker designs in stemware, one-off designer chandeliers, chess sets, punch bowl sets, diamond-cut ornaments and other exquisite trifles for the mega rich clients of famous interior decorators. It was our indulgence into a fantasy world.

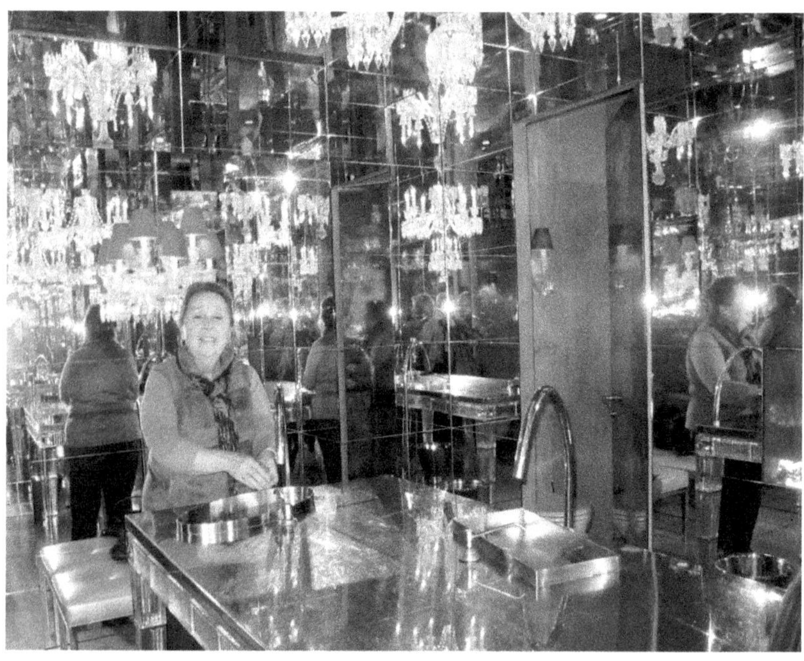

Light refreshments were available in a charming little tearoom. We ordered macaroons with our coffee. A visit to the ladies' powder room turned out to be an unexpected highlight. A narrow shelf under a mass of classic, bevelled mirrors covered an entire wall, where you could sit on elegant stools to fix make-up and hair. Each mirror had small crystal wall lights that aided the kindest reflection. Cherry red silk wallpaper was decorated with black flock, fleur-de-lys. The hand basins had crystal taps and gilded spouts, shaped like swans about to take flight. To complete our ablutions, a stack of soft hand towels lay beside each setting. It was all glitz, glamour and gilt. We waltzed out of there as if we'd returned from a weekend at the palace.

By five-thirty, we arrived back at Chemin Vert early for dinner, but we knew if we went straight home, we'd be too tired to venture out again later. Although we had a tenuous arrangement to see Nadia at a local church for vespers, that too, was not going to happen.

At the only café open this early for dinner, I ordered steak and chips with a garden salad. The steak was thin but tasty. This was followed by mousse with decoratively placed strawberries on a pond of berry *coulis*. Marina ordered *Boeuf Bourguignon* with glazed carrots on the side and salad, followed by a slice of pear tart, which she very much enjoyed. Cappuccino rounded off the meal before we headed back to the hotel. There was only enough energy left for our journal entries and a little photo culling before bed.

The following morning, Marina told me that the instant my head touched my pillow, I was asleep. I smiled at her comments. *Not a wonder, after a remarkably busy day.*

Chapter 31
A High Day

The feast of the Protective Veil of the Blessed Virgin was a high day and we'd made plans to meet up with Anthony, a relative of Marina's, after the service. In France, as in Italy, the service starts at ten, an hour later than what we are used to in Australia. This gave us time for a leisurely breakfast before getting ourselves to the *Cathédrale Alexander Nevsky* on *Rue Daru*, in *Courcelles*. The journey required two changes of lines on the Metro but by then, we were expert commuters.

The church, situated in the Russian centre of Paris, is a short walk from the station. We passed by a bookshop, an epicurean food store, a gift shop and two restaurants. I noted items on the menu, Chicken Kiev and *Stroganov de Veau*. I earmarked these as possible dishes for our lunch with Anthony.

The 1861 church with five domed spires[232] was built in the neo-Byzantine style, to cater specially to the growing population of permanent and visiting Russians to Paris. Tsar Alexander II had added 200,000 francs from his own purse to the building fund.

The interior is richly decorated with frescoes and mosaics, which reach high into the central apse. Many precious icons written by eminent iconographers hang on the walls. These were donated by members of the nobility who had fled to Paris after the Bolshevik Revolution of 1917.

In 1918, Pablo Picasso married Olga Kokhlova in this church. Years later, this cathedral saw the funerals of film director Andrei Tarkovsky and the composer Michel Legrand, artist Vassily Kandinsky, and authors Ivan Turgenev and Ivan Bunin, who was a recipient of Nobel Prize for literature.

Due to it being a special day, the church was decorated with an abundance of fresh flowers. It soon filled with people and incense. As there were no pews, the capacity was increased. This day, five clergy and a bishop, all resplendent in rich vestments, conducted the service with the assistance of six altar boys and readers.

I'd been looking forward to hearing the choir and it was every bit as good as I'd expected. I lamented being born too late for Nicolai Gedda's wonderful tenor[233] to grace this ensemble in person.[234] He was the 10th-best operatic singer of all time. He sang here at *Rue Daru* in the 1950s and '60s. At that time, the soloist led the most important hymns while the rest of the choir supported in the background.

I can only imagine the depth of emotion one would feel being in attendance during some of the Lenten and Easter services. I'm thinking particularly of a hymn known as 'The Penitent Thief'. I imagined how three soloists—baritone, bass, and tenor—sang in front of the Crucifix, recalling the words of penitence uttered by the thief. Immersed in the moment, with Gedda as tenor, I imagined it would be like stepping into Heaven itself.

233 Gedda was the most recorded tenor of our time. His tenor was said to be elegant; his C# matched that of Sutherland. His technique was flawless, with darker colours and was a joy to hear.

234 Gedda was born in Sweden. His mother was Swedish, his father Russian—a music teacher and choir master. He sang with the choir at the Russian Orthodox Cathedral of Alexander Nevsky in Paris. He spent 26 years with the Met and was also popular at *La Scala* in Milan.

Pavarotti once said, 'There is no tenor alive with a greater upper register than Gedda.'

It seemed to have been so long ago, another time altogether. I bought a couple of CDs of the church choir featuring Nicolai Gedda as soloist. Years later, I learned he was still alive at the time of my visit. He died in 2017 at his home in Lausanne, Switzerland aged 91 years. That was five years after our visit to Paris.

Marina caught sight of her watch. She nudged me—noon already—and Communion had just commenced. People were jam-packed but we managed to make our way out to the exit, where Anthony stood waiting patiently. Marina suggested we go across the road for lunch, but he insisted his wife, Maxine, was expecting us at home. Anthony's car was parked in the next street and we left straight away.

Anthony and Maxine lived with their daughter Kathleen and Paprika, a dog of mixed parentage. Their lovely cottage was situated in the semi-rural outskirts of Paris. Maxine was an unpretentious lady—slim and tall, like her husband. She was a cellist and music teacher. She belonged to a string quartet that performed at aged care homes on weekends. Unfortunately, our visit clashed with the gig Maxine had that day. So after giving some instructions regarding the meal to Anthony, she left. Paprika moped by the door, awaiting Kathleen's return.

We started with a little champagne and nibblies while Marina and Anthony caught up on family matters. Lunch was delicious. The roast beef, done to perfection, was accompanied by rice and green beans. Anthony quizzed us on our sightseeing and what we hoped to do in the coming weeks.

We chatted over a cheese platter of local cheeses, dried fruit and fresh walnuts that Maxine had left. We enjoyed this while we finished the dry oaky red from the Rhone Valley, which we'd been enjoying throughout the meal. Marina had arranged to spend a couple of days with Anthony and Maxine while I was attending a cooking Master Class in Toulouse. They spoke of visiting *Fontainebleau*, which was their nearest chateau.

Although still drizzling outside, we doggedly continued our plan to visit *Cimetière de Sainte Genevieve des Bois*.[235] Waiting for us at the gate was Anthony's friend, Catherine, who would be our guide at the cemetery. She was an unassuming young lady in a hooded raincoat, gumboots and backpack. She held a large black umbrella aloft. We already knew the historical background, so she was able to take us to specific graves.

We found the resting place of several Romanov Grand Dukes. I almost passed by the humble grave of Prince Felix Yusopov.[236] He was complicit in Rasputin's death. His family came from great wealth—they were richer than the Romanovs—but his grave with its simple inscription was unadorned like that of a simple pensioner. Felix's wife Irina, who was the first granddaughter of Alexander III and niece of Nicholas II, was buried similarly alongside her husband.

The grave of the most famous military person I saw was that of General Wrangel. He famously led the White Movement against the Bolsheviks. We saw the resting places of artists[237]

235 Many trees were planted to create an authentic Russian feel to the cemetery. It is estimated that there are more than 5,000 graves.

236 Felix died in 1967 and his wife Irina in 1970.

237 Like the Impressionist Konstantin Korovin, whose work I'd seen at the Hermitage in St Petersburg.

and writers[238], including two recipients of the Nobel Prize for Literature. I found the resting place of prominent people from the nobility including relatives of people I knew.[239]

For a time, we parted to wander in different directions in silent contemplation. The cemetery was laid out in an orderly fashion with monuments, paths and plots showing signs of regular maintenance. What set it apart was the abundance of trees, mainly birches. It was the song of the birch leaves fluttering in the breeze, that soft mournful whisper reminding visitors of the roots of those interred.

There were the graves of film director Andre Tarkovsky and several stars from the world of ballet, including those of Nijinsky, Sergei Lifar and Mathilde Kschessinska. Not only was she an outstanding ballerina but was also the former mistress of Nicholas II before his marriage. So many great names, all at rest here many miles from home.

Catherine and Anthony stood waiting amid a sea of concrete, marble and granite. As I neared, I saw a splash of bright colour. It was an unusual monument, the resting place of Rudolph Nureyev—a raised sarcophagus on a plinth of polished black granite covered with a luxurious oriental carpet made of glimmering mosaic tiles. The craftsmanship was stunning. The design reflected his Tartar roots. It was a good note on which to end our visit.

238 The first Russian recipient of the Nobel Prize for Literature was Ivan Bunin in 1933, with Joseph Brodsky receiving his in 1987.

239 Nekrasov and Somov were forebears of people I knew back in Australia.

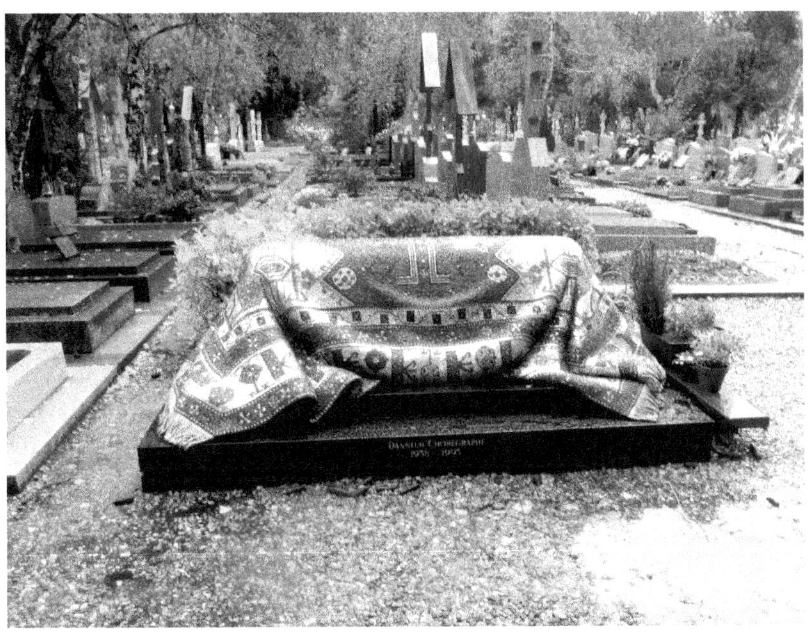

Catherine insisted we have afternoon tea at her place, where her parents waited to meet us. Her husband, Denis, greeted us at the door. The whole family had lived in Paris since 1920 and had little connection with their roots. Her father was keen to converse with someone in Russian.

Catherine's mother loved to cook her old family recipes. She'd made us a *Charlotka*—a dessert invented in the early 1800s by the French chef Marie-Antoine Carême. It consisted of a light sponge cake with layers of cinnamon-flavoured chopped apple. The top was decorated with thin slices of unpeeled apple wedged into the cake. My family made a similar one but used ladyfinger biscuits around the perimeter then filled it with berries and sponge cake.

Our visit was most enjoyable but the old couple was quite sad when it ended. Anthony explained that delay would mean we'd be stuck in traffic returning to the city after the weekend. He was right. As we neared Paris, traffic became gridlocked. With many apologies, he veered off the freeway and deposited us at a railway station. On parting, he warned us to watch out for pickpockets and scammers.

'The best way to avoid trouble is to look as if you know where you are going. Look like a local, not a tourist,' were his parting words.

After two stations, we changed to the Metro, with which we were more familiar. A short ride later and we were in Chemin Vert. After a day filled with many culinary experiences, there was no need for dinner. Instead, we headed straight to the bar. Our favourite concierge was in attendance to make coffee and serve us with some good cognac. He was very chatty and we stayed longer than intended before retiring for the night.

The next morning, after breakfast we were back on the metro to *Ile de Cite*. Our destination was *San Chapelle*. Built as a royal chapel, its sole purpose was to keep safe the precious relics associated with the Passion of Christ. Most important were the *Crown of Thorns* and the *Image of Edessa*.[240]

The small church is a two-storey gem of Gothic architecture renowned for its stained-glass windows. *How many stained-glass windows do we need to see?* I promised Marina they'd be worth the effort, besides, this €5 excursion was a fine way to spend the morning. The crowded Metro had me on edge. However, we managed the two-line changes, the escalators and the lifts without incident.

240 A piece of cloth with the miraculous imprint of the face of Jesus. Also known as the first icon or the 'icon not made by human hands'.

San Chapelle was classed as a national monument and was in the courtyard of the Palais of Justice site. At street level, we could see the spires and a statue of the Virgin Mary standing in the forecourt.

Although two-storey, the church was smaller in comparison to any others I'd seen in France. Inside, we were greeted with a kaleidoscope of colourful decorations with ample gilding. Fleur-de-lys on an azure background covered the walls and gold stars featured on the low ceiling. Columns were painted in rich cinnabar, emerald, purple, cobalt and gold.

The precious relics[241] were kept on the upper level, which was reserved for the royal family and clergy. The lower chapel was for the palace staff. The colours used in the stained-glass windows were stunning, but I was disappointed to see other visitors barely pausing to look at them. Instead, they hurried upstairs.

On this occasion, herd mentality did not discourage us and we followed. The room was bathed in jewel-like colours streaming through the stained glass. The sight was overwhelming. I thought I'd stepped into the Heavenly Realm itself. The walls were a bank of slender stained glass windows depicting scenes from Genesis to the Resurrection. Each pane was delineated with fine gilded columns which made the whole appear both intricate and weightless. The rose window at the western end could only be described as a flamboyant colour wheel. It depicted Christ's second coming at the end of time to judge the living and the dead.

The church has wonderful acoustics and is the venue for Baroque and classic concerts. These are held only twice each

241 Sainte Chapelle was built by the French king Louis IX to house the *Crown of Thorns*. The relic was transferred to Notre-Dame in Paris and survived the devastating fire of 2019.

week. Unfortunately, we didn't know this beforehand and had no more flexibility left in our schedule. Since then, I've had excellent reports from friends whom I've directed there.

We had time for a quick lunch before our shopping tour to direct fashion outlets (DFO). I'm not a shopper. I figured by batching the necessary shopping together, it would be taken care of in one trip.

Across the road from the tour office, we noticed a nice-looking bistro and thought it ideal for a quick lunch. Our celery soup, which was hot and tasty, arrived together with sandwiches. I had *Croque Monsieur,* which is ham and cheese on sourdough toasted in a sandwich press. Marina had *Croque Madame,* which was the same but with the addition of a poached egg, which was perched on top.

Judging by the size of the coach, I decided it was a popular excursion. As soon as the bus was filled with a lot of noisy women speaking in every imaginable language, we were on our way. The shopping complex comprised four streets of shops all in a gated industrial site. There were so many labels—Hugo Boss, Kookai, Calvin Klein and Lacoste. Marina bought some items for her two sons and husband.

We made a thorough investigation of the Christian Lacroix, Givenchy and Celine handbags so temptingly displayed. The aroma of new leather led us to powderpuff soft jackets, berets and gloves. Shoes with impossible heels, designed by Chloé, Marc Jacobs, Repetto, Vivier and other brands I'd not heard of, all begged us to buy. On sale were men's, ladies' and children's apparel, perfumes and accessories. I tried on some heavily reduced items. The sizes were impossibly small, while the prices were ridiculously large. It didn't help that we'd just had lunch and I wondered at the wisdom of eating beforehand.

Marina managed to find things of interest in each store. I thought the whole thing was a rip-off. We were flies lured into the cobweb and the only way out alive was to buy, buy, buy. I noticed other shoppers from our bus were loaded with bags. I'd bought nothing; the goods on offer were either not to my taste or not to my purse.

On the periphery of the shopping madness, a room full of shoes materialised as if by magic. I was drawn to the row upon row of tables heaped with shoes. I gave them a cursory once-over. Just before I retreated, a pair of black suede shoes with medium heels commandeered my gaze. They sat like wallflowers, dejected, on a table abutting the wall of a dead-end row. I examined one shoe. It was my size. I tried it on. It felt comfortable. I picked up the box to check the size and noticed the style was my name. *They've got my name on them, so I'll have to buy them.* I put on the other shoe and searched for a mirror to see the overall appearance.

The shopkeeper came up. 'Last pair, I have no other sizes,' she said.

'*Merci, Madame. Combien*?' They were French and not cheap.

Overall, of the many day tours we'd enjoyed, the discount shopping precinct was the only dud. It wasn't cheap and the brands were mediocre. I say this though, I did buy the shoes and they have been an enormous success.

On the way home, the driver played some happy French tunes—'*La Mer*', which we all knew as 'Beyond the Sea'. This was followed by the very appropriate rendition of '*Les Champs Élysées*', about the street renowned for its high-end labels, the very same labels we shoppers had bought, albeit at a slightly discounted price.

Chapter 32
Cabaret

Jubilant shrieks and youthful buffoonery came from the breakfast room, which was filled with German backpackers. They were preparing to take off on a day trip. Marina and I barely managed to find a seat for a quick coffee and croissant to set us up for our unaccustomed tussle with peak-hour commuters on the Metro.

I think we could have alighted nearer our destination, but the extra walk was pleasant since it had stopped raining and the sun was trying hard to peep through the clouds. We headed past the gold-embellished dome of *Invalide*. This was the final burial place for Napoleon. Interestingly, it was near *Pont Tsar Alexandre III*, where we were headed.[242]

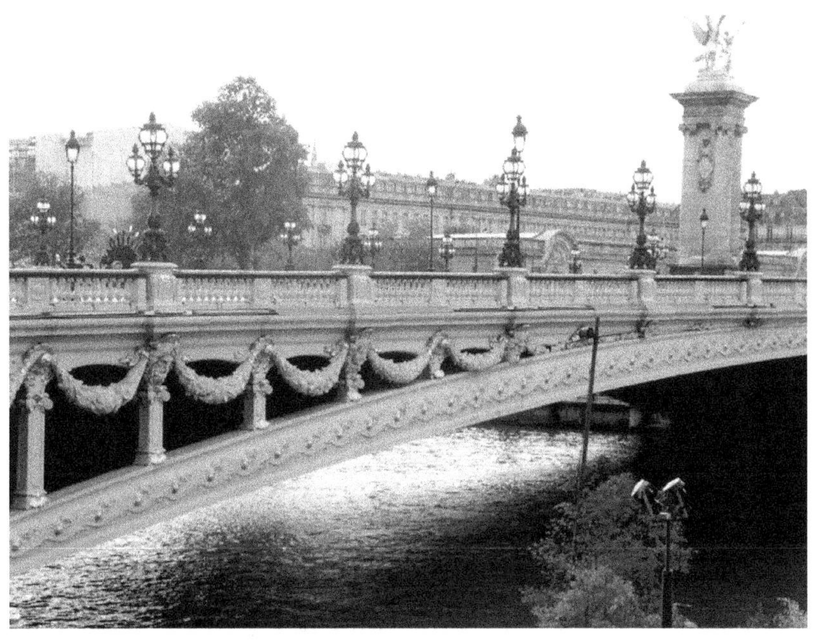

This bridge is regarded as the most beautiful and extravagant in Paris.[243] It was inaugurated in 1900 together with the *Grand Palais, Petite Palais* and *Invalides* for the World Exposition. Gilded bronze statues decorate the pylons. On the right bank, the statues commemorate the sciences, whereas the left bank celebrates commerce. The centre arches of the bridge are adorned with gilded nymphs holding a memorial shield to the Franco/Russian Alliance. For me, the most decorative features were the garlands adorning both faces of the bridge.

We marched towards *Champs Elysée*, past the *Grand Palais,* now used as government offices, and the *Petite Palais,* which houses the Museum of Fine Arts. Both were built in the French *Beaux-Art* architectural style. The cast lamp posts, found all over Paris, are a masterpiece of Art Nouveau style.

We strutted up one side of the *Champs Elysée*[244] to the *Arc de Triomphe*.[245] This arch is one of the most famous symbols of Paris and serves as the finish line for the *Tour de France* cycling race and is the focal point for the Bastille Day military parades. Theatres, cafés and boutiques flank the boulevard. The *Arc de Triomphe* is in the centre of a large and extremely busy roundabout. We failed to notice the entry to the underground walkway, so had to pose for photos on the edge of the footpath with the arch in the distance.

Finally, we managed to cross the wide boulevard to check out the window displays with enticing brand names emblazoned on the buildings. Names like Cartier, Louis Vuitton, Tiffany, Bulgari and many of the ones we had seen at the discount outlet. However, this stock was from a different colour palette and style. The wonderful menswear stores of Emanuel Ungaro and Zegna were well over our budgets. Instead, there were Levi, Lacoste and Armani.

One window held us captive. The model at the centre wore smart casual attire—trousers in a sort of plaid pattern of black and slate on a dove-grey background with a fine line of cherry. The ensemble was set off with a cashmere sweater, artistically draped across the mannequin's shoulders. A matching plaid cap completed the outfit, but for one further accessory—a French bulldog, on a lead, with matching coat and hat. This scene had us chortling with laughter. So smart but so ridiculous and our commiserations went out to any unfortunate dog made to be rigged out in that way.

244 It is French for elysian fields and was built to honour Napoleon's victories.

245 With the current volume of traffic, the street is considered one of the most polluted in the world. It's closed for traffic the first Sunday of every month until a project to green up the city with more gardens and trees is completed, hopefully for the 2024 Paris Olympic Games.

Further along, people were milling around. As we gained ground, we were treated to the sight of a sleek, mailbox-red Ferrari alongside a canary-yellow Lamborghini. Two young *Mafiosi* types, rigged out in leathers, were offering a ride at €89 per 20 m. I'm not sure if it meant 20 minutes, 20 miles or something else. The cars, like two floozies, were touted on the sidewalk, but we were not so naïve as to be taken for a ride.

From muscles to mussels—*Leon Bruxelles,* a café chain nearby, was offering a three-course lunch special at €13.50. Inside the well-patronised eatery, it was a very slick operation. We sat up at a bar, elbows on the table, just like everyone else. The patrons might have been office workers. They looked as if they were on their short lunch break.

A garden salad with a ranch-style dressing arrived quite quickly and when we'd finished eating, it was followed by a bowl of garlic mussels surrounded by steaming-hot broth. Freshly baked bread was offered to sop up the flavoursome juices. The waitperson—you're not allowed to call them *garçon* anymore—offered us a decent house white to accompany the meal and we dug in like chickens lined up at a feeder. For dessert, we were offered a *crème brûlée* or chocolate mousse. Quick and tasty, it was the perfect lunch.

Back home, after a quick change of clothes, we returned to town for a sensational evening in Paris. There were 30 of us on this night-time tour. Our guide, Simone, reminded me of my French teacher, Miss Pandu, from high school days. She was short in stature and wore her dark hair in a sort of coconut cut. The only thing large about her was her voice—it was high-pitched and instantly drew our attention.

Before boarding the bus, she noted our addresses for the complimentary return to our hotels at the end of the night. *What a clever idea after a night of partying.* We sat upstairs on the big, red London-style bus for the lights of the city segment of the tour. Most of these spots we'd already been to, but at night, statues were floodlit and trees festooned with fairy lights—there was an air of magic to the city.

The Eiffel Tower[246] was our first stop. The views from the structure were spectacular. Marina was in seventh heaven, taking non-stop photos to the left and right, so we almost missed the lift to go to the first-floor restaurant. By the time we arrived, all the seats in our designated area were taken. We had to share a booth with another couple.

I'd forgotten that everything happens for a reason. Margo and Mike introduced themselves. They were younger than us. Newly engaged. Margo, a petite blonde, seemed familiar. She sounded Australian too. *Everyone has a double.* Mike was tall and lanky with a deep sonorous voice, and as it turned out, a cheeky sense of humour.

'I detect a slight Australian accent. Where are you girls from?' he asked.

'Yes, we're from Sydney,' I replied.

'So are we.' Margo guffawed in surprise.

'I'm from the Central Coast,' I said.

'And I'm from Concord,' said Marina, quickly adding, 'but I used to live on the Central Coast.'

'No way,' said Mike. 'I'm in Blackwall.'

'Blackwall? Me too,' I replied.

We gaped at each other, then laughed at this chance meeting.

246 The tower is the focal point for New Year's celebrations and Bastille Day.

It turned out that Mike lived in the next street to me, and Margo was manager of the club I belonged to. Marina and I had another friend whose son worked at the club. A member of Margo's staff, she had high praise for him. What a coincidence. Mike had an online business and Margo had taken annual leave. They'd been to London to visit Mike's family and were having a couple of days in Paris on their way home. We chatted a little about where we'd been and what we'd seen. Then dinner arrived.

'It seems our holiday is one long episode going from one table to the next,' Marina said, and we laughed at that too.

The first course was a small portion of beef terrine perched on a lettuce leaf. Our main was poached chicken breast with a light *jus*, sprinkled with slivered almonds and accompanied by smoothly mashed potato and crisp green beans. Red wine and water were included in the set menu. The choice for dessert was a sort of raspberry flummery on a coconut crumb base or the classic chocolate mousse. I thought the mousse too pedestrian, so ordered the cerise coloured flummery and was not disappointed with the pleasantly tart taste.

With the breathtaking view of Paris as a backdrop, this had to be the highlight of our trip so we were happy to stay at the restaurant for the rest of the night. But there was more to come. The bus ferried us to the River Seine where a *bâteaux-mouche* or river boat was waiting to take us on a cruise.

As we glided along the calm waterway and under the many bridges that cross the river, Simone used the PA system to do a running commentary. She told us the Seine empties into the English Channel.

'There are 37 bridges and many more walkways that cross the Seine,' she said. 'The most extravagantly decorated is the

Pont Alexandre III.[247] The oldest standing bridge was built in 1607. Ironically, it's called *Pont Neuf*[248], which means the new bridge.' As our boat passed under each of the bridges, Simone gave a summary. '*Pont d'Jéna* is named after Napoleon I's victory in Jena.'

I sat gazing through the window of the boat, as mesmerised by the magic cruise as a child would be during their first visit to Disneyland.

'*Pont de la Concorde* was built to replace the ferry,' continued Simone. 'It ran from the *Tuileries Palace* to the main square. The bridge was built using the stones from the demolished *Bastille*.'[249]

Marina continued taking photos while I listened to the commentary. I enjoyed the sights but didn't take any photos. I knew mine would be dark and disappointing. Marina would be sure to share hers.

'*Pont des Arts*, built in 1804, is the famous love-lock bridge. The custom is now prohibited due to safety concerns. The bridge connects the *Louvre* to the *Institut de France*.'

Everyone gawked to see the sight. *Perhaps they'd heard of it and were hoping to add their own contribution to the array of locks.*

'What is the prohibited custom?' asked one of the teenagers near me.

'Urban myth has it that when a couple inscribes their names on a padlock, attaches it to the bridge and throws the keys into the Seine, their love will last forever,' answered Simone. 'In

247 The bridge is 160 metres long and 40 metres wide. It connects the *Champs Élysée* with the *Invalides* buildings and the Eiffel Tower.

248 *Neuf* means the numeral nine, but it also means new or unused.

249 *Pont de la Concorde* is 153 metres long and 18 metres wide, connecting *Quai d'Orsay* on the Left Bank to Paris's largest square, *Place de la Concorde*.

2015, the tradition was prohibited in order to relieve the bridge of the crushing weight posed by so many locks.'

The hour passed quickly and we were soon back on the big red bus, wending our way to Pigalle, a red-light district, where we had a booking at the Moulin Rouge.

Marina was a bit reticent, but I assured her she would not regret this once-in-a-lifetime experience. Moulin Rouge was the place where Comte Henri de Toulouse-Lautrec[250] and his fellow artists and writers of the time used to gather. They found inspiration and often their models for all the wonderful paintings and posters they created and which we admire.

Our guide had been there many times. 'When I see Lautrec's posters. I'm immediately transported to the Moulin Rouge.[251] The subjects of his paintings lived in Pigalle and worked in the dance halls, cabarets and brothels.'

Someone behind us said Pigalle and Montmartre were Lautrec's favourite haunts.

'Correct, and Lautrec made it known he was unlike other artists in Montmartre. He didn't paint portraits, instead, he portrayed characters. He loved the underworld culture, the anonymity of masked balls where—of course, with his body—he could never be anonymous.'

'Will we see the can-can?' someone asked.

'Yes,' Simone replied. 'The can-can is synonymous with the Moulin Rouge. A racy dance introduced by the courtesans of the area and danced to a furious rhythm in sensuous costumes.[252]

250 Henri was born a count. At age 15, he suffered two major falls that left him disfigured. This was most likely the reason for him leaving his privileged life. He died at age 36, most likely due to alcohol and debauchery.

251 The Moulin Rouge was opened in 1889. It was burnt down by fire in 1915 and rebuilt in 1925 in its present form.

252 Today, there are around 80 dancers and 1000 elaborate feathered and sequined costumes.

Many of the dancers today are Australian. The costumes are stunning and the choreography is effervescent.'

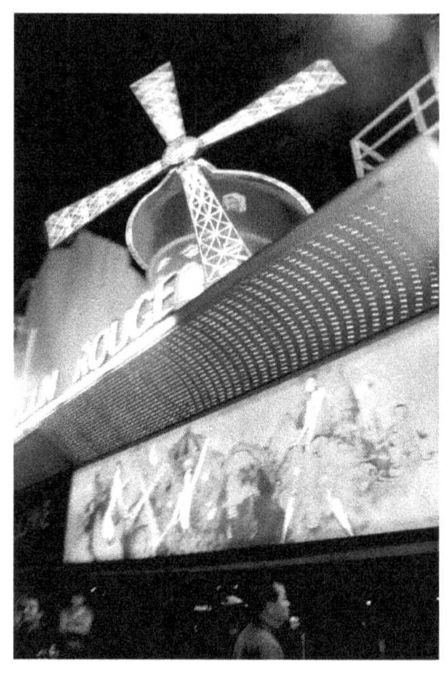

We pulled up to the iconic windmill, its name emblazoned over the entry door. The vanes of the mill were covered in bright pink neon and flashed their promise of a fun time within. Tickets were on sale for a combination of dinner and show or, alternatively, just for the show. The street was well-lit and nearby eateries were doing a steady trade. Beyond the immediate area I noticed the street lighting was quite dim, and I thought it looked ominous.

On arrival, we were shown to a large table in an area cordoned by a low barrier. After settling into our reserved seats, the waiter served us flutes of champagne. The fast-paced show, with many scene changes, was every bit as spectacular as I'd imagined. The singers and dancers, with feathered headgear and jewelled costumes that left little to the imagination, kicked up their legs in time to piercing shrieks.

There were circus acts and jugglers, acrobats and magicians. Wiry fellows balanced atop pyramids of strong men whose oiled muscles were delineated in the bright spotlight. Drinks flowed and a general feeling of unrestrained merriment coursed through the auditorium. It was a great night and we'd have loved to stay on, but the audience for the late-late show was already queued outside.

Tour buses waited at designated areas to collect their groups. The whole transportation issue was a feat of precision. On the way home, some of our fellow revellers slept while others, still on a high, continued singing and laughing.

It was 2:00 am when Marina and I were dropped off. Our hotel was securely locked for the night. A moment of panic swept over me. *How will we get inside?* A single light shone over the front door revealing a small doorbell. Our lovely concierge, who was doing the night shift, let us in and we went straight to our room.

He was still on duty when we appeared in the breakfast room.

'What are you two doing here?' he asked, clearly surprised we were not having a sleep-in after our big night out.

'We'll sleep on the bus,' I managed to say. 'Is there any coffee?'

'I'll put the kettle on,' he offered. 'Do you want a croissant each to take with you?'

'Yes, please,' Marina managed to say. 'We're off to Versailles and Giverny.'

'Have to get into town first, by Metro,' I added.

Chapter 33
Versailles and Water Lilies

We waited patiently for the tour office to open, only to find we were in the wrong place. Our tour was leaving from their other office—two blocks away. Several people were ahead of us and many more followed. Those at the head of the queue had the best choice of seats on the bus. I was at the window and Marina chose the aisle, which gave her an adequate view through the front windscreen.

The slowest part of the journey was getting through the morning traffic in the city. After we passed the *Arc d' Triomphe,* my eyes grew heavy and my head leaned on the window. The sound of soft chatter through the bus lulled me to sleep and I didn't wake until we arrived in Giverny some 84 km north-west of Paris. Marina shook my arm.

'Was I snoring?' I whispered.

'Not at all. We're on the outskirts of Giverny,' she said.

Just then our tour guide, Pascal, addressed us. He was a quietly spoken, retired professor of art history from the Sorbonne. As a teacher, he had the ability to project his voice, drawing everyone's attention. He told us Giverny was a backwater made famous by the celebrated impressionist, Claude Monet. As the village came into view, old, rendered houses with flower-filled yards vied for our attention amidst several quaint cafés and hotels.

After agreeing where to meet, we were free for an hour to enjoy Monet's house and garden. My first impression was of lush green foliage towering all around us like a jungle. I expected to see something more structured, perhaps not as formal as the Renaissance gardens we'd seen in the Chateaux region, but something of that ilk. However, we felt a special reverence for our destination and meandered in silent contemplation. It was easy to see where the artist found inspiration. During the 40 years Monet lived in Giverny, he'd nurtured his garden to reflect a palette of colours that changed with the seasons.

We traipsed along a winding path to the tranquil pond filled with waterlilies—the subject of his most famous works. Without a doubt, the biggest drawcard in the garden was Monet's Japanese style bridge where visitors gathered to be photographed. In fact, there are two identical bridges covered with succulent wisteria blossoms—a sumptuous lure for bees.

'Just like the huge paintings we saw at the *Museé de L'Orangerie,'* I said to Marina.

'Look at the willows.' She pointed across the water to the bank of trees. Their fern-green tresses moved languidly in the breeze.

A decent clump of bamboo in the middle of the pond added some oriental charm. As we continued along the well-trodden track, we stopped from time to time to admire various groups of plants that appear on his universally admired canvases.

The gardens flowed from one focal point to another. We emerged in the rose garden, to stroll through an arbour covered in a profusion of climbing roses. Their heady aroma wafted through the air. Here, the garden beds were laid out in geometric order and were filled with dahlias, peonies, narcissuses, primulas and crocuses. I imagined how it would look in Spring. *Tulips, poppies, lupins and rich purple irises waiting to transfer onto his waiting canvases.*

The pathway ended at the door of the cottage. Virginia Creeper and rambling roses crept up the whitewashed walls. They framed the second-floor windows. Climbers continued around the veranda posts to meld with the bottle-green window shutters.

Inside, the rooms looked as if Monet still lived there and had just stepped out.[253] The kitchen, tiled in blue and white majolica tiles, looked warm and homely. Shiny copper pots hung in a neat row above the stove. A beautifully set, rectangular table in the middle of the buttercup yellow dining room awaited the arrival of dinner guests.

Upstairs, the children's bedrooms were simply furnished. Each had a view through the open windows to some portion of his much-loved garden. Alongside was the blue sitting room—a suntrap, warm and inviting, where the Monets had sat with family and friends. The walls were covered in paintings by fellow Impressionists. These were interspersed with Japanese memorabilia. I was immediately drawn to Katsushika Hokusai's iconic painting called *The Great Wave*. Although painted in 1906, the work produced by this artist continues to inspire, so much so, it has developed pop art status.

We left the house with a better understanding of the artist and the era in which he'd lived. Monet's garden was a timeless beauty. During the last 16 years of his life, the garden

253 Photography is prohibited inside the house. Several attendants were stationed in doorways.

was his sole delight. *I think he might have loved his garden a bit more than his art.*

Lunch was in Vernon, a little hamlet 24 km away at a quaint country cottage by a fast-flowing stream. It was called *Le Restaurant du Moulin* because of the huge waterwheel attached to the side of the building. The proprietor, a tabby cat, met us at the gate and led us through the cottage garden to the front door. Once over the threshold, the *maître d'* took over from the cat.

Because we had a group booking, we were seated in a private room to enjoy a delicious three course meal made specially for us. The first course was local trout, a pale pink coloured slice on a leaf of cos lettuce. The flavour so fresh, I wondered if the chef had dropped a line in earlier that morning. We helped ourselves to white or red wine from carafes on the table.

A tiny scoop of lime and tomato-flavoured sorbet was presented to refresh our palate before the main course, which was roast chicken served with a splash of thin pan juices. A platter of roast vegetables was placed in the centre of the table for us to share. For sweets, a slice of the perennial classic, *tarte tatin*, completed the classic menu.

Having eaten like royalty, we were ready to visit the palace of Versailles. With full stomachs and an hour's drive, we could relax, take in the scenery or have a little nap. Marina and I wondered how this famous palace would compare to those we'd already seen here in France and other grand European palaces we'd seen elsewhere.

As we neared our destination, Pascal gave us a little background. 'Like most of the major palaces, Versailles started out in the time of Louis XIII as a modest hunting lodge.'

'That's one hell of a big hunting lodge,' said someone behind us.

'His grandson Louis XIV built the original palace on the property in 1668,' continued Pascal. 'Subsequent generations added and embellished the building. He employed landscape architects to design the enormous parkland that led all the way to the forest.'

'Is that where they hunted?' asked Marina.

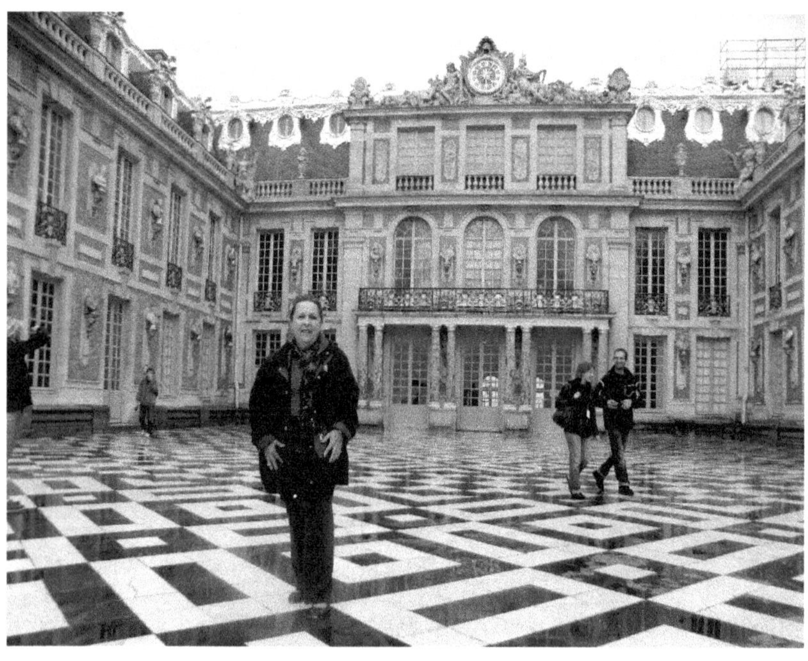

'Yes, in the adjoining forest,' Pascal answered. 'Royalty from other countries came to Versailles to hunt with Louis. They returned home inspired to build similar grand palaces of their own.'

When we arrived, we saw Versailles was bigger.[254] I think Versailles has the greatest number of fountains and statues in its park. Peterhof in St Petersburg, built in 1703, is not as big but I think more beautiful. The fountains are turned on every day for the whole of summer whereas the fountains of Versailles only function of weekends during the three months of summer.[255] Schönbrunn Palace in Vienna is another similar palace built in the early 18th century, with beautiful avenues, themed gardens and working fountains.

We entered the U-shaped palace of Versailles via a paved courtyard that led straight into the Hall of Hercules. The ceilings are exceedingly high. Large arched windows provide luminosity to huge ionic columns and dark-coloured marble panels. I thought the room was somewhat masculine, both because of its size and décor.

The nearby chapel with its magnificent marble inlaid floor, was built on two levels, the upper for the royal family and the lower for the court. I noticed that the ionic columns on the ground floor were replaced with delicate Corinthian columns upstairs. The interior was painted white with gold highlights, while the altar was a masterpiece in gilded bronze. We noted other rooms that were dedicated to different Olympian deities.

These rooms led to a long gallery known as the magnificent Hall of Mirrors. This is the most famous room in the entire palace[256] and was designed to highlight Louis XIV's power and prestige. A bank of enormous arched windows alternated with

254 Versailles, with 700 rooms, occupies eight million square metres of ground. The gardens are the largest in Europe.

255 There is no natural water source on the estate. A complicated pumping station was developed to deliver water from afar.

256 The Hall of mirrors is 70 metres long, 10.5 metres wide and the ceiling 12.3 metres high and has 357 mirrors.

ornately gilded mirrors and were reflected by the mirrors on the opposite wall. The high, coffered ceiling is infilled with frescoes depicting his many victories in battle. These are framed by gilded cornices and further decorated with cascades of stuccoed garlands. A forest of enormous Bohemian crystal chandeliers added to the dazzling display of opulence. The amount of gilding in this room was immense and was testament to the unbelievable wealth of the French court of the time.

The room was used for state occasions and was also the place where, in 1919, the Treaty of Versailles was signed. The royal apartments, decorated with Gobelin tapestries, ran parallel to the former rooms that we visited. I remember thinking the wall papers, curtains, valances and canopies, covered with intricate garlands of roses, lilacs and tulips, made the room look overcrowded. The design on the Gobelin tapestries was repeated on the upholstered chairs and footstools.

The theatre is used for recitals, plays and operas. Though it seats 750 people, it is considered small, even referred to as—cosy. The intricately carved and gilded seats are covered in sky-blue velvet are an overt expression of sheer luxury. The orchestra pit can be lowered to extend the floor and transform the area into a ballroom or banquet hall. I saw the same idea used at Drottningholm Palace[257] in Sweden. European royalty was in close communication and copied each other's ideas. Though Drottningholm is a smaller and more feminine venue, this innovative idea was easily copied.

The Coronation Room is memorable for its huge canvases. I particularly remember the painting called *Napoleon's*

257 Built in 1662 and known as the Swedish Versailles, Drottningholm Palace is the home of Sweden's royal couple. It is surrounded by a huge park where other retreats may be found. Near the Chinese Cottage is a dining room built over a kitchen where the table is set and lifted to the diners on the upper level.

Coronation.[258] The artist's interest in antiquity was evident in the artwork, where he has succeeded in drawing a parallel between ancient Roman emperors and 'that small Corsican' who'd dragged French legions throughout Europe to feed his own lust for power.

We didn't have enough time to look properly at the palace. It was larger than comparative palaces that I'd been fortunate to visit. The gardens were a huge park, a place to wander around for hours. We glanced at what was essentially a green expanse. However, had the fountains been turned on, I might have had a more positive impression.

At Peterhof, which compares more closely to Versailles than the other palaces I'd spent one leisurely visit inspecting the park, orangery and fountains and a second day viewing inside the palace and the Grand Trianon.

Le Nôtre, who during the 17th century had been lauded as the god of landscaping, was commissioned to design the 100-hectare parklands of Versailles. His secret was to use the rule of perspective by including follies, trianons, paths, groves and avenues, with numerous ponds and fountains.[259] They are focal points to his geometric parterre gardens. He created pure fantasy from the marshlands that surrounded the palace.

A monumental Neptune fountain was featured in Versailles, Schönbrunn and Peterhof, which became pure magic under the spray of water. The fountains were off when we visited Versailles[260] but having seen the other two, I could imagine what it would be like.

---

258 Napoleon took charge by crowning himself.

259 Versailles has 1400 fountains: a greater number than other palaces.

260 A constant supply of over one million gallons of water is required for the pools, ponds and the grand canal, which alone is 1.6 metres in length. This remains a hydraulics problem and is the reason why the fountains are only turned on at weekends and only in the summertime.

As we left the complex, the bus slowed down to allow us to have a glimpse of the trianons. These were cottages the king would use as a retreat or when he wanted a little more privacy to entertain a small group of intimates.

Marie Antoinette was 19 when she married Louis XVI. She found the position of queen daunting, with all its intricate etiquette and ritual. She had a little farmhouse built at the end of the property by the side of the lake, where she sought retreat with her children. There they played at being farmers. The pretty little thatched cottage camouflaged by leafy trees was surrounded by smaller cottages in an English country garden and was known as Marie Antoinette's hamlet.

Chapter 34
Ballet de l'Opéra

At precisely 7:40 am, the phone woke me. It was Nadia. She was already in the foyer. I felt a bit worse for wear after the previous day's touring. Marina was like a coiled spring—she jumped out of bed, dressed quickly, and went down to meet Nadia. This gave me time to gather my equilibrium under the soothing jets of the shower.

The three of us spent the next couple of hours enjoying a leisurely breakfast and deciding what to do. This was our last day in Paris, but apart from the ballet that evening, nothing else was planned. In truth, my vertigo had become worse and I needed to crawl back into bed. Upon my insistence, Marina and Nadia took off to see *Sacre Coeur* and Montmartre.

By lunchtime, I felt much better so polished off the food left over from the previous evening. I sorted out unwanted brochures, booked a taxi for my early morning transfer to Orly Airport and repacked, ready for my trip to Toulouse. I was looking forward to three days of French cooking classes while Marina visited Anthony and his family. We were scheduled to meet in Nice after that.

Marina and Nadia returned at five. I was already dressed for the theatre and chatted to Nadia over a coffee at the bar.

Marina returned and we said our last goodbyes. Nadia had become more than a good friend; she was more like a sister and we hoped to see her when she visited her family in Sydney.

No longer novices, we appeared so much more comfortable at the *Opera Garnier de Paris*. While sipping champagne, we perused the program. That evening's performance was the last night for the triple bill: *Serenade, Agon* and *Le Fils Prodigue,* as choreographed by George Balanchine.[261]

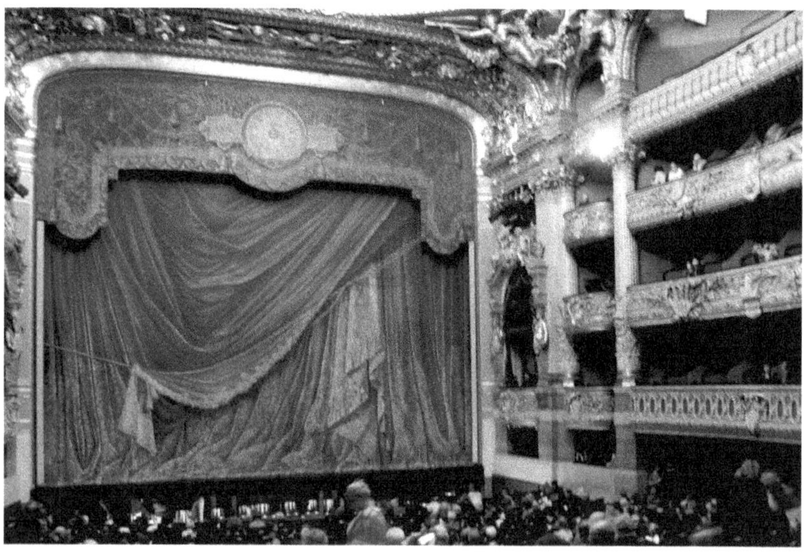

Our seats were the first row in the *loge* or boxes, on the same level and directly opposite the centre of the stage. We wore our finest and noticed how people peered at us through their opera glasses, wondering who the heck was seated in the royal box.

The first ballet was *Serenade,* created in 1935 to the beautiful music of *Serenade for Strings in C Major Opus 48* by Tchaikovsky. *Serenade* was Balanchine's first full length ballet in America. The costumes were ethereal, like those in *Les Sylphides.* The difference in production was that in *Serenade,* the scenery was non-existent. This was to ensure the audience remained fully intent on the music and dancing, without distraction. It also drew a comparison between traditional and modern ballet.

After a short interval or *entr'acte,* the audience returned to *Agon,* which is said to be the quintessential contemporary ballet. Balanchine collaborated with Igor Stravinsky on many other ballets before the creation of *Agon.* The score is specifically composed for 12 technically accomplished dancers. Their costumes plain, black and white leotards, worn as if at rehearsal. No sets, no tutus and the music typical Stravinsky—discordant and dynamic.

The highlight for me was the *Pas des Trois,* with one male and two female dancers completing intricate formations. The program indicated the ballet remains as cutting edge today as it was back in 1957.

The second interval allowed us to stretch our legs. The final ballet was *Le Fils Prodigue.* The story is based on the story of the prodigal son, as told in the Gospel of St Luke. Originally choreographed in 1929 to the music of Sergei Prokofiev, *Le Fils Prodigue* was created for Diaghilev's *Ballets Russes.*

In some way, it mirrored Balanchine's own life. He left home to wander the world until, at the very end of his days, his country of birth welcomed him back once more, albeit for one last performance. When Balanchine died, a tribute was held by the Kirov ballet in recognition of his work.

After the ballet, we went back to the *Café de la Paix* for *Crêpes Suzette* and Tsarina's Orange Pekoe tea, most likely named for

Nicholas and Alexandra, who may have at some time been patrons. It had been a memorable end to our time in Paris.

In the morning, I left Marina to settle the hotel account at leisure, while I proceeded to board a flight to my next adventure in Toulouse. I'd never flown with Easy Jet. They were a budget airline, and deemed my on-board bag was in addition to my small shoulder purse that contained only my passport, wallet and a lipstick. I'd bought this bag in Italy, specially to hold a book, wallet, hand cream and lollies on board, but they insisted it be sent as additional baggage.

I moved aside of the boarding queue and stuffed most everything into my jacket pockets then folded the bag and held it under my arm while I boarded through a different boarding aisle. Once in the plane, I shifted it all back into my Italian bag. It had merely been a slight inconvenience.

Chapter 35
Food, Glorious Food

The flight was barely 40 minutes in duration. Upon landing, I found my way to the meeting lounge where two other ladies were waiting for me to join them.

Paula was a redhead from New York who wore extremely high heels. *Will she cook in them?* I gazed at them in wonder.

The other lady, Sally, was a small woman in comfortable loafers. She was from Newcastle, in England's north-east. Both seemed to enjoy a competitive sort of banter, trying to outdo each other. They sat in the back and I sat up front with the driver.

Our destination was the small village of Gramont, 105 km from Toulouse airport. As we drove, a flock of kestrels and golden eagles shadowed us overhead. We drove by vineyards, beyond which were ancient forests. The route was certainly scenic but there was no respite from Sally and Paula's verbal sparring in the back. I added an occasional comment so as not to seem stand-offish, but I could see I had little in common with either of them.

After an hour and a half, we veered down a country lane through a corridor of charming limestone cottages with slate roofs. The wooden shutters were wide open; I assumed to catch any breeze. The driver pointed at the only grand building. This, he said, was the Chateau Gramont.

We stopped in front of a farmhouse at the end of the road. When the driver gave a short toot of his horn, the front door opened and we were greeted by our hosts, David and Bernard, who run the Gascony Cookery School. Inside we met another five aspiring cooks, two young men and three ladies. Satya and Jill from Sydney both worked at the same IT company. *Hoorah, I have compatriots.* Indeed, they were both intelligent professionals on holidays enjoying a fortnight in the south of France. They'd just returned from a week in Nice, which happened to be my next destination. One of the men was from London and the other from Brussels. The remaining lady was Swiss.

The school was a complex of buildings that had been a bed and breakfast with the main house and restaurant attached. My room was lovely. It was with ensuite and decorated in French Provincial style, the bed with huge European pillows and a down-filled doona. I sank into it. The pillows reminded me of my early childhood when my family had stayed with Grandma. She was a stickler for being self-sufficient. Her huge property had room enough for a cow, chooks and ducks. I remember drinking milk still warm from milking the cow and helping to stuff pillows with soft, fluffy feathers.

Lunch was buffet-style on the back terrace where a large table set for 10 awaited. The spread included a charcuterie platter, freshly baked bread rolls, tomatoes and cucumbers picked only moments earlier from the vegetable garden below. The tomatoes, bright red and bursting with flavour, reminded me of when I was eight or nine. I would pop into my neighbour's place after school. They would cut into wedges a couple of the ripest, juiciest tomatoes from their garden for us to enjoy. The taste and texture so delicious they remain with me forever, an indelible memory.

Beyond the terrace, with my cuppa in hand, I gazed out at a patchwork of green and yellow hills. Here and there a clump of dark, ancient forest provided a contrast. There was half an hour to fill before our first class. Not long enough to doze off but a perfect opportunity to get my bearings and to take in more of my surroundings.

I decided on a short walk and made my way up the main road, indeed the only road. Large tubs of annuals decorated the area around the post office and church. *A nice touch of community pride.* An aroma of newly mown grass and clipped hedges led me to the cemetery nearby. There's something about reading the plaques that I enjoy. They give me a sense of the history of a place. On this visit, my understanding was limited to the names and dates, because the rest was in French. Nearby, an angular building with a tower intrigued me. *I'll have to come back to have a better look when I have more time.*

Back at the farmhouse, the others had already donned their aprons and were leaning on the marble table ready for our first class—knife skills. It's not my forte but I was the best at chopping garlic sufficiently to turn it into a cream. Others were better with the onions. We learned what the different knives were for, how to sharpen them and how to store them.

The group split into two. Satya, Paula and I went to Bernard's kitchen to make *foie gras* and *cassoulet*. I'm not a sweets maker so this class was to my taste.

Skin-side down, the duck sizzled a jolly tune as the fat rendered and the flavour developed. A comforting aroma filled the kitchen. We followed Chef Bernard's direction with the pâté and *cassoulet*.

That done, the two groups came together to make *Sucre Pâtée,* which is a classic pastry for sweet tarts, not something I'd known or made before. When ready, the pastry was left to rest in the fridge. At the end of the session, we gathered for a natter over a glass of rosé before retiring to spruce up for dinner.

When we regrouped, David led us to the wine museum, where a large archive of ancient tools used for growing, harvesting and winemaking had been amassed. Equipment from early days included several stills, wine pumps, faucets, a corker and a scalder. I kept comparing this equipment to the modern winemaking and bottling methods I'd seen recently in the wine regions around Reims and the South of France.

Dinner in the restaurant started with a light soup made with chicken, vegetables and *cèpes.*[262] This was followed by *foie gras* and freshly baked bread, then a lemon sorbet to cleanse the palate. *I like the idea because it ensures flavours from different courses don't interfere with each other.* The red wine was a robust local. It went well with the *cassoulet* and the cheese platter that followed. An almond confection was served for dessert. After such a meal and an eventful day, I slept soundly.

I planned to skip breakfast, just have a cup of coffee. When I arrived in the breakfast room, the others were already tucking in. I reached for some orange juice to rehydrate. This led to muesli because it was homemade, and coffee. While I chatted with the others, someone put a warm croissant in front of me. I ate that too.

Cooking class began at nine. Apples were to be peeled, cored, chopped and poached in a small quantity of water. Once again, we broke into two groups. Some went with Bernard to make *tarte tatin* and *croquembouche.*

Satya, Jill and I stayed with David to fillet plaice, which is quite flat, rather like sole. We gutted, filleted, deboned and removed the skin. The off-cuts were placed over some chopped and sautéed onions, leeks, shallots and water to make a reduction to use as the base in our *velouté* sauce.

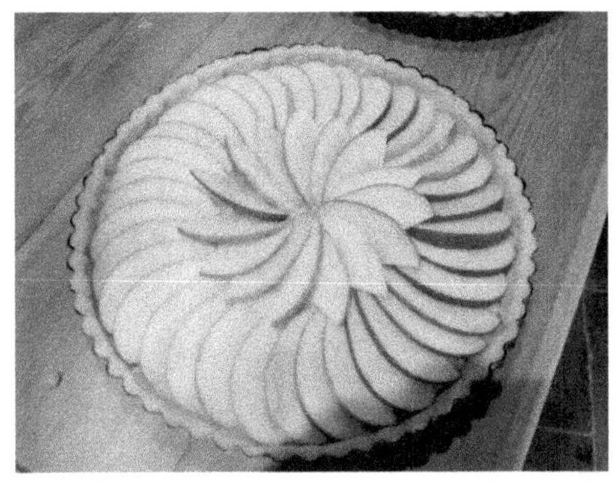

The next task was to roll out the pastry we'd made the previous day. There were technical aspects for this process that were new to me. The pastry had to be an even thickness to line a fluted flan dish perfectly before it could be baked blind. Chef David showed us how to work from the centre out to the sides. Such a simple tip yet it made an extraordinary difference. The apples we'd made earlier were mashed and combined with almond meal and other ingredients, then turned into the cooled flan cases.

It was a morning well spent. Lunch began with a welcome aperitif of chilled and spritzy rosé. We sat down to a freshly picked garden salad. What could be more refreshing? Confit of duck breast, the fat rendered and the paper-thin skin, crisp and caramelised. Stuffed roast potatoes, done to a turn with other root vegetables, all contributed to a satisfying repast. I don't know how we found room for dessert but could not refuse *tarte tatin* with vanilla ice cream and a tiny sprinkle of cinnamon.

The flan was every bit as delicious as it promised. This proves we truly eat with our eyes. I'd not eaten any bread and had little of the duck, but still I was stuffed. A siesta was most welcome.

At four in the afternoon, we were back with Bernard to make seven recipes. First, a basic custard, then crème caramel, *crème brûlée,* chocolate mousse, crêpes, choux pastry puffs with a filling of soft farm cheese and chopped aromatic herbs. There was also the suzette sauce for the crêpes. It was not the first time in my life that I'd made all of these except for the *crème brûlée.* Bernard taught us what to look for in a good *brûlée.* As for the crêpes, I'd never been able to flip pancakes, but he insisted that I could and should try to do it without delay.

'I've watched you,' he said. 'You know your way around a kitchen. You can do it.'

Flattery will get you everywhere, Bernard. I smiled with newfound confidence. With his encouragement, I did it. I flipped my crêpes as well as anyone else.

After a quick change for dinner, we gathered in the restaurant for predinner drinks with an array of nibblies, tiny smoked duck tapas, prunes wrapped in ham, olive and mixed nuts. An aperitif called *Pousse Rapiére,* unique to the region, was prepared for the group. This delicious nectar consisted of one-part white Armagnac, flavoured with orange, then topped with six parts champagne and served in a special flute. Though deceptively mild, I'm told more than one can be deadly.

The first course was a salad with lardons and coddled egg. It reminded me of the first real Caesar salad I'd eaten years ago at a place called *Le Mascaron* in Toronto. I was young, the wife of an up-and-coming executive, travelling on business, and was seduced by the theatre created by the waiter who prepared the salad at our table. Since that day, I'd not ever experienced another Caesar salad like it.

Our main meal was the delicately flavoured white fish that we'd prepared in the morning. Crisp, green beans and steamed fluffy rice were a perfect complement to the plaice. A cheese platter followed to accompany the remains of our wine. This was followed by the apple tart we'd made earlier. The flan—a crisp biscuit—was filled generously with fragrant apple pulp. Coffee and snifters of Armagnac rounded off what could only be called an epicurean banquet.

The next day, I sat alone with my coffee on the terrace. Morning mist still blanketed the valley below and the horizon held a golden hue as it melded into the clear azure sky. Some of the group went into town, but I wanted to enjoy my surroundings a little while longer.

Later, I wandered through the village, along cobbled paths and past a few cottages built with irregular stones. *I wonder why they do that?* The chateau's even stonework contrasted with these houses. I thought the chateau must be newer but a plaque near the front gate indicated it was built in the 14th century. I saw turrets and arrow slits, which hinted at a turbulent medieval past. I recognised some similarities to the chateaux I'd seen in the Loire. Pilasters, fluted columns, pediments and entablatures, indicative of the Renaissance period had been installed over the windows and doors during a later renovation.

The day remained warm but humid. I walked along the main road. There was not a soul in sight, although several cats and a dog kept following me.

On my left was a sign, *Musee de Miel,* or honey museum. However, it appeared more like a farmhouse. Surrounded by acres of land, it was someone's home. I grew up in a semi-rural environment on an exceptionally deep block. Like my grandmother, we too had chooks, ducks, fruit trees and vegetables, but down at the very back were four beehives. The taste of unadulterated honey in the comb was a treasured childhood memory.

The place was closed. There were no cars and a mist had begun to form. Since it was Sunday, I decided not to knock at the front door. A small dog saw me loitering outside of his domain and raced out of his hiding place. He stopped at the closed gate to bark fiercely at me.

Meanwhile the larger, stalking dog joined in. I was disturbing the peace so I turned back. The mist became a fine drizzle and I quickened my pace.

As I passed the church, its bell chimed to announce noon. My escort stopped by the entrance to howl and bark at the noise. We parted there. I needed to get back for a hot shower and change of clothes before lunch.

Our shoppers had returned earlier with a box of *petit fours* for the group to share later with coffee. Lunch commenced with a homemade pizza topped with mussels and peppers. *Crêpe suzettes* were served for dessert.

The time came to exchange contact details and say our last goodbyes. Satya and Jill gave me directions to a restaurant in Nice that featured truffles. It had been recommended to them and they'd thoroughly enjoyed it.

At the airport, I went through the business of measuring hand luggage. My bag was a bit too thick so I removed my folded raincoat from the pocket and wore it. As I made my way through customs the lady spotted a thin leather strap on my shoulder under the raincoat.

'What's that?' She pointed.

The purse was very small—15 cm by 15 cm—barely large enough for my passport and ticket. I showed it to her.

'Put in hand luggage,' she said.

I agreed, nodded, smiled and stepped through the gauntlet. In the boarding lounge, I saw one of the men from the cooking course and told him of my boarding debacle.

He laughed. 'That's nothing. On Ryanair, the hand luggage is also weighed.'

Finally, a flight arrived and disgorged its passengers. Without further delay for cleaning, we were herded on. I settled into my seat feeling very satisfied with the few days I'd spent at the cooking school.

Chapter 36
Nice

We flew over the spectacular coastline of the French Riviera. Below us, the Mediterranean Sea's smoothness was broken by shards of white sails atop a myriad of yachts that were held back from the land by a wide girdle of pebbly beach.

A quaint little hotel on the *Promenade des Anglaise,* the best address in town, was to be our home for the next few days. Marina, who had arrived ahead of me, was particularly concerned that the only room available was even smaller than the broom cupboard we'd left behind in Chemin Vert. Nor was there a bellboy or lift, just a narrow staircase for us to drag our luggage to the second floor.

The picture window in our room had uninterrupted views of the esplanade, where the fronds of tall palm trees rustled in the breeze. I was reminded of Picasso's painting, *Pigeons in Cannes,* which featured a similar palmed view of the sea through his window. This alone made it worth the effort. I giggled, trying to make light of Marina's worry.

'The hotel only has two floors,' I said, 'and we're on the second floor. It means we're in the penthouse. We have a room with a view, though we'll hardly be here to appreciate it.'

After a quick unpack, we headed out along the palm-lined esplanade past a couple of impressive hotels and restaurants, towards the old town and busy quay. We passed by the Art Deco styled Le Negresco Hotel. At the entrance stood a mosaic covered statue of a jazz trumpeter wearing a multicoloured jacket in a bold, geometric pattern reminiscent of Mondrian's paintings. The figure promised a fun time to be had inside the restaurant.

We crossed the road to look at the beach where the last lounges and umbrellas were being folded up for the night. Little bars that had served drinks during the day were closing, but the sea still sparkled invitingly under the setting sun. We vowed to return during the day.

When we reached the quay, cafés and restaurants were already touting for business. Blackboards and placards with menus and specials were displayed to tempt those passing by. The menus were remarkably similar, and the prices varied only marginally. Marina was captured by the loudest spruiker offering a special discount or free drink. Being my usual cautious self, I was put-off by these aggressive tactics, which are to be found everywhere in the world when there are tourist dollars to be had.

The eateries seemed a replica of each other, so I reluctantly agreed with her choice. We started with a *Kir Royale* aperitif to sip while we waited for the first course. When the *Salad Niçoise* arrived, it proved to be quite tasty, so I relaxed.

Since one of the region's major industries is fishing, I anticipated a tasty *bouillabaisse*, but it turned out to be a dud. The grey dishwater-coloured broth was tasteless. It contained diced potatoes, a few pieces of white fish and two off-cuts of calamari. I wanted to send it back but restrained myself. I knew it would create a scene and spoil our night. At least the red wine was nice.

For dessert we ordered *crème brûlée*. However, it turned out to be exactly what Bernard said it should not be. This dessert resembled a junket but was jelly firm and not at all soft and mousse-like. To add further insult, the toffee was already melting. The flavour was passable so I swallowed my disappointment. After some tea, we called it a night.

Awakening to our magnificent sparkling sea view was magic. The sky was cloudless, the air warm. It was an ideal morning for breakfast on the lawn-covered terrace. Juice, coffee and croissants were a perfect combination. We relaxed there for a little while, mesmerised by the boundless sea before embarking on our scheduled day tour.

A four-wheel drive picked us up from the hotel. Our fellow travellers were all from Australia. There was a mother and daughter from Sydney and a couple of girls from Melbourne with their friend from Queensland.

Michael, our driver and guide, was a university student from Germany. He told us in his deep baritone voice that he enjoyed guiding during his semester breaks.

'My friends, they do bar work or wait tables in restaurants. But my work is more interesting. I meet people like you, from far away. One day I will come to see your kangaroos.'

Michael stopped at various vantage points so we could photograph the coastline, the busy port and some of the beautiful old buildings. Our first destination on the *Cote d'Azur*, was the charming little enclave of Èze, which is made up of winding alleys and narrow walkways. They nestle along the edge of a rocky outcrop. Little cafés, hotels, shops and art galleries are shoehorned, like eagles' nests, into niches of the Alpes-

Maritimes. This mountainous region forms the border between France and Monaco.

Èze and Grasse are known for French perfume. The Fragonard Parfumier Laboratory has been in Èze village since 1926. An ancient still took pride of place at the front door but there were more modern examples inside. Steam distillation was the earliest method for extracting essential oils. However, the new cold processes enable more delicate flowers to be used.

Creating a perfume can take years. It is a job for only a few gifted noses. The chemists explore all the olfactory families from the floral, fruity, chypre, woody and oriental aromas then introduce the appropriate styles in specific measure. I imagine it to be like creating an orchestral symphony—first violins, brass, perhaps a little timpani for drama before leaving a lasting note. A good fragrance can become your signature, be that elusive something which lingers even after you have become a memory.

Perfume is produced on commission to individual fashion houses who market it under their own brand. The factory in Èze, makes solid and gel perfumes as well as the eau de toilettes, soap, cosmetics, serums, hand creams and more. Perfume is used in everyday products: shower gels, massage oils, candles, diffusers, balms and household products.

Eons ago, my husband was an industrial chemist. He belonged to the worldwide Cosmetic Chemists Association. The members of this association worked for many multinationals who commissioned fragrances for their laundry and cleaning products, pharmaceuticals, ointments and balms. Every product has a smell, an aroma, mostly pleasant but if not, then the addition of a perfume can correct it. For example, when upholstering furniture, producing handbags or other consumer goods, the fragrance of leather is used on synthetic material to mimic the real thing.

At the end of the tour, we were able to purchase from a wide selection of Fragonard products. I was surprised to see they had license to sell Manuka Royal Jelly face cream from New Zealand, and Moroccan Argan oil. I chose perfume for myself, soaps and hand creams for gifts. I'd bought enough to receive a lovely gold purse-sized perfume atomiser as a bonus. Ten years later, the perfume is as fresh and alluring as the day I bought it but I've never been able to buy perfume to pour into the atomiser. Only spray is available these days.

Our next stop was over the border in the Principality of Monaco.[263] Set in the Alpes-Maritimes, Monaco is a tax haven and billionaires' playground. It is best known for the Monte Carlo Grand Prix, the Casino of Monte Carlo, and the fairy-tale story of Grace Kelly, who married Prince Rainier III in 1956. They are now at rest alongside each other in the Romanesque Monaco Cathedral.

I couldn't help but be impressed by the immaculate condition of the town. The roads seemed as if they had just been laid. Any dust was immediately swept up. Pretty patches of flowers surrounded every building. Each tree and hedge was trimmed to an inch of its life and no weed left to spoil the garden beds. Most buildings faced the panorama of yachts and super-yachts, catamarans, and cruisers[264]; a display of unimaginable wealth, bobbling on the calm sea.

263 Vatican City is one square kilometre, whereas Monaco is two square kilometres. In 1962, Monaco changed from a hereditary monarchy to a constitutional hereditary monarchy. Prince Albert is the present head. Monaco is the most expensive, wealthiest and most densely populated country.

264 The annual boat show held by the yacht club is an important event. With each year, the boats increase in size and cost.

Across a paved court is the palace where the Grimaldi family live. The entrance is flanked by two sentry boxes and a row of ornamental cannons. The changing of the guard is held there and it is the launching place for official parades. What surprised me was the absence of a fence or other barrier. We could wander in to have a sticky-beak or knock on the front-door to borrow a cup of sugar.

In the absence of formality, we walked straight in the door. It led to a courtyard, where signs indicated a suitable route for tourists. I don't know what I expected—perhaps a fairy-tale world—instead the first room, which was a large reception area featuring interesting display cases and a potted history of Monaco. The following rooms were furnished in a way that made them appear more lived-in instead of a repository of artifacts in a museum.

The royal apartments included a throne room filled with the Grimaldi family history, portraits and accoutrements. After seeing so many grand palaces, chateaux and mansions, the Grimaldi residence, though lovely, was a little underwhelming.

The group scattered in all directions to enjoy an hour and a half of free time. Marina and I resolved to have a quick lunch from a café in the village. Since we wanted something simple like sandwiches, we settled on Croque Monsieur. As we sat there observing the world go by, the music of tinkling water from somewhere nearby helped us to relax and clear our heads. On our way out, we investigated the source of the water. It turned out to be a fountain around a resplendent statue of St Nicholas.

'He's following us,' I commented.

'Keeping us safe,' Marina added.

We followed a path that led to St Martin Gardens. Strategically positioned benches invited visitors to pause and admire the cliffs covered with lush overhanging greenery. Further along, we encountered modern bronze statues. Each was surrounded by a bed of colourful annuals. These splashes of colour further enhanced the park.

We came upon a statue of a little girl seated on a chair. What captured our imagination more than the statue was the name of the sculptor, Hans Jorgensen. The surname was that of a dear friend of ours who'd passed away far too early. Another example of this artist's work was that of an eagle, wings spread wide as if it were about to launch into flight.

For me, the most notable statue was that of the bronze mariner, said to be Albert I, resplendent in a sou'wester while standing at the helm. The hem of his raincoat was blown by a wild mistral coming in from the stormy sea.

We surfaced outside the oceanographic museum, which is also renowned for work in human palaeontology and its exploration of the Mediterranean Sea. A yellow submarine once used by Jacques Cousteau stands proudly outside of the museum in an area called the Octopus Garden. It was built in 1966, the same year as the Beatles released their hit song 'Yellow Submarine' followed by 'Octopus's Garden' on the *Abbey Road* album.

Five minutes after boarding the four-wheel drive, we arrived in Monte Carlo. Michael suggested various tourist attractions before we were let loose to explore.

As we neared the Casino[265], immaculately dressed punters emerged from luxury cars of the like we rarely see back home. There were more 'look at me, look at me' cars than parking spots. Everyone jockeyed for position. It seemed a toss-up between who you were and how much you've got. Marina pointed to

265 The Casino of Monte Carlo was established in 1863 as a gambling house.

a classic, burgundy-coloured Rolls Royce coupe with cream leather seats and polished maple dashboard.

'What sort of car is that?' she asked.

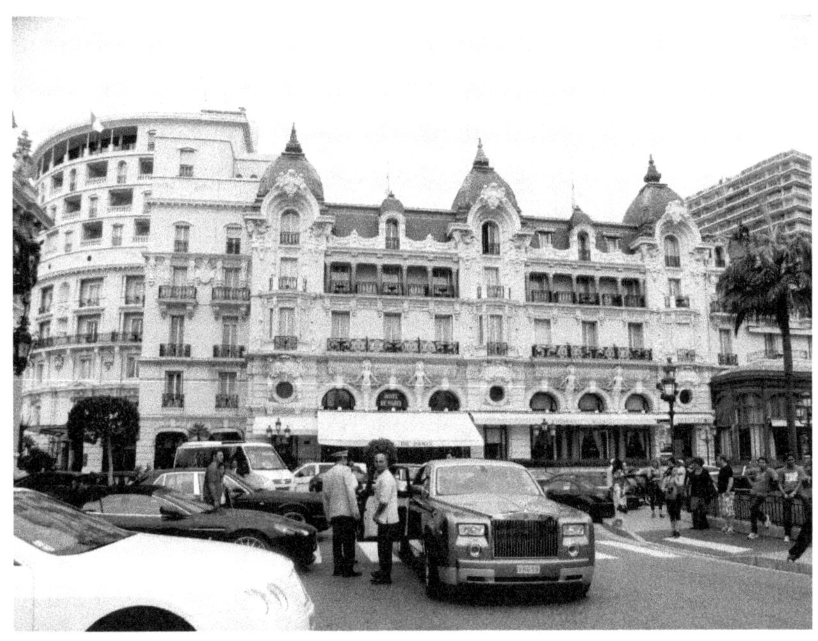

I pretended not to hear. People milled around admiring the luxury vehicles parked at the steps of the casino's grand entrance. I pulled at her sleeve to ensure she remained alongside; I didn't want to lose her in the crowd as I guided her into the gambling haven. She resisted going in, but I cajoled her to merely step into the foyer, to at least be able to say we'd been there with the rich and infamous.

Later I discovered that Charles Garnier, the chief architect of the Paris Opera Garnier, had also been commissioned to design the theatre known as the *Opera de Monte Carlo*.[266] If only I'd known this at the time, Marina might have been less reticent to enter this gambler's paradise and we might have wandered through to the back of the casino to take a look.

Prince Albert, I encouraged fledgling arts to the principality. The annual visit of Diaghilev's *Ballets Russes* benefited from the endeavour. In 1932, between the two world wars, the directors of the company had a falling out. After litigation, the name *Ballets Russes* was retained by Wassily de Basil. Whereas *Ballets Russes de Monte Carlo* became the official ballet company of Monte Carlo. Monaco was regarded as the cultural centre of Europe so attracted the best artists.

Ballets created then, such as *Afternoon of the Faun*, with music by Debussy, and *Rite of Spring*, with music by Stravinsky, continue to be performed in theatres all around the world. Vaslav Nijinsky's choreography for both ballets continues to be used. The *crème de la crème* of ballet dancers and choreographers worked at one time or another with this group. In the 1940s, after the war, many of the artists migrated to other countries, where they established what are now world-renowned ballet companies.[267]

Inside the foyer of the casino, the mega-rich milled around. They were familiar with their surroundings and acknowledged friends who were also there for a flutter, to have fun and to be seen. Monégasque citizens are not allowed to gamble at the

267 Alicia Markova founded the English National Ballet, Ninette Valois founded the Royal Ballet and Sadler Wells, where Vera Volkoff introduced the Vaganova method. Voganova graduated from the Imperial Ballet School, which later became the Leningrad Choreographic Institute. Boris Volkoff founded the Royal Winnipeg Ballet. Balanchine the New York City Ballet. Sergei Lifar was credited with technical restoration at the Paris Opera Ballet. Anna Pavlova from *Ballets Russes* visited Australia with colleague Eduard Borovansky. They decided to stay and together with JC Williams and the Elizabethan Theatre Trust, set up the Australian Ballet company. Irina Baronova, one of the Baby Ballerinas from the *Ballet Russes de Monte Carlo*, made Australia her home. She died in 2008 in Byron Bay, NSW.

casino because the government doesn't want them to become impoverished. They prefer the visitors to do that.

Only a third of the population are actual citizens. Judging by our clothes, it was obvious we were fresh off the tour bus. Burly bouncers knew the high rollers and ensured their privacy by deciding who they allowed into the hallowed halls of this den.

Before we left, Marina noted the wonderful chandeliers. 'Probably Baccarat,' she said.

Across the road was the grand Baroque-style *Hotel de Paris*, which we thought might be a suitable spot for a coffee. Inside, beyond reception and past the magnificent floral arrangement that stood on a round table in the middle of the foyer, we noticed the unhurried pace of the establishment and feared it could be a problem for our limited time. It didn't feel right so we decided to do some window shopping along the high street.

Elegant shop windows displayed a variety of luxury goods: Lalique, Louis Vuitton, Dunhill. I remember once buying a Dunhill lighter as a parting gift for a special friend. Further on, was Hermes boutique with their wonderful accessories: bags, gloves and scarves.

'I wonder how much a scarf would cost?' asked Marina as we both drooled longingly at the display in the shop window. 'I don't see any price tags.'

'My mother used to always say, "If you must ask how much something costs, then you can't afford it." Don't you agree?' This time she chose to ignore me.

There were very few shoppers to be seen. The only people were those walking small dogs on leads. We were intrigued to see the flash and sparkle of their jewellery.

'Do you think it's real?' Marina asked.

I didn't know what to say. We glanced at each other in disbelief and kept walking. After a while, we realised it was not unusual. Their clothes were straight from the runways of Paris and Milan, as were the shoes with impossibly high heels. Later, Michael explained that because of the high security, Monaco is the only country where billionaire residents and visitors feel safe to wear their jewels in public. In the interest of their safety and privacy, paparazzi and all professional photography is banned.

Further on were the boutiques of Prada, Cartier, Dior, Valentino and lastly, a high-end family business, the exclusive house of Orlov Jewellery. In the window was the most fantastic emerald and diamond bracelet I'd ever seen, the design Art Deco-inspired. I wondered if the piece was new or estate jewellery, and what other delights they might have on offer behind the closed door of the store. I'm sure they wouldn't waste their time on we poor tourists, besides, it was time to leave. The fantasy was over and we returned to the four-wheel drive and the rest of our little group.

Our next experience was to complete the Grand Prix circuit; the same route where the famous car race is held. One of the Melbournian girls wanted to know when the first race had been run.

'The first winner of the Monte Carlo Rally was Henri Rougier in 1911, over 1020 km in a Turcat-Méry,' said Michael.

'Didn't they call it a Grand Prix in those days?' asked the Sydney mother.

'There are two races, the Grand Prix and the rally,' answered Michael. 'The first Monaco Grand Prix[268] for Formula 1 cars was held in 1929. It was held over a gruelling 3367 km[269] and was won by W Williams in a Bugatti. He was a bit of a mystery man; there was little known about him. Some said he was a chauffeur who hired out his car to rich people, yet others thought him a wealthy sportsman. He turned out to be a private fellow, William Grover[270], from a humble background.'

Soon we crossed the border and were back in France. The fine morning we'd experienced had not lasted and it had drizzled for most of the day. After a short rest at the hotel, we were ready for dinner.

We were booked at the truffle place recommended by Satya. When we arrived at this humble café tucked away in a side street, the chestnut-brown walls and iron lace-decorated door did little to excite us. Marina appeared dubious and suggested we search for an eatery by the quay, but I insisted we eat as planned.

Marina was worried about truffles. She reminded me of a fad style of restaurant from the 1990s called Death by Chocolate and she didn't fancy chocolate for her dinner. When that issue was sorted out, we laughed at the contradictory meaning of the word.

Terres De Truffe prepared meals using the king of ingredients—the truffle. We began with a small complimentary serve of pureed vegetable soup enhanced with a drop of truffle

268 Today the Grand Prix is one of the most notable events in Monaco. It raises upwards of $100 million every year.

269 That is an estimate of 78 laps of the circuit.

270 He was a chauffeur who changed his career path to car racing then changed his name to William Grover-Williams. In WWII, he was a saboteur for the Allies. Sent to a concentration camp, he was executed in 1945.

oil. The waiter placed a dish of butter curls in the middle of the table and offered a choice of bread rolls from a large basket. We chose square-shaped rolls sprinkled with sunflower seeds. They were crisp on the outside, warm inside and had a nutty flavour.

The service was quick. My main consisted of a creamy truffle risotto and was topped with *Coquille St Jacques*.[271] The presentation didn't disappoint. The creamy white scallops with their contrasting orange roe not only looked delicious, but added another level of flavour to the rice, which in a lesser establishment might have been stodgy.

Marina ordered grilled salmon. Palest pink with a crispy skin, it was served on a ratatouille base, all liberally sprinkled with dark grated truffle. I thought the ratatouille an unusual accompaniment, but she loved eggplant, and commented that its faintly tart taste was a perfect complement to the fish.

Our wine, *Moulin de la Lagune*, a full-bodied red from Bordeaux, was expensive, but what the heck, it was the perfect accompaniment for our gourmet meal. A lesser wine would have been an insult to the truffles.

We skipped dessert in favour of a pot of tea, which was served with little chocolate truffle balls. When they arrived, we laughed because all our truffle bases had finally been covered.

The earlier rain had stopped and the wet footpath glistened under our feet, making for a pretty walk home. A full moon shone above, its rays dancing on the sea. Along the other side of the promenade, brightly-lit hotels were alive with music and the sounds of revellers.[272]

Chapter 37
The Finale

Our last breakfast was on the terrace under a brilliant, cloudless sky. I spread marmalade onto a buttery croissant and sipped my steaming hot coffee, while Marina scrutinised a local map to check the route to our first destination for the day. A warm breeze from the sparkling sea ruffled the paper.

'It's not far,' she said with a satisfied smile. 'Take us no more than ten minutes, at a slow pace. I'll get ready while you finish breakfast.'

I could always rely on her sense of direction; she was a natural. We looked forward to visiting the church Nadia had recommended. She'd told us that since the 19th century, when the Russian nobility visited France, it was to follow the fashion of doing the Grand Tour, as established by the English upper classes. They especially enjoyed the French Riviera and while some holidayed, others made it their home.

Tsar Alexander II[273] visited in 1864. He was followed by his son and heir apparent, Nicholas Alexandrovich, who was 21 years of age and engaged to Princess Dagmar of Denmark. Whilst in Nice, the heir caught cerebrospinal meningitis and died shortly after his diagnosis.

His younger brother, Alexander III, became the heir apparent and married Princess Dagmar. The marriage resulted in six children, including the heir to the throne, the last emperor—Nicholas II. A new church was needed to accommodate the growing Russian community that had settled in Nice. Nicholas II inherited the project and funded it from his own purse. The church was consecrated in 1912.

Today, *Cathédrale Saint-Nicholas de Nice*, built in the Muscovite style, sits like a grand jewel surrounded by lush parkland on the Avenue Nicholas II. This runs off *Boulevard du Tsarevich*. It was named for the heir apparent, who died there in 1865. The five domes of the church were covered in coloured tiles and each was topped with a gilded cross. The pink hued terracotta of the building was a contrast to the many greens of trees, palms and shrubs in the garden.

At the wrought iron gates, we were met by the resident cat, who rubbed against our legs in welcome, then accompanied us along the path up to the main entrance, where he stopped at some invisible boundary. Inside, we lit candles and venerated icons. The walls of the cavernous interior were covered in frescoes that reached high into the domes. Light streamed from the main apse onto the altar and gilded iconostasis. A group of tourists had gathered and I heard their guide say this cathedral was the largest Russian Orthodox church in Western Europe.

After the group departed, Marina and I were left alone with the volunteer caretaker. When she learned we were from Australia, she gave us special attention.[274] She showed us antique icons of the Apostle Peter, Archangel Michael and St Alexander Nevsky, then led us to the church's most precious

274 There is a museum of the early Russian colony in Nice. It is held in the crypt of the church.

relic—an icon of St Nicholas the Wonderworker.[275] It was the very icon that had hung in the corner of the room where Nicholas Alexandrovich Romanov had stayed and died. The icon was of his patron saint.

The building had been subsequently demolished to make way for the construction of a new church. A small memorial chapel was erected on the spot where Nicholas Alexandrovich had died and was the same icon attached above the exterior door. However, the icon was not made to withstand the elements, and it slowly became so black you could no longer see the image. The icon was removed to an obscure place in the altar.

One day in 1930, someone noticed the image on the icon had begun to return, but malformations like drops of varnish from the wood had also appeared. Today, this most revered icon is kept in a prominent place in the body of the church for ease of veneration. Several parishioners said that their prayers for intercession, made before the icon, were answered. We left our lists of names with the caretaker for commemoration at the next memorial service.

From the church, it was a short walk back to the quay. There, a flower market[276] was in full bloom. Row upon row of stalls with red-striped awnings offered produce from an inviting palette of flowers, fruit and vegetables.

Though summer was long gone, there was still much colour to enjoy—bright red cotoneaster berries, purple irises,

275 The same saint whose relics I'd visited in Bari on the first day of my trip and it seemed that on my last day, I was again blessed to be in his presence.

276 This was the first flower market in France. It opened in 1897. It operated daily except Mondays, when a vintage flea market took over.

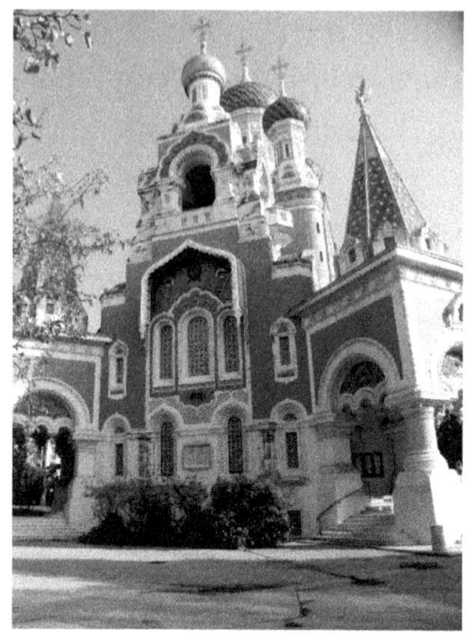

dahlias and pink oleander. The fragrance of mimosa, lavender and jasmine lured us deeper into the maze. Of course, there is always a demand for roses and the variety of colours on display was vast. These had been cultivated in hot houses, although the milder weather in the South of France allowed a longer floral season. Potted plants were also on sale: cacti, succulents, bonsai, cyclamens and a line-up of potted orchids.

A tempting array of ripe and fragrant fruit was on offer: rosy apples, pears, all sorts of citrus and shallow straw boxes of freshly picked berries. Vegetables vied for our attention—shiny purple eggplants, marrows and emerald-green capsicums awaited a traditional meat and rice stuffing. Zucchinis lay next to bright yellow zucchini flowers. They seemed barely large enough to fill. Sun-ripened tomatoes; their bright red colour reminded me of the delicious tomatoes from my father's garden. Fat haricot beans sat next to slender green beans and further along were bunches of snake beans draped nonchalantly over the edges of the vegetable barrow.

Leafy fresh and fragrant herbs were still growing in their little pots and others were in protective cellophane packages. Parsley, rosemary, sage and waxy green bay leaf branches were laid out on tables. Many mushrooms were on sale; some white, others grey, or rust, in a variety of shapes—flat or domed, frilled or smooth, some like little tendrils reminiscent of bean sprouts.

This cornucopia of produce would surely tempt any savvy French cook to buy for their marinade or sauté pan.

The mouth-watering aroma of bread baking led us to a stall outside of the bakery. On offer were loaves, cobs, batons and flatbread. The stall next door offered soups, spices, olives, jams, spreads and honey still on the comb alongside boxes of soft dates. I so love them stuffed with brie. My tummy began to grumble.

Marina skipped from one delicious offering to another, picking up items to smell or touch. I too was captured by the ambience of the market with all its colour, tantalising aromas and by the antics of the stallholders, who jovially bartered for our custom.

I knew my friend so well, I could read her thoughts. *Let's buy these and what about those?* she'd say. *You go find a spare table. I'll bring us something nice.*

I confess to being momentarily tempted. *Sorry, my friend, not today.* I'd booked lunch well in advance at Cap Ferrat. So with some difficulty, I diverted her with a takeaway coffee to have at the bus stop while we waited for the bus.

The number 81 public bus route follows the crest of the peninsular, at the end of which is some of the most expensive real estate on the planet. There, perched on the ridge, is the Baroness Beatrice Ephrussi de Rothschild's dream home, which she built in 1912—an Italianate Palazzo where the *crème de la crème* of society gathered at her *soireés*. Back in those days, to be invited meant to rub shoulders with Charlie Chaplin, Winston Churchill, Edith Piaf, David Niven, Jean Cocteau and F Scott Fitzgerald. I wondered if the mansion and her lavish parties had inspired Fitzgerald to write *The Great Gatsby*.

House parties, when more intimate friends had stayed, included sailing across the bay to the *Casino de Monte Carlo* for a flutter. The baroness loved to gamble both at the casino and the races. She was the daughter of the banker and art collector Baron Alphonse de Rothschild. She was only 19 years old when she married Maurice Ephrussi, who was 15 years her senior. Maurice, from a banking family in Odessa, was an inveterate gambler enjoying the high life. They had no children to indulge so travelled extensively, amassing an enviable compilation of fine art and artifacts, especially porcelain, sculpture and old masters.[277]

The bus stopped right outside the mansion. A fortress of tall hedges hid the house, and I asked the driver if we were at the correct address.[278] He gestured towards an open gate and we alighted. A long driveway covered in crazy paving bound with flower beds and tall shrubs led us through a stuccoed archway. Beyond the fence was the Villa Ephrussi, painted in the same pink shade we'd seen earlier that morning. Columns and other embellishments, in contrast, were painted a crisp white. All were surrounded by lush botanical gardens.

At the ticket office, the attendant recommended audio devices because of the extensive number of artworks on show. But first on the agenda was lunch. Our reserved table was on the terrace surrounded by greenery where we sat entranced by the view of *Bay de Villefranche-sur-mer*. Pretty umbrellas provided shade and we were taken care of just like any of the baroness's guests would have been.

'On holiday?' asked the waiter. 'A special occasion, maybe?'

'Belated birthday for my friend,' I replied.

277 They divorced after 21 years of marriage. On her death in 1934, she left the estate to a foundation in her name so that it could become a museum. An estimated 130,000 people visit her mansion each year.

278 It is only 10 km from Nice, along a steep winding road to the Villa Ephrussi. Bus 81 also stops at Villa Kerylos, owned by an Ephrussi relative. Somerset Maughan also owned a villa here. Now privately owned, it is unavailable to view. Villa Ephrussi consists of a mansion and gardens covering seven hectares of land.

He returned with two flutes of champagne. '*Je vous félicite,*' he said, handing Marina her glass.

We both ordered the same salads. They resembled works of art: mesclun leaves, peppery rocket, crisp bean shoots, succulent slices of chicken breast, golden mango cheeks, red and yellow cherry tomatoes, and big fat king prawns. This exotic concoction, dressed with a light sprinkle of vinaigrette dressing, filled edible baskets that were made from egg white and rice flour. Tiny violets decorated the plate. We sent our compliments to the chef; the salad was truly ambrosia. This was followed by a slice of apple and strawberry tart to accompany our orange pekoe tea.

After the light but elegant lunch, we moved inside the house. The interior of the palazzo was set on two levels around a central atrium. We switched on our audio devices and were guided by a pleasant female voice.

'Rose pink Verona marble columns form an Andalusian-style colonnade around the grand salon. This is where Baroness Ephrussi held her lavish parties.'

The quadrangle flowed through to the sumptuous gardens outside. I pictured intimate groups of guests chatting while sipping their champagne.

'Musicians, hidden from sight on the second-floor balcony, would play to entertain the guests below. The ceiling fresco, The Chariot of Love, pulled by doves, is by Tiepolo.'

We strained our necks to examine the subdued tones of the mythological scene.

'The interior was used in the 1983 James Bond film, Never Say Never Again.'

I noted that the Persian rugs on the floor remained thick and colourful.

'One of the carpets is from the Louvre, the other from the chapel in Versailles.'

The small salon is where guests had mingled to chat after the meal. The audio alerted us to the timeless Gobelin tapestries representing the adventures of Don Quixote. Various paintings hung on the walls. I stopped to admire a fireplace screen that once belonged to Marie Antoinette. In yet another sitting room, Louis XV and XVI gilded chairs were arranged to best capture vast sea views.

Upstairs, Beatrice's bedroom reflected her eclectic taste.

'The Venetian bed covered in Chinese silk is embroidered with flowers and birds. French furniture from the 18th century provided seating for close friends, whom the baroness often entertained in her boudoir.'

I caught sight of a wardrobe, its doors ajar, and wondered who'd left it open.

'Exotic Asian-inspired clothing and dresses still hang in her armoire. She followed the tradition of foot-binding, having her own toes, except the big toe, folded under her feet. The small slippers she wore are on display.'

We turned to each other, astounded at this bit of personal history, and gawked for several minutes at the strangely shaped slippers.

'I think the baroness was a little mad,' whispered Marina.

I smiled back in agreement. 'Utterly eccentric.'

'She wrote letters in her room at a writing desk that once belonged to Marie Antoinette. The adjoining room is used to exhibit her acquisition of Fragonard drawings, mostly botanical specimens.'

'The artworks are pen and ink with a colour wash,' said Marina. Watercolour was a medium Marina used to great effect. Two of her paintings hang in my son's house.

'Jean-Honoré Fragonard was born in Grasse and was a favourite of the baroness. In 1926, the perfume factory was named after him.'[279]

279 Our visit to Villa Ephrussi entitled us to a 10% discount on perfumery purchases at the factory. Unfortunately, we'd already visited the factory.

The tapestry room led to the Monkey Room, so called for its Meissen figurines.

'In the cabinet, we see an orchestra of monkeys, some dressed as musicians, others like clowns. They are engaged in various activities but are loved mostly for their sheer buffoonery.'

I agreed. Most were cute chimps, but some had sinister expressions, while others were being very naughty.

'An incredible collection of rare porcelain is displayed in the dining room. Most pieces are from the Royal Manufactory of Sévres near Paris, Meissen and Vincennes.'

Objets d'art appeared in curio cabinets positioned randomly in the corners and nooks of the room. I was particularly taken by the fine lyre-backed chairs. The lovely games table was another piece from the estate of Marie Antoinette.

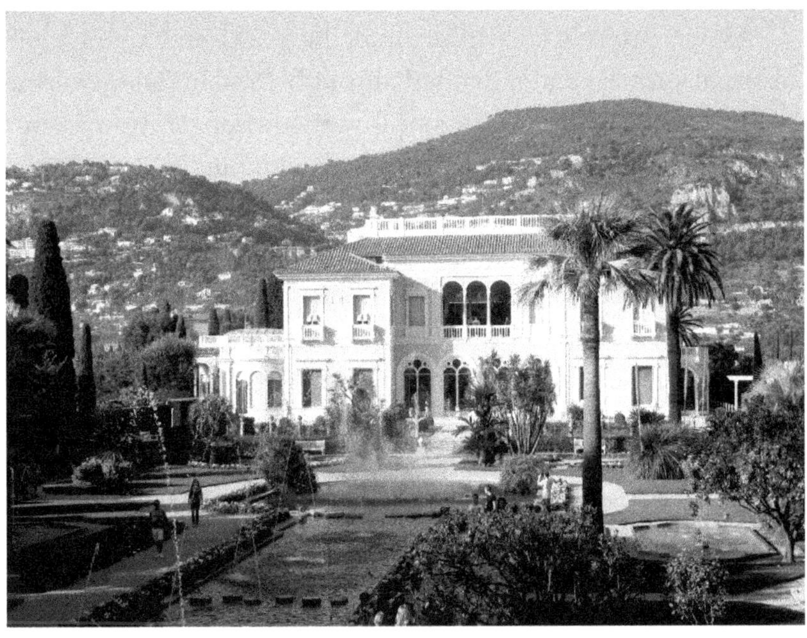

An announcement over the public address system broke our concentration. The main fountain was about to be turned on. We stepped out to take our places in the formal French garden to view the display. Jets of water flanked the sides of a long pool[280] while the spray ebbed and rose in time with the music. During one of Baroness Beatrice's fabled parties, Anna Pavlova danced to Chopin's nocturnes around a moonlit water show. I tried to imagine the sheer magic of the scene and how enchanting it must have been to witness the spectacle.

The formal French garden, where we'd begun our walk, was the first of nine geographic-themed gardens. With the sea on both sides of the peninsular, the garden took on the appearance of a ship's deck. Clipped hedges, topiaries and exquisite urns perched on pedestals decorated the lower section of the gardens. At the highest point is a pretty folly called the Temple of Love. Inside the classic rotunda, a white marble nude gazed at water gently trickling down a set of shallow stairs.

As we progressed further into the park, aromas of pine, eucalypt and lavender wafted through the air. They were a heady welcome to the Provençal garden. Long rows of olive trees, cypress pines and agapanthus stood rooted in a soft carpet of herbs.

We lamented that the rose garden, which boasted 100 varieties, would have been best visited in summer when the flowers on the arbour would have been flourishing. Though already October, there were enough blooms to enthral us, their honeyed perfume still evident among the flower beds. Songs of bees became more pronounced as they neared each stamen to gather their precious harvest.

280 It was like the set up at the John Paul Getty Museum in Santa Monica—a long shallow pool surrounded by exotic plantings. I don't recall there being a fountain or water feature.

An oasis of tall cacti was an unexpected sight in the Mediterranean surroundings. Their spikes became erect like soldiers in response to our intrusion. Gigantic succulents stood sentinel amongst masses of tiny pigface that trailed lazily over embankments. Beyond these were agave and other foreign trees and shrubs. We paused at a stone plinth, hoping to soak in some of the ambience, and were surprised to see grevilleas and bottlebrushes.

Our aimless saunter had changed direction and we found ourselves heading back to the mansion. There was still much to enjoy along the way. Up ahead stood a barbary fig tree so heavy with flowers its bough had bent in half. Further on was something we didn't expect to see—a Japanese Zen garden with raked sand and stretches of pebbly ground.

A stone bench begged us to stop a while to embrace the peace-filled surroundings. At every turn there was the music of water rippling over rocks, dripping into a wooden bucket or gushing into a lily pond. We sat for a little while, allowing the sounds to soothe us. It felt like having a head massage. At the far end, an ornamental bridge was positioned over a pond with koi. It reminded us of Giverny. Stone lanterns and bonsai money trees completed the exotic scene. We left this peace-filled place with great difficulty.

Each garden had been designed to be different; each a reminder of a trip or holiday that Baroness Beatrice had enjoyed. The variety and beauty seemed endless. Around the corner stark stone statues with fearsome faces glared. They reminded me of Mayan artefacts. Architectural pieces accumulated but not used during the construction of the villa were grouped in this overlooked back lot. The beauty of the sculptures was not wasted—gnomes, Gothic arches and even the scary gargoyles all found common ground amongst the camphor laurels and bay trees. In spring, I imagined this area came alive with the colour of azaleas, camellias and rhododendrons.

Back at the entry to the villa, the Sévres garden melded seamlessly with the Spanish garden. A covered patio with a tiled floor provided an ideal environment for water-loving plants. Here in happy cohabitation, papyrus from Egypt, Arum lilies, pomegranate trees and strelitzia stood proud and formal, while pink bougainvillea and heady honeysuckle climbed pergolas.

We spent all day at the villa. The interior was fascinating and the variety of artefacts overwhelming. There were many things we'd not seen previously and that we're not likely to ever see again. But it was the serenity of the gardens, where we'd spent the most relaxing few hours together, that will remain vivid in my memory.

The bus arrived straight away and ten minutes later, we were back in Nice. There was time enough to pause at the beach, sit with a beer in hand and watch the sun set on our amazing day. Bright pink and orange splashes across the sky promised another perfect day in this paradise, albeit without us. My trip was at an end but Marina was continuing to Munich to visit family and friends.

With mixed feelings, we dawdled along the esplanade towards our hotel. Marina pointed out a restaurant called *Le Crocodile*. She'd had lunch there on the first day before my arrival. The door was wide open and the lights were on. Though we had no reservation, we wandered inside.

'Ladies, you are most welcome, but we ask you to finish by eight as we have another booking for this table,' said the waiter.

'We've been out all day and will be keen for an early night, so no worries,' said Marina.

We started with another salad, this time with creamy avocado slices, a delicious contrast to the crisp lettuce leaves. For the main, we ordered Duck *Confit* with a side of green beans and potato. I suspect the duck was merely roasted. There is a difference between the two cooking styles that not all diners would discern, but since my cooking course, I'd become rather fussy. Marina ordered *crème brûlée*, which arrived with a caramel sauce over it. We sent it back. It returned this time minus the sauce, sprinkled generously with sugar and blowtorched to produce a crunchy toffee. We relaxed over a pot of tea before returning to the hotel to pack.

My transfer to the airport arrived at seven the next morning. Marina was scheduled to leave at nine. The trip is only seven kilometres, but I think the taxi drove via the scenic route. He was pleasant and we chatted about his recent visit to Sydney. He carried my luggage into the airport although he didn't have to. I wondered if it was to make amends for the circuitous route he'd taken.

An hour and a half later, I was in Paris, queueing for my flight to Dubai, where I could stretch out for a sleep before my long leg back to Sydney.

My daughter, Christina, met me at Sydney airport. 'What drugs are you on, Mum?' She laughed. 'You seem so calm, so rested.'

I was glad to see her and laughed too.

The following day, I had a ticket to the matinee performance of *Lucia di Lammermoor* at the Sydney Opera House. It was my regular subscription and I hoped I wouldn't fall asleep during this lovely opera.

At interval, I bumped into two good friends. 'Looking great, said Sandra. 'I told you, didn't I? That place is magic.' She had an all-knowing smile on her face. 'Champagne all round,' she said, handing me a flute.

Dear Sandra, she was a character, lots of fun. She's the friend who went to Venice for a holiday but stayed six years. She passed away a few years ago but I have good memories of many a dinner party and lunch shared.

Back home, everything returned to its normal groove, except for me. I was not the same person who had left on this trip. Something had changed.

There was much to unpack. I'd seen wondrous things—iconic buildings, stained glass windows dazzling in the daylight. I'd enjoyed flutes of champagne at emotionally charged concerts in historic theatres, even listened to the clatter of the city and enjoyed the silence of the countryside. I'll always remember marble lined apses in ancient churches, their fresco covered walls and the aroma of incense and beeswax.

I cling to the history passed down thru the ages and recall the fascinating tales shared by local guides like those of Capitan Guido on the Lake Como cruise. The glitz and glamour of the French Riviera, the cars, boats and mansions of the mega rich were breathtaking. I especially treasure the little gems that serendipitously came my way and for which I'm eternally grateful.

Then there were the mouthwatering regional dishes lovingly prepared to time-honoured family recipes. I recall my feeling of trepidation at the cooking school when I was challenged to flip the crepes. So many experiences savoured and filed in readiness for recollection.

There is much I want to remember. The long-departed fragrance of fresh herbs and flowers in full bloom at Cap Ferat and Giverny and so much more besides.

My journey had begun at the *Chiesa San Nicola* in Bari and throughout my trip, St Nicholas kept making his presence known, as if guiding me along the way. On the last day, as if in fond farewell, Marina and I were blessed to venerate his precious icon at the *Cathédrale Saint Nicholas de Nice*.

I returned home feeling supreme satisfaction. For me, this had been the grandest of Grand Tours.

About the Author

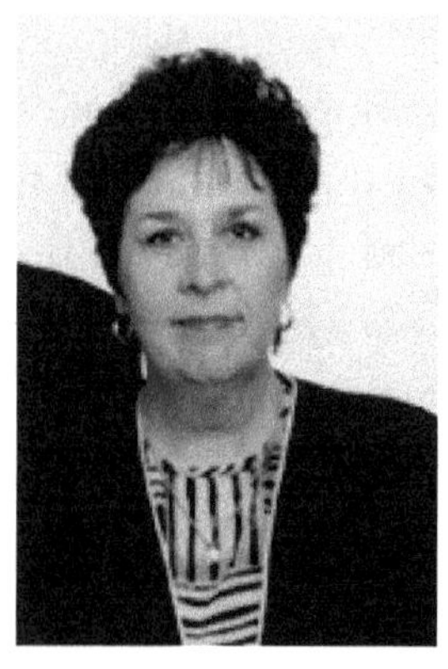

Anya Nielsen has a Bachelor of Adult Education from University of Technology Sydney.

She has written and published two travel memoirs:

Russian Embers, published 2014
An Unexpected Fork in the Road, published 2015

Six of her short stories were published in the following anthologies:

Seniors Stories Vol 4 - in 2018 (a competition run by Seniors Card)
Seniors Stories Vol 5 - in 2019 (a competition run by Seniors Card)
Seniors Stories Vol 7 - in 2021 (a competition run by Seniors Card)
Wyong Writers annual anthologies 2018 to 2023
Winner of Poetry Competition – Haiku 2021 (Wyong Writers)

In 2012 she spent a month in Italy, visiting many churches, museums and art galleries. She included the north and South of Italy including Sicily. Everywhere she went she tasted the bounties of the region. Similarly, she spent three weeks in

France even attended a cooking school. Her short time in Spain included Madrid and Barcelona.

She is a member of the Fellowship of Australian Writers,
A member of Wyong Writers and their weekly Scribblers group.

Anya has a daughter and son. A dog and a cat. When not writing or travelling Anya loves to cook for her family and friends.

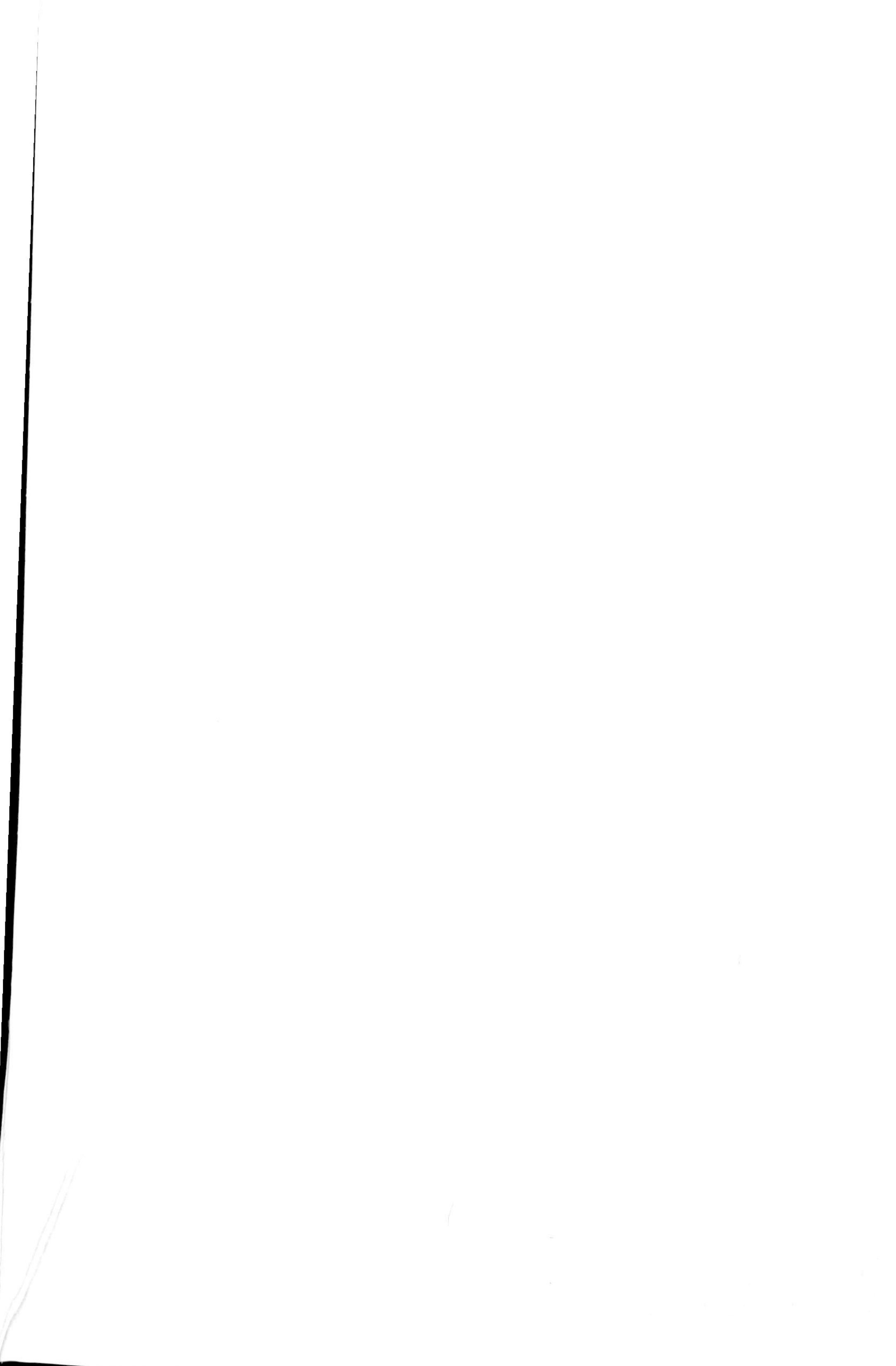

www.ingramcontent.com/pod-product-compliance
Lightning Source LLC
La Vergne TN
845155LV00028B/272

* 9 7 8 1 9 2 3 0 3 8 3 6 3 *